The Acts of the Apostles
A Devotional Commentary

M J Flower

The St Giles Commentary Series

Grosvenor House
Publishing Limited

The right of M J Flower to be identified as the author of this
work has been asserted in accordance with Section 78
of the Copyright, Designs and Patents Act 1988

The book cover is copyright to M J Flower

This book is published by
Grosvenor House Publishing Ltd
Link House
140 The Broadway, Tolworth, Surrey, KT6 7HT.
www.grosvenorhousepublishing.co.uk

A CIP record for this book
is available from the British Library

ISBN 978-1-80381-694-4

In Memory of
Daniel Edward Flower
1970–2004

CONTENTS

About the Author

M J Flower, BA (Hons); MPhil, raised a family before reading Theology and Philosophy of Religion at the University of Exeter, where she also completed a research thesis on the social theory of John Millbank. She jointly established the Institute for Christian Studies in Exeter, and worked extensively with the South West Training Ministry for the Diocese of Exeter, training and supporting Readers and non-ordained ministers. She spent many years as a Churchwarden at St Leonard's Church in Exeter, and sat on the Deanery Synod as a lay member. She has spent more years than she would like to count leading and contributing to Bible Study and Home Groups and continues this work while happily retired in Buckinghamshire, living close to a very wide circle of friends and three generations of her family.

She is the author of *The King and the Kingdom: A devotional commentary on the Gospel of Matthew.*

Preface

In the first book, O Theophilus, I have dealt with all that Jesus began to do and to teach, until the day when He was taken up, after He had given commandment through the Holy Spirit to the apostles whom He had chosen. To them He appeared, and presented Himself alive after His passion by many proofs, appearing to them during forty days and speaking of the kingdom of God. (Acts 1:3)

Paul writes to Timothy, 'Present yourself to God as one approved, a workman who has no need to be ashamed, rightly handling the word of truth'. (2 Timothy 2:15). This is the ambition of Luke and of all those who wait on the Lord to receive from Him a measure of understanding of His Word, and of His activity in the lives of men and women. Standing before this portion of the word of truth, the word of God, the Acts of the Apostles, we know that we are standing on holy ground, and prayerfully submit to the guidance and inspiration of the Holy Spirit as we look more closely and more intensely at what He has given us in His word.

Our prayer is always,' May the words of my mouth and the meditation of my heart be always acceptable in your sight, O Lord, my strength and my Redeemer.' (Psalm 19:14).

Introduction

The Author of The Acts of the Apostles

Luke does not claim authorship of this book, as does Paul, for example, when writing to various churches as an apostle, or as one of a group of elders, or as a servant of Christ Jesus, or as a prisoner. Paul's identification of himself was necessary for those to whom he was writing. But Luke prefers anonymity, no doubt expecting that no emphasis would therefore be placed on him, but on others, as he focused on participants in the story of the early days of the spread of the gospel, men such as Peter, Stephen, Barnabas and Paul, and women such as Lydia and Dorcas.

However, traditionally, the author of the Acts of the Apostles has been identified as the Luke who is mentioned in the last days of Paul's life as the 'beloved physician; (Colossians 4:14), as the Luke who is mentioned in 2 Timothy 4:11 as 'only Luke is with me', and as a fellow worker with Paul in Philemon 24.

In contemporary scholarship, the author of Acts has been regarded as being an unknown, unidentifiable person because of perceived inaccuracies in the portrayal of Paul, as of a different character from that observed in Paul's writings. This is an important dispute, for it suggests a need to assess the historical accuracy of Acts, which may not necessarily be determined by the 'we' passages in Acts 16:10; 20: 5-15; 21:1–28:16. which clearly give the impression that Luke is accompanying Paul at certain stages of his life and ministry.

This may also affect the supposed date of composition. Traditionally, Acts has been dated from the early sixties of the first century, the point at which Paul was imprisoned in Rome for two years. But the possibility of an unknown author also leads some scholars to favour a later period of composition, perhaps in the nineties. (For a fuller discussion see Marshall pp 17; 84).

However the 'we' passages do convey the impression that the author was an eyewitness of the events he describes and that the information he gives is correct. He was in a good position to see at first hand what was happening in the early church and at the same time to receive additional information both orally and literally.

C.K Barrett, p 56, makes the point that writing and receiving letters was very common in the 'Pax Romana', the period roughly from 30 B.C. to 235 A.D. This is illustrated by the letters of Paul, and may well be illustrative of the way in which the gospels were dispersed. At an early stage after the death, resurrection and ascension of the Lord Jesus, there may well have been those who were witnesses of the events, recorded in the Gospels, to which of course Luke had contributed with his Gospel; and also in the Acts of the Apostles

This is not to say that there were no problems associated with Luke's depiction of the early church, but that Luke's intention was to report the acts of the apostles, and perhaps more importantly the acts of the Holy Spirit, in such a way that these early Christians had a foundation for their faith, and for their mission to those around them, both Jews and Gentiles. What Jesus had begun to do and to teach, (Acts 1:1), the Holy Spirit would continue to do, so that Jesus would be glorified. (John 16:14). It was not to be expected that Luke was setting out rules and regulations for the conduct of this new phenomenon, the phenomenon of the church, but only attempting to preclude any possibility that such regulation was or could be valid. The only motivating force behind all that activity was the power of the Holy Spirit.

Though Luke's theology may be pre-emptive of the fuller significance of the continuing work of the Holy Spirit as shown in the epistles, yet the foundation was being laid for fellowship and understanding among believers, as recorded for example in the Apostolic Decree of Acts 15; as Jews and Gentiles came together to fast and pray in Acts 13 1:3; to pray in Acts 12:5,12; to break bread together in Acts 20:7; and baptize new believers in Acts 9:18; 10:48 and 19:5.

Luke is setting out what purports to be a truthful record of how the disciples went about fulfilling the commission given to them by Jesus on the mountain in Galilee; (Matthew 28:2) and the promise He gave them as they waited near Jerusalem, that they would receive power after the Holy Spirit had come upon them. (Acts 1:8,12). The commission and the promise together would supply all that they needed for the work which He wanted them to do.

What motive could Luke possibly have for writing fiction? Or promoting his own theology? There have been critics of his writing on both these grounds. But Luke was not a historian, nor a theologian, but an author; a witness to the Graeco-Roman times in which he lived, and an eyewitness to much of what he describes.

Luke is seeking to go back to the beginning of the church in an attempt to establish its foundations; faith in the Lord Jesus Christ and total reliance on the guidance and empowering of the Holy Spirit; and to prevent the infant church from being led away from these basic principles. Luke was not writing a theological document, explaining these principles as he went along in theological terminology, but was describing what life could be like when lived in the Holy Spirit; His vibrating, energizing, accomplishing, transforming power becoming an important feature in the lives of many.

Luke almost certainly had historical information of which we are not aware, even as he undoubtedly had when writing his first volume, the Gospel of Luke. This however does not make him an historian. For example, details of the account of the conversion of Paul vary from one account to another, because of the perceptions of the people to whom first Luke, in Acts 9, and then Paul in Acts 22 and 26, were testifying of the change that had come about in Paul's life through his experience on the road to Damascus. This seeming discrepancy *may* lead to doubts about the historical accuracy of Acts as a whole, but there is sufficient material in Acts which may be corroborated by other, external sources, and surely lends weight to the suggestion that even reliable historians sometimes make errors, or may have received conflicting accounts of the same incident. And it was the case that each of these accounts of Paul's conversion was tailored to the needs and experience of those who heard them.

Luke was not indifferent to history or theology, but these disciplines were outside his remit. It is impossible to fit Acts into any literary genre, for it is different from them all as a genre in its own right, but we do see historical, theological and biographical features in his work.

Our tendency to categorise literary works must not be allowed to interfere with what the Holy Spirit is wanting to show us as we read this portion of God's word. He is, we know and believe, the executive Person of the Trinity, and is concerned with the outworking of the life of Christ in the life of every believer. Without reliance on Him, any kind of study of God's word will be fruitless. With HIm, our eyes are opened, our hearts are enlarged.

Without Acts, we could never have known how the early church functioned, nor how the gospel spread from Jerusalem throughout Asia Minor and strategic cities of Europe like Athens and Corinth.

Luke has given us an invaluable gift.

Acts 1:1-2. The Dedication

In the first book, O Theoplhilus, I have dealt with all that Jesus began to do and to teach until the day that He was taken up. (Acts 1: 1, 2).

Both the Gospel of Luke and the Acts of the Apostles are dedicated to someone called Theophilus, who is not mentioned elsewhere in the New Testament. In the Gospel, Theophilus is described as having been taught the truth 'concerning the things which have been accomplished among us', (Luke 1:1), and that the Gospel had set in order 'what has has been delivered to us', that is, Luke, 'by those who were witnesses from the beginning'. (Luke 1:2).

In this way, Theophilus would have the certainty, the confirmation, of all that he had received as information, 'the things of which you have been informed'. (Luke 1:4)

From this introduction to Luke's Gospel, we could assume that Theophilus was someone who had recently joined the church, or was perhaps an outsider, seeking for the truth of the gospel.

Alternatively, Theophilus could be seen as a representative figure whom Luke addresses, as evidenced by the name 'Theophilus', which could mean either 'Beloved of God' or 'Lover of God', and that Luke was writing a general document to all who love God and who are aware of His love for them.

These addressees may have been Gentile Christians, for whom Jewish traditions may have been obscure, needing some explanation, or for Jewish Christians, to emphasise the continuity between the historical past of their tradition and the new experience of life in the Spirit. But whether an intended reader, Theophilus, or a representative group, Luke intends that the work which he is about to undertake should be seen in its proper light; not something which once occurred in the life of Jesus and then came to an end, but as an ongoing expression of His life in the lives of those to whom He came; to those who have become followers of Him.

The same person is addressed in both the introduction to Luke's gospel and the Acts of the Apostles, as 'Most excellent Theophilus' in Luke, and 'O Theophilus' in Acts. The vocative form was the normal way of addressing a person of rank or importance, and this mode of address indicates that though, as Paul writes, not many wise, not many powerful, not many noble are called (1 Corinthians 1:26), there were indeed some in the church who were. Though the name Theophilus may have religious significance, and may therefore have been regarded as representative, it may well have been a particular person whom Luke had in view, the same intended person in Acts as in Luke.

The courteous term, 'most excellent Theophilus' indicates that although numerically, there may not have been many of noble birth or those exercising an upper class influence in the early church, there may have been some. We do not learn that the ministry of Jesus, and the ongoing ministry of the church under the power of the Holy Spirit, consisted only of ministry to slaves and other lowly members of society.

We conclude that Luke was concerned with a fairly mixed group of believers, poor and lowly as well as important and influential, Jewish as well as Gentile Christians. Theophilus, if he was an actual person, as much as any lowly follower of Jesus, needed equipping to know the facts of Jesus' ministry, HIs ministry of 'doing' and 'teaching', (Acts 1:1), and how that ministry was to be continued in the infant church.

Theophilus needed certainty. He needed encouragement. He needed the Holy Spirit.

Acts 1:5 The purpose of Acts

We have been blessed over the centuries and into more recent decades with brilliant scholars, and exegetes of the scriptures who have studied long and hard to help us to understand the importance of the teaching of the word of God. We thank God for them all; for the enrichment they have brought us, for the understanding of His precious word they have afforded us. And in them, we include Luke.

Luke and the other Gospel writers are the first in a long line of those who have sought to establish the veracity of the claims made by him and the other evangelists; the truth of what Jesus began to do and to teach while here on earth, that what He began to do and to teach is confirmed by what happened after His ascension into heaven; and that what He had accomplished through His death and resurrection, the salvation of all who come to Him by faith, is now to be proclaimed throughout the world by the emerging church.

As the church began to evangelize, it needed an orderly account of the operation of the Holy Spirit to strengthen faith, for many were discovering, as Jesus Himself had forewarned them, that the cost of discipleship was high. Luke makes no apology for telling it like it is. It is only with hindsight that we realize that all the persecution and opposition against the followers of Jesus served only for the expansion of the gospel as these faithful Christians gave up everything for His sake and the sake of the gospel. Jesus had never promised that to follow Him would be easy, pain free, trouble free. But He had promised that

He would never leave them, even to the close of the age. (Matthew 28:20). 'And lo, I am with you always, even to the end of the world, the close of the age', was His promise to them.

The promise was never rescinded, never broken, whether in the joy and exultation of receiving the Holy Spirit on the Day of Pentecost, in Acts 2:4, or in incidents like the trial of Paul before the Sanhedrin in Jerusalem, when in spite of all that Paul is enduring, he is able to say 'the Lord stood by me and said 'take courage, for as you have testified about Me at Jerusalem, so you must bear witness also at Rome'. (Acts 23:11).

In every circumstance, God never fails

To say that the presence of the Holy Spirit was with the early church all the way is to do limited justice to His ordering of all things. The first task was to establish a foundation in Jerusalem; to constitute the church, to unite and consolidate the believers in love for one another. Then, throughout Acts, we see ways in which the good news of the kingdom of heaven is taken to the Gentiles, God's plan of salvation for all the people of all the nations, the eternal life of Jesus Christ offered to all, the Holy Spirit doing what Jesus had said the Holy Spirit would do, convict the world concerning sin, and righteousness and judgement because the ruler of this world is judged. (John 16:8)

Luke was the chosen vessel through whom the expansion of the knowledge of Christ was set out in a simple literary pattern, and in such a way that the life and teaching of the early church should prove an inspiration and source of instruction in a world which had never seen the like before. After the resurrection and ascension of Jesus, and the coming of the Holy Spirit, what began as a disparate group of people became a new family, meeting in each other's homes to pray together, to break bread together, to listen to the apostles teaching. (Acts 2:42).

If we consider that 'what Jesus began to do and to teach' (Acts 1:1) is a slightly inadequate summary of Luke's gospel, or even of the life and work of the Lord Jesus, and therefore a not very impressive introduction to the work of the Holy Spirit in Acts, we must remember that to those to whom the teaching and and acts of healing mercy came, they were absolutely confirmatory of the status of Jesus as the Son of God.

Peter, an eyewitness of the compassion of Jesus for the weak, the sinful, the lowly of every age, class and ability, declares in his second letter,' we did not follow cleverly disguised myths, (R.S.V.), cunningly devised fables (K.J.V), or tales, (NASB) when we made known to you the power and coming of our Lord Jesus Christ, but were eyewitnesses of His majesty. (2 Peter 1:16). Peter recognised that in seeing Jesus on the mount of transfiguration, the disciples had seen an epiphany, a manifestation of Jesus as Son of God, as Jesus Himself had said to Philip, 'he who has seen Me has seen the Father'. (John 14:10).

While He lived among them, they had glimpses of who He was; the 'Son of Man' as He described Himself, fulfilling all the Old Testament scriptures; the 'Son of God' as He healed the sick and cast out demons; the 'Lord' as He walked on the water and they recognized who He was and worshipped Him. The One who began to do and to teach and through the Holy Spirit would continue so to act in this way begins to seem an extraordinarily accurate description of what He continued to do in Acts.

The Greek term for the Acts of the Apostles is 'Praxeis Apostolon'. It has also been known as the 'Acts of the Holy Spirit', but perhaps we should also consider the 'Acts of the Trinity', for all three Persons of the Godhead are at work in the volume we know as the 'Acts of the Apostles'. God is at work in His church. Believers encounter and meet with God as Father, Son and Holy Spirit. Jesus said, 'I will build My church and the gates of hell shall not prevail against it', (Matthew 16:18), and this word remains firm, as do all the sayings of Jesus. We believe Him and His word. His work did not come to an end in the imprisonment of his servant Paul in a Roman prison in A.D.62, at the end of Acts, (Acts 28:16), but is still continuing; all that He is continuing to do and to teach, narrative and discourse, the good news about what He does and what He proclaims.

Acts Chapter 1

Acts 1:1-14. The promise of the Holy Spirit and the ascension of Jesus

In the first book, O Theophilus, I have dealt with all that Jesus began to do and to teach until the day when He was taken up, after He had given commandment through the Holy Spirit to the apostles whom He had chosen. To whom He had presented Himself alive after His passion by many proofs, appearing to them during forty days and speaking of the kingdom of God. And while staying with them, He charged them not to depart from Jerusalem but to wait for the promise of the Father, which, He said, you heard from Me. For John baptized with water, but before many days, you shall be baptized in the Holy Spirit. (Acts 1:1-5).

Jesus was taking His disciples right back to their beginnings, to the baptism in water by John the Baptist, and promising them a further baptism, a further immersion, in the Holy Spirit, immersed in Him as they had been in the water of the River Jordan.

Could they possibly understand what He meant? They believed that they understood something of God. Jesus had introduced them to God as their Father, (Matthew 6:9), someone to whom they could pray as children to their Father, who would answer them, supply all their needs, keep them close to Himself and close to one another.

But until now, the Holy Spirit had not been part of their thinking, although Jesus had often spoken of Him. Jesus had said to them. 'The Holy Spirit is *with* you'. This they could understand. for they knew He had been with their prophets of old. But Jesus went on to say 'And He will be *in* you'. (John 16:17). They did not know exactly what that meant, but Jesus had said it and they could trust Him.

1

He said, 'Before many days, you will be baptized in the Holy Spirit'. And whatever He meant by that they knew it was a gift He was giving them out of His love for them. It was alright to be baptized in the Holy Spirit. Their failure to support Him at the time of His arrest when they all forsook Him and fled, (Matthew 26:56), had convinced them that the way of discipleship was not a journey they could take alone. They needed so much more. They needed the Holy Spirit to take them forward, to accomplish all that Jesus had commissioned them to do on that mountain in Galilee, to live the life of the kingdom, and preach the gospel to every creature. (Mark 16:15).

For forty days after His resurrection He had been with them, suddenly appearing, sharing a meal with them and then going again, speaking to them of His favourite subject, the kingdom of God, its entry requirements and its ultimate fulfillment; (Acts 1:3), how men and women may enter it; how they how they might live in it; how the total realization of what was yet to come, would come in God's good time, giving them hope and the expectation of His worldwide power and glory, when He would be all-in-all, God manifestly seen and heard and heaven's Beloved One.

So much had happened and all so quickly. Six weeks ago, Jesus had hung on a cross. Six weeks ago, He had risen from the dead. During that time, they had become used to Him suddenly appearing and saying,' My brothers, do you have anything to eat?' (Luke 24:42), proving that He was indeed not the flesh and blood they had known and loved, but a new, glorified though scarred Body, yet the same Jesus. So when they had come together, the disciples asked Him, 'Lord, will You at this time restore the kingdom to Israel? (Acts 1:6). After all that had happened, and His speaking to them of the KIngdom of God, this was surely not an unreasonable expectation. It would not have surprised them in the slightest to see Him suddenly coming on the clouds with power and great glory. (Matthew 24:30). But this was not yet the time. He said to them, 'It is not for you to know the times and seasons which the Father has fixed by His own authority, but you shall receive power when the Holy Spirit has come upon you and you shall be witnesses to Me'. (Acts 1:6-8).

2

Nevertheless He had something of great significance to show them before they received the Holy Spirit and became witnesses to Him in Jerusalem, and in all Judea, not just in Jerusalem, but also in Samaria where the people worshipped God in a substitute way because of their history; and also to the uttermost parts of the earth. (Acts 1:8).

One day they had gone with Him to the mount called Olivet, which is near Jerusalem, (Acts 1:12). He had already told them that it was not for them to know the times and seasons which the Father had fixed by His own authority. (Acts 1:7). Disappointed though they may have been, they were encouraged, if a little hesitant, when He said that they would receive power when the Holy Spirit came upon them and they would be witnesses to Him. What did this mean? They loved Him. They believed Him and they trusted His word, but what did He mean by witnessing to the ends of the earth?

They had had a foretaste of this; they remembered how Jesus had sent them out under His delegated authority as apostles, 'sent ones', to take the good news of the kingdom of heaven to' the lost sheep of the House of Israel'. (Matthew 10 5:6). This had not altogether been a comfortable or successful experience. They had met with opposition, rejection, hostility, even though there had been wonderful times when they were aware that what they were saying to these people had not been their speaking but the Holy Spirit speaking through them. Was Jesus now suggesting that they do the same thing again? They had experienced the Holy Spirit working with them on that earlier occasion. Was this what Jesus was wanting for them again?

No. Jesus had an entirely different plan for them this time. He said, 'you shall receive power when the Holy Spirit comes upon you, and you will be witnesses to Me, in Jerusalem and in all Judea, and Samaria and to the end of the earth'. (Acts 1:8). When they will have had the experience of the Holy Spirit coming upon them, when they will have been baptized, immersed in Him, what a difference that will make. On one occasion Jesus had explained this to them. He had said, the Holy Spirit is *with* you and shall be *in* you. This was now beginning to make sense to them. (John 14:17).

They were not given much time to think about it. When He had said this, as they were looking at Him, He was lifted up and a cloud received Him out of their sight. (Acts 1:9)

Peter, James and John had seen something similar on the Mount of Transfiguration. Wait a little, they may have said, He will return. Had He not also during those forty days and nights after His resurrection often suddenly appeared when they were least expecting Him? He will return.

But not this time. As they were gazing into heaven as He went, behold, two men stood by them in white robes and said. 'Men of Galilee, why do you stand looking into heaven? This same Jesus who was taken up from you, will come in the same way as you have seen Him go into heaven'. (Acts 1:11).

This same Jesus, the One whom they knew and loved, but risen, and ascended, and glorified, will come again!

Left to themselves, they would perhaps have stayed there for a long time, looking up to where they had last seen Him, and had a last glimpse of their heavenly Friend. This was a crossroads point in their lives. Did they still want to remember earlier times, to live in the remembrance of all that He had said and done while He was with them? Perhaps they yearned for those happy days they had spent together before He went to the cross. The angels had said He would come again, but when? They wanted Him *now*. Peter had suggested the making of three shrines when they had seen Jesus on the Mount of Transfiguration. Perhaps if they really had to wait for His return they could build a shrine for Him and He could dwell there forever with them. They could spend their time thinking about Him, praying to Him forever, for there was no doubt in their minds that He was who He said He was, whom He claimed to be, the Son of God.

But God is moving on. He is doing a new thing, and these beloved disciples are about to experience something tremendous, because He is going to use them in the very beginning of His new plan and purpose for mankind as they wait on Him.

They now remembered something else He had said. 'Do not depart from Jerusalem, but wait for the promise of the Father'. (Acts 1:4). If they had learned nothing else in their three years with Him, they had learned the importance of obedience. Jesus Himself had said of His relationship with His Father,' I do always those things that please Him'. (John 8:29). To be obedient was not necessarily the easiest thing to do, but for them, as for Jesus, it was predicated on love; love for the Father; love for Jesus; and on the absolute confidence that whatever He commanded was not just the best thing to do but the only rational thing to do. It was the Father's will, part of His plan for their lives and for the blessing of others.

So they returned to Jerusalem from the mount called Olivet, which is near Jerusalem, a sabbath day's journey away, a fifteen or twenty minute walk, about three quarters of a mile. So short is the distance sometimes, between obedience to the will of God, and trusting in our own will and desires.

They had not far to go to Jerusalem, and when they had entered, they went up to the upper room where they were staying. (Acts 1:12). Had they been disobedient, there would have been no continuing activity of the Lord Jesus through the Holy Spirit. Just as God allowed His incarnated Son to be born in a stable, in a far from settled political situation with very little of this world's goods to support Him, though with a loving mother in Mary, and a wise and obedient guardian in Joseph; so He was allowing the whole future of the emerging infant church to hang upon the the thread of eleven men's obedience to Him. But they had seen His face, had heard His word, and their hearts were united in being together to honour Him. They returned to Jerusalem.

Were they staying in the 'large upper room furnished' to which Jesus had taken His disciples on the occasion of the Last Supper? (Luke 22: 12). It needed to be large, for all eleven of the disciples, individually named by Luke, were joined by the women and Mary the mother of Jesus and His brothers. (Acts 1:14). His earthly family integrated into His spiritual family; the proto-church as a fellowship with the named apostles at its heart, a new family. The disciples had seen His ascension, had heard His words of commission, and the promise He had given them and were now together talking together of all that they had seen and heard.

What had been the purpose of His ascension to heaven in the sight of His disciples? Was it just to demonstrate what they already knew, that Jesus was indeed the Son of God, or was it to make a clear distinction between His wonderful appearances during the forty days after His resurrection, and the time when those appearances must come to an end as indicated by the angel-men in white robes?

There was a sense in which they had to learn to do without Him, without His physical bodily presence with them. But as His earthly life had been wrapped up in unending fellowship with His Father, whom He could not see, so would theirs be from now on. The promise of the Father, the constant indwelling of the Holy Spirit would be their daily, hourly experience, even though they may not always have been physically conscious of Him.

The word *up*, that He was taken up into heaven, has troubled some who entirely reject the notion of a tripartite universe, with heaven at the top, hell at the bottom and the earth between. But the *up-ness* if we may call it so, was surely only a distinction in physical terms between heaven and earth, firstly, as we have seen, to demonstrate that the post-resurrection appearances of the Lord Jesus were now over, and secondly, that He was returning to another realm, the realm from which He had come to be with them, His original heavenly life, seated on His Father's throne. His ascension was a pictorial representation of a spiritual truth.

Acts 1:15-26. Waiting for the Holy Spirit

All these with one accord devoted themselves to prayer, together with the women and Mary the mother of Jesus, and with His brothers. In those days, Peter stood up among the brethren, (the company of persons was in all about one hundred and twenty), and said, Brethren, the scripture had to be fulfilled. (Acts 1; 14-16).

Resolutely, the apostles return to Jerusalem. Of those gathered together in the upper room, only the eleven apostles and Mary the mother of Jesus are mentioned by name. These together with the women, (Acts 1:14), constitute the core of the church and it is important that we know who the apostles are before their Acts are recorded; before the expansion of the church takes place; even before the Holy Spirit is given, and the consequence of receiving Him is declared by Jesus as the gift to be able to witness to their Lord. 'You shall receive the gift of the Holy Spirit and you shall be witnesses to Me'. (Acts 1:8).

Ephesians reminds us that as followers of Jesus, we are fellow citizens with the saints, and members of the household of God, built upon *the foundation of the apostles and prophets*, Jesus Christ Himself being the chief cornerstone. (Ephesians 2:19,20.) The list of the apostles in Acts corresponds, with only minor differences in the order of the apostles and the omission of Judas, with the list in Luke 6:14-16 These are the named apostles, chosen by Jesus Himself after a night of prayer, a night of close communion with His heavenly Father. The apostles and the women who had ministered to Him during His lifetime on earth, (e.g. Luke 10:38,39; 7:37); at His death and resurrection, (Luke 23:55), and including His earthly brothers and possibly even His sisters, (Matthew 13:55), 'all these with one accord devoted themselves to prayer'. (Act 1:14).

Jesus had Himself begun His ministry with the claim 'The Spirit of the Lord is upon Me', quoting from the prophecy of Isaiah, (Isaiah 61:1-3). If He began by allying Himself with the Holy Spirit, and recognizing His anointing, how much more did the disciples and the other men and women gathered together in that upper room, need the Holy Spirit as they became witnesses to Him. But it was necessary that there should be a time of preparation before the Holy Spirit was given. The preparation time for Jesus was after He had been baptized by John in the River Jordan, and had returned full of the Spirit, to fast for forty days in the wilderness, being tempted by the devil. (Luke 4:1,2). This was the preparation for His ministry.

A different preparation time was given to those gathered together in the upper room. Losing the physical appearance of Jesus to them after His ascension may well have seemed to be a wilderness experience for them, a real hiatus between the past and the future as they waited and watched and prayed for a new manifestation of Him through the Holy Spirit, for Luke also calls Him the Spirit of Jesus. (Acts 16:7). The Holy Spirit makes Jesus real to us.

These apostles whom Jesus had chosen had to be eyewitnesses of Jesus' ministry and of His resurrection. (Acts 1:3). These were their qualifications as apostles. It was on the foundation of their testimony that Luke could present the truth of the kingdom of God in this volume, as God had presented it to them in the person of His Son, (Acts 1:1), and that which He had begun to do and to teach. They were divinely chosen, divinely qualified and uniquely appointed to be His witnesses, and to become His apostles. At that time, in that world, an apostle was understood to be an ambassador, an envoy or delegate sent out with a message from the sender and under his authority. It was often a highly important political post. This is what Jesus is doing, sending out the apostles, His sent ones, for that is what apostle means, sent out with the most life-transforming message of all, under His authority, empowered by the Holy Spirit.

So for ten days, they' devoted themselves to prayer'. (Acts 1:14). Jesus had set them an example that prayer to His heavenly Father was absolutely vital. They could do no better than follow His example as together 'with one accord', with one heart and mind, they cast themselves on the love and mercy of God to take them through the time of waiting for the Promise, to guide them and assure them of His presence and of the constancy of His will.

Acts 1:15-26. The appointment of Matthias

In those days, Peter stood up among the brethren, (the company of persons was in all about a hundred and twenty) and said, 'Brethren, the scripture had to be fulfilled which the Holy Spirit spoke beforehand by the mouth of David concerning Judas, who was guide to those who arrested Jesus. For he was numbered among us, and was allotted a share in this ministry.

(Acts 1:15). For it is written in the book of Psalms, 'Let his habitation be desolate and let there be no-one to live in it,' and, 'his office let another take'. (Psalm 69:25; Psalm 109:8).

There was just one problem which Peter, no doubt in consultation with the other apostles, felt it was important to resolve. Peter felt it was necessary to appoint someone to take the place of Judas who had so signally failed to be the disciple whom Jesus wanted to follow Him, even to being the guide to those who arrested Jesus and thus betraying Him. (Luke 22:47,48; Matthew 26:47; Acts 1:6).

For this appointment, Peter needed the warrant of scripture. It would appear that during the ten days of prayer, many others had joined them so that they now had to move to larger premises. If there were now one hundred and twenty gathered together, they would have outgrown the upper room. (Acts 1:15). Perhaps Peter felt that it was now even more important that matters should be resolved in a scriptural way. Judas had been one of them, one of the disciples of Jesus. He had shared their food and whatever accommodation they had managed to find while they had been with Jesus, though He had warned them that foxes have holes, and the birds of the air have nests, but the Son of Man had nowhere to lay His head. (Matthew 8:20).

The loss of Judas had reduced the number of the disciples to eleven and the number twelve had a great significance for the Jewish people. To begin with, there were the twelve tribes of Israel, God's chosen people, arising from Jacob/Israel's twelve sons. When choosing the tribe of Levi to be the priestly tribe, setting them apart for the service of the Tabernacle, and therefore as priests having no geographical inheritance, God had chosen the two sons of Joseph, Manasseh and Ephraim to become both the replacement for Levi, while still recognizing Joseph's claim as one of the sons of Jacob/Israel.

Was this what Peter had in mind as well as the verses from the Psalms which he had quoted? Luke is anxious to give us the story of what had happened to this man Judas who under God had been the means of the suffering which the Lord Jesus had endured.

So he gives a parenthetical account of the betrayal of Jesus by Judas, and his subsequent death; which was suicide according to Matthew's gospel, 'he went away and hanged himself', (Matthew 27:5), or according to Luke's account, 'he fell headlong and burst open in the middle so that all his bowels gushed out'. (Acts 1:18).

These are not necessarily conflicting accounts. Stott writes that 'it is perfectly possible to suppose that after he hanged himself, his dead body fell headlong, assuming that the rope or the tree branch broke, or that he swelled up and in either case, ruptured'. Stott p55.

There is also the question as to who 'bought the field'. Luke writes 'Now this man bought a field with the reward of his wickedness and falling headlong he burst open and all his bowels gushed out. And it became known to all the inhabitants of Jerusalem so that the field was called in their language, 'Akeldama', that is, 'Field of Blood'. (Acts 1:18).

Matthew records that Judas, filled with remorse at what he had done, attempted to return the thirty shekels to the chief priests but they refused to accept it, but later the priests, unwilling to put the money into the treasury of the temple because it was blood money, bought with it 'the potter's field'. the field which later became known as the field of blood, a field to bury strangers in. (Matthew 27:3-10). Is it possible on these grounds to harmonize the two accounts? Did Judas buy the field or did the chief priests and the elders? Stott says that it is reasonable to suppose that the priests bought the field with the money which had belonged to Judas, the betrayal money which was the reward of his wickedness. (Acts 1:18). It therefore became Judas' field because it was bought with his money.

Peter was convinced that it was important to replace Judas, and this conviction he expressed to all the one hundred and twenty gathered together to pray. (Acts 1:15). Over the days of waiting for the promised Holy Spirit, the number had increased and it appeared that Peter had become their natural leader.

'Brethren; he said, using the term which generically included both men and women, for there was a holy sense of brotherhood among them as there always is when a group of people gather together in united persevering prayer; 'Brethren', he said,' this man Judas was numbered among us and was allotted his share in this ministry. (Acts 1:17). It is written in the book of Psalms, 'Let his habitation become desolate, and let there be no-one to live in it, and his place, his position, let another take. Brethren, the scripture had to be fulfilled which the Holy Spirit spoke long ago by the mouth of David concerning Judas, (Acts 1:16).

The first quotation from the Psalms describes what Judas had done and its consequences. The second quotation demands that it was necessary to replace him. These scriptures were enough to give Peter the guidance which he needed. Peter believed that the replacement of Judas, especially in view of his apostleship, depended upon two qualifications. First, the newly appointed apostle had to have been one of those who had 'accompanied us during all the time that the Lord Jesus went in and out among us, beginning from the baptism of John, until the day when He was taken up from us'. (Acts 1:21). And secondly, that he had seen the risen Lord, the risen Jesus. (Acts 1:22).

This second qualification might not be quite so onerous as it sounds. Paul mentions a time when He was seen by more than five hundred brethren at once after His resurrection, (1 Corinthians 15:6). But the most important problem was that to be an apostle, one had to be commissioned, sent out, by the Lord Himself. Neither Peter nor this group of devoted followers of the Lord Jesus had the authority to call out a man into apostleship. Only the Lord could do that. What should they do?

There were two men who fulfilled the criteria which Peter and the other brethren believed to have been set forth in scripture, Joseph called Barsabbas, and Matthias. (Acts 1:23).

Then they prayed. They prayed and said 'Lord, you know the hearts of all men, show us which of these two you have chosen to take the place in this ministry and apostleship from which Judas turned aside, (transgressed, crossed the line from right to wrong, leaving one place vacant and going to another place). (Barrett, p104).

Then they drew lots. This was an Old Testament way of discerning the will of God. (e.g. Leviticus 16:8; Numbers 26:55; Proverbs 16:33; Luke 1:9). They trusted that through this method, God would make His will known to them. And the lot fell on Matthias. (Acts 1:26).

First they had the leading of scripture. then they considered apostolic qualifications. Then they prayed believing that God who knows the heart, who is the only heart knower, would make His will known to them. (Psalm 139:2). Then they drew lots. The usual method of drawing lots was to place names in a vessel and allow one to fall out. This was the Old Testament device for determining or discerning the will of God and would soon be replaced by reliance on the Holy Spirit as they moved forward into the Day of Pentecost. And Matthias was numbered with the eleven apostles, though neither he nor Joseph were ever again mentioned in the Acts of the Apostles.

Acts Chapter 2

Acts 2:1-13. The Day of Pentecost. The Old Testament significance of Pentecost

When the day of Pentecost had fully come, they were all together in one place. And suddenly a sound came from heaven like the rush of a mighty wind, and it filled all the house where they were sitting. And there appeared to them tongues as of fire, distributing and resting on each one of them. And they were all filled with the Holy Spirit and began to speak in other tongues as the Spirit gave them utterance. (Acts 2 1-4).

The Feast of Firstfruits together with the Feast of Weeks, later known as *Pentecost* celebrated God's provision for the children of Israel, the first fruits of the beginning of the harvest season. Initially, after they had left Egypt and spent forty years in the wilderness, God provided the land to be ploughed and sown. Then He provided the harvest which followed. Offering their firstfruits to the Lord was a recognition of His grace to them, a symbolic gesture of worship to the God of their provision, and of their dependence on Him.

On the Day of Pentecost, the priest waved a sheaf usually of barley, before the Lord. Barley was usually the first grain to mature. This indicated that the worshipper offered thanksgiving to God as the source of his livelihood. God was the owner of the land. The people recognised His right to do as He pleased with it. Psalm 24:1 says 'the earth is the Lord's and the fulness thereof'. His people are thankful that through it, through His provision for them He supplies them with their daily needs.

This harvest celebration, the Feast of Firstfruits and the Feast of Weeks are conflated in Numbers 28:26, and in Leviticus 23:9,15. Leviticus states that the people shall count from the morrow after the sabbath, from the day when they brought the sheaf of the wave offering, seven full weeks, counting fifty days after the seventh sabbath. These precise instructions are later celebrated as Pentecost, coming as it does fifty days after the Sabbath of the Feast of Unleavened Bread or Passover. The Feast of Weeks or Pentecost concentrated on the grain crops. Special loaves of bread were made with leaven, (Leviticus 23:17), and waved before the Lord in the sanctuary, the tabernacle. There were also specific instructions for the provision of the poor and strangers, for them to be able to gather the gleanings after the harvest, as is demonstrated in Ruth 2:2 and Leviticus 23:22,23; to share with others what God had given them.

It was no haphazard choice on the part of God to send His Holy Spirit upon the followers of Jesus at Pentecost. Jesus had been crucified at the time of Passover, fifty days previously; the forty days of His appearances to His disciples, followed by the ten days in which they had prayed for the coming of the Holy Spirit. All the types and figures of the Old Testament were finding their fulfilment in Jesus. He was the corn of wheat which fell into the ground and died so that it could bring forth much fruit. (John 12:24). Jesus said that He was the Bread of life, (John 6:35), that 'he who comes to Me shall never hunger, and he who believes in Me shall never thirst'. And He also declared very firmly that man cannot live by bread alone but by every word that proceeds from the mouth of God. (Matthew 4:4, quoting Deuteronomy 8:3).

That Jesus was the Bread sent down from heaven (John 6:51) 'of which a man may eat thereof and never die', we may dimly understand, and this wonderful truth may have special significance as the object of special worship on the Day of Pentecost, Jesus symbolically waved before the Lord in worship and thanksgiving for the bounty of God's provision in sending Jesus. We may feed on Him, know that He sustains us, provides for us our daily nourishment of His peace, His grace in our hearts. Feeding on Him means that we do not hunger. Believing in Him means that we never thirst. He satisfies all our need.

But there is another and connected truth. Jesus had spoken of a corn of wheat falling into the ground and dying that it might bring forth much fruit., symbolically identifying Himself as the corn of wheat. Through His death, the church, which at this time consisted of one hundred and twenty people, was being born; they were the first fruits of the amazing, incredible, overwhelming harvest which was to follow from the death and resurrection of Jesus. The Day of Pentecost was *fully* come.

The coming of the Holy Spirit, coinciding with the Feast of Pentecost, celebrated that although at the beginning, only one hundred and twenty people were baptized in the Holy Spirit, God had a greater company in mind. There was a gathering together of all peoples, from all corners of the earth to this pilgrim feast in Jerusalem. And by the end of Peter's sermon, 'there were added that day 'about three thousand souls'. (Acts 2:41), who believed Peter's word that 'the promise was for them and their children and to all that are far off, everyone whom the Lord God calls to Him'. (Acts 2:39).

These had been the *pilgrims* to Jerusalem, and also 'there were, *dwelling* in Jerusalem, Jews, devout men from every nation under heaven', people who were resident in Jerusalem as well as those who were visitors. 'And at this sound, the multitude came together, and they were bewildered because each one heard them speaking in his own language'. (Acts 2:5). These were devout Jews and proselytes, who had come to Jerusalem to participate in one of the three most important Jewish festivals. So many of these people were strangers, emphasizing that this was God's plan 'for every nation under heaven'; (Acts 2:5). God loved and loves His chosen people still. But He wanted His love to be received and accepted by so many, many more. The coming of the Holy Spirit, His work in the lives of believers was not just for the few. God wanted to pour out His Spirit on all flesh, as Peter said when quoting the prophet Joel (Joel 2:28-32), an Old Testament prophet who had understood God's desire for a world wide people to know Him, to be part of the family of God.

God does nothing haphazardly. He chose this particular festival of fruitfulness for the coming of the Holy Spirit to show His apostles that as the Lord Jesus had commanded them to preach the gospel to the ends of the earth, (Acts 1:8), so they would be empowered by the Holy Spirit to do so, and so also would the Holy Spirit be given to all who would receive Him.

The third wonderful truth which was being fulfilled on this amazing day of Pentecost was that Pentecost was the only festival for which peace offerings were specifically prescribed. (Leviticus 23:19), though they were also offered at great events like the ratification of the covenant, and the dedication of the tabernacle, the tent of meeting, and the temple. (Exodus 24:5; Numbers 7:17; I Kings 8:62). The peace offering was offered when someone was seeking or enjoining peace with God. So at the Pentecost of Acts 2, God was declaring that peace with Him was especially available, especially possible, for all; peace with God through our Lord Jesus Christ. (Romans 5:1). Once far from God and dead in sin, they could now know the reality of living in His care and love. They could have peace. They could be reconciled to God,

God had provided land and therefore food for His people. He had provided for the people of Israel and for the poor, the needy and the stranger. He had provided peace, *shalom*. What Had He not provided for His people? And on the Day of Pentecost, He was providing, not only for His people, but for all who would come to Him, the gift of His Holy Spirit to comfort, to strengthen, to guide, to counsel, to dwell in them and empower them.

All we have needed Your hand has provided. Great is Your faithfulness, Lord to us. (Lamentations 3:22)

Acts 2:1-4. The Coming 0f the Holy Spirit

When the day of Pentecost was fully come, they were all together in one place. And suddenly, a sound came from heaven like the rush of a mighty wind and it filled all the house where they were sitting. And there appeared to them tongues as of fire, distributed and resting on each one of them. And they were all filled with the Holy Spirit and began to speak in other tongues as the Spirit gave them utterance. (Acts 2:1-4)

Until now, the time spent in prayer together may have seemed ordinary, pedestrian almost, though well intentioned, earnest, and above all, expectant. But now, it suddenly became ecstatic for the one hundred and twenty people who had been praying for the coming of the Holy Spirit, who were 'gathered together in one place'. The Holy Spirit rushed through the house where they were sitting like a whirlwind. The whole house was filled with the sound and as they looked at one another, they could see what appeared to be 'cloven tongues as of fire, and it sat upon each of them' (K.J.V.).

Far from being alarmed or frightened, they were filled with joy as they began speaking in other tongues as the Spirit gave them utterance. (Acts 2:4). As they spoke to one another of the wonderful thing that was taking place, they were amazed to find they were speaking in this unknown language, yet were able to understand each other perfectly. Is this what Jesus meant when He said that the Holy Spirit will come upon you?' they may have tried to say to one another. But they could only speak words of worship and praise to Him who had given them this great gift, this wonderful miracle which enabled them to worship Him, while being aware of each other.

The Day of Pentecost was fully come. We have noted that this was seven weeks or fifty days after Passover. These three festivals, the Feast of Weeks, otherwise known as Pentecost; and before Pentecost; the time of the Passover; and later the Feast of Tabernacles or Booths were the times of the year when the Jews celebrated their heritage and looked forward to their ultimate destination as the people of God. These were the Hebrew names for these three festivals.

Three times in the year, the observant Jew made his way to Jerusalem to the temple, to celebrate these three most important feasts of the Lord as a commandment which Moses had received from the Lord. 'Three times in the year shall all your males appear before the Lord your God'. (Exodus 23:17). This festival of Pentecost was the next great festival after Passover. It was a time when Jerusalem was crowded with pilgrims from all over the world, each using his or her own language.

The tower of Babel in Genesis 11:1-9, had ensured the dispersion of human beings by the confusion of languages. On the Day of Pentecost, the confusion is dispersed, reversed by the miracle of the coming of the Holy Spirit as the visitors to Jerusalem heard these people speaking in their own language. 'They were amazed and wondered, saying, "Are not all those who are speaking Galileans? And how is it that we hear, each of us in our own native language? Parthians and Medes and Elamites and residents of Mesopotamia, Judea and Cappadocia, Pontus and Asia, Phrygia and Pamphylia, Egypt and the parts of Libya belonging to Cyrene and visitors from Rome both Jews and proselytes, Cretans and Arabians, we hear them telling in our own tongues the mighty works of God. And all were amazed and perplexed, saying to one another, 'What does this mean?" But others mocking said, 'they are filled with new wine'. (Acts 2:8-13).

Some of these visitors may have been descendents of Jews who had been carried away into exile and had not returned to Palestine. Others were from Asia Minor and yet others from Arabia, North Africa, Egypt and Libya. Some were racially Jews. Others were proselytes, observers of Jewish law and admitted into full fellowship with Israel on being circumcised. Barrett comments (pp 85,86), that the Jewish authorities in Palestine seem to have sanctioned the use of any language in reciting the 'Shema'; 'Hear, O Israel, the Lord our God is one God'. The praise of God did not have to be in Hebrew or even Aramaic, (an ancient Semitic language which predates Hebrew, but which in the exilic and post-exilic period (sixth century BCE) became the vernacular of the Jews).

In the great festivals when so many pilgrims from the Diaspora, the Dispersion of theJews, were present, the praise of God would be heard in many and various tongues and dialects. Now these pilgrims were hearing these words of praise in their own language, and by Galiileans who were notoriously hard to understand. Barrett writes, the reversal of the curse of Babel is surely in the writer's mind. (Barrett, p 86)

How long this ecstatic experience lasted, we do not know, but from 'the day fully come' (verse 1), about six o'clock, to 'the third hour of the day', (verse 15) about nine o'clock, is three hours. Just as the disciples had been reluctant to leave the mountain side from which Jesus ascended into heaven, so it was quite possible that they were unwilling to leave that special place where they had been filled with the Holy Spirit. (verse 4). But they could not ignore what was going on outside.

Some scholars have surmised that they went to the Temple, as did Peter and John in Acts 3:1, or possibly that they had been in the Temple when the Spirit came. But certainly, there is a transition from a private event, 'in the house where they were sitting', (verse 2), to a public demonstration of the mighty power of God in enduing this group of people with the gift of tongues.

It is possible that this group of the followers of Jesus left the house where they had been staying and moved to the Temple to praise God and this would be the explanation of 'the multitude whio came together', being able to hear the believers 'telling in our own tongues the mighty works of God'. (verse 11). But the location is not given to us by Luke. The believers may simply have moved out onto the street. The wonderful tongues of fire which had sat upon each of them had apparently subsided, and the mighty rushing wind of the Holy Spirit had also dispersed, but they were left with the ability to praise God in other tongues, 'as the Spirit gave them utterance', (verse 4) declaring in these tongues the mighty works of God. (verse 1).

Acts 2:5-13. The amazement of the crowds

And all were amazed and perplexed, saying to one another, 'What does this mean?' But others mocking said,' They are filled with new wine'. (Acts 2:12, 13).

The multitude which heard them speak was a mixed multitude. Some of them were Jews and some were proselytes, men and women who had discovered in Judaism a way to God which they had not found in the Greek and Roman pantheons, and had converted to Judaism. They had come from the east (Parthia or Persia), from the west, Mesopotamia, from eastern Asia Minor and westward to the province of Asia.; from Asia Minor to Africa, Egypt and Libya and all they could do was marvel as they said, 'how is it that we hear, each of us in our own native language, the mighty works of God? (Acts 2:11). Are not these men Galileans? (Acts 2:7).

No wonder they were amazed and wondered. It was divine intervention, it was a miracle, and the very term miracle indicates that this was not a usual happening but quite outside their normal experience. It was also a different experience from that which became a normal worship experience later when the church met together and gratefully used the gifts of the Spirit. (1 Corinthians 14:26). The wonderful experience of being baptized in the Holy Spirit is a unique initial experience in the life of the believer. He or she moves on from there to life in the Spirit, and he or she learns to live his or her life out from that which the Holy Spirit has placed within, even the life of faith in the Son of God who loved us and gave Himself for us. (Galatians 2:20).

Though this experience on the Day of Pentecost was a different experience from that which many of these believers were to enjoy as part of their worship when they met together later as a church, speaking in tongues continued to be part of their worship, according to 1 Corinthians 12:4. Paul describes how the gift of tongues to one person could be allied to another who had the gift of interpretation of tongues. (1 Corinthians 12:10). This was a way in which God could communicate with His church and the church be edified, built up. (1 Corinthians 14:5). The gift of tongues is always associated with the building up of the Body of Christ, the church. (1 Corinthians 14:12). In Acts 19, Luke describes a group of believers who had only been baptized into John's baptism. 'And when Paul laid his hands on them, the Holy Spirit came on them, and they spoke with tongues and prophesied'. (Acts 19:6).

This phenomenon was very precious when the church was gathered together, but was subsequent to the inception of the church on the Day of Pentecost. Christians often speak of the birthday of the church, the day when the Spirit came to demonstrate His invisible presence among them, His power to cleanse and heal, to minister His saving grace as they receive from H[m by faith. The Holy Spirit glorifies Jesus (John 16:14), and brings men and women to God, their heavenly Father. He is the gifted Holy Spirit, gifted by the Father through the Son to those who love Him. How great is that gift! (John 14:26).

Paul did indeed write that the gift of tongues are a sign, not for believers but for unbelievers, (1 Corinthians 14:22), who coming into an assembly where people were speaking in tongues would assume that they were mad, especially if speaking in tongues was accompanied by prophecy. But they would soon come under the conviction that God was among them indeed as 'the secrets of their hearts are disclosed, and falling on their faces, would worship God'. (1 Corinthians 14:22-24).

Paul does however acknowledge that an unbeliever's first reaction on hearing the gift of tongues might well be, 'You are mad! This is the same kind of reaction from the crowd on the day of Pentecost, as Peter standing up with the other eleven, gets up to speak to the multitude. (Acts 2:14). Though some were saying, 'what does this mean?', others mocking said 'they are filled with new wine', (Acts 2:13) 'they are drunk'. This gave Peter the opening he needed. He says, 'these men are not drunk as you suppose, since it is only the third hour of the day', nine o'clock.

The normal time for the Jewish breakfast was the fourth hour of the day, ten o'clock. We can guess that on that morning they had no breakfast at all! It could certainly appear that these disciples were drunk, but they were 'drunk' with the Holy Spirit, completely satisfied in Him as He reached down into the very core of their being so that nothing else seemed to be of any importance in that moment of time, especially not food or drink.

Speaking with their own tongue, their own language, would have seemed entirely inadequate. Only Spirit given, Spirit inspired language could express all that was in them of joy, of thanksgiving, of worship to their heavenly Father. They felt it was not so much their speaking as the Holy Spirit speaking *through* them, but *beyond* and *above* them, ecstatically. This was ecstatic utterance. It was completely outside their present experience, or any experience they had ever encountered before. They were taken up into a completely new realm. But they felt no fear, only comfortably in the place where they had always wanted to be, entirely encompassed by their loving Lord, more fully aware than they had ever been of His love for them, and their love for each other.'As the Spirit gave them utterance', (Acts 2:4), they talked of what God had mightily done, of His power, of His might, of Himself.

It was inevitable that when Peter got up to speak, he refuted the suggestion that the disciples were drunk, but immediately turned to the Prophet Joel, for Joel had prophesied that the whole purpose of God in sending the Holy Spirit upon men and women was *salvation*. Joel prophesied saying, 'In the last days, whoever calls upon the Name of the Lord will be saved'. (Acts 2:17).

In the last days, it shall be, God declares, I will pour out My Spirit upon all flesh, and your sons and daughters shall prophesy, and your young men shall see visions, and your old men shall dream dreams, and whoever calls on the Name of the Lord shall be saved. (Acts 2:21).

Whoever shall call on the Name of the Lord. God is extending His salvation to whoever calls upon the Name of the Lord, 'this Jesus whom you have crucified, but whom God has made both Lord and Christ'. (Acts 2:36). This is the purpose of the coming of the Holy Spirit. Some of those who had heard the believers speaking in their own languages were amazed and perplexed, saying to one another 'What can this mean? (Acts 2:12). To Peter, filled with the Holy Spirit, and inspired by Him, was given the understanding to explain to them the meaning of what they had seen and heard.

Acts 2:14-36. Peter's appeal to the multitude quoting Joel

But Peter, standing with the eleven lifted up his voice and addressed them, 'Men of Judea and all who dwell in Jerusalem. Let this be known to you and give ear to my words. For these men are not drunk as you suppose since it is on;ly the third hour of the day; but this is what was spoken by the prophet Joel. 'And in the last days, it shall be, says God, that I shall pour out My Spirit upon all flesh'. (Acts 2:11-17).

Until three years previously, Peter had been an ordinary fisherman, going about his work, living an ordinary life among the people who lived along the shores of the Sea of Galilee, supplying them with much needed protein in their diet. Then he met Jesus. Or did Jesus meet him? Jesus later said, You did not choose me but I chose you and appointed you. (John 15:16). He could have refused the call of Jesus upon his life, for Jesus never coerces anyone, but when Jesus saw Peter and his brother Andrew casting a net into the sea, for they were fishermen, and said to them, 'Follow Me', they immediately left their nets and followed Him. (Mark 1:16-18; Matthew 4:18-20).

Luke says, 'they left *all* and followed Him', (Luke 5:11). This was total commitment=t to an itinerant preacher who had suddenly appeared on the scene, an act of faith and a life transforming decision which they had never regretted.

For three years, Peter had heard Jesus teaching, had seen His compassion for those who were sick, or disabled or hungry, had heard Him preaching the good news of the kingdom of God and at the end, had seen His arrest and condemnation to death on a cross and His glorious resurrection and ascension.

Was there anything he would not do for such a Master? such a Lord?

Inspired by the Holy Spirit, Peter stood up with the eleven, lifted up his voice and addressed the multitude. (Acts 2:14). His first care was for 'the men of Judea and all who dwell in Jerusalem'. They may well have seen the crucifixion of Jesus, and the crucifixion, death, resurrection and ascension of Jesus was the focus of what Peter was explaining to them, but he began with an Old Testament prophet, for Old Testament, Hebrew prophecy, would have been familiar to them as Jews. The crucifixion of Jesus would not have been particularly outstanding to them. Crucifixion was a common occurrence in Jerusalem under Roman occupation and one crucified man among others not especially worthy of consideration. But this crucifixion was different, followed as it was by the resurrection of Jesus and His ascension.

This crucifixion marked a new epoch in human history. This was the beginning of the 'last days', and the coming of the Holy Spirit was inaugurating this new epoch, the days of the church.

So Peter quoted the Old Testament prophet Joel, for Joel had a revelation from God that *in* the last days, God would pour out His Holy Spirit upon all flesh. The period of time under the old covenant initiated by Abraham had been fulfilled. The beginning of the time of the new covenant in His blood which Jesus had come to give His disciples had begun as God poured out His Holy Spirit on 'all flesh'. These are the last days.

The Holy Spirit had always come upon the Lord's prophets, priests and kings whenever they needed the anointing of the Holy Spirit for the accomplishment of a task which God had given them. But Joel had a vision that in the last days, He would not be restricted as in former times, but would come upon 'all flesh', (Acts 2:17). He would come upon sons and daughters, young men and old men, menservants and maidservants, all classes and members of society. All these, all flesh, would come under an outpouring of the Holy Spirit. They would prophesy, see visions, dream dreams.

But this was not all. At the *end* of the last days, the whole cosmic universe would be affected. God declares, 'I will show wonders in the heaven above and signs on the earth beneath, blood and fire and vapour of smoke. The sun shall be turned into darkness and the moon into blood before the day of the

Lord comes, the great and manifest day. And it shall be that whoever calls on the Name of the Lord shall be saved, (Acts 2:17-21; Joel 2:30-31).

Peter was quoting this terrifying prophecy of Joel's, not to minimize what was then happening, the *first* of the 'last days' when the Holy Spirit was being outpoured and men and women in Jerusalem at that time could see evidence of His outpouring in the gift of tongues; but to explain that this was *only the beginning* of what God had in mind ultimately for all creation. The last days had begun with the outpouring of the Holy Spirit, the final epoch of God's involvement with the world and the people whom He had created to be with Him forever. But He knew that many would reject what He had done for them, would not respond to His loving, providential care of them. So at the end of the epoch, these last days, God will give mankind a final opportunity to turn to Him. And it shall be that whoever calls on the Name of the Lord shall be saved. (Acts 2:21; Joel 2:32).

In Joel's time, conditions in Palestine had deteriorated considerably within the Jewish community which had been left behind while others went into exile in Babylon. They were made even more difficult by a plague of locusts which stripped every plant bare, destroying the harvest and the vines and the fig trees, and leaving famine in its wake.

Joel implores the people to turn to God, to cry to Him, (Joel 2:12-14), for he recognizes that this tragedy, this plague of locusts has to be seen as a reminder of His judgement for their apathy, but also could be could be an opportunity to return to Him, relying on God's intense love for His people. And as Joel is prophesying, he sees the people turning to their God in fasting and weeping and mourning (Joel 2:12) while God replies, 'I will restore the years which the locusts have eaten. (Joel 2:27). I am the Lord your God and there is no one else, and My people shall never again be put to shame. And I will grant you a further blessing. I will pour out My Holy Spirit at the dawning of the Messianic age. I will use visions and dreams and prophecies to give you revelation of Myself' (Joel 2:25,29).

And I will give all My people a second chance. There will be multitudes in the valley of decision. People who have not yet turned to me will have an opportunity to repent as they see the sun darkened and the moon turned into blood and the stars withdraw their shining and realise that the valley of decision is also a valley of judgement. (Joel 3:14,15)

And Joel proclaims and Peter echoes it, 'but all who call on the Name of the Lord will be saved'. (Joel 2:32; Acts 2:21). The Holy Spirit has come.

During these last days, until the Parousia, the coming again of the Lord Jesus, God will continue to reveal Himself to His people. But when the Day of the Lord comes, it will be preceded by signs in sun and moon and stars, and upon the earth distress of nations in perplexity at the roaring of the sea and the waves; men fainting with fear and with foreboding of what is coming on the world; for the powers of the heaven will be shaken. And then they will see the Son of Man coming in a cloud with power and great glory. (Luke 21:25-27).

This will be the end of the last days, the final day, the day of the Lord.

But we have not yet seen the end of the last days. The last days, the days of opportunity for repentance and faith and turning to the Lord are still mercifully with us. But the day of the Lord will come at a time when we are not expecting Him, when time will be no more, when there will be a new heaven and a new earth in which dwells righteousness. (2 Peter 3:9). There are always those 'scoffers', who say, 'Where is the promise of His coming? (2 Peter 3:4). But the Lord is not slack concerning His promise, but is forbearing, not wishing that any should perish but that all should come to repentance. (2 Peter 3:9)

Peter is even now offering the gift of repentance to these 'men of Israel' (Acts 2:22), for he wants them to know that the gift of the promise of the Holy Spirit is for them and for their children, and to all who are far off, everyone whom the Lord our God shall call to Him. (Acts 2:39). And Peter explains that the name of the Lord upon whom they should call is Jesus.

Acts 2:22-36. Peter speaks of Jesus of Nazareth

Men of Israel, listen to these words. Jesus of Nazareth, a man attested to you by God with miracles and wonders and signs which God performed through Him In your midst as you yourselves know..... this man, delivered over by the predetermined plan and foreknowledge of God you nailed to a cross by the hands of godless men and put Him to death. But God raised Him up again.

Peter says that this is why the men of Israel should call on the Name of Jesus of Nazareth, of whom they had all undoubtedly heard, whom 'you yourselves know', (Acts 2:22), who was a man attested and legitimated by God with many signs and wonders which God had done through HIm in their midst. Jesus bore upon Him the authority of God and all He said and did was projected from His relationship to God.

Peter unflinchingly continues, this Jesus, delivered up according to the definite plan and foreknowledge of God, *you* crucified and killed by the hands of lawless men. But God raised him up having loosed the pangs of death because it was not possible for Him to be held by it. (Acts 2:23, 24.).

These lawless men, who did not obey the law of Moses, whose very nature was rebellion against law, even the law of God, had carried out the dreadful task of actually crucifying Jesus, but they, (and we) were all complicit. Death entered the world through sin. (Romans 5:12). It can only occur where there is sin, and Jesus knew no sin (2 Corinthians 5:21). How then could Jesus die?. Hebrews tells that through the Eternal Spirit He offered HImself without blemish to God so that men and women could be purified, redeemed, and forgiven (Hebrews 9:14.15, 22), and Jesus now appears in the presence of God on their behalf, always living to make intercession for them. (Hebrews 7:25)

So it was necessary for the salvation of men and women that He should be crucified, offering Himself up to the Father as a living sacrifice wholly acceptable to Him, employing the lawlessness of those who crucified Him to further the definite plan and foreknowledge of God, (Acts 2:23).

Acts 2:25-36. Peter's appeal to the people quoting David

God raised Him up, having loosed the pangs of death because it was not possible for Him to be held by it. For David says concerning Him,' I saw the Lord always before me, for He is at my right hand that I may not be shaken'. Therefore my heart was glad and my tongue rejoiced, moreover my flesh will dwell in hope. For Thou wilt not abandon My soul to Hades, nor let Thy Holy One see corruption. (Psalm 132:8-10).

Peter further explains why it was impossible for Jesus to be held by death. He claims that David, speaking prophetically, recognized Him as the Holy One whom it was impossible for God to abandon to 'corruption', (the word for Sheol), or to Hades, (the Greek equivalent), the soul of a Holy One. (Psalm 16:10).

As a prophet, David could only point to the Holy One who should come. He did not know the Name of Jesus. But there has only ever been one Holy One, the Lord Jesus Christ. David confesses, I saw the Lord always before me, because He is at my right hand I shall not be moved'. (Psalm 16:8; Acts 2:25). He saw in a vision, or it was revealed to him, this risen Lord whom death could not hold, who would be the source of joy and hope and security to David as he dwelt in the presence of the risen Lord whose name he did not know, but the reality of whom was so real to him. (Psalm 16:26,28).

'Brethren', says Peter, lovingly including these people into this new family, this new experience, 'Brethren, I may say to you confidently of the patriarch David that he both died and was buried, and his tomb is with us to this day'. This was in fact true. They would have known that David's tomb was in the south of the city, near Siloam. (Bruce p 94). Peter continues, David was not speaking of himself, but of one who should come, who would be one of his descendents. (Acts 2:30; 2 Samuel 7:16; Psalm 132:11,12).

This One would not be abandoned to Hades, for God would raise him up. (Acts 2:31). The fact of the resurrection of Jesus, could be confirmed by all those standing with Peter on this Pentecost day, who had been witnesses to their risen Lord and could testify that this was indeed the One of whom David had been prophetically speaking, according to Psalm 132:11, the oath that God had sworn to David. It was a covenant of grace that He had made with him, that the one who was descended genealogically from him should be the Anointed One, the Messiah. (Luke 3:34; Matthew 1:1.) Peter is keen to emphasize that *Jesus* was the One whom God had raised up from death, and also raised by His Father to His right hand, the right hand of God; and had received from His Father the gift of the outpouring of the Holy Spirit which He had promised, 'which you now see and hear'. (Acts 2:33).

This was the preaching of the gospel under the power of the Holy Spirit. This was what they were both hearing and seeing. *This was the first preaching of the gospel* ever undertaken by a servant of God under the power of the anointing of the Holy Spirit.

The gospel begins with the Lord Jesus as Jesus of Nazareth, designated as the Son of God by the manifestation of the mighty works of power which God did through Him, the power of God which resided in Him, (Acts 2:22), but who was predestined by God to be crucified and killed by the hands of lawless men, but who is now risen from the dead because God raised Him up and exalted Him to glory, to the right hand of God. (Acts 2:22- 24,33). This is the gospel.

This however is not God's final word concerning His Son. All this has taken place, not to establish the credentials of Jesus, as if He somehow needed to qualify or verify His position as the Son of God, but to declare God's further purpose. It was only necessary to summarize the life, death and resurrection of Jesus because without these tremendous happenings, the Son of God, incarnated as the Son of Man and giving Himself

29

as a sacrifice for sin, God's ultimate purpose could not be achieved.

Jesus had returned to His Father in order to claim the promise of the outpouring of the Holy Spirit, and this He accomplished when He was raised up to the right hand of the Father, a position revealed to David in Psalm 110:1. The Lord said to my Lord, sit at My right hand till I make your enemies your footstool'. This is the exaltation text.

Because of His exaltation Peter was able to conclude that 'Jesus, the One whom you crucified, God has made both Lord and Christ'. (Acts 2:36). The work which Jesus had begun on earth would be continued by a band of men and women on whom the Holy Spirit had been outpoured. And the first group to be given that privilege were also given the gift of speaking in tongues. That was the evidence that the Holy Spirit was with them.

The Lord, YAHWEH, said to my Lord, ADONAI, sit at my right hand, till I make your enemies my footstool. (Psalm 110:1). Yahweh is the covenant Name for God, the covenant made with Moses at the burning bush and meaning; 'i am that I am'. Adonai means Lord', and is used by Jewish religious leadership when to use Yahweh could compromise the taking of the Lord's Name in vain, violating the second commandment.

Psalm 110:1 is the basic exaltation text. Christ had emptied Himself, laid aside his glory which He had with the Father before the world was, (John 17:5), so that He could become a man and die, for only as a man could He redeem men and women. He emptied Himself from God to man, and was restored to God again, for He had become the Saviour, Jesus, and God had exalted this One and given Him a name above all other Names, that at the Name of Jesus, every knee should bow and every tongue confess that Jesus Christ is Lord, to the glory of God the Father. (Philippians 2:7-11).

Though Jesus had emptied Himself of equality with God at His incarnation for the sake of sinful men and women, God was fully restoring that equality to Him. Peter is saying with all the emphasis of which he is capable that God has made Him both

Lord and Christ, the One in whom all the fulness, the *pleroma* (Gk) of the Godhead resides bodily, (Colossians 1:19), and in whom God was able to reconcile all things to Himself, whether things in heaven or things on earth, making peace through the blood of His cross. (Colosians 1:20).

For whose sake did He empty Himself? Certainly for the sake of His Father. Jesus had chosen to go this way so that His Father would be glorified. He said 'I seek not my own will but the will of Him who sent Me. (John 5:40). But *also* for the 'men of Israel' to whom Peter was speaking, *and for all* who call on the Name of the Lord that they might be saved, (Acts 2:23). For as Peter said later, there is no other Name under heaven given among men whereby we must be saved'. (Acts 4:12).

This is the gospel, the foundation truth on which the church is built. This Jesus, whom you crucified, God has made both Lord and Christ; *Lord*; as representing the ineffable Name and character of God; *Christ*; as representing His Messiahship, His anointing with the Holy Spirit, His being sent by God on a mission to call out a people from the ends of the earth for Himself. It explains why the early church so loved to call Him 'Christ', so that Christ became for them almost an alternative name rather than a title; this one whom God raised up, who has become so precious to them. Paul writes to the Corinthians, 'We preach Christ crucified, a stumbling block to Jews and folly to the Gentiles, but to those who are being saved, Christ the power of God and the wisdom of God'.

But how we love the Name of Jesus, The angel said to Joseph at His conception, 'You shall call His Name Jesus, for He shall save His people from their sins;. (Matthew 1:21). We know how much we need salvation, and that Jesus has come to bear away our sins on His Body on the tree, as Peter encourages us in his first letter. (1 Peter 2:24).

The preaching of the gospel begins with Jesus who at His baptism in the River Jordan heard His heavenly Father say, 'This is My beloved Son in whom I am well pleased, (Matthew 3:17). And it continues with Jesus pouring the love of God into the hearts of men and women through the Holy Spirit,

(Romans 5:5), bringing them into relationship with Him and through them raising up a people who would love Him, love one another and seek to walk His way. This is what the Acts of the Apostles goes on to describe so vividly and comprehensively. Acts 2:14-36 gives a superb summary of the gospel as Peter is inspired by the Holy Spirit.

But there is a sense that though Peter has begun at the beginning with the earthly ministry of Jesus and His death, resurrection and ascension and ends with His exaltation to God's right hand, claiming the promise of the outpouring of the Holy Spirit; this is not the full story. God was about to do a new thing through His Holy Spirit, to bring into being *a worldwide church,* for the Holy Spirit had come to enable generations as yet unborn to know and understand what Jesus has done, and done for them. He started on the Day of Pentecost with a small group of one hundred and twenty people and 'there were added *that day* about three thousand souls' (Acts 2:41).

Acts 2:37-40. The call to repentance

Now when they heard this, they were pierced to the heart and said to Peter and the rest of the apostles, 'Brethren, what shall we do?'. Peter said to them, 'repent and be baptised in the Name of Jesus Christ for the forgiveness of your sins, and you will receive the gift of the Holy Spirit. (Acts 2:37).

The Holy Spirit had inspired Peter with a complete summary of the gospel. But it was not his words alone that caused men and women to cry out 'Brethren, what shall we do?' (Acts 2:36). The Holy Spirit was moving in convicting power among them, as Jesus had said He would, convicting them concerning sin, and righteousness and judgement. (John 16:8,9,).

In their distress they cried out to Peter and the rest of the apostles, 'Brethren, what shall we do?' They were cut to the heart, convicted of terrible guilt that such a One had been crucified at the instigation of their own religious leaders, an agonizing and cruel death for someone who had been innocent (or even for someone who was guilty), to whom Peter had just borne witness that He was the Son of God, their promised Messiah.

Though not personally responsible for the death of Jesus, they had a strong and sudden conviction that they were guilty of sin, of rebellion against God. Although they were here in Jerusalem to celebrate one of the three prescribed feasts of the Lord, their hearts were not upright before Him. Peter had said that God had made Jesus both Lord and Christ, (Acts 2:36). But He was not *their* Lord. Jesus had not been for them their promised Messiah. They were still waiting for Him to come, still waiting for the prophecies to be fulfilled, for 'the One who should come'. (Matthew 11:3).

Peter was telling them that He *had come*, that Jesus was indeed the Messiah, the Christ, for so God had always intended. 'Let all the house of Israel know assuredly that God has made Him both Lord and Christ'. (Acts 2:36). He was the One sent from God to be a ransom for sin; and by His sacrifice of Himself on the Cross to buy them back to God from all that was of sin in their lives, to a different life, eternal life which God supplied to them. They could be a forgiven people. They could be clean in His sight. They are suddenly faced with the reality of who He is. Jesus is the Christ. And their perhaps inadvertent rejection of Him has brought them under the judgement of God.

'Brethren, what shall we do?' they said.

Peter had not far to look for an answer to that question, the most important question that anyone could ever ask.

He remembered John the Baptist who had preached repentance, to which many had responded, declaring openly their repentance by being baptized in the River Jordan. And John had also proclaimed with great certainty that the One who would come after him, the Lord Jesus, would baptize them with the Holy Spirit and with fire. (Matthew 3:11). But even more importantly, after His baptism and period of temptation in the wilderness, Jesus went about all Galilee, preaching the kingdom of God and saying,' Repent, for the kingdom of God is at hand'. (Matthew 4:17).

So Peter, following in his Master's footsteps said to them, 'Repent and be baptized every one of you in the Name of Jesus Christ for the forgiveness of your sins, and you shall receive the gift of the Holy Spirit. For the promise is to you, and your children, and to all who are far off, everyone whom the Lord our God calls to Him'. (Acts 2:38,39).

Peter and those who were with him on the Day of Pentecost had prayed for and received the Gift of the Holy Spirit. Those who were in the crowd *outside* had 'heard and were amazed and wondered', when they heard them speaking in tongues. How much more privileged were those who had been *inside,* in the house when the Spirit came. But Peter did not want to keep this wonderful gift to himself and his friends. He did not want an exclusive esoteric club, available only to the initiated. Inspired by the Holy Spirit, he extended the invitation to all those gathered together. 'Repent', he said 'and be baptised in the Name of Jesus, and you will receive the gift of the Holy Spirit, and not only you but your children as well, and not only those here today, but for those who are not here with us on this wonderful Day of Pentecost, for the Lord is going to call many more to Himself'.

Peter was convinced that this was what God had in mind. His covenant with Noah, (Genesis 9:9), with Abraham, (Genesis 13:15; 17:7; Galatians 3:16), and with David, (Psalm 18:50; 89:34; 132:11). all spoke of God wanting to extend His loving provision to 'many nations'. Isaiah 57:19 speaks of the Lord wanting to give 'peace, peace to them that are far off and to those who are near'; on the basis of contrition. The conjunction of those far off and those who are near agrees so graciously with the words of Joel 2:32, *whoever* calls on the Name of the Lord shall be saved; the Lord calling them to Himself as in Isaiah 57:15. Barrett says 'they call upon Him who has already called them. (Barrett, p 156).

But Peter did not stop there. 'He testified with many other words and exhorted them saying,' Save yourselves from this crooked generation'. (Acts 2:40). By their rejection of their Messiah this crooked generation had incurred the righteous judgement of God. (Matthew 23:36; Luke 11:50). But Jesus had provided a way to escape judgement. It was the way of repentance. He had offered this way to the religious leaders throughout His ministry but they had rejected it as they had rejected Him. Back in the time of Isaiah, the Lord had said to His people, 'All the day long I have spread out My hands to a rebellious people', (Isaiah 65:2), the loving Lord pleading with His people to come to Him. Isaiah again reminds the people, 'The Lord's hand is not shortened that it cannot save, nor His ear dull that it cannot hear, but your iniquities have made a separation between you and your God and your sins have hid His face from you'. (Isaiah 59:1).

But God has given men and women, His people, free will. They may choose to come to Him, but equally they may choose not to. But on this occasion they came. Three thousand souls that day were added to the infant church, (Acts 2:41); all those who had received the word and were baptised.

This was the first Christian church. The call was to all, but the response was from every individual person whose heart the Holy Spirit had touched. Through baptism they had placed themselves under the authority of Jesus Christ for they had been baptised in His Name. They had turned away, *metanoia*, repentance, *from* a life of disobedience to God, which is sin, and turned *to* the One who could forgive sin and give them eternal life; not only a future life, but a life which begins now with repentance and goes on forever, the life of the Lord Jesus within them, as Paul writes, 'the life I now live, I live by the faith of the Son of God, who loved me and gave Himself for me'. (Galatians 2:20).

The swollen population in Jerusalem at that time because of the festival had led to three thousand souls turning to Christ, which with the one hundred and twenty of Acts 1:18, formed the nucleus of what God was about to do as the primitive church grew from day to day. (Acts 2:47).

The scope of the gospel and its acceptance will go on growing throughout Acts, throughout the world, and down through the centuries.

Acts 2:41-47. Life in the early church

So those who received his word were baptized and there were added that day about three thousand souls. And they devoted themselves to the apostles' teaching, and fellowship, and to the breaking of bread, and the prayers.

These new believers adopted a way of life that has been familiar throughout all periods of Christian history. To begin with, these newly baptized believers wanted and needed instruction, for they wanted to learn more of what Jesus had taught while He was on earth. There had been times when His teaching had been public, as for example, the sermon on the mount; but there were other occasions when He and His disciples had withdrawn to a more private place where He could share with them what His Father was saying to Him. (Matthew 13:10; John 6:67; Mark 8:27).

In this way the apostles' teaching became authoritative, because it was the teaching of Jesus through the apostles. So these new believers sat hungrily at the feet of the apostles. Please tell us more, they would plead. We want to know about Jesus, what He said and what He did.

Sometimes, the apostles' teaching was augmented and authenticated by 'many wonders and signs done through the apostles'. (Acts 2:43). Jesus had given them authority for this. After calling the twelve disciples, He gave them authority over unclean spirits, to cast them out, and to heal every disease and every infirmity, and 'preach as you go saying, the kingdom of God is at hand'. (Matthew 10:1, 7). As the apostles received the Holy Spirit, the authority which Jesus had given them became energized within them, and this authority was certainly recognized by these new believers. They devoted themselves to the apostles' teaching.

But they also discovered that they had become a fellowship of believers. Fellowship, *koinonia*, means sharing, participation. The outworking of this fellowship led to the sharing of their possessions with each other, and eventually with anyone who had need. (Acts 2:45). But the initial sharing, the initial fellowship was the sense of belonging to each other, of sharing a common experience, giving them a common life together. They were together, they had each other to love and care for, to support. They had become a loving church, a loving community of the people of God. They devoted themselves to the fellowship. (Acts 2:42).

As they enjoyed this fellowship together, they discovered that they wanted to share their meals together too, and as they did so, what more natural than that they should remember the last meal that Jesus had with His disciples, when He broke bread with them saying,' this is My body which is given for you. Do this in remembrance of Me. (Luke 23:19; Matthew 26:26; Mark 14:22). It was a way of remembering Him together. He had also said,' This is My commandment that you love one another as I have loved you' (John 15:12). So they broke bread together 'in their homes' (RSV), 'from house to house' (AV), expressing their fellowship and love for each other and constantly renewing their loving remembrance of Him. (Acts 2:46).

Even up to the time of Paul's writing to the church in Corinth, it appears that this was a common practice among believers; that it was a real as well as a symbolic meal. (1 Corinthians 11:21). Only later did it become ritualised as a specific Christian sacrament, known variously as Holy Communion, or the Lord's Supper, or the Eucharist. There has of course been much theological thinking about the precious significance of the broken Body and poured out Blood of the Lord Jesus. We get the impression, or the sense, that for these believers, breaking bread together mostly consisted in remembering HIs love for them as He gave his life for them on the Cross, sharing together the wonderful thing that had happened to them of salvation from their sin and of faith in the Lord Jesus Christ.

They rejoiced in the revelation of His love for them and the joy of their love for one another. They devoted themselves to the breaking of bread. (Acts 2:42).

They devoted themselves also to the prayers; the many requests agreed to by all, for Jesus had said, 'if two of you shall agree on earth about anything you ask, it will be done for you by

My Father in heaven. (Matthew 18:19). He also said, whatever you ask in My Name, I will do it, that the Father may be glorified in the Son. If you ask anything *in My Name*, I will do it'. (John 14:13,14).

They are beginning to learn the power and authority behind that Name. As they pray into the Name of Jesus, they are praying into the whole character and purpose of God; His faithfulness and steadfast love; His will to be done on earth as it is done in heaven. They can say 'Amen' to one another's prayers because 'Amen' is one of the Names of Jesus. (Revelation 3:14); Jesus who said, 'Lo, I come to do your will, O my God. (Hebrews 10:7).

They were praying in the Spirit. They were praying with understanding also, (1 Corinthians 14:15), praying as we do for friends and family and for those who are as yet outside the kingdom, for those far away and for those at hand, for the governing authorities, (Romans 13:1). They were praying through immediate circumstances, being comforted and counselled by the Holy Spirit as He had promised and perhaps again singing in psalms and hymns and spiritual songs, making melody in their hearts to the Lord, always and for everything giving thanks to God the Father through Him. (Ephesians 5:15).

What wonderful times of prayer these would have been, this close intimacy with each other and with the Father in the Name of Jesus. They devoted themselves to prayer. (Acts 2:42).

These were the halcyon days of the church, 'days of heaven upon earth', (Deuteronomy 11:21. AV), seldom if ever to be repeated. They believed together, prayed together, ate together, partaking of food with glad and generous hearts, praising God and having favour with all the people. And the Lord added to them daily, those who were being saved. (Acts 2:47).

They shared their homes and possessions and distributed them to those in need, so that no-one either in or out of the group was left out of the daily provision even if it meant selling such things as they had in order to supply their need. (Acts 2:45). Marshall says. 'Everyone held his possessions at the disposal of others whenever the need arose. (Marshall p 84).

They were also to be seen in the Temple precincts, a large space in which to come together outside of their homes. (Acts 2:46). But whether learning, loving, sharing, praying, they were witnessing to their new life in Christ, to such an extent that they had favour with all the people, and under the power of the Holy Spirit, to rejoice day by day that there were others who were being saved.

This primitive church could not help but expand. The primitive church was a Pentecost church and was soon to be tested to the limits of its authenticity, even as Jesus had promised. The fear which fell upon all who heard Peter's sermon (Acts 2:43), was no invisible or fleeting impression but something which continued into the days ahead as people saw the effect of the signs and wonders done by the apostles, (Acts 2:43) as a vindication of the gospel invitation and validation that this was indeed the work of the Holy Spirit. Karl Barth writes, (Church dogmatics 3.4,49), 'the church has no reason for existence apart from the kingdom of God, the call and word of God and the power of the Holy Spirit'. (quoted by Barrett p 172).

This is indeed the reason for the church's existence, and its continued existence relies on the word of God and the operation of the Holy Spirit, constantly challenging the lives of men and women so that they might be saved and added to the church, God's redeemed community.

Acts Chapter 3

Acts 3:1-10. The healing of the lame man at the beautiful gate of the Temple

Now Peter and John were going up to the Temple at the hour of prayer, the ninth hour. And a man lame from birth was being carried, whom they laid daily at that gate of the Temple which is called Beautiful, to ask alms of those who entered the Temple. Seeing Peter and John about to go into the Temple, he asked for alms. And Peter directed his gaze at him and said, 'Look on us'. And he fixed his attention on them expecting to receive something from them. But Peter said 'I have no silver or gold, but I give you what I have. In the Name of Jesus of Nazareth, walk'. (Acts 3:1-6).

And he took him by the hand and raised him up, and immediately his feet and ankle bones received strength. And leaping up he stood and walked and entered the Temple, walking and leaping and praising God. (Acts 3:7-9).

It appears that it had become customary for members of this new community to meet together in the temple. (Acts 2:46). Peter and John were on their way to the temple expecting to enter by the beautiful gate. This was possibly the Nicanor Gate, which led from the court of the Gentiles into the women's court and was familiarly known as the Beautiful Gate because it was constructed of Corinthian bronze, a huge structure, seventy five feet high, with magnificent double doors, 'far exceeding those plated with silver and gold', as Josephus the historian writes in his volume 'The Jewish War'. (quoted by F.F Bruce, p 104). It was on the eastern side of the temple and would be approached from the Mount of Olives, or from the villages on that side of the city.

Distance from the villages may be the reason why it was not until the ninth hour, three o'clock in the afternoon, before the lame man was seen to be carried by his friends and laid at the beautiful gate of the temple. Legally, according to Mosaic Law, he would not have been permitted to enter the temple precincts because of his disability but would have been allowed to sit at the entrance and beg for alms.

It may have been that Jesus had passed by him as He went in and out of the temple. yet had not laid His healing hands upon him; but His timing is always perfect. Until now it had not been the right time for the lame man to be released from this life which he had been compelled from necessity to live for forty years since his birth. (Acts 4:22). Now he was not only going to be healed, but his healing was going to bear witness to the saving power of the Name of Jesus.

Luke uses the terminology,' lame from his mother's womb', and also notices how long the man had been in this condition, and we remember that Luke was the beloved physician, (Colossians 4:14), retailing this episode in the life of the newly emerging church as a medical as well as a spiritual phenomenon. This man is paralysed. He cannot move by himself and has to be carried to the gate of the temple. HIs only means of subsistence is to sit, or perhaps lie, and beg alms from those who frequented the temple.

Acts 3:1. The ninth hour

It was the ninth hour.

It was the time of the evening sacrifice. Perhaps Peter and John had made an appointment with the other apostles to meet at that hour, for the time was significant. They were beginning to understand many things which had formerly been a mystery to them. They now saw the force of the declaration made by John the Baptist that Jesus is 'the Lamb of God who takes away the sin of the world'. (John 1:29), and realised that the daily offering of the morning and evening sacrifices in the temple, the offering of a lamb without blemish to God, the continual burnt offering, (Numbers 28:3,4.) was symbolic of the offering up of the Lord Jesus as an offering to God, the Lamb of God, not on an altar but on the cross.

Jesus is the sacrificial Lamb. The cereal offering representing His humanity, and the libation offering symbolising His blood poured out for the forgiveness of sin, were offerings made in conjunction with the offering of the Lamb. (Numbers 28:5,7-8). All the ritual and ceremony since the time of the tabernacle in the wilderness and now in Herod's beautiful temple had been passed on from generation to generation and yet was only a shadow of what was to come. (Hebrews 8:5). The reality was Jesus. Everything speaks of Him. He fulfilled all that was behind the sacrificial system. He fulfilled all the law and the prophets. (Matthew 5:17). He was the first and the final word. He was and is, the Logos.

The morning and evening sacrifices were a reminder to the Jewish people that God was meeting with them and speaking to them. As with the tabernacle in the wilderness; as with Solomon's temple; as with the post exilic temple and now with Herod's temple; there was in the midst of the people of God a place sanctified to the glory of the Lord, consecrated to Him, where His people could meet with Him.

This ninth hour, the time of the evening sacrifice had become very precious to the Jews, for it was the fulfilment of the promise which God had made to them. 'I will dwell among the people of Israel, and I will be their God. And they shall know that I am the Lord who brought them out of the land of Egypt that I might dwell with them. I am the Lord their God'. (Exodus 29:38-46).

This was their Redeemer. He had redeemed them; delivered them, from slavery. Amazingly, Peter and John had become aware that all the types and figures of the Hebrew scriptures had been fulfilled in Jesus. He was the spotless Lamb of God who was slain. They were going up to the temple, but not for the hour of sacrifice but for the hour of prayer. (Acts 3:1). There was no need of further sacrifice for sin, (Hebrews 10:18), for this One with whom they had lived and talked for three years was now revealed to them as the Lamb of God, sacrificed for them, not on an altar but on the cross, as it had been revealed to John the Baptist at the outset of Jesus' ministry, the Lamb of God who takes away the sin of the world. (John 1:29). Where there is forgiveness of sin, purchased for all mankind on the cross, there is no longer the need for a constant offering for sin. (Hebrews 10:18). By the single offering of Himself, Jesus has perfected, made complete for all time those who are sanctified, (Hebrews 10:14); delivered, redeemed, sanctified them through the precious blood of the sacrifice of Christ on the cross. Peter and John went up to the temple at the ninth hour for prayer.

Acts 3:1. The two apostles witness to the power of the Name of Jesus

Now Peter and John were going up to the temple at the ninth hour, the hour of prayer. Acts 3:1).

The apostle John plays little part in this narrative but he is important as a witness and shares in the arrest and imprisonment meted out to Peter and John by the religious authorities. It had always been a principle of Jewish law that out of the mouth of two or three witnesses, every word should be established. (Deuteronomy 19:5). Jesus too had sent out His disciples two and two into every town and place where He Himself would come. (Luke 10:1). Peter and John went together to the temple to pray.

Peter and John and James had become an inner circle within the group of the twelve disciples. They had been with Jesus at the bedside of a dead child. (Matthew 9:25). They had been with Him on the mount of transfiguration. (Matthew 17:1; Luke 9:29), and in the Garden of Gethsemane, (Matthew 26:32; Mark 14:33). They were the two or three witnesses out of whose mouths every word would be established. On this occasion it was Peter and John.

Though Acts 2:43 had spoken of 'many signs and wonders' which had been done by the apostles after they had been filled with the Holy Spirit, and Acts 2:47 speaks of the believers having favour with all the people, it was not until the significant healing of the lame man, and perhaps even more significantly, Peter's speech to the people who had seen the lame man 'walking, leaping and praising God, (Acts 3:9), that the chief priests and the captain of the Temple, and the Sadducees decided to come and arrest them.

Now Peter and John were going up to the temple at the hour of prayer. The contrast could not be greater between them, and the lame man. They had an ability to walk through the gate of the temple to their time of prayer, and this helpless man lying at the gate of the temple, however beautiful, was confined to being outside the beautiful gate. He would have preferred to be walking about Jerusalem, or going to the temple himself, or having an employment which gave him a purpose in life, and going home to a loving family. But because of his disability, he was an outsider from his own culture; from his own religious beliefs. He could see Peter and John walking purposefully towards the temple though he may not have known about the wonderful time of prayer which they were about to share with others of the amazing church which the Holy Spirit had brought into being. All he could do was to hold out his hands for a gift.

But none of them had any money. In this respect they were the same. The lame man had none. He had to beg for alms for his very existence, for if no-one gave him money he would starve. The apostles had no money either. 'Silver and gold have I none', said Peter, 'but what I have I give you. (Acts 3:6). 'In the name of Jesus Christ of Nazareth, rise up and walk'.

Peter was confident that what he had would fully meet the poor man's need, for what he had was the authority of the Name of Jesus. Peter knew that the Name of Jesus was a powerful Name, and he believed that that Name, by faith in that Name, would make the poor disabled man well; that he would be healed.

This formerly weak, vacillating Peter had become empowered by the Holy Spirit. The proposed miracle was a risk that he was taking, but it was the risk of faith, faith in the Name of Jesus. He commanded the man, 'in the Name of Jesus, walk! (Acts 3:6). And he reached out his hands and lifted him up.

Immediately, the miracle happened. HIs feet and ankle bones received strength. Here again, Luke the physician is intrigued by his medical condition. It appeared that his diseased feet and ankle bones were the source of his paralysis, and it was those which needed to be made strong. When Jesus had called His disciples to Him, they rose and followed Him. This man had needed help to rise and follow the Lord Jesus, but God had provided for him the help which he needed. Peter held out his hands to him and lifted him up.

It is possible that Luke knew the medical phraseology, had perhaps investigated the nature of the disease, had perhaps been involved in the gradual improvement of such a condition in others. Luke, the narrator of this miracle, was filled with amazement at what had happened to this lame man. He could identify with those who were filled with wonder at the signs and wonders which had been the evidence that God was doing a new work, but also *continuing* the work which Jesus had so recently done among them before His death and resurrection. That which Jesus had begun to do and to teach before He was taken back to heaven, the Holy Spirit was continuing to do, through the faith of His followers and their trust in Him. (Acts 1:1).

The people too were filled with wonder and amazement at the healing of this man, as they saw him walking and leaping and praising God, the one whom they recognised as having 'sat for alms at the beautiful gate of the temple'. (Acts 3:10). As Peter and John breathed a sigh of relief that the Name of Jesus had been fully vindicated, that in His Name the man had been really and truly healed, that Jesus had been magnified and glorified in the sight of these people, they remembered the words of the Lord Jesus, 'with men this is impossible, but not with God, for with God all things are possible'. (Matthew 19:26).

In the Name of Jesus, the man was fully healed. He not only walked but leaped!, 'walking, leaping and praising God'. (Acts 3:8). For he recognised that it was not Peter and John who had healed him, but God. The man had had a personal encounter with Peter, and that was unusual for him, for people often passed him by indifferently, or mechanically offered charity as part of their religious duty. But Peter had said, 'Look on us'. (Acts 3:4). And he had fixed his attention on them expecting to receive something from them.

But Peter wanted him to know that this was more specifically an encounter with Jesus, that this was not just an offer of help routinely offered. It was a life changing experience of the love of the Lord Jesus for this man personally in whose Name Peter and John had commanded the blessing of wholeness. And to affirm that this was individual to him, Peter took him by the right hand and lifted him up.

The Lord is always scrupulous in maintaining *personal* salvation, and *personal* healing. Though His mercy and love are universal, and available to all, it is to the individual man, woman or child that He gives the invitation, 'Come to Me'. (Matthew 11:28). It has truly been said that God has no grandchildren. Each one who comes to Him becomes His child. 'To all who received Him, who believed in HIs Name, He gave the power (RSV), the right, (AV), to become the children of God. (John 1:12).

The man immediately followed Peter and John into the temple. He was no longer disabled, and had the right now to enter the temple; and as it was the ninth hour, to witness the evening sacrifice. But he knew where his future now lay. It was not with the religious culture in which he had been born, but with these people of God who were meeting together for prayer. And we may speculate that his friends who had brought him and carried him to the beautiful gate of the temple, and seen the miracle which had taken place, would want to join him as he went into the temple.

However, they were not able to get very far. While the previously lame man clung to Peter and John, (Acts 3:11), 'all the people ran together to them in the portico, or porch or colonnade, which is called Solomon's'. This was a kind of cloister which ran along the eastern wall of the temple, where Jesus Himself had sometimes walked. (John 10:23).

The people needed answers to the many questions they wanted to ask Peter, and Peter was grateful for the opportunity to speak to them about Jesus.

Acts 3:10-26. Peter and John in Solomon's portico

They were taking note of him as one who used to sit at the Beautiful Gate of the temple and they were filled with wonder and amazement at what had happened to him. (Acts 3:10).

There appears to be a lapse of time between the end of Acts 2 and the beginning of Acts 3, and it is impossible to know for sure how long the infant church had 'favour with all the people'. (Acts 2:47). Apparently, the activities of those believers quietly going about from house to house and praising God in the temple, had not seemed to the religious authorities to be a threat to them and their way of life, and especially no threat to their centuries old religious certainties, even though there had been signs and wonders done amongst them by the apostles. (Acts 2:43).

What then could they fear from two 'uneducated common men'? (Acts 4:13). All that they knew about them was that they had been with Jesus, a man who had recently been crucified on the ground of blasphemy, but who had been a nuisance to them for some time; they thought it could have been about three years. He had been preaching some alternative way of religious life from their own, and assuring people that through repentance and faith they could even enter into a personal relationship with God.

They had known through their scriptures that some of their most important ancestors had known God in that way, but those people had been an exception, chosen by God to do something extraordinary for Him. It was surely presumptuous for an ordinary person to claim such distinction. Was the Law of Moses, those wonderful scrolls which they treasured and kept so carefully in their synagogues, not sufficient for these people? In their view, some people were never satisfied. They were always wanting something new, something outrageous, something revolutionary. Of course they had a magnificent temple, but it had been restored not by a Jewish king but by an Idumean. Nevertheless it was a worthy place in which to carry out all the sacrifices and rituals commanded by Moses.

Really, who did Peter and John think they were?

According to their rigid, rigorous standards, Peter and John were uneducated. Like all Jewish boys, they would have attended a rabbinical school until the age of twelve, when after their bar mitzvah, they would be regarded as men and allowed to sit with the men in the synagogue away from the women and children. They would have learned the Torah, the law of Moses contained in the Pentateuch, the first five books of the Hebrew Bible, off by heart, and having learned it in childhood would never have forgotten it.

But culturally, only those who had proceeded academically to study the Law and the many commentaries on it by accredited rabbis over many years, almost word by word, would have been accounted educated.

Peter however, had an asset which these clever rulers of the people, the scribes and the elders, did not have. He had received the gift of the Holy Spirit. And when all the people were gathered together to Peter and John in Solomon's portico, (Acts 3:11). they were anxious to hear Peter's explanation of what had happened to the man who had been lame and was now fully restored to health. They were filled with amazement at what had happened to him, and they wanted to understand. Peter saw their amazement and needed no encouragement to begin to address the people. (Acts 3:12).

Acts 3:12-36. Peter's second speech to the House of Israel

While he was clinging to Peter and John, all the people ran together in the portico called Solomon's, full of amazement. But when Peter saw this, he replied to the people, Men of Israel, why are you amazed at this, or why do you gaze on us, as if by our own power or piety we had made him walk? (Acts 3:12).

Peter addressed the people as 'Men of Israel'. It may be that many or even most of those who had come up to Jerusalem for the Feast of Firstfruits, that is, the Feast of Pentecost, had now returned home, taking with them all that they had seen of the outpouring of the Holy Spirit and Peter's enlightening speech to them on that day. They may even have been among the three thousand who had been added to the church at that time, and for a time enjoyed with others the fellowship, the apostles' teaching, the breaking of bread and the prayers. (Acts 2:42). But business and family responsibilities may have caused them to leave Jerusalem and return home.

The 'men' of Israel was a generic term. Those whom Peter now addressed of course included women and may have included some who had witnessed the outpouring of the Holy Spirit on the Day of Pentecost, but these 'men and women of Israel' may have been simply residents of Jerusalem whose daily life took them through that part of the temple, and who happened to be there on the day of the healing of the lame man.

But they were Jews, God's chosen people. It was God's intention that the opportunity for salvation should be given to all, that 'whoever calls upon the Name of the Lord shall be saved', (Acts 2:21), whether Jew or Gentile, and that it was HIs will to pour out His Spirit on all flesh, in the last days. (Acts 2:17) But God never forgot His covenant with His people. Paul writes later, 'To them belong the sonship', (Romans 9:4), for God describes Israel as His first born son, (Exodus 4:22), and refers to Himself as a father to Israel; or Ephraim, (an alternative name for Israel), as His first born son. (Jeremiah 31:9). In Hosea, Israel is described as a child whom God loves. a son whom He called out of Egypt. (Hosea 11:1).

Paul proceeds in Romans 9:4: to categorise some of the reasons why Israel is still precious to God. He writes that to the Israelites also belonged the shekinah glory, which represented to the Israelites the presence of the Lord, which filled the tabernacle, the tent in the wilderness where God met with His people, (Exodus 40:34), and guided them as they journeyed through the wilderness as a cloud by day to protect them from the sun, and as fire by night for warmth and protection, and as a sign that He was continually with them.

Paul continues, to those Israelites also belonged the covenants, the giving of the law, the worship and the promises. To them belonged the patriarchs and of their race according to the flesh, is the Christ. (Romans 9:4,5). They are indeed a privileged people. Paul asks 'Has God cast off His people whom He foreknew? And answers emphatically, By no means! (Romans 11:1).

Paul's absolute conviction is that the power of God for salvation is to everyone who believes, *to the Jew first*, but it is also to the Greek, the Gentile. (Romans 1:16). The mercy of God does not come to an end with His provision of salvation for His ancient people, the Jews. Christ has come to take away the sin of *the whole world*, to the Jews first but also to the Greeks, the Gentiles, the nations who know not God, to all who hunger and thirst for His righteousness.

Peter too is convinced of this. 'Men of Israel', he says, for Jesus had come to the people of Israel first, and many had received Him, walking in the way of discipleship. On the day of Pentecost, Peter had made it quite clear that the precious gift of a personal and intimate relationship with God through the Lord Jesus, and in the power of the Holy Spirit, was not for Jews only, but 'for all whom the Lord our God shall call unto Him'. (Acts 2:39). Nevertheless, the people before Peter in Solomon's portico were 'men of Israel', and to them he began to explain how this man had received his healing. Peter speaks to the crowd, saying, 'His name through faith in His name has made this man strong whom you see and know; and the faith which is through Jesus has given the man this perfect health in the presence of you all'. (Acts 3:16).

Peter seemed surprised that the people should be so astonished at the miracle which had taken place. 'Why do you wonder at this?' he said, (Acts 2:12), as though such healing could be an everyday occurrence, as perhaps it had been in the earliest days of the church, although Luke does not say so. And then disclaiming any exclusive ability that he and John may be thought to have, Peter says 'why are you looking at us as though by our own power and piety we had made him walk? (Acts 3:12).

Peter has launched into his speech. He says, Men of Israel, why are you amazed at this, or why do you gaze on us as if our own power or piety had made him walk? The God of Abraham, and of Isaac and of Jacob, the God of our fathers, glorified HIs servant Jesus whom you delivered up and denied in the presence of Pilate when he had decided to release Him. But you denied the Holy and Righteous One, and asked for a murderer to be granted to you and killed the Author of life, whom God raised from the dead.

To this we are witnesses. And His name, through faith in His Name has made this man strong whom you see and know; and the faith which is through Jesus has given this man perfect health in the presence of you all. (Acts 3:13-16). Jesus, the author of life, the source of life; the finisher, *telos*, of the old life, and the originator, *arche*, of the new.

Peter continues by reviewing their status as inheritors of the example of Abraham, Isaac and Jacob, who were men of faith and walked with God. These 'men of Israel', whom Peter is addressing, were proud of their inheritance, claiming their inheritance as descendents of Abraham. On one occasion when Jesus had been speaking to the recalcitrant Jews of the freedom they could have if they looked in faith to Him; of the freedom from sin they could experience in Him; and of the eternal life which could be theirs,) they insisted, Abraham is our father. (John 8:30-51) They accused Him of having a demon, (John 8:38), and took up stones to stone Him for blasphemy. (John 8:59), but 'His hour had not yet come' to be killed, and He departed from them. (John 2:4; 7:6,30; 8:20).

Abraham, Isaac and Jacob had all been servants of God. But Jesus was different. God had now glorified His servant Jesus, (Acts 3:13) for this servant was also His Son. God had ordained that a different servant should arise in the person of His Son. He was the ultimate servant, submissive to His Father's will in everything.

This servant had been glorified by God through His death and resurrection. Peter acknowledges that it was through ignorance that they and their rulers had put Him to death. Though it was through the Jewish leaders that Jesus had been delivered up to the cross, had had His Sonship as the Son of God denied by Pilate and had been killed, God had raised Him from the dead. Peter declares that he and John and many others were witnesses of His resurrection. Paul later claims that there were over five hundred people who had seen the risen Christ, though the gospels do not mention this. (1 Corinthians 15:6).

The point Peter is making is that Jesus, the holy and righteous One (Acts 3:14), the Author of life who is bringing new life into the world, had been put to death by the Jewish leaders. But He who had embraced humanity at His humble birth, taking the Name Jesus, (Matthew 1:21), is the One who would save His people from their sins; was able to save them, even them, from their sins; and this Name, the Name of Jesus, by faith in this Name, had given this man perfect health in the presence of them all. (Acts 3:16).

Peter was saying that he and John were merely vehicles. They carried with them the Name of Jesus. They were absolutely and completely under the authority of that Name. All His character, all His ability to heal, to restore, to save, to forgive, is vested in that Name. His Name is as ointment poured forth, (Song of Solomon 1:3), the ointment which heals, which sets men and women free from the pain of sin and death, which anticipates and includes the comforting oil of the Holy Spirit's anointing. The Name of Jesus. This Name, through faith in His Name has made this man whole.

This was the explanation given to these people by Peter as to how this man, lame from birth, was healed. He and John were not routinely, or merely, invoking that Name. It is not a Name to be invoked casually or tasmanically, but in that Name is all that any man or woman could ever find of total fulfilment.

Nothing that Peter and John could have done of themselves would have helped the man. All they could do was to exercise faith in all that the Name represented. Bengel writes, through

Christ our faith is *from* God and is *in* God. (quoted by Barrett, p 200). The faith in question was not that of the lame man, who was only expecting money, not exercising faith. This was a trial of the apostles' faith, exercising faith in all that the Name stood for. First the Name, then the power and authority associated with the Name; then faith in the Name, the Name of the One in whom we live, the author of our life. (Acts 3:15,16.).

But Peter has more to say to them. 'And now brethren' he says. (Acts 3:17). The man was now healed. But what about them? The grace of God had been extended to the man in healing, but could they not also receive His grace?. Kindly, compassionate Peter, speaking to them as brethren, had already acknowledged that it was through their ignorance and the ignorance of their leaders that this dreadful yet wonderful event, the crucifixion of Christ, had taken place.

God had already foretold through His prophets that as the Christ, the Messiah, the Anointed One, the Lord Jesus would suffer. (Acts 3:18). The Messiah for whom they longed would undergo His passion, His suffering. He would be led like a lamb to the slaughter and there take upon Himself the iniquity of us all. (Isaiah 53:6,7). This was an opportunity for these 'brethren 'to turn to Him, to repent, to know that their sins could be blotted out and that times of refreshing would come from the presence of the Lord, for this refreshing always comes in His presence. (Acts 3:19).

This is the One who will come again for them. (Acts 3:20). Peter also understands the prophecy of Moses concerning Jesus as a Prophet. He is the One of whom Moses said, The Lord will raise up a prophet for you, like unto me. (Deuteronomy 18:15-16; Acts 3:22). The role of a prophet stretched from a prophet's concern with the details of daily life, through the proclamation of the eternal principles of the unchanging God, to the mysterious forthtelling of the distant future.

Jesus fully fulfilled every aspect of this definition. He is the Prophet who will watch over them, leading and guiding them by the word of God, someone to whom they may listen and receive direction in the way they should go while being concerned with their ultimate destiny. 'Listen to Him' says Moses. And Peter repeats, 'You *shall* listen to Him', (Acts 3:22), for their choice may have eternal consequences. They may listen to this Prophet, or they may choose not to. And if they refuse, they may be destroyed. (Acts 3:23).

This destruction comes, not from God, but from their own lifestyle, a life without God, for only the life of God, the life of Jesus within them will guarantee the blessing of which all the prophets from Samuel onwards had spoken, the privilege of being within the covenantal relationship with God received by Abraham through faith, (Genesis 15:6,18; Genesis 17:2; Galatians 3:9), but more than that, being also the first to discover and experience the joy of being in the new covenant, the promise of the Spirit by faith. (Galatians 3:14).

This is the covenant in the blood of Jesus poured out for many for the forgiveness of sins. (Matthew 26:28; Mark 14:24; Luke 22:20). And not only for them, but for all their posterity, their descendents, to bring blessing to all the families of the earth. (Acts 3:27; Galatians 3:8). Peter is telling these men of Israel that this blessing is validated and endorsed by the Lord Jesus Himself, the One whom God raised up; His Servant; and the blessing to His people is that He was sent to them first, to turn them from their wickedness. (Acts 3:26).

Peter is seeing in Jesus the Suffering Servant, (Acts 3:13,26), the fulfilment of all the Servant Songs of Isaiah. (Isaiah 42, 49, 50, 52-53). Peter's message is full of references to the resurrection of Jesus, His servanthood, the Messiahship of Jesus, the beloved Son of God. Isaiah 42:1 speaks of 'My servant, whom I uphold, My servant in whom My soul delights', and this is echoed in the baptism narratives in the synoptic gospels, Mark 1:11; Luke 3:22; Matthew 3:17, and also in the transfiguration narratives of Luke 9:35, and Matthew 17:5. 'This is My beloved Son. Listen to Him!.

Jesus identified Himself with the Suffering Servant of Isaiah 53 when He said in Luke 22:37, 'I tell you, this scripture must be fulfilled in Me. And He was numbered with the transgressors'. (Isaiah 53:12). Peter is confirming to the gathered crowd that Jesus is the Servant spoken of in the Servant Songs of Isaiah, the

One of whom not only Isaiah but the whole of the Hebrew scriptures speaks, as Jesus had said to the two men on the road to Emmaus, when 'beginning with Moses, and all the prophets, He interpreted to them in all the scriptures the things concerning Himself. (Luke 24:27).

Though HIs death and crucifixion had happened only a short while ago, Peter is insisting that Jesus is the anointed servant of God, spoken of in the scriptures. All the wonderful redemptive story spoken of by all the prophets had been fulfilled in the recent lifetime of these privileged people whom Peter called 'brethren'.

But because it was so recent it was perhaps harder for them to understand. Some of them may have seen Jesus while He was still among them. They may have heard Him speak, may have been one of the five thousand or four thousand at the impromptu picnic when He broke and blessed the bread and the fish and gave it to them. Some may have seen Him crucified, or seen Him raised from the dead, or had known others who had. Was this man really the One spoken of in their precious scriptures? Peter could only repeat what he had said in his first sermon, though perhaps in different words, God has made this Jesus, whom you crucified, both Lord and Christ. (Acts 2:36), and this was in fulfillment of what God had spoken through his prophets. (Acts 3:18).

Historically Jesus had been crucified under Pontius Pilate, procurator of Judea from 26-36 A.D under the Emperor Tiberius, and who apparently committed suicide in 37A.D. Few remember him, except as the reluctant judge at the trial of Jesus, who condemned Him to execution. (F.F. Bruce p108; C.K. Barrett p 195).

But the word of the Lord endures for ever. (Isaiah 40:8). What God had promised He was able also to perform through His Servant, the Author of life, the Originator, the source of life without whom no life could have existed. (John 1:4; Acts 3:15) and who could never have been held by death, for death comes by sin, and He alone was the Holy and Righteous One. (Acts 3:!4).

Peter recognises that although the prophecies of the death, resurrection, ascension and exaltation of Jesus have been fulfilled, all the prophecies regarding Him have been by no means exhausted. There is Old Testament prophecy about a future Messianic reign. The New Testament speaks of this reign in terms of the Parousia, the second coming of Christ in the clouds of heaven with power and great glory. (Matthew 24:30).

There is much yet to be fulfilled, but the time will come when every knee shall bow to Him, and every tongue confess that Jesus Christ is Lord to the glory of God the Father. (Philippians 2:11). The time has not yet come but the purposes of God are constantly moving outwards and forwards into more than the future, into eternity.

And these men of Israel are sons of the prophets and of the covenant which God gave to Abraham, (Acts 3:25). They are the first recipients of this revelation, if only they will repent and turn to Jesus. They are first in privilege. They are first also in responsibility, to respond to what Peter is telling them, that this is the consummation of all history, the initiation of which is here before them. This must surely lead them to respond and enter into the new life offered in the Name of Jesus. They may not be sick in body, as the previously lame man had been, but they certainly needed the work of the Holy Spirit for the sickness of the soul, the cleansing, renewing power which Jesus had promised He would give.

Jesus had said that the Holy Spirit would take what was His and declare it to His disciples, for that is the work and purpose of the Holy Spirit, to glorify Jesus. (John 16:14,15.), and this was what He was doing through Peter. So the work of grace goes on, through the love of the Father, through the obedience of the Son and the fellowship, the sharing together of the Holy Spirit; God manifested as all three persons of the Covenant-keeping Trinity.

And at the Parousia, the second coming of Christ, *chronos* and *kairos* are brought together. These two Greek words for time, *chronos* indicating *the passing of time,* the time of waiting, tarrying, especially in anticipation of the consummation of all things at the second coming of the Lord; and the *kairos, the event in time*; the time appointed by God, the point at which God moves in history.

One day the light of the glory of God will split the universe asunder as Jesus returns in all His glory to take His people to Himself. This will be the *kairos,* the consummation, the event when the anticipation will be realized, when God moves in history to complete the history of the world, when *chronos* time, the time of waiting will come to an end, when the trumpet shall sound, (1 Thessalonians 4:16) when there will be no more delay, (Revelation 10:6), and time will be no more. Peter explains that this time is coming when the Lord will send Jesus, 'the Christ appointed for you whom heaven must receive until the period of the restoration of all things, all things about which God had spoken by the mouth of His holy prophets from ancient time'. (Acts 3:21). A glorious time for all those who love His appearing. (2 Timothy 4:8).

Acts Chapter 4

Acts 4:1-4. Peter and John are arrested

And as they were speaking to the people, the priests and the captain of the Temple, and the Saddcees came upon them, annoyed because they were teaching the people and proclaiming in Jesus the resurrection of the dead.

And they arrested them, and put them in custody until the morrow, for it was already evening. But many of those who heard the word believed, and the number of the men came to about five thousand. (Acts 4:1-4).

Even as Peter was speaking, he could see what appeared to be important people approaching John and himself, although the crowd continued to listen to what he was explaining to them. Peter recognised them as the chief priests, the captain of the Temple and the Sadducees, and realised that they represented a challenge to what he had been saying to the crowd; that they were annoyed by his teaching them about Jesus, and especially that Jesus was not dead but alive and had been raised up out of death to the place which only He could fill, the right hand of God.

These officials were annoyed (RSV), grieved, (AV), greatly disturbed, (Stott p 95). vexed, (Barrett p 215), exasperated (NEB). It appears difficult to find exactly the right word to describe the reaction of these religious people to what Peter was saying. They were a deputation of the aristocratic leaders of the people, approaching Peter and John. Politically, they were collaborators with the Roman occupation and could not afford to have a revolution on their hands, especially as they regarded Peter's teaching as having subversive implications. But within the group, the Sadducees were the ruling element of the Sanhedrin or Council, and differed theologically from the Pharisees.

The Sadducees were not looking for a Messiah, because they believed that the Messianic age had begun at the time of the Maccabean revolt in 167 B.C. Above all, they did not believe in the resurrection of the dead, which was of course the preeminent truth of what the apostle was preaching. (Acts 23:8; Matthew 22:23). There was much theological dissension between the Pharisees and the Sadducees.

No wonder they were annoyed, exasperated by Peter's preaching. In their view, these so-called apostles had no authority to preach, for no authority had been given to them by the Sanhedrin. They were preaching false doctrine, for Jesus could not be the Messiah if the Messiah had already come as the Sadducees believed and could certainly not have risen from the dead for to the Sadducees there there was no such thing as resurrection from the dead; and perhaps more urgently, they had a responsibility in view of the occupation by the Romans, not to appear to harbour revolutionaries, in case they lost the many privileges which the Romans had conceded to them, to practise their own religion.

By common consensus, this teaching must be stopped before it went any further. Until now, they had been content to allow this new phenomenon of people meeting together in the temple to pray and to listen to the teaching of the apostles, helping each other and listening with some absorption to what they were being taught, as harmless enough; but they had taken it a step too far.

It seemed to them that the man called Peter had become the leader of these people. Though it was chiefly his preaching that concerned them, they had an excuse for arresting him and his confederate John in the healing of a lame man who for years had sat at the beautiful gate of the temple. They had seen a lame man sitting or sometimes lying there as they passed in and out of the temple, had even occasionally thrown him a denarius or two, but that Peter and John should have healed him without their knowledge or permission could not be tolerated. It would be better if the apostles could be put away somewhere safe for a while, where they could not go about preaching and healing people, and then perhaps they would be forgotten. People would forget and the whole thing would blow over.

And anyway, who was this Jesus they were talking about? Just someone who had been condemned to death, and in their opinion, rightly so, for blasphemy. Nobody really important. Nobody to make a fuss about.

They were totally hostile, totally opposed to Peter and John on these grounds. They approached Solomon's portico where this teaching was going on.

It was easy for the common people to see who these dignitaries were, for unlike themselves, they wore rich robes and had a self important, arrogant air about them. Their clothes alone, if nothing else, marked them out as of the aristocratic class. (Luke 16:19; James 2:2). Some were priests, chief priests who may have formed part of the temple guard, having some responsibility for its security. The captain of the temple had outright oversight over the priests, and was next in rank to the High Priest. They were accompanied by the Sadducees who as we have seen represented a policy of collaboration with the Roman authorities, and who strived for purity of worship, in defiance of the encroaching Hellenism of the nations around.

Under orders from the captain of the temple, whose task it was to maintain order in the temple, Peter and John were arrested. The power of arrest had been given to the Sanhedrin, the governing body of Judaism, where there were offences against Jewish law, but not the power to carry out the death penalty. This remained within the jurisdiction of the Roman governor. The offence of Peter and John, was the perceived stirring up of riotous behaviour on the part of Peter and John, and therefore a cause of possible retaliation on the part of the Roman authorities. This was reason enough for them to be put into custody overnight, for it was now the evening. (Acts 4:2) From the point of view of the captain of the temple, this was the wisest thing to do, for many of those who had been listening to Peter's preaching had been persuaded by it to believe the gospel, and turn to the Lord, 'and the number of men came to about five thousand'. (Acts 2:41).

Acts 4:5-12. Peter and John before the Council

On the morrow, their rulers and elders and scribes were gathered together in Jerusalem, with Annas the high priest and Caiaphas and John and Alexander, and all who were of the HIgh Priestly family. And when they had set them in the midst, they inquired, 'By what power or by what Name did you do this? (Acts 4:5).

Although this had been a life changing experience for the lame man, it had been a fairly minor incident of legal or religious insubordination on the part of the apostles as far as the Sanhedrin was concerned But 'on the morrow' it became a full scale examination (Acts 4:5), when the rulers and elders and scribes gathered together with the former High Priest Annas and his son-in-law Caiaphas, (John 18:13), the present High Priest, and other members of the priestly family. (Acts 4:5,6).

The full Sanhedrin consisted of seventy (or in some source material, seventy one) members, in an attempt to identify itself with the seventy elders of Numbers 11:16. It was divided into three groups, rulers, elders and scribes. Scribes were teachers of the law, rabbinic scholars. They were mostly of the Pharisaic group, thereby contributing to religious dissension and tension within the Sanhedrin.

The high priestly family and members of the ruling elite were Sadducees. The elders, *presbyteros*, was the word most generally used for members of the Sanhedrin, referring back to early Israelite history when the 'elders of Israel' had been those who occupied an influential and representative position in the nation, at the centre of its life, (Exodus 3:16; 24:1; Numbers 11:16, etc), although the term and its rationale had undergone significant evolution, especially since the return from the Babylonian exile (598-538 BC). Until the destruction of Jerusalem in 70 AD, the Sadducces generally remained the ruling element in the Sanhedrin. (Adapted from F.F. Bruce. The Acts of the Apostles p 117-118).

It seems unnecessary at first to state, as Luke does, that these people were gathered together in Jerusalem, for we know that that was where the Sanhedrin were located, and also that it was in Jerusalem that the Holy Spirit came upon the early church. But no word of scripture is ever without significance. The gathering together of these religious rulers *in Jerusalem* emphasizes that what appeared to be an episode of interest was actually of tremendous theological importance. *Jerusalem was the place chosen by God to put His Name there*, Zion, the city of God. Psalm 87:1-3, says 'Glorious things are spoken of you, O city of God. Psalm 78:68 speaks of 'Mount Zion, which He loves'; and Psalm 48 of Jerusalem being 'beautiful in situation, the joy of the whole earth' because it is 'the city of our God'.

Zion was a natural fortress which provided the location for the ancient Jebusite city of Jerusalem. Within the central plateau on which it was situated was the 'stronghold of Zion', (2 Samuel 5:6:-10), which David conquered and which became known as 'the city of David'. The whole area was often referred to as 'Mount Zion'. It became the site where David placed the Ark of the Covenant containing the ten commandments, (1 Kings 8:1,9), and where Solomon later built the temple, for God had promised David that his son would build Him a house. (2 Samuel 7:12,13). In a sense, Zion replaced Sinai as the focus of God's presence with his people as they migrated from the rural and agricultural wilderness of Canaan into the more urban settled nation of Israel.

The members of the Sanhedrin were the inheritors of an ancient tradition, but also the contemporary representatives of this place, the place of all that God had designed for the presence of His glory to rest and remain; the city and the temple; God present with His people as they worshipped Him. It was in their custodianship of the city where God had put His Name that these tremendous historical and theologically important events were taking place, and yet they had no impetus or desire to discover for themselves what God was doing through His Holy Spirit.

This contemporary group of the spiritual leaders of the people of Israel did not present a united front. There were conflicting views between the different members of Sanhedrin as to the interpretation of the Messianic passages of the sacred Hebrew scriptures. It was scarcely surprising that as recorded in Acts 3:11-26, Peter's sermon was anathema to them, and not just because it was a matter of interpretation. But Peter really had only one message. It was all about Jesus. If they really wanted to know about a good deed done to a paralysed man, this is what happened. (Acts 4:10). The means of healing, the power of the healing, and the Name through which the healing took place become synonymous. It was the Name of Jesus. Jesus is the means and Jesus is the Name.

It was they who had crucified Jesus. They meant it for evil, but God meant it for good, (Genesis 50:20) for God had raised Him from the dead. They were the builders who had rejected the Stone which became the head of the corner, (Acts 4:11) because they regarded Him who was the Stone as flawed in some way and unable to take the weight of the building, but God had made Him the head of the corner, the chief corner stone which held the whole building together. (Psalm 118:22; Acts 4:.11). Peter in referring to this Old Testament passage is claiming before these Sadducees Messianic status for Jesus, which the Sadducees would have wholeheartedly rejected. The Psalm quoted by Peter continues, 'This is the Lord's doing and it is marvellous in our eyes'.

What Peter is saying is really very simple. All this that was happening was what Jesus had 'begun to do and to teach', (Acts 1:1), followed by His betrayal, death and resurrection, His ascension and exaltation, (Acts 1:2-11), and the outpouring of the Holy Spirit on the Day of Pentecost, (Acts 2:1-4), resulting in the growth of a new phenomenon called the church. But what Peter was saying was being opposed as unorthodox and possibly blasphemous by the religious authorities, by those in Jerusalem who were guardians of what Jerusalem should have represented as the site of the spiritual life which God had given them; keepers of the covenant which God had made with His people on Mount Sinai.

Peter is trying to explain to them that this formerly lame man is a man who knows nothing of their different religious views, knows nothing of their political affiliations and their need to maintain a good relationship with the Roman occupation. Peter is saying, this was the man's need, to be restored to having a purpose in life; some employment; perhaps a family; to be self-sufficient and independent. This is what *Jesus* has done for this poor man and He has used us as His instruments. We are under His authority, the authority of One who is now at God's right hand; and under the authority of His name, the Name of Jesus. This is the Lord's doing and it is marvellous in our eyes, as we trust it is in yours. It is not our doing, we take no credit for it. But we want you to know that there is salvation in no-one else, for there is none other Name in heaven given among men whereby we must be saved. (Acts 4:12)

The spiritual importance of the trial of Peter and John by the Sanhedrin in Jerusalem cannot be too highly stressed. It was the antithesis of law to grace, of death to life, of love to judgement. On this occasion, and because we know what later transpired, it could be regarded as a preliminary examination, but its intention was deadly. The members of the Sanhedrin wanted to destroy this new found way of approaching the scriptures, and they wanted to do that immediately. And like those reported in the gospel narratives, (Matthew 12;14; Mark 14;1; John 7:59; 10:39; 11:53), they wanted to destroy all that pertained to Jesus.

Firstly as we would have expected, they questioned Peter's authority. They say, 'by what power or by what Name did you do this?' Peter's glowing face would have told them. Peter, filled with the Holy Spirit, said to them, courteously and respectfully, 'Rulers of the people and elders'. Then he began to tell them about how the lame man was healed in the Name of Jesus; that Man who had been the founder of this sect with all their apparently transgressive ideas about the Messiah whom the Sadducees believed had already come, and the Pharisees who were unconvinced by the Sadducean doctrine but who could not believe that when the Messiah did come, He would be brutally tortured to death as the criminal blasphemer Jesus had been, but would come to Jerusalem in splendour, as a king should.

Peter did not hesitate. While reminding them of the details of the healing of the lame man, he attributed all the glory of the miracle to Jesus, the one whom they had crucified, whom God raised from the dead, 'by whom this man is standing before you whole'. (Acts 4:10). This is when Peter quotes Psalm 118:22, identifying Jesus with the stone which they, the builders, have rejected as not being strong enough to carry the weight of the building because it was flawed in some way, but was actually the one perfect stone which alone could hold the building together when placed as the cornerstone, the head of the corner. (Acts 4:11).

And Peter declares, 'there is salvation in no one else, for there is no other name in heaven, or under heaven, given among men, whereby we must be saved'. (Acts 4:12)

This was only the beginning of the persecution which was going to be the experience of the apostles over many years. Suffering for the Name of Jesus, as He had warned them, was the cost of discipleship. (Matthew 10:16-20). But Jesus had also promised them that when they were delivered up to councils, were flogged in their synagogues, were dragged before governors and kings, for His sake, to bear testimony before them and the Gentiles, they need not be anxious how they were to speak, or what they were to say, for it would not be they who spoke but the Spirit of their Father speaking through them. (Matthew 10:20).

This promise is now fulfilled, as it would be time and time again for the apostles, including on this occasion for Peter, as he spoke to the Sanhedrin, 'filled with the Holy Spirit'. (Acts 4:8).

The Sanhedrin was arranged in a semi-circle so that the members might see each other. (Barrett, p225). And Peter and John were placed in the midst. (Acts 4:7). Scornfully they look at Peter and John. 'By what power or by what Name did you do this?' they ask. This is a double question. It raises the fact of the lame man's healing, while at the same time introducing the validity of the authority upon which the healing took place, and this of course involves the Name of Jesus, the one whom the apostles claimed had been raised from the dead.

'Then Peter, filled with the Holy Spirit', had answered them. He was respectful, giving honour where honour was due as Paul recommends in Romans 13:7, and answered both their questions in order. 'Rulers of the people and elders', he says to them, 'you ask by what means or by what power this good has been done to a disabled man, by what means he has been healed. Be it known to you all, and to all the people of Israel that by the Name of Jesus of Nazareth, (giving Jesus His full title), whom you crucified, whom God raised from the dead, by Him this man is standing before you well'. (Acts 4:10). Peter is implying that His Name, through faith in His Name, is available to them also for salvation if only they will come to Him.

Peter uses a double negative. He says, there is salvation in no other, no one else, for there is no other Name under heaven given among men whereby we must be saved; 'no-one else', 'no other Name', declaring absolutely with strong affirmation the uniqueness of Jesus and His saving power. Whatever these Jewish leaders were trusting in would not bring them salvation. Only Jesus can do that. And He will, if they respond to Him. The lame man was healed physically. They may be healed spiritually if they come to Jesus.

It was with this incomparable boldness that Peter spoke to these important people, filled as he was by the Holy Spirit. (Acts 4:13). These men, Peter and John, had been fishermen. They were not cultured or experts in the Torah, the Jewish law. But the Sanhedrin took knowledge of them that they had been with Jesus. (Acts 4:13). Peter and John were not professional theologians, but they had sat at the feet of Jesus and heard His word, as did Mary, (Luke 10:39), the word of Jesus who was not a professional rabbi, but who spoke as the Son of man, the Son of God.

The Sanhedrin were astounded, particularly as the man who had been healed was standing beside them, (Acts 4:14), no longer clinging to Peter and John but standing upright on his own two good feet, and they could not deny his healing.

They had nothing to say in opposition to Peter. It was probably a new experience for them to be tongue-tied. They saw the need to come together to discuss this extraordinary happening. They were a disparate group of people by inclination, by influential religious position, by theology, by life experience; but they were temporarily united against what Peter and John had done, and who were claiming the miracle to be the work of someone who had been condemned to death as a heretic, as a blasphemer.

Impossible! they thought angrily. They commanded Peter and John to leave the council while they debated amongst themselves what was. to be done. (Acts 4:15).

Acts 4:13-22. Peter and John are dismissed

Now as they observed the boldness of Peter and John, and understood that they were uneducated and untrained men, they were amazed, and took knowledge of them that they had been with Jesus. (Acts 4:13).

There were two factors which it was important to consider. The first was the obvious one that the lame man who sat at the beautiful gate of the temple was actually healed, was no longer disabled and a beggar. This was undeniable.

The second was that this miracle had been performed publicly, a miracle that was 'apparent to all the inhabitants of Jerusalem', (Acts 4:16). Had the apostles attempted to heal the lame man and then failed, that would have been the end of the story, but it seemed as though everybody had seen him 'walking and leaping and praising God'. (Acts 3:8).

As always, as the current religious authorities, they had to be careful not to appear to the Roman authorities to engage in any kind of upheaval, especially of a religious nature. The Romans were an enlightened occupying power. They had given many concessions to the Jewish leaders and people, allowing them to practise their faith virtually unhindered, but there was a limit to their tolerance. The Jewish leaders wanted this little incident kept quiet so that it could quickly be forgotten. So far, no riot had occurred. If they just threatened Peter and John and let them go, warning them to speak no longer in this Name to anyone, (Acts 4:17), then perhaps the whole incident would die down.

Having made this decision, they called Peter and John back into the council chamber and charged them not to speak or teach in the Name of Jesus. (Acts 4:18). With all the power and authority of the Sanhedrin behind what they said, surely these uneducated, common men would be intimidated; would meekly assent to what was proposed to them, and be grateful that nothing worse than a night in the prison had happened to them.

They were unprepared for the reaction of Peter and John. Peter and John answered and said to them, 'Whether it is right in the sight of God to give heed to you rather than God, you be the judge. For we cannot stop speaking about what we have seen and heard'. (Acts 4:19,20).

Peter was suggesting to the Sanhedrin that there was an alternative way of looking at the healing of the lame man. Was this a miracle which had its origin in the work of God, or was it merely something haphazard which had happened to a man? If it was a human undertaking which had restored a man to health, then, as human authorities set over the people, the Sanhedrin was right to question it and forbid it. But if it was from God, then those who had received it from God, who were speaking of what they had seen and heard, were not at liberty to obey the authorities, for they had to obey the greater authority, the authority of God to whom they owed a greater obedience.

Peter later put it rather more succinctly. We must obey God rather than man. (Acts 5:29). However impressive, the Sanhedrin was still a human institution. It probably claimed to speak on behalf of God to His people, but could not appreciate what God was doing in 'these last days', (Acts 2:17), the days of the ascended, glorified Christ; the days of the outpoured Holy Spirit.

When the members of the council had seen the boldness of Peter and John, they had taken knowledge of them that they had been with Jesus. (Acts 4:13) The boldness, the confidence which the apostles had, was not defiance of the authorities, but the boldness of faith. They knew themselves to be absolutely and utterly within the will of God, so that whatever the outcome of their arrest they knew that God was with them; they were sure of the life of Jesus within them; they were under the anointing and the overshadowing of the Holy Spirit.

They could not deny the power which God had given them to speak in the Name of Jesus. They were changed men, a change which faith in Him had made not only possible but actual. They could not possibly obey a command given to them by their religious leaders if it clashed with what they believed God had told them to do. His word to them was paramount.

But for the Sanhedrin to accept Peter's argument was a step too far. All they could do was to threaten them and let them go, finding no way to punish them because of the people, for all men praised God for what had happened. For the man on whom this sign of healing had been performed was more than forty years old. (Acts 4:21,22).

The Sanhedrin may have found the preaching and healing performed by the apostles illegitimate, but for the time being, this had only been an unpleasant initiation for Peter and John. Their confrontation with the representatives of what had been their religious observance from their earliest years had only begun. There would be more to come as they continued to preach and teach in the Name of Jesus. At this time, the religious leaders could find no way to punish them. (Acts 4:21). That problem would be remedied in the future, as was the thread hanging over Peter and John as they were released.

Acts 4:23-27. The believers pray for boldness

When they had been released, they went to their friends and reported all that the chief priests and the elders had said to them. And when they heard this, they lifted up their voices to God with one accord and said 'O Lord, Sovereign Lord, it is you who made heaven and earth and the sea, and all that is in

*them..... And now Lord, take note of their threats and grant
that your servants may speak your word with all boldness,
while you extend your hand to heal, and that signs and
wonders are performed through the Name of your Holy Servant
Jesus'. (Acts 4:23, 24).*

Bruised and broken in spirit, because the salvation so freely
offered to these religious leaders in the Name of Jesus had been
rejected by these men who had such a powerful influence over
God's chosen people, Peter and John's footsteps led them to a
place where they could find comfort. They went to their friends.
(Acts 4:23), to their community, to their own people, to those
who had become their family; brothers and sisters who like
them were sons and daughters of the most high God through
faith in Christ.

Perhaps they expected sympathy, or at least a kindly pat on
the shoulder as they reported all that the chief priests, *archiereus*,
and the elders, *presbyteros* had said to them. (Acts 4:23). *But what
happened was an impromptu prayer meeting.* When they heard the
report, their friends immediately 'lifted their voices together to
God'. (Acts 4:24). Peter and John may have expected them to call
down imprecations upon he group of men who had attempted to
curtail, or preferably to extinguish altogether, the good news of
the gospel, that in the Name of Jesus, and only in that Name
could men and women be saved from their sin and enter into a
personal relationship with God as their Father through Jesus,
God's anointed one.

However, the prayer of those gathered together was lifted to
the Lord on a completely different basis. These young believers
who had so recently come to know Jesus as their Saviour, and to
know the power of the Holy Spirit in their lives, immediately
turned to their scriptures.' Sovereign Lord, Creator God', they
prayed.

So often in His word, God is spoken of as Sovereign Lord,
Creator God, the Creator of all things. From Genesis 1 onwards
He is known as the Creator, and if Creator, then supreme
God. All other so-called gods are subject to Him. The gods of the

nations round about were no gods. They were idols, but the Lord made the heavens. (Psalm 96:5).

This is what is meant by God. God is; He who is. It excludes the possibility of there being any other. Abraham's revelation was that He existed. (Genesis 12:1). The revelation to Moses was that He is YHWH, I am that I am. (Exodus 3:14). Sovereign Lord, these humble believers prayed. Sovereign Lord. (Acts 4:24).

Peter and John may have been disconcerted at first to find themselves in the middle of a prayer meeting, but how absolutely right was the reaction of these believers, for they knew that though all the principalities and powers and world rulers of this darkness were against them, (Ephesians 6:12), they were in the hands of God.

They are reminded of the second psalm, where the psalmist speaks of the heathen, the Gentiles, the kings of the earth and its rulers conspiring together, taking counsel together against the Lord, *and against His Anointed.* The psalm speaks powerfully of those who are hostile to each other on so many other grounds, but powerful people united in this conspiracy. So often, even in an Old Testament passage there is a word or a phrase which could only apply to the Lord Jesus. He is God's Anointed One, the Messiah, the Christ. He is the One against whom they are conspiring.

There is an anointing for David too, the sweet psalmist of Israel (2 Samuel 23:1), assumed to be the author of this psalm and God's servant, the mouthpiece of God's word, (Acts 4:25), and an anointing also for these believers as they experience the infilling of the Holy Spirit. (Acts 4:29), and discover what a privilege it is to be a mouthpiece of the Lord, His servant. So they pray, asking for God to give them the confidence to speak His word.

But Jesus is not only anointed as God's servant; Jesus is His Son 'designated the Son of God in power, according to the Spirit of Holiness, by His resurrection from the dead. Jesus Christ our Lord. (Romans 1:4).

Nevertheless, under this anointing, David was able to speak by the Holy Spirit. (Acts 4:25). These new servants of God, these new believers were asking for boldness, for courage, so that they too could speak His word, while He stretched out His hand to heal, and signs and wonders could be performed through the Name of His holy servant Jesus. (Acts 4:30). Jesus was His holy servant, the holy and righteous one as the Servant Songs of Isaiah testify. (Acts 3:14). He said of Himself, 'the Son of man came not to be served, but to serve, and to give His life as a ransom for many'. (Matthew 20:28). This was the substance of their prayer. They prayed for boldness, for courage. They prayed that the will of the Lord might be done. They prayed that there would be signs and wonders performed, not so that they could enjoy a *frisson* of excitement, but so that the name of Jesus would be glorified and His authority vindicated.

The whole purpose of the life of Jesus had been to bring salvation to the men and women upon whom He had set His heart, and though Herod Antipas, 'that fox' (Luke 23:7; Luke 13:31, 32), and Pontius Pilate with the Gentiles and the people of Israel, had set themselves against the Lord and against His Anointed, the believers were only expecting that what God had foreordained, would happen; 'to do whatever Thy hand and Thy power had predestined to take place.' They prayed with greater earnestness, 'And now Lord', look upon their threatenings and grant to your servants to speak your word with boldness'. (Acts 4:29). And when they had prayed, the place in which they were gathered was shaken, and they were all filled with the Holy Spirit and spoke the word of God with boldness. God had shown that He had heard and would answer their prayer.

What a time of prayer that had been. They were absolutely certain that God was in charge, that His foreordained plan was being worked out, and that by His grace they were included in that plan. All that they really asked of Him was the boldness, the courage to do, as His servants, whatever He required of them to do. And when they prayed, the place in which they were gathered together was shaken as with an earthquake, *esaleuthe*. And they were all filled with the Holy Spirit, and spoke the word of God with boldness. (Acts 4:31).

They may have understood that the 'shaking' of the earthquake was a sign of Divine assent to their prayer, and of course it was. But how much more significant was the renewed infilling with the Holy Spirit which they were experiencing; a repeated, re-commissioning of them; the encouragement of their ability to speak the word of God with boldness. God had answered their prayer.

There can be nothing more wonderful than the knowledge that He hears and answers prayer. And so they can also expect that through them He will indeed stretch out His hand to heal and perform signs and wonders through the Name of Jesus. They *'went on'* (continuous tense) speaking the word of God with boldness, not only among themselves, but to all who would listen.

Acts 4:32, 35. All things in common

Now the company of those who believed were of one heart and soul, and no-one said that any of the things which he possessed was his own, but they had everything in common. (Acts 4:32).

This newly energised company, encouraged by the answer to their prayer, the physical shaking of the place where they were gathered together, indicating the presence of God with them as a group, and then the personal infilling of each one by the Holy Spirit, drew them together. (Acts 4:31). They were a company of those who believed, who were of one heart and soul. (Acts 4:33). They enjoyed complete unity and unanimity. All that they possessed in material terms became the possession of all. Why hold on to something if someone else needed it? The important thing was to give testimony to the resurrection of the Lord Jesus, and this they did with great power, and great grace was upon them all.

To have been in that company must have seemed like heaven on earth. All that mattered was their witness to the Lord Jesus and their love for one another and for Him, expressed in the sharing of what each had so that no-one was needy. 'There was not a needy person among them, for as many as had possessions of lands or houses sold them and brought the proceeds and laid them at the apostles' feet'. (Acts 4:35).

Not all would have been possessors of lands or houses, perhaps very few, for the believers came from all walks of life. There may have been many who relied on daily or weekly wages for the necessities of life but had been caught up in this new and wonderful way of living and were able to share what they had with others.' Distribution was made to each as any had need'. (Acts 4:35). But their focus was not on their need, or on their willingness to share what they had, but only to witness to the Lord Jesus. (Acts 4:33).

This overriding impulse was in the heart of a man called Joseph. This man was so remarkable in the eyes of the whole church that they had given him the name of Barnabas, which means 'son of consolation', or 'son of encouragement'. Comfort, consolation, counsel, encouragement, are the characteristics which Jesus attributed to the Holy Spirit. (John 14:16).

Barnabas was of a priestly family. He was a Levite from Cyprus, where there was a considerable Jewish settlement. As Mark was his cousin, (Colossians 4:10) he may have had connections in Jerusalem, and he may have stayed on in Jerusalem after the feast of Pentecost, which may explain his presence there. Barnabas did not have much, but he had a field. He sold the field, and brought the money and laid it at the apostles feet. (Acts 4:37).

Barnabas later played an important part in the spread of the gospel, (Acts 9:27; 11:22,30; 12:25, and throughout chapters 13, 14, and 15). He was Paul's partner until their separation in Acts 15:39.

Even at this stage in the life of the early church, Barnabas was seen by the apostles as having the gift of comforting people, encouraging them, and not only other believers but those outside the church too. It seems that the Holy Spirit also recognised this as He separated Paul and Barnabas to the work to which He had called them, the missionary work which would have such tremendous repercussions wherever the Holy Spirit led them. (Acts 13:2). And all this had its modest beginning in a simple committed act of making a contribution to the funds of the Jerusalem church. He brought the money and laid it at the apostle's feet.

These are blessed days in the life of the early church. Despite the increase in numbers, the early church continued to be of one heart and mind and to hold things in common, just as they had from the beginning. (Acts 2:24). Because the Holy Spirit was in control the believers were guided by Him as they lived alongside each other, sharing what they had, encouraging one another. Consciously or unconsciously, they were following the teaching of Jesus who had said 'Love one another as I have loved you. By this shall all men know that you are My disciples if you have love for one another. (John 13:34,35). They could not help but love one another. The love of God, both the love *from* Him and the love *for* Him, had been poured into their hearts by the Holy Spirit whom He had given to them. (Romans 5:5). The early Christian theologian, Tertullian, (c155–c220 AD), is reputed to have said, 'See how these Christans love one another!'

It was wonderful to have great power resting on them as they gave testimony to the resurrection of the Lord Jesus, and equally wonderful to know that abundant grace was upon them all. (Acts 4:33). All of them, the formerly wealthy as well as the formerly needy, sharing together what they had and rejoicing together in the grace of the Lord Jesus, His ineffable presence and benediction, the suffusion of His grace and favour towards them, the quiet power of God reaching out to all around them. Abundant grace was upon them all. (Acts 4:33).

Acts Chapter 5

Acts 5:1-11. Ananias and Sapphira

But a man named Ananias with his wife Sapphira sold a piece of property and with his wife's knowledge, he kept back some of the proceeds and brought only a part, and laid it at the apostles feet. (Acts 5:1).

There must have been many, like Barnabas, who sold what they had to give what they could to the common fund of the church in Jerusalem, and we have no knowledge as to why Luke especially marked out Barnabas unless it was to contrast him with Ananias and Sapphira. It may of course have been simply Luke's intention to give the background to Barnabas' future ministry, taking the gospel as he had to many places where the Name of Jesus was unknown, so that he could share the blessing of life in the Holy Spirit, life in Jesus, with others, just as he had shared the blessing of enabling some provision for the needy ones of the Lord's people.

But Ananias with hIs wife Sapphira sold a piece of property, and with his wife's knowledge he kept back some of the proceeds and brought only a part and laid it at the apostles feet. But Peter said to Ananias, 'why has Satan filled your heart to lie to the Holy Spirit and to keep back part of the proceeds of the land? While it remained unsold, was it not at your disposal? How is it that you have contrived this deed in your heart? You have not lied to men but to God. (Acts 5:1-4)

Ananias and Sapphira wanted it to be known that they too were among those with a generous heart towards the poor in the community. But their generosity was tainted with pride and ambition. They wanted to be somebody in the church, to be recognised as that interesting couple who had given so much to the church.

Jesus had made this obscure statement 'Let not your right hand know what your left hand is doing'. Jesus is advocating a simple, secret, humble giving, but also a kind of spiritual carelessness, an attitude of not dwelling on what the believer has found it in his heart to give, but grateful that he had that resource, and had given without demonstrating his ability to do so. In humility the believer has given, knowing that all blessings come from God, but are given that they might be shared. The believer is trusting God for the provision of his own needs, and rejoicing that God could use him to meet the needs of others.

This of course had been the attitude of Barnabas. It was not so with Ananias and Sapphira. Ananias means 'the Lord is gracious', and Sapphira means 'Beautiful'. God had really been gracious to Ananias, giving him a beautiful wife. And they had apparently been living in the glow, the atmosphere, of what the Holy Spirit had been doing in the church, especially the love of the brethren for each other. How wonderful to be part of all that! But somehow they wanted more. They wanted recognition. They conspired together, (Acts 5:9), and had the idea that giving a lot of money to the church would assure them of at least a place of honour, if not importance in the company of believers. But they were hesitant about going too far. They had to think of their future. Suppose this experiment did not work out quite as well as these people seemed to think? They would not give all the money, just a part of it.

Ananias sold a piece of property and with his wife's knowledge he kept back some of the proceeds, and brought only a part of it and laid it at the apostles feet. (Acts 5:1,2). How sensible of us, he may have thought, not to go too far, to become too extreme. You can get too carried away by the emotion of the thing, thinking that you can live like that, everybody helping everybody else. You have to draw the line somewhere, be practical, use a little compromise.

But Peter saw through this miasma of lies and deception. In his view, this was just as serious a temptation by Satan, the adversary of God, as had been the temptation of Adam and Eve in the garden of Eden. Adam and Eve had been tempted to take upon themselves the interpretation of the word of God to them. 'Has God said?' said the serpent. 'Are you really sure that you want to obey that silly rule He has given you? He is only afraid that you will become like Him if you eat of that particular tree. Make up your own mind. Do what you think is best for you'. (Genesis 3:5).

Adam and Eve were at the beginning of mankind, at the beginning of the plans which God had made to have a people for HImself. Peter and John, the apostles and the other believers, had come into God's extended plan, a people for Himself from all the nations of the world, the beginning of a worldwide church. We are not surprised that God's adversary should have tried to thwart God's plan now even as he had from the beginning. Peter was aware of this which is why he said to Ananias, 'Why has Satan filled your heart to lie to the Holy Spirit?'

God had made no rules for the early church, but the commandment to love the Lord your God with all your heart and with all your soul and with all your strength and with all your mind; and your neighbour as yourself, (Luke 10:27; Deuteronomy 6:5; and Leviticus 19:18), remained as true as it had ever been. Jesus commented that on this, the commandment to love the Lord your God, the greatest commandment of all, depended all the law and the prophets. (Matthew 22:36-40).

The temptation for Ananias and Sapphira was to misinterpret the word of God. Their love for God should have dictated their love for their neighbours, but they had put themselves first while pretending concern for others. Just like Adam and Eve, they were manipulating the word of God. Did it really matter if two members of the church out of five thousand (Acts 4:4) should seek to deceive the Holy Spirit? To lie to Him? Peter obviously thought it did. We are not told how long the early church had lived in love and consideration of others before the incident of Ananias and Sapphira took place. It may have been weeks or months, even perhaps a matter of years. But Peter felt that it was only too soon that the tragedy had happened. Even as Ananias laid the money at the apostle's feet, Peter knew in his heart that the gift was not gifted at the prompting of the Holy Spirit, but was a bribe, an attempt to gain recognition.

Peter said to Ananias, 'Ananias, why has Satan filled your heart to lie to the Holy Spirit and to keep back part of the proceeds of the land? While it remained unsold, did it not remain your own? And after it was sold, was it not at your disposal? How is it that you have contrived this deed in your heart? You have not lied to men but to God'. (Acts 5:3,4.).

When Ananias heard these words, he fell down and died and great fear fell upon all that heard of it. (Acts 5:5). It seemed like a dreadful punishment. But the sin was in itself dreadful. To lie to the Holy Spirit is to infer that the truth is not truth; it is not absolute, but can be 'managed', even twisted if necessary to further one's own purposes.

The Holy Spirit is the Spirit of truth, (John 14:17), and Jesus says that the world cannot receive Him because it neither sees Him nor knows Him. The disciples to whom Jesus is speaking in John's gospel do know Him, for before His ascension, the Holy Spirit dwells *with* them and after the Holy Spirit has come upon them at Pentecost, will be *in* them. (John 14:17). Jesus is saying that if the Holy Spirit has come upon you you belong to Him and walk in the truth. But if you have not known the indwelling of the Holy Spirit within you, you may try to do and say all the right things, but He will say 'I never knew you. Depart from Me, you workers of iniquity'. (Matthew 7:23; Luke 6:46). They call Him 'Lord', but do not acknowledge His lordship over their lives, and this discrepancy is a lie, a deception. They may even deceive themselves, but they cannot deceive the Holy Spirit.

This is an infant church, full of members whose past lives probably held many incidents and instances which by the grace of God had been dealt with at the cross of the Lord Jesus, where He had given His life so that they could be forgiven. The members of the church had been filled with the Holy Spirit, but they still needed establishing in the faith. Peter had a vision of a church which was absolutely honest and truthful in its dealings with one another and the outside world, but most of all, in its dealings with God. Of course God is not deceived. God is omniscient, and knows all things. But in this body of people, newly entered into the kingdom of God, experiencing kingdom living, there had to be no compromise or half measures. They needed to be honest with each other and honest with God. This evil thing had to be cast out from them. Ananias fell down and died.

This does not mean that Peter had the power of life and death. Peter was sensitive to the Holy Spirit. Ananias'death was brought about by the Holy Spirit to whom he had lied. It was the work of the Holy Spirit in judgement, just as the healing of the lame man at the beautiful gate of the Temple was the work of the Holy Spirit in healing, for He always responds to the Name of Jesus.

Completely open to the work of the Holy Spirit, completely filled by Him, Peter's words, as Ananias heard them, led not only to this man's death, but to great fear falling upon all who heard it. (Acts 5:11). There had to be integrity, openness, transparency among the believers if they were to give witness to the resurrection of Jesus. (Acts 4:23). No shadow or obfuscation should fall upon His precious Name, for if the message of His caring, saving power was not clear then men and women would not be saved. Those who may at first have been attracted by the message of salvation would ultimately be repelled by the dishonesty of those who proclaimed it, and the purpose of Jesus in coming to this earth, in going to the cross, in giving up His life for them would be more than damaged in their eyes. It would be nullified, made of no account to men and women who desperately needed the assurance of sins forgiven, of peace with God through the Lord Jesus Christ.

Ananias had brought about his own death. The young men rose and 'wrapped him up', (a medical term in Greek, *sunesteilan*, indicating Luke the doctor again), and carried him out and buried him.

Peter has a shepherd heart. He cares deeply about what happens to people, (1 Peter 5:1-3), but when Sapphira comes in after three hours, he *has* to ask her whether she and Ananias had sold the land for so much. She had the opportunity here to confess, to tell the truth, to repent, at the words of this compassionate apostle. But probably out of loyalty to her husband, she said 'Yes, for so much'.

Peter's voice must have been full of sorrow, even as he sternly rebuked her, and his question to her was one of genuine puzzlement as he said, 'How is it that you have agreed together to tempt the Spirit of the Lord?'. He is saying, why did you do it? You surely have no knowledge of the Holy Spirit if you imagine that you can put His holiness, His power, His love, the absolute sincerity of His dealings with us, to the test. Try as you will, you will find the Holy Spirit genuine through and through, and it is this genuineness that condemns you. This is a serious attempt to undermine the work of the Holy Spirit among His people, and 'even now, the feet of those who buried your husband are at the door, and they will carry you out'. (Acts 5:9).

Immediately, she fell down at his feet and died. When the young men came in, they found her dead, and they carried her out and buried her beside her husband. (Acts 5:10). And great fear came upon the whole church and over all who heard of these things.

We might have expected that great sorrow would have come upon the church, (the *ekklesia,* the first time this term is used in Acts). But in fact it was great fear. (Acts 5:11). They were reminded that what they had committed themselves to was not an experiment in communal living, nor to an extended course in theology as they listened to the apostle's teaching, nor to exciting ecstatic times of prayer, but to a relationship with the living God. God, not as an ideological proposition or a far away transcendent Being, but as a Person. A Person who not only dwelt with them, but in them too. This was actual, personal, real, life changing and costly.

By what wonderful means they were enabled to live and walk in the Spirit, they did not know. They could only know that this was so, that this was what Jesus had promised. The Holy Spirit had come. (John 15:26). They walked by faith, not by sight, (2 Corinthians 5:7), by faith in the atoning work of Christ which removed the barriers between them and God, and enabled the Holy Spirit to be at work in their lives.

Ananias and Sapphira had apparently not understood this, had attempted to go their own way, had refused to commit their lives completely to the Holy Spirit; and had come to an inevitable end, for the principles of the kingdom which Jesus had laid out had to be maintained. (Matthew 4:17). 'Repent', He had said, 'for the kingdom of heaven is at hand'. This was the first principle. Repentance for sin is the foundation stone upon which the kingdom of God is built, where God is King, where He is Sovereign Lord, ruling every aspect of a believer's life, for if He is not Lord of all, He is not Lord at all. (Hudson Taylor). The way of repentance and obedience to the will of the King in their lives had been circumvented by Ananias and Sapphira.

The foundations of the church in Jerusalem were being laid. How important it was that this terrible event concerning Ananias and Sapphira should be openly acknowledged by the whole church, so that members of the church should be in no doubt of their greater blessing of being able to stand before their heavenly Father in total openness.

John put it so clearly in his first letter. 'If we say we have fellowship with Him while we walk in darkness, we lie and do not live according to the truth. But if we walk in the light as He is in the light, we have fellowship with one another, and the blood of Jesus, His Son, cleanses us from all sin. (1 John 1:6;7).

Acts 5:12-16. Signs and wonders

Now many signs and wonders were done among the people by the hands of the apostles. And they were all together in Solomon's portico. None of the rest dared to join them, but the people held them in high honour. And more than ever, believers were added to the Lord, multitudes both of men and women. (Acts 5:12-14).

The narrative of the early church continues after the important interruption by Ananias and Sapphira, revealing to these new believers how delicate and yet how powerful are the dealings of the Holy Spirit with those who have committed themselves to Hs authority.

The church continued to meet in Solomon's portico, (Acts 5:12), a larger space than could be provided by peoples homes, or any other building available to them, as 'many more believers were added to the Lord, both men and women'. (Acts:14). The concern for women in the gospels, contrary to the patriarchal practices of this society, especially in Luke's gospel, continues in Acts. The apostles were beginning to be held in honour by the people, (Acts 5:13), who were beginning to accept that to Peter and the apostles was given the authority to perform signs and wonders, to such an extent that they even carried out their sick friends into the streets and laid them on beds, or stretchers or pallets in the hope that as Peter passed, at least his shadow might fall on some of them. Also the people from the cities round about Jerusalem were coming together, bringing with them people who were sick or afflicted with unclean spirits, and they were all being healed. (Acts 5:16).

There were some however, whom Luke calls 'the rest', (Acts 5:16) who held them in high honour but did not dare to join them, for joining the group in Solomon's portico was tantamount to a declaration that they too had become believers, and for them this was a step too far, leading ultimately to letting go of oneself to God and to the authority of the Holy Spirit. Ananias and Sapphira had demonstrated that this was no light commitment.

Yet the temptation to join themselves to the believers was strong. It was at *the hands* of the apostles that the miracles were being performed (Acts 5:12), suggesting that each miracle was an individual, personal one as perhaps the apostles laid their hands on each one for healing; each one was a particular person with particular needs of body or spirit, so that that person was healed. But even Peter's shadow was perceived to have a healing effect. Not only in Jerusalem, but in the villages around, news of what was happening in Jerusalem caused people to bring all those who were sick, and those suffering with unclean spirits to come to this place of mighty healing power.

Peter's shadow was not some magical effluence flowing from him to others. He did not possess this power in his own right. It was the power of the Holy Spirit working through him and reaching out to those who were sick in body and soul, even without Peter needing to touch them or even speak to them, because the need at this specific time was great. But the power of the Lord was present to heal, (Luke 5:17), God confirming and establishing the word of the gospel by signs following. (Mark 16:20. AV)

All were healed. None who ever came to Jesus or to His Spirit filled servants were turned away or went home unfulfilled. *All were healed.* They came. They were healed. They went home rejoicing.

Acts 5:17-42. The second arrest and examination of the apostles

But the high priest rose up and all who were with him, that is, the party of the Sadducees, and filled with jealousy they arrested the apostles and put them in the common prison. But at midnight, an angel of the Lord opened all the prison doors and brought them out and said,' Go and stand in the temple and speak to the people all the words of this Life'. And when they heard this, they entered the temple at daybreak and taught. (Acts 5:17-20).

It was inevitable that before long, such activity should come once again to the attention of the religious authorities, They had forbidden Peter and John to speak in the Name of Jesus, and here they were, filling Jerusalem with this heretical teaching, (Acts 5:28), and in addition bringing 'this Man's blood upon us', for Peter had claimed that it was through their delivering up of Jesus to the Roman governor that Jesus had been crucified. (Acts 3:13).

They could not allow this revolutionary behaviour to continue, especially in view of the numbers of ordinary citizens who were now involved. The high priest, and all who were with him, that is, the party of the Sadducees, rose up and were filled with jealousy at the behaviour of the apostles because it was beyond their understanding and their ability. They arrested the apostles and put them in the common prison. (Acts 5:17). Whether they included all the apostles or just Peter and John is not clear, but prison bars were not sufficient to keep them in custody. At night, the angel of the Lord opened *all* the prison doors and brought them out, and said, 'Go and stand in the temple, and speak to the people all the words of this Life'. (Acts 5:19,20).

As Peter and the apostles (Acts 5:29) followed the angel through the passages and corridors of the prison until they were once again outside in the fresh air, they must have wondered if this was really a good thing. They knew that they would have to be put on trial for what they had done, for they had deliberately disobeyed the terms of their earlier release. Would not leaving the prison make matters worse? They would inevitably be condemned to some form of punishment. Leaving the prison and going to speak to the people would magnify the charges against them.

But the one who was leading them out of prison was the angel of the Lord. This was divine intervention. God Himself was giving them this opportunity to speak yet again to the people 'all the words of this Life'. (Acts 5:20). The doors of the temple were opened at daybreak for the morning sacrifice. Gladly they entered the temple at daybreak and taught. (Acts 5:21).

In the morning, the High Priest, probably Annas, (Acts 4:6), remembered that he had these men in custody. This, he thought, concerned the whole council and senate of Israel, (Acts 5:21), the Sanhedrin, and so he called them all together, while he sent a message to the prison to have the apostles brought.

But the officers, the Temple guards, could find no trace of them. They returned to the council, reporting that the prison was securely locked, that the sentries were standing at the doors, but when the doors were opened, the prisoners were gone. (Acts 5:23). 'When the captain of the temple, the officer in charge of the temple guards and the chief priests heard this report, they were much perplexed', (Acts 5:24), which is probably a bit of an understatement. The captain of the temple knew that the security of the prison was, and had to be, tight. In fact it was more than his job was worth for there to be any error to be made in the detention of these prisoners, for there was always the risk of retaliation from the Roman occupying power if anything untoward was allowed to happen. Together with the chief priests under his authority, he wondered what this would come to. (Acts 5:24). What would Annas and the elders do?

But then there was a report from someone who had gone early to the temple who said,' The men whom you put in prison are standing in the temple and teaching the people'. (Acts 5:25).

At last, there was something that the captain of the temple could do. Taking the temple guards with him, he went to the temple and brought the apostles back to the Sanhedrin, but very carefully, without using force, for the apostles went with them willingly, and besides, the people held them in honour and the guards were afraid of being stoned by the people. (Acts 5:26). There seemed to be a tendency on the part of the populace to throw stones. Having arrived safely before the council, the High Priest began to question them.

Acts 5:27-42. The second trial before the Sanhedrin

When they had brought them, they stood them before the council. The High Priest questioned them saying, 'We gave you strict orders not to continue teaching in this Name, and yet you have filled Jerusalem with your teaching and intend to bring this Man's blood upon us. But Peter and the apostles answered, 'We must obey God rather than men'. (Acts 9:27-29).

In obedience to what the angel had told them, the apostles had been standing in the temple and speaking to the people' all the words of this Life', (Acts 5:20), the new life of Jesus offered by Him to all who would trust in Him. *All the words.* They were to hold nothing back for fear of the religious authorities, or from being tactful, telling people what they wanted to hear. They would not worry about wounding people's sensibilities. This was the full gospel which they were proclaiming. All the words they were speaking were to help people to understand the message of the gospel, that God was holding out to them the gift of Life. They were the words of life, life in His Son, offering redemption and the abundant life which Jesus came to give. (John 10:10).

The apostles were hardly surprised when they were arrested again, and once again taken into custody. They were taken before the Sanhedrin and once again stood within the semi-circle as the Council surrounded them, and as Annas the High Priest questioned them in an almost petulant tone of voice. Surprisingly, he made no mention of their disappearance from the prison, his chief complaint being their disobedience to the earlier charge that they should teach no more in this Name. (Acts 5:28). He said, 'we strictly charged you not to teach in this Name, yet you have filled all Jerusalem with your teaching and intend to bring this Man's blood upon us'. It is noteworthy that the High Priest avoided the use of the name 'Jesus', identifying Him merely as 'that Man', surely indicating that the precious Name had become anathema to him.

Peter had already demonstrated the power of that Name and Annas the High Priest was unwilling to run any risks by using it. But he failed to remember what Peter had been saying after the healing of the lame man, that it was not only this Name, but faith in this Name that had made the lame man whole. (Acts 3:16). Annas was safe in his unbelief, for he had no faith in the Name of Jesus.

Yet here was the paradox. If the Man's Name was of so little account, why was Annas concerned that Peter appeared to 'intend to bring this Man's blood upon them'.? (Acts 5:28). Jesus was one of many who were crucified under the Roman occupation. Why was His blood any different from any of theirs?. This was the crux of the matter, the dilemma which Annas was facing, but as a not incompetent politician, he preferred to regard Peter's intention as a personal accusation, that he and the Sanhedrin were to blame for the death of Jesus.

In their previous trial, Peter and John, with Peter as spokesman, had indeed said to Annas and his son-in-law Caiphas, and the council gathered together, that 'this Jesus, *whom you crucified*, God has raised from the dead'. (Acts 4:10). Perhaps Annas had been turning these words over in his mind and was afraid of divine retribution if this was indeed so. Had God actually raised a Man from the dead? In addition to any religious speculation he was experiencing, there was also the possibility that he was likely to have a popular uprising on his hands, for there were those who held the apostles in high honour. (Acts 5:13).

In their earlier trial, Peter had already set forth before the Sanhedrin the reasons why he could confidently say, 'we must obey God rather than men. (Acts 4:19,20). He had said to them, 'Whether it is right in the sight of God to give heed to you rather than God, you be the judge. For we cannot stop speaking about what we have seen and heard'.

Now he recapitulates in an abbreviated form what he had said before, 'we must obey God rather than men'. He says, 'the God of our fathers, the continuity we have with all that God was doing through the patriarchs, Abraham, Isaac and Jacob, and all who came after them, He has now completed, and though you killed Jesus, the One who was the predetermined pinnacle of all God's dealings with His people, God raised Him from the dead and exalted Him at His right hand as Prince (AV), Leader, (RSV), and Saviour, to give repentance to Israel and forgiveness of sins. These are the gifts of God to you, repentance and the opportunity for forgiveness. And we are witnesses of these things, and so is the Holy Spirit whom God has given to those who obey Him'. (Acts 5:29-32).

Each of these premises or statements was anathema to the Sanhedrin. To begin with, their own authority is being questioned. Peter is suggesting that he and the apostles are being obedient to God, with more than an implication that these religious leaders of the people of God are disobeying Him, these men who regarded themselves as the ones supremely qualified to know the mind of God.

Secondly, Peter is speaking in terms of the God of their fathers, the Transcendent One, the Holy One whom they worshipped daily in offerings and sacrifices, but who was remote and unattainable. But, Annas is saying to himself, Peter is absolutely sure that this same God was actively, contemporarily and recently committed to the life of one Man and that Man a blasphemer, (Mark 14:64), and a heretic, for which reason He was condemned to death; and that God had personally raised this Man from the dead and exalted Him to a place at His right hand in heaven. This is surely blasphemy on Peter's part.

And that thirdly, that God was now, at this moment, ready to give them repentance and forgiveness of their sins through the death of this Man, whom God had raised from the dead.

And finally that Peter and the other apostles had actually witnessed these things. (Acts 5:32). They were witnesses to all that Jesus began to do and to teach. (Acts 1:1). They were witnesses to His showing Himself alive by many proofs after His resurrection during forty days and speaking of the kingdom of God. They were witnesses to His being taken up into heaven. (Acts 1:3).

But the apostles were not alone in being witnesses of these things. So was the Holy Spirit, whom God had given to those who obey Him (Acts 5:32). All that the Holy Spirit had done through them, the signs and the wonders, the healing of many people, the many who had heard the teaching of Peter and the apostles and become believers (Acts 5:14), all this was the work of the Holy Spirit as He witnessed to Jesus through those who obeyed Him, witnessing to the gospel, the good news of peace with God and sins forgiven through Jesus, God's Man, God's Son.

The reaction of the Sanhedrin, not only to Peter's words, but to the implication of what he was saying was completely predictable. They were 'enraged' (RSV), and wanted to kill Peter. They were 'cut to the heart' (AV). The Greek word literally means 'to saw through, to saw asunder', and denotes strong emotion. (Barrett p291). They wanted to kill him then and there.

Acts 5:34-39. Gamaliel's counsel

But a Pharisee named Gamaliel, a teacher of the law, respected by all the people, stood up in the council and gave orders to put the men outside for a short time. And he said to them, 'Men of Israel, take care what you propose to do with these men'. (Acts 5:34,35).

But Gamaliel. (Acts 5:34). It is God's 'but'. The High Priest was a Sadducee, and the party of the Sadducees was the largest party in the council. They were the aristocratic party with much influence among Jewish aristocratic families. They insisted that there was no resurrection from the dead, (Acts 23:8), which inclined them even further to resist the claim of this newly formed group of people that their leader had been raised from the dead.

The Pharisees on the council, especially the scribes who were teachers of the law and of the Pharisaic party, though without that strong objection to resurrection, still could not, or would not, believe that God had raised from the dead a criminal who had been crucified on the grounds of blasphemy. They certainly could not accept that Jesus was the long awaited, long foreordained Messiah of whom their scriptures spoke because in their understanding, He failed to comply with the Mosaic law, and in fact claimed to be above the law. They did not understand His saying that He came not to abolish the law but to fulfil it. (Matthew 5:17). To change in any way the law on which their whole lives, and the spiritual life of the nation depended, was intolerable.

Nevertheless, there were those in the council who had a deeper understanding, among whom was Gamaliel. He was a Pharisee, willing to listen to these men and examine what they had to say. Though he was a Pharisee and therefore not of the majority party in the council, he was a celebrated and revered teacher of the law, and at his suggestion, the apostles were 'put outside for a while' (Acts 5:34) while the situation was more easily discussed without the inflammatory presence of these despised men.

In closed session, Gamaliel now advocated a cautious approach to the problem of these apostles. He gave the example of two leaders with substantial numbers of followers whose movements had come to a premature but predictable end. One, called Theudas, had been slain, after which his followers dispersed and the movement came to nothing; and the other example was Judas the Galilean who had led a revolt against the tax system imposed by the Roman authorities, and who had also perished and his followers scattered. (Acts 5:37).

Gamaliel concluded that since the leader of this new movement, Jesus, was also dead, there was no point in taking action against the apostles. Just like Theudas and Judas, the followers of Jesus would soon disperse and give no more trouble.

But he also issued a caveat. He said, in effect, there is always the possibility that the movement originated by Jesus is not like that of Theudas and Judas. It may actually be a movement initiated by God. So be careful! In attempting to destroy this movement, you may be destroying the work of God, you may be fighting against Him, and you will not be able to overthrow Him, or them.

Willingly or not, the members of the Sanhedrin 'took his advice'. (Acts 5:40). The apostles were severely beaten, presumably on the grounds of causing an uproar among the people, and were again charged not to speak in the Name of Jesus, and were let go. (Acts 5:40). This may have been the 'forty lashes less one' which Paul also experienced. (2 Corinthians 11:24), because they had offended against the Jewish law. Forty lashes could mean death. The 'less one' was a flogging to the brink of death and therefore considered a merciful punishment. But this terrible punishment filled the apostles with joy, rejoicing that they had been considered worthy to suffer for the Name of Jesus. (Acts 5:42). Their injuries did not prevent them from teaching and preaching 'every day' in the temple and at home, preaching Jesus as the Christ. (Acts 5:41,42.).

Acts Chapter 6

Acts 6:1-7. The appointment of the seven

Now in those days when the disciples were increasing in number, the Hellenists murmured against the Hebrews because their widows were neglected in the daily distribution. And the twelve summoned the body of the disciples together and said, 'It is not right that we should give up preaching the word of God to serve tables. Therefore brethren, pick out from among you seven men of good repute, full of the Spirit and of wisdom whom we may appoint to this duty. (Acts 6:1-3).

The apostles have laid the foundation of the church. Now in number being five thousand members, (Acts 4:4), and increasing in number, (Acts 6:1); living in an atmosphere of teaching, preaching, prayer and caring for one another and for others who have not yet come into the kingdom, they have nevertheless become an administrative problem. The apostles are still teaching in the temple, whether for the convenience of having the larger amount of space which the temple provided and in addition, or because, that is where the roots of their faith lay, in the Old Testament scriptures, from which Christians from the early church onwards have found enlightenment and blessing, for it is the word of God.

The church is still meeting almost exclusively in Jerusalem, though the dispersal of people back to their homes on or after the Day of Pentecost suggests that the gospel, the good news which Peter preached on that day, would have been disseminated far and wide.

The question is, where does the church go from here? How is it going to develop as it must surely do? Jesus had made it abundantly clear to His disciples that He had all the nations of the earth in view as the missionary purpose of their lives as they witnessed to Him. At His ascension into heaven He had said to them, 'You shall be witnesses to Me in Jerusalem, and in all Judea, and Samaria, and to the utterrmost parts of the earth'. (Acts 1:8).

The apostles had truly borne witness to Him in Jerusalem. They had suffered for His sake. As Tertullian (c 155-225) wrote in his *Apology,* 'the blood of the martyrs is the seed of the church'. (*The Lion Book of Christian Thought:* Tony Lane; p17). The church in Jerusalem continued to grow; and for God's purposes to be fulfilled, other servants of His needed to be appointed to 'serve tables'. (Acts 6:2). Among the seven men who were anointed by the Holy Spirit for this ministry were Stephen and Philip.

So at this period of the expansion of the church there were two problems. The first problem was the administrative one. The disciples were increasing in numbers, and of course this was a wonderful problem to have, but it made the burden of caring for all these precious new believers an acute one.

Arising from this was the second problem. Within the church there were two groups of believers, the Hellenistic Jews, those with a Greek background, and the Hebrews. They were distinguished in this way by their language and culture. The Hellenists were Greek speaking Jews and the Hebrews spoke largely Aramaic, an ancient Semitic language pre-dating Hebrew which had become the vernacular of the Israelites when returning from exile, and which had become the common language of Palestine, though it was possible that both languages could be used by both in the cosmopolitan empire that was Rome.

However, there began to be a quiet murmuring, a quiet note of complaint among the Greek speaking Jews. (Acts 6:1). These believers had probably come from the Diaspora, that is, the Dispersion of the Jews into settlements all around the Great (Mediterranean) Sea. They were concerned that the widows among them were not being properly cared for. It is not difficult to imagine that these women had left their homelands and their families in order to accompany their husbands to Jerusalem and that their husbands had subsequently died, leaving them without provision or support. There were probably many others in extreme poverty in Jerusalem. The social position of widows was always a difficult one as we understand from James 1:27 and 1 Timothy 5:9. They were often poor, desolate, unprotected, and neglected.

This should not be a situation allowed to continue among those who loved the Lord. The Hellenists took their problem to the Twelve. (Acts 6:2). The church must not be allowed to become a source of derision, of mockery to those outside the church. It must at all times be seen as a body of believers who obeyed the command of Jesus to 'love one another as I have loved you' (John 13:4).

The widows, whether Hellenists or Hebrews were to be loved and seen to be loved and provided for if they had no other means of support, for love is not primarily an emotion, but an act of the will. Love is kind. Love bears all things. Love never fails, Love is of God, for God is love. God can use even the poverty of these lonely, neglected, dear people to bind the church together in love.

The first problem was largely a problem of time. With such a large group of people to provide for, how could the apostles also give themselves to prayer and the ministry of the word? Both of these activities were of the utmost importance. But it was equally important that no-one should be discriminated against, left out of the daily distribution. How to reconcile these two important issues, the important ministry of teaching and prayer to which God had called the apostles, and equally the care for the most vulnerable members of the community?

The apostles, the leaders of the new and expanding church, were the link with Jesus Himself, and derived their authority through Him. But this was not an autocratic assembly. The twelve apostles did not assume that they had the answers to all the problems arising in the church, as in any human organization there were bound to be.

They gathered all the disciples together to determine what ought to be done. No doubt with much prayer and looking for guidance to the Holy spirit, the decision was made by the whole body of believers. The twelve apostles should be left free to continue the ministry of the word of God, for God was revealing so much to the church through their ministry, and that these men, their leaders, should devote themselves to prayer, for no progress could be made, nothing could proceed or prosper or be accomplished without close intimate fellowship through the Holy Spirit with their heavenly Father and the Lord Jesus.

In addition seven men full of the Holy Spirit and wisdom could be appointed to 'serve tables', to do the practical work which was so necessary, as the twelve had suggested. 'Brethren', they had said, 'choose from among you seven men of good repute, full of the Holy Spirit and wisdom whom we may appoint to this duty', the duty of being a servant of the church. (Acts 6:3).' But we will devote ourselves to prayer and to being servants of the word'. (Acts 6:4).

This was in effect a rededication of the apostles to that to which God had called them, and what they said pleased the whole multitude. (Acts 6:5). It was a proposal, a way forward which was satisfactory, which pleased everybody. It was the solution to both problems.

And they chose Stephen, a man full of faith and of the Holy Spirit, and Philip, Prochorus, Nicanor, Timon, Parmenas and Nicolaus, a proselyte of Antioch. The mention of Nicolaus of Antioch was an indication of how far the gospel had spread. These men they brought before the apostles; and after praying they laid their hands on them, commissioning them for the task which was ordained for them, the care of the church. The word of God kept on spreading and the number of the disciples continued to increase; and a great many of the priests were becoming obedient to the faith. (Acts 6:6,7).

So important was this work which these seven men were appointed to do, that the believers appreciated that they needed to be commissioned to it by the Holy Spirit, by prayer and the laying on of hands, for the work of caring for the church was just as important as preaching and teaching. And inevitably, the solution of the problem led to the expansion of the church.

As the word of God increased, God continued to reveal Himself more and more through His word. The number of believers multiplied greatly in Jerusalem and included many of the chief priests who had formerly been opposed to the faith. (Acts 6:7). And Stephen, full of grace and power was performing great wonders and signs among the people. (Acts 6:8).

The church had acquired a flexible governing body, the twelve apostles and seven men full of the Holy Spirit and wisdom, through whom God could also do signs and wonders in addition to 'serving at tables'. Acts 6:1-7 is a significant bridge to the rest of the Acts of the Apostles, or alternatively, the acts of the Holy Spirit through the apostles.

Luke speaks of the ministry of the word, *diakonia ton logos*, (Gk) but also the ministry of the table, *dikonein tratiezais*, (Gk) *diakoneia* meaning ministry, service, help, support; the root word for deacons. Jesus Himself said that He came not to be served but to serve, and to give His life as a ransom for many. (Mathew 20:28).

Whether what one is given is the ministry, service of the word, or the ministry of tables, there has to an element of giving up one's life in order to perform this ministry, not of course as Jesus did in becoming a ransom for many; as He did, for His blood bought sons and daughters who have come into His kingdom through faith. But nevertheless, these were men called to serve His people whatever the personal cost, both the cost and the privilege of being a servant of the church, of loving others as He has loved them, washing their feet metaphorically and sometimes literally. Jesus took a towel. (John 13:4). He said to them, 'By this shall all men know that you are My disciples if you have love one for another'. (John 13:35)

These two ministries have not always been regarded as of equal value in the church, but there should be no tension between them. In the Jerusalem church, the seven were chosen by the whole body of the disciples, so that the whole church could have confidence in them, as the apostles appointed them to 'this duty'. (Acts 6:3).

The names of the seven men are given and they are all without exception, Greek names. But this does not mean that they were Hellenist Jews. Among the twelve, there are also Greek names. (Andrew, Philip, Bartholomew). Stephen is a reasonably common Greek name and he and Philip (not the apostle Philip) are the two of the seven who subsequently have narratives written about them.

Of the other five little is known, though Nicolaus is described as a full convert to Judaism, a proselyte, (Acts 6:5), meaning that he had been admitted to Judaism through circumcision and the offering of sacrifice. Acts 6:5 says that he was from Antioch, and Acts 11:19 informs us that those who were scattered abroad because of the persecution that occurred in connection with Stephen made their way to Phoenicia and Cyprus *and Antioch,* speaking the word to none but Jews only. Perhaps Nicolaus had been one who later returned to Antioch after the persecution, and perhaps he was also one of the prophets and teachers in the church at Antioch when Barnabas and Saul were sent out by the Holy Spirit on their first missionary journey. But this is conjecture for which we have little or no evidence. We can say however that Nicolaus was a man governed by his quest for the truth, which he first found in Judaism and afterwards more fully as he embraced salvation in Christ.

These seven men stood before the apostles as they gathered round them and prayed and laid hands on them, in blessing and authorization to the service of the church.

And once again the Lord confirmed His word to them with signs following. (Mark 16:20. AV). As the apostles continued to preach, and the widows were relieved of their poverty, 'a great many of the chief priests were obedient to the faith'. Once again, a tragedy had been averted.

Acts 6:8-7:60. The attack on Stephen

And Stephen, full of grace and power was performing great wonders and signs among the people. Then some of those who belonged to the synagogue of the Freedmen, as it was called, and of the Cyrenians and of the Alexandrians and those from Cilicia and Asia, arose and disputed with Stephen. But they could not withstand the wisdom and Spirit with which he spoke. (Acts 6:8-10).

Stephen was already a man 'full of faith and of the Holy Spirit'. (Acts 6:5), but the laying on of hands by the apostles had conferred on him the authority of one who was chosen by God for this service to Him. Under this authority, Stephen 'full of grace and power', did great wonders and signs among the people. He had been chosen to wait on tables, to be a servant of the church, a ministry of great privilege and also great responsibility. The Holy Spirit had enlarged his ministry. It may have been similar to the signs and wonders wrought by the hands of the apostles in Acts 5:12, when more believers were added to the Lord, and the sick and afflicted with unclean spirits were healed. (Acts 5:16).

That Stephen, full of grace and power, was able to do great wonders and signs was his spiritual gifting, the gift of the Holy Spirit to him. He was given the grace of the Lord Jesus and the power of the Holy Spirit.

As Luke had already explained in the narrative concerning Peter and John before the Sanhedrin, performing signs and wonders among the people was bound to lead to a degree of opposition. The rulers of the synagogues were especially aggressive, though it seems that it was not so much the signs and wonders but Stephen's teaching which troubled them.

It is not quite clear from the text whether there was one synagogue of which all these Jewish leaders were a part, or whether there were several synagogues in Jerusalem, a probability in a large city. Barrett describes synagogues as primarily institutions for the reading and exposition of scripture, for prayer and for instruction, but they also served as a meeting place, and might even have residential accommodation on the premises. (Barrett p 323). Bruce is particularly interested in the Libertines, (RSV), or Freedmen (NASB). A Libertine could be either a freedman or the son of a freedman of the imperial household; alternatively the Libertines may have been Roman freedmen descended from Jews sent by Pompey as prisoners to Rome and soon liberated. The synagogue which Paul attended prior to his encounter with the Lord Jesus on the Damascus road may have been a synagogue of the Libertines, or have had Libertines as members of it, and Paul's father or remoter ancestor may have received his manumission in that way, giving Paul the right to claim to be a Roman citizen. (Acts 22:28. Bruce pp 156, 157).

On one reading of Acts 6:9, there appeared to be at least five synagogues in Jerusalem, unless verse 9 is understood as one synagogue attended by five different groups of people, which may even have included some who were descended from freed slaves arriving originally from Cyrenia, Alexandria, Cilicia and Asia.

It may be that the Holy Spirit used the signs and wonders which Stephen was enabled to perform, to draw attention to what he was saying. This was a challenge to the synagogue or synagogues, for as we have noted, the purpose of the synagogues was to read and expound the law of Moses while the sacrificial element of the Jewish faith took place in the temple. Around the synagogues, the life of the community flourished. Stephen was challenging not only the purpose of the synagogues but the position and functions of their leaders.

These men arose and disputed with Stephen, but they could not withstand the wisdom and the Spirit with which he spoke. (Acts 6:9,10). Just as the High Priest had done with Jesus, these men brought forward people who were prepared to perjure themselves as witnesses to what Stephen was reputed to have said. They accused him of speaking blasphemies, 'blasphemous words against Moses and God'. (Acts 6:11). And they stirred up the people and the elders and the scribes, and they came upon him and seized him, and brought him to the council. (Acts 6:12).

The men of the synagogue had tried disputing with Stephen. It was a skill they had learned long ago and at which they were particularly accomplished. But they could not withstand the wisdom and the Spirit with which He spoke. The Holy Spirit was fulfilling again, as He had with Peter and John, the promise of Jesus to His disciples. 'When they deliver you up, do not be anxious about what you are to speak, or what you are to say, for what you are to say will be given to you in that hour. For it is not you who speak but the Spirit of your Father speaking through you'. (Matthew 10:19,20.) It seemed that the only recourse open to these men of the synagogue was to 'secretly instigate men who said' '"we have heard him speak blasphemous words against Moses and against God"'. (Acts 6:11).

Even these perjured witnesses had difficulty with the concept of blasphemy, for blasphemy can only be against God, blaspheming His Name, stating that God was other than almighty, all powerful, the Creator of the world and humanity; that God was not Who He claimed to be, everlasting God. Stephen could not do this as he was speaking by the power of the Holy Spirit.

To speak of blasphemy against Moses was also a false accusation. Moses was meek,' more than all that were on the face of the earth', (Numbers 12:3), and the Lord said to his brother Aaron and sister Miriam, 'why were you not afraid to speak against My servant Moses, with whom I speak mouth to mouth and not in dark speech, and he beholds the form of the Lord? (Numbers 12:8). Aaron and Miriam were punished for speaking against Moses, but they were not being accused of blasphemy against Moses but rebellion against the servant of God whom He had chosen.

For all their clever rhetoric and logic, these men of the synagogue could no more speak against Stephen than Aaron and Miriam could speak against Moses, for he too was a servant of the Lord. In their helplessness, their inability to overcome Stephen's words, the men of the synagogue and Stephen's accusers stirred up the people and the elders and the scribes and brought him to the council, the Sanhedrin. (Acts 6:12). Their accusation against him had been expanded to say,' this man never ceases to speak words against this holy place and the law, for we have heard him say that this Jesus of Nazareth will destroy this place and will change the customs which Moses delivered to us. (Acts 6:14).

And gazing at him, all who sat in the council saw that his face was like the face of an angel. (Acts 6:15).

At last we have come to the nub of the problem. It is actually Jesus whom they are resisting, rejecting. This is informative because it throws a light upon what the apostles have been teaching and preaching, the teaching of the kingdom of God and kingdom living, the proclamation of the gospel to all who believe, those who have received the word with joy as they gathered together in the temple.

Stephen is a man of faith. Since there is no mention of him in the gospels, we may assume that he came to faith in the Lord Jesus through the ministry of the apostles, perhaps through Peter's speech on the day of Pentecost, or his speech to the crowd after the lame man had been healed at the beautiful gate of the temple, or the preaching of the apostles after they were found preaching at daybreak in the temple after they had been released from prison by the angel.

For it is a spiritual principle that faith comes by hearing, and hearing by the word of God. (Romans 10:17). From these, admittedly, only assumptions, we may understand that Stephen had relatively recently become a follower of the Lord Jesus, yet he had been able to speak of Jesus of Nazareth, and the temple, the holy place and the law of Moses. In fact he was accused of 'never ceasing to speak of the holy place and the law', and in his speech he shows that he had a wide knowledge of the Hebrew scriptures, not forgetting that the Holy Spirit was enabling him to witness to the love and mercy of Jesus for these people who needed Him so badly. His accusers were limited by their Roman overlords in their authority to punish Stephen as they thought he deserved, and so he was brought to the council.

They had of course completely misunderstood what Stephen was saying. The Jews were the chosen people of God, and He had allowed them to build Him a house, a place where He could put His Name. (1 KIngs 8:29; 2 Chronicles 6:20). It was true that

Jesus had spoken of the destruction of the temple, which happened in 70 A.D. He had said to the disciples when they pointed out to Him the beauty of the temple,' Truly I tell you, there will not be left one stone upon another that will not be cast down'. (Matthew 24:1,2).

Stephen had spoken of the destruction of the temple as a warning to these scribes and Pharisees of the judgement that was to come upon those who had been given the covenant, and the law and the promises. (Romans 9:4). They were indeed the chosen people of God, but they trusted in themselves that they were righteous and despised others. (Luke 18:9). They failed to recognize their hypocrisy, their laying of burdens hard to bear on others. (Luke 11:46). The temple was important to them as evidence that their way of life conformed to the law as given to them by Moses. They were contemporaries of this 'Jesus of Nazareth', who thought He knew better than they did; and whom they misunderstood to say that He would destroy their beautiful, precious temple, their 'holy place'. (Acts 6:13).

Jesus had not of course said that He would destroy the temple, but that it would be destroyed. The message of Jesus to them time and time again, was 'Repent, for the kingdom of heaven is at hand! The kingdom, the kingdom of heaven, the kingdom of God, was that close to them if only they would repent and enter in through the door marked 'repentance'. Jesus wanted these people, His people, to come to Him and receive new life from Him, to enjoy a future far more satisfying and glorious than their present attempts at being righteous, if only they would repent and believe the gospel, and receive the forgiveness of their sins.

'But they would not'. (Matthew 23:37; Luke 13:34). This is perhaps one of the saddest phrases in the whole of the New Testament. They would not.

It was also true that Jesus would 'change the customs which Moses delivered to us', (Acts 6:14), but again, they had completely misunderstood what Jesus had said and what Stephen had been trying to explain to them; that the customs, the traditions, the law, and the sacrifices, were symbolic of the greater truth which was to come, for they were all fulfilled in the life, death and resurrection of the Lord Jesus; Jesus the promised Messiah of whom they had surely read in their scriptures.

Jesus had come, not to abolish the law but to fulfil it. (Matthew 5:17). The sacrifices, the offerings and even the law itself were but types, figures of the true. (Hebrews 9:24. AV). Gifts and offerings could deal only with disobedience to outward rules, regulations, even commandments, although the sin for which the offeror was asking for forgiveness as he brought his offering to God was real. But such offerings could do nothing for the inward knowledge, the consciousness of failure before God and His holiness, described so movngly by David as he confesses his sin before a merciful God. 'Against Thee, Thee only have I sinned and done that which was evil in Thy sight. Have mercy upon me, O Lord'. (Psalm 51:41.). And God was merciful to David as He is to all who call upon Him.

Only the knowledge of God's redeeming grace in the sacrifice of His Son, the knowledge of sins forgiven because of the shed blood of Christ, the life He poured out upon the cross, can remove the ache of a conscience which is constantly aware of the blemish which lies upon it; which can only be removed by that precious blood.

Who would not want the customs and traditions changed which led only to condemnation? But these men had rejected Stephen's words and in so doing had condemned *themselves,* with a constant perception that they were not doing enough to gain God's favour. The constant repetition of the sacrifices may have given them temporary respite. 'But Jesus appeared *once for all* at the end of the age to put away sin by the sacrifice of Himself'. (Hebrews 9:26). Though they had tried and tried again these men were rejecting the provision God had made for them in Jesus and which Stephen was now attempting to help them to understand.

What was the council to do? AS they sat there gazing at Stephen 'all who sat there saw his face like the face of an angel'.

(Acts 6:15). Like the face of Moses when he came down from the mountain after communing with God, Stephens's face radiated the glory of the Lord whom he worshipped and who was with him at this trial before the Sanhedrin. (Exodus 34:29).

Acts Chapter 7

Acts 7:1-53. Stephen's speech

And the High Priest said, 'Is this so? And Stephen said, 'Brethren and fathers, hear me. The God of glory appeared to our father Abraham when he was in Mesopotamia, before he lived in Haran, and said to him, 'Depart from your land and from your kindred and go into the land which I will show you. Then he departed from the land of the Chaldeans and lived in Haran. And after his father died, God removed him from there into this land in which you are now living. (Acts 7:1-4).

Stephen heard the scribes and elders and the false witnesses refer to Jesus contemptuously as 'Jesus of Nazareth', the One whom Stephen could only think of as his Lord. In his defence of his teaching about his Lord, Stephen did not seek to exonerate Him, but to clarify what He had done in rejecting the temple as the place where God could only and exclusively be found, for He was not limited to any one place.

If God limited Himself at all, it was only to the One who was the Home of God, the Lord Jesus, the place, the Person, who had made Himself available so that human beings could also find a home in Him as they dwelt in Him and He in them. This was where He could always be found, not in a building however beautiful, though many did find Him there, but, as He had prayed to His Father, 'I in them and Thou in Me, that they may be one, even as We are one'. (John 17:22,23.). And in John's ultimate revelation, that in the new Jerusalem, the holy city which came down out of heaven from God, there was no temple, for its temple is the Lord God Almighty and the Lamb (Revelation 21:22).

These things may be hard to understand, as Peter himself discovered (2 Peter 3:16). But Stephen had been given this revelation that the temple days were over for the Jerusalem church. Though their roots continued to lie in Judaism, and continued to be inspired by all the wonderful things that God had been described as doing through His servants in the Hebrew scriptures, the church was now moving on. The scriptures could not be a limitation imposed upon them to understand what God was doing now, for He was doing a new thing; building a church which was not dependent on a place, or a land, not even on Jerusalem with its beautiful temple, and especially not on a comprehensive set of traditions, customs and laws.

Stephen's message to the Sanhedrin was one of liberty; of freedom from the law if only they would receive it. It was an inspired message, as the shining of his face testified.

Stephen foresaw the inevitability of a break between Judaism and the church and in this way prepared for the gospel, the *kerygma*, to be extended to the Gentiles, the proclamation of the gospel requiring the response of faith. He is courageous in his affirmation that the Jewish people had always been stubborn and rebellious, and their rejection of the Righteous One, (Acts 7:52), has brought this rebellion from the past into the present. At the end of his speech he says, 'You do always resist the Holy Spirit. You are a stiff necked people, uncircumcised in heart and ears'. (Acts 7:51). Without rancour, he seeks to demonstrate that there had always been another way to live in intimacy with God. Though they were the leaders of God's people, they had never learned effectively how to come into His presence.

Acts 7:1-8. God appears to Abraham

So Stephen begins with Abraham, who had neither temple, nor law, nor land, but who walked before God. (Genesis 17:1). He continues with the twelve patriarchs, including Joseph; the time of slavery in Egypt and their exodus under Moses; the tabernacle in the wilderness and the conquest of Canaan under Joshua; and David's request that he might build Him a house which was refused so that David's son Solomon should build Him a house.

Stephen might at that point have brought the history of Israel up to date, but he had said enough. The reaction of the Sanhedrin was immediate and violent.

Stephen's speech is one of the longest in the Acts and profitable as an insight into what God had demonstrated of His love and care for His people from the time of Abraham onwards. Far from blaspheming against God, the charge which they had brought against him, Stephen was attempting to disclose to the ones whom he addresses as 'Brethren and fathers' (Acts 7:2), how the whole purpose of God from Abraham onwards was bound up with the vindication and coming of the Righteous One whom they had rejected, and of His all-sufficiency for all mankind. Nothing and no-one else was necessary to the purposes of God, no law, no prophet, no temple, no land. Only Jesus.

The high priest had said to Stephen 'Is this so? Are the charges against you true?'

It is difficult to see from Stephen's speech whether he ever actually answered the High Priest's question, for his is not a forensic defence of his own teaching, or an attempt to avoid what he must have known that the apostles had suffered before him after their interrogation. HIs speech is an *apologia, a defence,* a reasoned explanation for his Christian teaching, his teaching about Christ, a clarification and expansion of all his earlier teaching, but in tone, respectful and conciliatory.

He began his speech gently by calling them 'brethren and fathers', even though Annas the High Priest's question to him 'Are these things so?' had really invited him to commit himself before being heard. In effect Annas was saying 'Do you plead guilty or not guilty to the charges brought against you?' Stephen could have pleaded 'not guilty'. But his opening words include himself as a Jew like themselves in the accusation which he is bringing against the leaders of Israel by calling them 'brethren, fathers'. He is identifying them as his brethren, but his respectful words do not prevent the Sanhedrin from condemning him even before he speaks.

'Brethren and fathers', he says, 'hear me'. Listen to me. What he had to say to them is not in his own defence but a defence of the gospel, a continuation of what he had already been preaching. He was not trying to prove that he was not blaspheming. His object was to show them that God was doing something new in their midst. The temple that was so important to them that to have it was an indication that God was with them, and that therefore they were His special people was to be replaced by a new temple, as Jesus had said in John 2:20, the temple of His Body, which became the church. (1 Corinthians 12:27).

He also refuted the accusation that Jesus wanted to abolish the customs and the traditions, the law delivered by Moses the giver of the law, for the law displayed the character of God and the means whereby they could partake, in measure at least, of His character. Jesus had said that He came *not to abolish the law but to fulfill it.* (Matthew 5:17).

To the elders and scribes who had originally brought the accusation against Stephen, these concepts of the temple and the law were of paramount importance. They believed that they had insurmountable evidence that Stephen was trying to undermine every aspect of their religious life. It is perhaps understandable that they felt more than a little frustrated by Stephen's insistence on a new move of God which they feared could destroy their whole purpose in life. They considered that everything of value to them was being undermined by what Stephen was teaching.

Stephen's purpose in this discourse was to show that God had set his heart not so much upon a holy place as upon a holy people; a people who reflected His holiness. He wanted them to understand that God is constantly at work in the history of His people, and that in the life of Jesus is the ultimate expression of His purpose for them. So he goes back to the very beginning of their history, to Abraham. (Acts 7:2).

But the real beginning was God. God appeared to Abraham. The God of glory, the visible display of the divine presence, the self manifestation, self-revelation of the transcendent God; who does not live in buildings, even such buildings as the temple, appeared to Abraham when he was in Mesopotamia, before he lived in Haran, in the land of the Chaldeans, a people who practised astrology and polytheism. From Mesopotamia after the death of his father Terah, he moved to Canaan via Haran.

Chaldea was where Abraham's family and ancestors had lived. Though Ur of the Chaldees held an important place in his life, with its familiar culture and associations, yet, by faith, Abraham 'obeyed to go out to a place which he was to receive as an inheritance, and he went out, not knowing where he was to go'. (Hebrews 11:8). Surrounded as he was by the culture of polytheism, he rejected the polytheism and the idolatry of the Chaldeans, because God had spoken to him, the one true God, the God of glory who had appeared to him.

From ancient times, Mesopotamia had been regarded as the land between two rivers, the Tigris and the Euphrates, but by the Greeks was considered to comprise an even larger area to the south, which included Babylonia. The city of Babylon represented all that exalted itself against God from the building of the tower of Babel onwards. (Genesis 11:4; Revelation 17 and 19).

God was delivering Abraham from that. He was removing him from Ur, where He had made Himself known to Abraham. God had said to him, 'Depart from your land and from your kindred and go into the land that I will show you. Then he left the land of the Chaldeans and settled in Haran. From there after his father died, God had him move to this country in which you are now living'. (Acts 7:4).

God spoke to him again in Haran after the death of his father Terah, a period of some years. God was taking out of the nations a people for Himself, but He is the God of eternity as well as the God of time. He was prepared to wait until the death of Terah before Abraham was sent once more on a journey of faith to the land of Canaan. Stephen says 'After his father died God removed him from there into this land in which you now live'. (Acts 7:4). Abraham did not choose where he was to live; God did. But God was in no hurry. There were two removes along the way to the land of promise, some years apart, God dealing tenderly with Him. (Matthew Henry p2089). Abraham had only to follow wherever his God would go.

God was preparing Abraham to receive the covenant. He had called him out of an idolatrous culture and he had obeyed. He had challenged Abraham's links to that culture through his family and all that was dear to him, and he had obeyed. He had heard the voice of God and he trusted God. He obeyed, and his faith was the precursor of the covenant of circumcision which God gave him as a sign that he belonged to Him.

God is not confined by land, by distance, by time. He has His purposes in view and He will fulfil them, and by His grace He sometimes allows a man or a woman to be part of what He is doing.

God is certainly not confined to living in a temple as these men of the Sanhedrin seem to think. The temple was a gift to them as a mark of His grace. How desperately sad that it should have brought them into a bondage to it. God wanted His people to communicate with Him freely. God had communicated with Abraham long before there was a temple, or the law. God gave him no inheritance in the land to which He called him, 'not even a foot's length'. (Acts 7:5). What He did give him was the covenant. God was covenanting to be a God to Abraham and his descendents, even though he had as yet no heir. God said to Abraham, 'I am God almighty, El Shaddai. Walk before Me and be perfect, blameless. And I will make My covenant with you and will multiply you exceedingly'. (Genesis 17:1,2). And he believed God, and it was counted to him as righteousness. (Genesis 15:6).

God almighty, El Shaddai, is proclaiming His own self sufficiency. He is perfect and He is the God who will guide and continue to care for His people as they walk before Him. It was to be an everlasting covenant, (Genesis 17:7), between God and Abraham and his descendents after him and circumcision was to be the sign of the covenant.

So the circumcised Abraham became the father of the circumcised Isaac, and Isacc the father of Jacob, and Jacob of the twelve Patriarchs, (Acts 7:8), the originators of the twelve tribes of Israel, drawing them into the covenant. Stephen implies that Abraham had no temple, no law and no land, but he had something infinitely more precious. He had a covenant with Almighty God, his God. God had promised to be his God as he walked before Him. And Abraham was the father of the Jewish nation, a nation that walked in the light of the knowledge that God was their God, the one who would always protect them while they walked with Him.

'Our father Abraham' said Stephen, (Acts 7:2), aligning himself with his accusers as a participant in the covenant and in the history of God's dealings with His people, long before the law was given or the temple built.

Acts 7:8-10. The story of Joseph

Abraham became the father of Isaac, and circumcised him on the eighth day, and Isaac became the father of Jacob, and Jacob of the twelve patriarchs. The patriarchs became jealous of Joseph and sold him into Egypt, but God was with him and rescued him from all his afflictions and granted him favour in the sight of Pharaoh, king of Egypt and he made him governor over Egypt and all his household. (Acts 7:8-10).

Stephen continues his theme of God's activity on behalf of the men whom He has chosen. He has brought the history of Israel from Abraham up to the time of the twelve sons of Jacob, who was renamed Israel, 'prince with God', or 'he who strives with God', by God. (Genesis 32:28). Jacob's eleventh son Joseph was cruelly treated by his ten older brothers. They sold him into Egypt, but God was with him. (Acts 7:9). Rejected by his brothers, suffering at the hand of Potiphar's wife, and his subsequent imprisonment, Joseph is finally vindicated.

Stephen's summary barely does justice to what God was doing through Joseph, but it makes an important point. Just as God had chosen Abraham and promised to be with him, so God also chose Joseph from among his brothers. He would also choose Moses, the man who was the meekest man on the face of the earth and with whom the Lord spoke face to face. (Numbers 12:3). He would also choose David, a man after God's own heart who would do all His will. (Acts 13:22), for God had in mind not just a chosen vessel to Him, as Paul was, (Acts 9:15), but a chosen *people* who would do all His will.

God chose Joseph and God was with him, (Acts 7:9). He rescued him out of all his afflictions and gave him favour and wisdom before Pharaoh, who made him governor over Egypt and over all his household. (Acts 7:10). God was equipping him for the task He had given him.

God had intervened in the life of Isaac, Jacob, and now Jacob's son, for He had an eternal purpose in view, a people who were redeemed, who were to be taken out of a culture of idolatry, the culture of the nations around and redeemed to Himself. He was their redeemer. His people were precious to Him. And now they had come to Egypt through Joseph. The prophet Hosea says of God 'out of Egypt have I called My son' (Hosea 11:1), And this purpose He would fulfil.

But God had informed Abraham that it was going to be four hundred years before the people inherited the land, the land of Canaan. God was in no hurry to fulfil His purpose, for Israel had a lot to learn.

The Canaan of Joseph's childhood and family life was not an empty land when Abraham moved into it. Genesis 14 speaks of a five state coalition of Canaanite city states which attempted to rebel against the imperial lordship of Chedorlaomer, and his four-state coalition from Mesopotamia. (Genesis 14:1-12). (Gerald Janzen p31). Salem, later Jerusalem, was an ancient Canaanite city ruled by a priest king, called Melchizedek, king of Salem, king of righteousness, king of peace. (Psalm 76:2). It was not until Joshua that the conquest of Canaan took place. But silently, surely, God was working his purpose out; without haste and with infinite patience. His people had to live through their Egypt experience to discover who God truly is.

Since the land which God had promised to Abraham was an important part of the Israelite inheritance, the place where God was to deliver the law to His people and provide a place for His presence with them, the story of Joseph is significant.

Joseph was a young man of seventeen when he perceived that God had chosen him above his brothers through the dreams which he had. (Genesis 37:2-11). He knew that God was with him. He knew that the Lord was with him in Potiphar's house. (Genesis 39:2). He knew that the Lord was with him in prison. (Genesis 39:21). And Pharaoh had to acknowledge 'can we find such a man as this in whom the Spirit of God is?' (Genesis 41:55). When the famine came, Pharaoh said to the Egyptians, 'go to Joseph'. (Genesis 41:55). When his brothers came down to Egypt for the second time, Joseph was aware, not of himself and the great position he had been given but of God. He said, 'God sent me before you to preserve life, to preserve for you a remnant on earth'. (Genesis 45:5,7). 'It was not you who sent me here but God'. (Genesis 45:8).

And at the end of his life he could say to his brothers, 'As for you, you meant it for evil against me, but God meant it for good. (Genesis 50:20). Thus he reassured them and comforted them. So great was his faith in the loving kindness and faithfulness of God that he made mention of the exodus of the Israelites from Egypt and gave directions concerning his burial, not in Egypt but in Canaan, the promised land. (Hebrews 11:22). As he was about to die, he said, 'God will visit you and bring you up out of this land of Egypt to the land which He swore to Abraham, to Isaac and to Jacob. And you will carry my bones from here. (Genesis 50:24,25).

God keeps His promises. Joseph had been faithful to God throughout his time in Egypt and God had been faithful to him. But God now wanted to bring His growing people into the land which He had promised to give them. During the next four hundred years, they increased from the seventy who went down into Egypt with Jacob. (Genesis 46:27). They had become so numerous a people that they had been enslaved by the rulers of Egypt who were terrified that they might rise up against them, particularly as they did not worship the gods of the Egyptians, but their own God.

Joseph had no holy place, no temple, no law, no land except that land which had been given to his family to live in by

Pharoah, but which continued to belong to the Egyptians. But he had God, the God who determined the course of history, (Barrett p 348), but also the intimate personal God who was with him.

Through Joseph, God's people went down into Egypt and stayed there for four hundred years. (Genesis 15:13). During that time, they had become a nation, living comfortably to begin with in the land of Goshen, a part of Egypt where they could live apart from the Egyptians, for Joseph had described his family to Pharoah as shepherds, and shepherds were regarded with contempt by the Egyptians as being of a lower class occupation. To be a shepherd was beneath the dignity of an Egyptian, 'every shepherd was an abomination to the Egyptians', (Genesis 46:34). Joseph was completely honest as he anticipated the speech of his brothers with Pharoah. He advises them to say to Pharaoh, 'Your servants have been keepers of cattle from our youth even until now, both we and our fathers'. (Genesis 46:34).

This was true. Abraham had been a shepherd. (Genesis 13:2). Isaac had also been a shepherd. (Genesis 26:14). Jacob was concerned for his flock of sheep. (Genesis 33:13). Later we read that God took David His servant from the sheepfolds, from tending the ewes that had young. God brought him to be the shepherd of Jacob His people and Israel His inheritance'. (Psalm 78:70), God always wanted the leaders of His people to be the shepherds of His people. He Himself is described as the Shepherd of Israel, One who leads Joseph like a flock, (Psalm 80:1) the One who feeds His flock like a shepherd, gathers the lambs in His arms and gently leads those who are with young. (Isaiah 40:11).

God, the ultimate shepherd, appoints for His people shepherds who will care for them as He does. Without a shepherd heart for 'the people of His pasture and the sheep of His hand, (Psalm 95:7), no-one can truly be a shepherd of God's people. Joseph was born into a shepherd family, and was concerned for his family, but not for his family only, but for the people of Egypt who without help would be suffering the effects of famine even as the nations around were suffering. *The people of all the earth came to Egypt to buy grain from Joseph, because the famine was severe in all the earth.* (Genesis 41:57).

But Joseph knew from God that this was not the ultimate destination of God's people. He knew that they would eventually leave Egypt and settle in the land which God had promised to them, 'the land in which you are now living' as Stephen reminded his hearers.

By faith, Joseph made mention of the exodus of the Israelites, and gave direction concerning his burial. (Hebrews 11:22). And as the time of the fulfilment of the promise drew near which God had granted to Abraham, (Acts 7:17), 'at that time Moses was born', God's people had grown and multiplied in Egypt, and it was time, God's time for Him to move again in raising up another of His servants, another shepherd. (Exodus 3:1), as He pursued His intentions for them. At last, God is going to have a people for Himself, and He is going to give them not only the land, but also the Covenant, and the law, the revelation of the character of God, through Moses.

Acts 7:17-45. Stephen speaks of Moses

But as the time of the promise drew near, which God had granted to Abraham, the people grew and multiplied in Egypt, till there arose another king who had not known Joseph. He dealt craftily with our race and forced our fathers to expose their infants, that they might not be kept alive. At this time, Moses was born and was beautiful before God. (Acts 7:17-20).

Far from speaking against Moses, which had been one of the charges brought against him by the Sanhedrin, Stephen goes on to demonstrate that this man too was a servant of God, raised up by Him for the deliverance of His people.

The birth and early life of Moses was miraculous. He was born into a Levite family which subsequently became a priestly family when the tabernacle was erected. He was the son of Amram and Jochebed, and he had an older brother Aaron, and a sister Miriam. (Exodus 6:16). Pharaoh, a pharaoh or Egyptian ruler who had not known Joseph, had commanded that 'every son born to the Hebrews you shall cast into the Nile, but you shall let every daughter live'. Exodus 1:22).

Amram and Jochebed already had Aaron and Miriam when Moses was born so that the edict had not applied to Aaron; though God had a special work for him to do also. But Jochebed only partially obeyed the royal edict. She did put Moses into the River Nile when he was three months old, the river which the Egyptians worshipped as a god, but protected him from the river by a basket of bulrushes covered with bitumen and pitch which of course rendered it waterproof.

At that time the Egyptians were great civil engineers. They were building enormous store cities, Pithom and Raamses, (Exodus 1:11), and needed the Israelites as slave labour, so it seems counterproductive that they should rid themselves of a future potential labour source. But fear encourages people to do strange things. 'They were in dread of the people of Israel'. (Exodus 1:12), probably because they were becoming so numerous.

But with so much building going on, it would not have been difficult for Jochebed to obtain bitumen and pitch, to make Moses' cradle watertight; but with what weeping and tears and faith in God's protection of her baby would she have instructed Miriam to stand at the water's edge, to see what would become of him, (Exodus 2:4). She knew that the Nile was no god and that she was committing her baby into the hands of the true God.

God provided Moses not only with a surrogate mother in the daughter of Pharaoh, but restored him to Jochebed to be nursed and cared for. He grew and became familiar with all the wisdom of the Egyptians and was mighty in words and deeds. (Acts 7:22). 'When he was forty years old, it came into his heart to visit his brethren, the sons of Israel'. He was the adopted son of the royal princess, but he knew that by birth, he was also an Israelite. (Acts 7:23). He was protected by his status, but they were not, and when he interfered between an Israelite and an Egyptian, it was clear to which people he belonged.

At that time, he had not had that encounter with God which he was later permitted to have. He thought that his position at court, his education, even his own personal wisdom, were sufficient for him to be able to help his fellow Israelites. But even had he been able to help them, it would have at best an amelioration of their condition. God was planning on a complete escape from slavery for His people. Moses' own initiative, his own strength would never have been sufficient. He needed God to lead him as he led the people out from slavery into the promised land. But until he met with God at the burning bush he was content to do what he could for his people and was surprised that 'they did not understand that God was giving them deliverance by his hand'. (Acts 7:25). When one Israelite was having an altercation with another, and he interfered again, he was challenged by the man whom he was trying to turn from his violence, with the words, 'will you kill me as you killed the Egyptian yesterday? (Acts 7:28). And Moses fled.

The time of the promise had drawn near at the time when Moses was born. (Acts 7:17, 20), but Moses was forty years old before he fled to Midian to escape the anger of the Egyptian authorities; and it was forty years more before he encountered God in the burning bush; the God of time, the God of judgement. How unsearchable are His judgements and His ways past finding out! (Romans 11:33). Moses was now eighty, and God still had work for him to do.

Acts 7:29 describes Moses as having found sanctuary in Midian with Jethro who became his father-in-law. (Exodus 3:1). He had a wife, Zipporah, and two sons, a family and an occupation as shepherd, and he was content. He was far enough away from Pharaoh's court, and the time had been long enough for all his previous years of irresponsibility to be forgotten.

But God had not forgotten, and his timing is always perfect. From his birth he had been chosen by God. He had been granted what few Israelites would have been given at that time, instruction, education, in all the considerable wisdom of the Egyptians and was mighty in words and deeds. (Acts 7:22).

Possibly without realizing it, Moses had been in a course of preparation by God all this time, for all that he had to do in His Name. Just as Abraham and Joseph had found, life in intimate communion with God was a pilgrim life for Moses. Abraham had left Ur of the Chaldees for Canaan. Joseph had left Canaan for Egypt. Moses had left Egypt for Midian. God is always, constantly, moving on, in the case of the patriarchs geographically, as well as spiritually, and His servants must keep in step with Him, where He is going, what He is doing.

Stephen is reminding these elders in Jerusalem that God is doing a new thing in Jerusalem. Why were His people and the leaders of His people not moving on with Him? says Stephen Whatever these servants of God in their ancient history had gained, they had counted it but loss for the privilege of knowing God, as Paul also said in a different context. (Phillipians 3:8). God was offering the Jewish leaders a way to Him through the One whom they despised, Jesus of Nazareth. But though they had rejected HIm, God was giving them another opportunity to receive Him through Stephen's preaching. They did not need temples, or laws, even laws given by Moses, that man of whom God said that he is faithful in all His household, a man with whom He could speak mouth to mouth, even openly and not in dark sayings; and who beholds the form of the Lord. (Numbers 12:7,8).

All the Jewish leaders needed was God and the gift of being able to live their lives in obedience to Him as had Abraham, Joseph and Moses.

But for Moses to be able to lead the people out of Egypt, he needed two things. He needed a personal encounter with God, and he needed His commissioning for the task to which He had called him. So at the age of eighty, when he was keeping the flock of Jethro, his father-in-law and had led his flock to Horeb, the mountain of God, 'the angel of the Lord appeared to him in a flame of fire out of the midst of a bush, and lo, it was burning yet it was not consumed'. (Exodus 3:2).

Horeb is also identified as Mount Sinai, as Stephen does, calling it 'the wilderness of Sinai'. (Acts 7:30; Deuteronomy 29:1).

But as the history of the exodus unfolds, we learn that Sinai or Horeb was the mountain from which the Lord delivered His 'living oracles' to His people through Moses. (Acts 7:35). God wants all His children to know Him personally. This mountain was where Moses had a meeting with God which changed his life. This same mountain was the place where the children of Israel said to Moses, 'you speak to us and we will hear, but let not God speak to us lest we die. (Exodus 20:19). So often the reaction of the Lord's people has been like that of the Israelites. How the Lord longs for His children to come to Him but they so often prefer to go through a mediator, to a man or woman whom they perceive to have the mind of God. 'Come to *Me*', says Jesus, 'and I will give you rest'. (Matthew 11:28). And many do. But so many go through an intermediary while Jesus waits for them to come to Him.

So Moses received from God the living oracles which He gave to the Israelites, (Acts 7:38), oracles or commandments which were based on the revelation which He had given of Himself to Moses at the burning bush on Horeb as the 'I AM'. or 'I am that I am'. 'YHWH', (Exodus 3:14).

God takes the initiative by giving Moses His Name. I AM, a personal relational subject. It is a statement of both His existence and His pre-existence, the ontology of His eternal-ness, of the eternity of the being of God. It is His self-identification. It is not a label, as names may be, but an expression of His character, and His character concealed as well as revealed. It reveals Him as 'being', but conceals His otherness, His transcendence, His immutability, His fullness, the fullness of His being and activity as Creator and Sustainer.

W. Johmstone writes. 'The rest of the book of Exodus is the exposition of the character of YHWH, the God and the Name, (Johnstone, p103), the inexhaustible God; for there was so much more to come as Moses continued to walk with Him. (Exodus 33:11,17-23), and so much more as He continues to reveal Himself even to us as we follow Him.

On the mountain of Horeb, God was the fiery flame which needed no external stimulus to keep it burning, for it burned with its own life force, a living omnipresent, omnipotent flame. This was God. Where Moses was weak, though obedient, God would be all-powerful, Almighty God, and His personal Name is YHWH, translated throughout the Hebrew scriptures as 'the Lord', our sovereign Lord, the I AM. This Is the God who is commissioning Moses, the One who says 'I have surely seen the affliction of My people that are in Egypt and heard their groaning and I have come down to deliver them'. And He says to Moses 'Now come, I will send you to Egypt' (Acts 7:34).

Stephen continues '*This Moses* whom they refused', (Acts 7:35), thus emphasising the same response of the Sanhedrin to Jesus as the Israelites had to Moses. Peter had said to this same Sanhedrin '*This Jesus* whom you crucified' (Acts 2:23). He was the One who had come to deliver His people, just as Moses had been chosen, commissioned by God to do.

For the next forty years, Moses led them out of Egypt and through the wilderness, having performed wonders in Egypt and at the Red Sea. (Acts 7:36), just as Jesus had done throughout Galilee and Judea. God had spoken with Moses on Mount Sinai and with the Israelites and through Moses they had received the 'living oracles', (Acts 7:38), just as Jesus had preached His living word.

Of course, there was a vast difference as well as a similarity between Jesus and Moses. Moses had given the Israelites the opportunity of worshipping God through sacrificial animals and the keeping of the law. Jesus came that He might sacrifice Himself, that through His sacrificial offering of Himself on the cross, He might create a new way for men and women to come to God and worship Him.

Could Stephen have pointed up the difference between Moses and Jesus more clearly? Or indicated to these experts in the law more exactly that God was doing a new thing through the death of Jesus on the cross?

Stephen continues with the comparison. He says, there was a congregation, an *ekklesia* (Gk) in the wilderness, the congregation of the followers of Moses, but they did not listen to him. 'They refused to obey him and thrust him aside'. (Acts 7:39;

Numbers 14:2) and even made themselves a Golden Calf to worship instead of worshipping the Lord who had done so much for them. And this idolatry did not cease with the wilderness period. Because of their idolatry, the prophet Amos, (Amos 7:14, another shepherd), writing on the eve of the Assyrian invasion which brought to an end the Northern kingdom of Israel in 722 B.C, is quoted here by Stephen in Acts 7:42. 'Did you bring to Me sacrifices and offerings forty years in the wilderness, O house of Israel?.

O house of Israel. This was God's house, the people among whom He dwelt, where He was at home. They constantly strayed to false gods. Their hearts, their inner beings, were constantly rebellious against God. They did not have a temple in the wilderness but they had the tabernacle, the tent of witness (Acts 7:44), a witness to the everlasting covenant between God and His people, the tent which was at the very centre of their various tribal compounds, always witnessing to them of His care for them, His presence among them. But still they rebelled. Bruce comments,' Both Moses and Jesus, though rejected by their brethren, were chosen by God to deliver them'. (Bruce p171), and this was Stephen's message to them and what made the Jewish leaders so angry.

God did not need a tent, or a temple in which to appear to Moses, and to commune with him. He had already spoken to him from a burning bush. His self-revelation is never confined or restricted to one place. But God provided for His pilgrim people a pilgrim tent that they could take with them wherever He was leading them. He went before them by day in a pillar of cloud to lead them along the way, and by night a pillar of fire to give them light, that they might travel both by day and night; the pillar of cloud by day to give them shade from the sun, and the pillar of fire by night to give them warmth, did not depart from before the people. That was God's care and protection of His beloved people. (Exodus 13:21,22).

How precious was the tabernacle to them. Before Solomon was to build the temple, he was given wisdom and understanding beyond measure, and largeness of mind like sand upon the seashore. (1 Kings 4:29), and explicit instructions as the house of the Lord was built. (1 Kings 6:11). But the temple had as its prototype the tabernacle in the wilderness. As Moses was about to erect the tabernacle, he was instructed by God saying, 'See that you make everything according to the pattern that was shown you on the mount', (Hebrews 8:5), 'a sanctuary that I may dwell in their midst', (Exodus 25:8).

Both the temple and the tabernacle were provided by God for His people, His glorious provision of a national focus for worship. They were constructed in accordance with God's will. They were a constant reminder of His presence with them. From the crossing of the River Jordan into the promised land to the time of David and Solomon, it appears from Acts 7:46 that the use of the tabernacle persisted until the time of David, 'who found favour in the sight of God and asked leave to find a habitation for the God of Jacob' (Acts 7:46). But it was Solomon who built a house for Him. (Acts 7:47).

Acts 7:48-53. Stephen's speech concluded

Stephen had received a revelation from God which he was glad to share with his 'Brethren and fathers', (Acts 7:2), even though it was a court of law that provided the opportunity. God had revealed to him that though He had provided so much for His servants and for His people, the temple, the law and the land, these gifts had now become institutionalized.

His people had become rigidly bound to them, to Judaism, to the land, the law and the temple. They had resisted the Holy Spirit who had been given to them to keep them true to God and not to His gifts. (Acts 7:51). They had replaced the Giver with His gifts. Stephen was anxious to remind them of what they had already heard from Peter, that 'this Jesus. whom you crucified', had come to set them free from their bondage' (Acts 4:10).

This new phenomenon, the gathering together of people under the power of the Holy Spirit, was not entirely a new thing, for God had always moved among His people. The work, the ministry, the teaching of Christ and His sacrifice on the cross were a continuation of what He had always done for His people, supplying the means of drawing them nearer to HImself, to becoming no longer to be known exclusively as the children of Israel but His children, the children of God, having a relationship with Him as their Father, as Jesus was their Saviour, their deliverer, their redeemer, taking upon Himself all that separated them from God, bearing their sins in His own body on the tree. (1 Peter 2:24).

Why would they not accept what God had done in sending Jesus? This new thing that God was doing had its origins in the past, through Abraham and the patriarchs, through Joseph, through Moses. But God had now a more important purpose in view, and it included substituting all the institutions which had become so precious to them, for the reality of the word of God, and more importantly, the word of God incarnated in a Man of flesh and blood, in the flesh of Jesus, as John later described Him as 'the word became flesh and dwelt among us, and we beheld His glory, the glory as of the only begotten of the Father, full of grace and truth' (John 1:14).

God had given His people so many gifts, and though they had always resisted His Holy Spirit, and had killed the prophets who announced beforehand the coming of the Righteous One, Jesus (Acts 7:52). God was now giving them His ultimate gift, the gift of His Son. 'For God so loved the world that He gave His only begotten Son that whoever believes in him should not perish but have everlasting life'. (John 3:16). He is a giving, generous God who does not want that any should perish but that all should come to repentance and receive eternal life. (2 Peter 3:9)

So He has sent Stephen to them, to remind them that He is the same God, the God of Abraham to whom He promised land for his descendents; and gave the wonderful gift of the covenant, sealed by circumcision as a sign that he and his family belong to Him, but to whom He gave no temple, no law, or in fact, no land.

He is also the God of Joseph, through whom, at the end of his life God offered the gift of redemption from slavery in Egypt, but who had no temple, no law and no land, but always the overriding conviction that God was with him.

He is also the God of Moses, through whom the now fully established nation receives the law and the tabernacle, the place of God's presence with His people 'which our fathers brought in with Joshua when they dispossessed the nations which God thrust out before them'. (Acts 7:45). Under Moses they had the law and the tabernacle, the forerunner of the temple. Under Joshua, they also had the land, God had completely fulfilled all His promise to them, and so it was until the time of David, who so wanted to build God a house and was refused. But it was his son Solomon who built Him a house, (Acts 7:46,47).

But these wonderful provisions which God had given to His people He was replacing with something more glorious. The Greek of John 1:14 could be translated, 'the word became flesh and *tabernacled* among us'. Just as the tabernacle was the place where God met with and was present to His people, so they may now meet with and be present to Him through His Son. a much greater tabernacle. All that God had provided for His people is completely fulfilled in His Son. The temple and the tabernacle were a witness to Christ. Everything within them spoke of Him. They were a witness that God was with them. But He has now come to them in the person of His Son.

God was never, ever limited to a place, even a holy place. He does not live in houses made by hands, as the prophet says, 'Heaven is My throne and earth My footstool. What house will you build for Me, says the Lord?' (Isaiah 66:1; Acts 7:48). Other deities might be so accommodated but not God, as even Solomon recognized (I Kings 8:27). Abraham, Joseph and Moses all enjoyed communion with God which did not require a dwelling place for God, but God had allowed the Shekinah glory, the glory of His presence to be in the burning bush, and in the midst of His people in the tabernacle, (Exodus 40:24), and at the completion of the temple. (2 Chronicles 7:2).

Stephen is saying to the Sanhedrin, Can you not see that the Shekinah glory is no longer needed? That God's presence with His people rests with His Son? That what God is moving towards is the glory of His presence in the people whom He has redeemed through he death of His Son, who though, as Paul later understands it, they are only earthen vessels, vessels of fragile clay, yet they have within them 'the light of the knowledge of the glory of God in the face of Jesus Christ'. (2 Corinthians 6:7), That individually they fulfill the function of a temple, a place where God resides, (1 Corinthians 6:19), and when they are all together they are a temple of the living God. (2 Corinthians 6:16).

God has a different kind of temple in view, not buildings which are the work of men's hands, but living temples in which He can dwell by His Spirit. He says, I will dwell in them and move among them and be their God and they shall be My people, but not only in them, for am I not the Lord whose dwelling place is My throne in heaven? (2 Corinthians 6:16).

The Sanhedrin had accused Stephen of blasphemy against Moses and God, (Acts 6:11); of saying that Jesus of Nazareth will destroy their holy place, the temple, 'and will change the customs which Moses delivered to us'. (Acts 6:14). But now, Stephen is accusing these men, the religious leaders of the people of God. 'You are stiff necked', he says.' You refuse to bow before God, you are uncircumcised in heart and mind'. Your body may be circumcised but there is that in your heart and in your hearing which needs dealing with, which needs to be cut out. You do always resist the Holy Spirit who has spoken to you time and time again through His prophets and you have killed them and persecuted them although they were bringing you the assurance of the coming of the Righteous One, Jesus, whom you have betrayed and murdered. And this is especially heinous because to you were given the law, so precious that it was given by angels, and you have not kept it. (Acts 7:51-53).

As he spoke these words to them, his face was shining like an angel, but his words were full of deep sorrow. He was not using invective against them, even though he appeared to be attacking their most cherished beliefs, suggesting that like their forefathers they had rebelled and grieved the Holy Spirit.

125

(Isaiah 63:10). They had not found in Jesus all that their hearts were secretly needing to know of the reality of God, of a loving God present and real and at work in their lives. Jesus had been there to show them the way. 'I am the way' He said. (John 14:6). He had now gone to be with His Father, but through the Holy Spirit He was still available to them, for the work of the Holy Spirit is always to glorify Jesus. (John 16:14).

The God who had been so close to Abraham, to Joseph and to Moses wanted to be close to them too, but when they heard these things they were enraged, and they ground their teeth against Stephen. They could not accept the Spirit by whom he spoke. (Acts 7:54)

Acts 7:54-8:1. The death of Stephen

It is possible that Stephen had more to say, but he was cut short, for what had begun as an exposition of their history had become a serious implication of their complete misunderstanding of all in which they as religious leaders were engaged.

It was not simply that they were ignorant, but that having had so much given to them, so much history as a nation with God woven into their very beings as they daily performed their sacrifices and studied their scriptures, they yet failed to see the point of so much religious activity. Through it all, God had been seeking them out, wanting them to be worshippers of Him in Spirit and truth, wanting them to draw near to Him even as He drew near to them, wanting them to become His children, not in the name of Israel, as Israelites, but in the Name of Jesus through whom they could receive forgiveness of sins as they repented and were drawn into His KIngdom, the kingdom of heaven, for this was what Jesus came to do.

The time had come. Stephen 'full of the Holy Spirit, gazed into heaven and saw the glory of God, and Jesus standing, not sitting, at the right hand of God' for He was wanting to see Stephen and welcome him home. (Acts 7:55). But they cried out with a loud voice and stopped their ears for they wanted no more of Stephen's speaking to them. They rushed upon him, cast him out of the city and rained stones upon him until he died, having laid down their garments at the feet of a young man whose name was Saul. And as they were stoning him Stephen prayed. He prayed as His Lord had prayed, 'Father into thy hands I commend my spirit' Luke 23;46; 'Lord Jesus, receive my spirit'. (Acts 7:59). And then he prayed for his executioners as Jesus had done. Jesus had prayed, 'Father, forgive them for they know not what they do'. (Luke 23:34). Stephen prayed 'Lord, lay not this sin to their charge, and do not hold their sin against them'. (Acts 7:60)

With his last breath, Stephen is acknowledging that even as God is the One to forgive sins, a truth which the Sanhedrin would willingly accept, so is Jesus. Jesus has the prerogative to forgive sins, therefore He too is God. And he is proclaiming the deity of Christ as he prays 'Lord Jesus, receive my spirit'.

And when he had prayed for those who had condemned him to death, he fell asleep. (Acts 7:60). And Saul was consenting to his death, leading some commentators to assume that Saul was a member of the Sanhedrin. (Acts 8:1)

Stephen had prayed, 'Lord Jesus, receive my spirit' as he stood before them. Now at the last, perhaps because that as the stones were being thrown at him he was becoming weaker; or because he was conscious that these men were committing a terrible sin against the Lord's messenger, one who had been anointed by Him, (Psalm 105:15), he could no longer stand. He knelt down and prayed for them also.

Both prayers show his utter conviction that Jesus was indeed Lord, that he had the power to receive Stephen back into heaven and that He had the power to forgive sin. He paid for this conviction, and in this conviction, he fell asleep, not in a comfortable bed surrounded by his friends, but on the hard ground, peacefully and full of confidence that he would shortly be joining his Lord in heaven. Though on that day, a great persecution began against the church in Jerusalem, including the ravages made by Saul against men and women, dragging them off to prison, it is not unreasonable to imagine that the death of Stephen, witnessed by Saul could have made a profound impression on him and that it could have had a preparatory effect on him as he travelled on the road to Damascus. God may well have been preparing His servant for the work to which He was calling him.

Acts Chapter 8

Acts 8:1-40. Persecution and dispersion

And on that day, the day of Stephen's death, a great persecution arose against the church in Jerusalem; and they were all scattered throughout the region of Judea and Samaria except the apostles. Devout men buried Stephen and made great lamentation over him. But Saul was ravaging the church, and entering house after house, he dragged off men and women and committed them to prison. (Acts 8:1-3).

The church in Jerusalem is scattered, apart from the apostles who were courageous enough to remain in Jerusalem and care for those who had no ability to become refugees, staying at considerable danger to themselves.

Devout men buried Stephen and made loud lamentation over him, and this too was a considerably risky thing to do as the ruling Jewish party believed that his death had been a judicious killing of one who had preached heresy. In giving Stephen this burial, his friends were drawing attention to his death as an unlawful killing of an innocent man.

Saul violently attacked the church, going into homes and dragging off men and women for punishment, handing them over to prison and many to martyrdom, (Acts 8:3), for men and women were equally offensive to their persecutors as members of the church.

This is the conclusion of the story of Stephen and the beginning of the story of Paul. Luke includes Stephen's burial between verses 1 and 2, for the immediate effect of Stephen's speech was the great persecution which arose against the church. Stephen had obviously not anticipated this, yet his speech had given the impetus for the persecution and the dispersion to take place; the *dispersion of believers* throughout

Judea and Samaria but also the dispersal, the *scattering of the word*, for those who were scattered went about preaching the word, the gospel. (Acts 8:4).

But Stephen's work was done. His revolutionary teaching had stirred up the religious authorities and given them a reason to destroy this new movement which they recognized to be hostile to their own beliefs and perhaps equally importantly, their way of life. Their persecution of the church unwittingly led them to implement the command of Jesus to His followers that they should be His witnesses in Judea, and Samaria, and to 'the uttermost parts of the earth'. (Acts 1:8).

Now all that remained was Stephen's burial which as we have seen was carried out by devout men as they mourned for him, grieving for him, for he had been a man of God and a brother in Christ. His life had made a great impression on them and though in the circumstances it was a dangerous thing to do, they were still determined to give Stephen a proper burial.

As for Saul, he made havoc of the church, ravaging it, (Acts 8:3), and many others followed Stephen into martyrdom. Christianity had originated in Jerusalem and Jerusalem remained the focal point of the church even after the persecution. But God was moving His church forwards and outwards. Judaism in the form of its religious leaders had shown an unequivocal rejection of the gospel, which was revealed to Paul as 'to the Jew first and also to the Greeks', (Romans 1:16). God was now using the group of 'seven' (Acts 6:3), to bring the gospel to the Gentiles. Judaism was rejecting the gospel, not altogether comprehensively, but certainly by the Jewish hierarchy. The Gentiles were gladly receiving the gospel as the scattered believers, including Philip, one of the seven, 'proclaimed to them the Christ'. (Acts 8:5).

Perhaps, in God's economy, it was important to have the Jewish reaction to the gospel before the mission to the Gentiles could develop. But not only Philip, but all the scattered believers were now going on a missionary journey (Acts 8:5), as they went about preaching the word, the *euangelion*, the gospel. They took with them and now proclaimed the gospel.

Acts 8:5-25. The gospel reaches Samaria

Philip went down to a city of Samaria and proclaimed to them the Christ. And the multitudes with one accord gave heed to what was said by Philip when they heard him and saw the signs which he did. For unclean spirits came out of many who were possessed, crying with a loud voice; and many who were paralysed or lame were healed, so there was much joy in that city. (Acts 8:5-8).

We know very little about Philip. He was not the apostle called by Jesus in John 1:43, and sent out with the other disciples in Matthew 10:3, or the disciple with the Greek name who was approached by Greeks who wanted to see Jesus. (John 12:22).

This Philip was Philip the Hellenist of Acts 6:5, the evangelist who was one of those seven selected by the whole church in Jerusalem to 'serve tables', to give attention to the social needs of the weaker members of the community; a man of good repute, full of the Spirit and of wisdom, like the other six. (Acts 6:3). And we read here in chapter 8, of Philip still concerned with the needs of those with illness or infirmity.

Because of their joint responsibility, for of course Stephen was also one of the seven, Philip and Stephen were undoubtedly very close, and on the death of Stephen and the subsequent persecution of the church, Philip went down to the city of Samaria. It may be that Philip had heard Stephen preach and had realised that Stephen was gradually seeing something very profound about Jesus.

As Jesus of Nazareth, Jesus had raised up a group of His inner disciples who were beginning to understand who He was; the Son of Man, having a totally human nature, and the Son of God, totally divine. This wonderful truth began to dawn upon them to such an extent that they were rejoicing in His death, His resurrection and exaltation to the throne of God.

Now, as Stephen had preached before his death, there could be a deeper, fuller way of proclaiming Him to unbelievers, who had only known Him, or had heard rumours of Him, as Jesus of

Nazareth. Philip proclaimed Him as the Christ; not in any way disparaging the Name of Jesus, for as Peter had said, 'there is no other Name under heaven given among men whereby we must be saved', (Acts 4:12). But in referring to Him as the Christ, Philip was declaring 'the whole counsel of God', even as Paul later did, (Acts 20:27), the Messiahship of the Lord Jesus as the Anointed One of God, foreordained from before the foundation of the world, (1 Peter 1:20, K.J.V), to be made by God both Lord and Christ, 'this Jesus whom you crucified'. (Acts 2:36).

Jesus is His precious Name, Christ is His precious title, expressing both His character and His destiny, and His sovereignty.

And the Lord confirmed the word which Philip brought to the people of Samaria with signs following, (Acts 8:7; Mark 16:20), as He had in Acts 2:43; 5:12 and 6:8; and as the believers had prayed that He would do after Peter and John had been released from prison. (Acts 4:29).

Many people in the multitude who listened to Philip were healed or set free and there was so much joy in the city, that a man named Simon, a sorcerer who had previously practised magic in that city was caught up in the proclamation of the gospel. He believed and was baptized and was continually with Philip. (Acts 8:13).

Simon had amazed the nation of Samaria saying that he himself was somebody great, and the people gave heed to him, agreeing with him that he was that power of God which is called Great. (Acts 8:10). This could mean that they believed that there was some kind of emanation from him which was divine or supernatural. It could also mean that 'great' *magos* referred to a priestly tribe of Persian origin known as *Magi*, who were astrologers but with magic powers. Perhaps all that Simon was claiming for himself was that he was a *magus*, an ordinary man with magical powers but not with divine power.

But Simon wanted something more. He wanted what Philip and Peter and John had, for he perceived that though his power was 'great', what they had was greater. (Barrett, p407; Bruce p184).

Acts 8:14-24. Peter and John visit Samaria

Now when the apostles at Jerusalem heard that Samaria had received the word of God, they sent to them Peter and John. (Acts 8:14)

Samaria occupied a middle religious position between Jews and Gentiles. They were not fully Jews. They had their own adherence to the Torah, the Law of Moses, and their own temple on Mount Gerizim. Gerizim means 'a waste and desert place', but it had become the mountain of blessing, a refuge for these displaced people. (John 4:20; Deuteronomy 11:29). But they were not fully Gentile either, for though they had been under the ethnarchy of Archelaus, from 4 BC-6 AD, and the community had become highly Hellenized, it was as much Jewish as Greek and as much Greek as Jewish. (Barrett p 402).

The Samaritans were a confused people. From the time of the troubled political situation of the 8th century B.C, they had worshipped God but also worshipped other gods. 'They feared the Lord, but also served their own gods after the manner of the nations from whom they had been carried away.' They were not Israelites but refugees whom the king of Assyria had brought from other countries which he had conquered and placed in the Northern kingdom of Israel; 'placed them in the cities of Samaria instead of the people of Israel', in 722 B.C. (2 KIngs 17:24.33). Their worship, their ethnicity, their understanding of themselves and their approach to God was mixed.

After the exile of the 6th century BC, when the Jews were allowed to return to their homeland, they were unwilling to receive help from the Samaritans to rebuild the temple. (Ezra 4:1-3), and in the 4th century BC the Samaritans built their own temple on Mount Gerizim. The Samaritans were despised by the Jews, summed up in the comment in John 4:9. 'The Jews have no dealings with the Samaritans'.

But Jesus Himself had initiated the mission to the Samaritans. He longed to include them in the proclamation of the gospel. At the time of His ascension He had said to

His disciples, 'You shall receive power after the Holy Spirit has come upon you, and you shall be witnesses to me in Judea, *and in Samaria,* and to the uttermost parts of the earth'. (Acts 1:8).

And He had begun the mission with one woman. John 4:4 says He *had* to pass through Samaria. There was a compulsion on Him to bring back into the fold of God those who had only a partial understanding of the word of God, and none at all of the kingdom of God, and He chose a woman of Samaria who came to draw water at the well of Sychar, or Shechem. (John 4:6; Genesis 33:18).

This woman did not come to draw water in the early morning with all the other women, for she was a woman with a shameful history, who preferred the isolation of the well at midday. Jesus, wearied as He was with the journey, yet had only compassion and the gift of redemption for her as He sat on the well. How long He spent talking to her we do not know, but we know that she left her water pot and went away into the city saying to the people, 'Come, see a man who told me *all* that ever I did'. (John 4:29). And many Samaritans believed in Him because of her testimony. He stayed with them for two days and they declared to the woman, 'it is not because of what you said that we believe, for we have heard for ourselves, and we know that He is indeed the Saviour of the world'. (John 4:42).

Though this incident may have taken place some four or five years earlier, Philip was chosen to go to the city of Samaria where Jesus had gone before. How they welcomed him, listening to his word, rejoicing in all the signs which he did in the power of the Holy Spirit, (Acts 8:6), confirmation that though forgiveness of sins was a highly personal and hidden response of faith; an internal work in the heart of the believer; miracles of healing and exorcisms could not be denied, but were obvious to all. They were the outward external signs of an inward, invisible grace. The multitude were of one accord, (Acts 8:6), united in their response to Philip's teaching; united in their joy.

The Samaritans had been expecting the Messiah, (John 4:25,29), and many had received Jesus as Saviour of the world, the one whom they called the Restorer, identifying Him with the

Prophet of Deuteronomy 18:15. But not all Samaritans would have seen Jesus on HIs visit to the well of Sychar, or have heard the testimony of the woman who said that He had told her all that she had ever done. (John 4:29), and her conviction that this was indeed the Christ.

But as we have seen, there was a man called Simon who had previously practised magic in that city. Perhaps those Samaritans who were ignorant of what had gone before thought that Simon could be the fulfilment of that prophecy, the promise of the coming Prophet of Deuteronomy 18:15, for he amazed the nation of Samaria, saying that he himself was somebody great, (Acts 8:9), though he did not claim to be the prophet of Deuteronomy.

His name has come down to us as Simon Magus. Originally, Magus was a title of respect, but it is now used for someone who is a charlatan, false, counterfeit. Luke mentions others in Acts who were similarly counterfeit; the false prophet named Bar Jesus in Acts 13;6; the girl with a spirit of divination inActs 16:16; the seven sons of Sceva in Acts 19:14. These all had a following of those who believed that they had a genuine supernatural power. Simon too had amazed them with his magic, but it only glorified himself. The work which Philip did was through the Holy Spirit and brought healing and peace to many, and caused Simon's 'greatness' to appear somewhat redundant.

Whatever Simon's greatness had consisted of it was now obvious to him that there was something greater, As people 'believed Philip' as he preached the good news of the kingdom of God, and the Name of Jesus Christ, they were baptized both men and women, and Simon himself believed. After being baptized he continued with Philip, just as the formerly lame man had clung to Peter and John after being healed at the beautiful gate of the temple. (Acts 3:11).

Acts 8:14-24. The visit of Peter and John to Samaria

Now when the apostles in Jerusalem heard that Samaria had received the word of God, they sent them Peter and John, who came down and prayed for them that they might receive the Holy Spirit. For He had not yet fallen upon any of them, they had simply been baptized in the Name of the Lord Jesus. (Acts 8:14-16).

There were apostles in Jerusalem who had not fled at the persecution which arose after the death of Stephen. Concerned though they were for those who were scattered abroad throughout the region of Judea and Samaria. (Acts 8:1), who had become refugees, there were also others remaining in Jerusalem who were under constant threat of opposition from the religious authorities. These were people who needed the support and comfort which the apostles so willingly gave.

But they became aware that the Lord was doing a new thing in Samaria, that despised place where people were neither truly Jews nor truly Gentiles. So when the apostles in Jerusalem heard that Samaria had received the word of God, they sent to them Peter and John.

Peter and John had seen at first hand what faith in the Lord Jesus could accomplish in the life of believers. With what joy they hurried down to Samaria, longing to see Philip and encourage him, and to give him the assurance of their fellowship with him in the gospel. They were aware that God had a plan for Samaria, and they wanted Philip to allow them to be part of what God had shown him, that He had provided a place in His kingdom for all men and and women, irrespective of their religious, non religious or cultural background, if only they would respond to the gospel. This vision which Philip had he could share with his brothers in Christ, labourers together in the harvest of Matthew 9:38, workers together with Him and with each other, just as they had been from the beginning.

Peter and John came down from Jerusalem to Samaria and when they came the first thing they did was to pray for the believers that they might receive the Holy Spirit, 'for as yet He had not fallen on any of them' (Acts 8:15,16). And as they prayed, they laid their hands on them, for when the Spirit comes, He comes to individuals. When He came at Pentecost, the tongues of fire *rested on each of them.* (Acts 2:2). It is the individual person whom the Holy Spirit wants to fill, and He needed the hands of the apostles on each person to receive Him.

'Then the apostles laid their hands on the believers and they received the Holy Spirit', (Acts 8:17), after having been baptized in the Name of the Lord Jesus, (Acts 8:16).

These men and women were already His. They had been baptized in His Name, signifying that they now belonged to Him. Now the Holy Spirit had confirmed to them their inclusion in the body of Christ, His church. There was no distinction between the believers in Jerusalem and the believers in Samaria, whatever their background or former way of life. They were all one in Christ Jesus. There were not two churches but one.

The gift of the Holy Spirit was not simply the sign of an inward spiritual experience but an immediately obvious conferral of power upon the Samaritan believers, and this was what Simon noted.

Though Simon had become a believer and had even been baptized in the Name of Jesus, the pride and ambition he felt were still with him. If such power could be given to 'ordinary' men and women by the laying on of the apostles hands, why could he not also have this power? Simon offered the apostles money, saying, 'Give me also this power that anyone on whom I lay my hands may receive the Holy Spirit'. (Acts 8:19.) He had failed to recognize that Peter and John had no power of their own. Full of the Holy Spirit as they were as they laid their hands on these believers, they were but channels, transmitters of the Gift which the Lord Jesus had promised. (John 15:26).

God cannot be bribed with money, with gifts, with promises of future behaviour. It is an insult to Him; a presumption. He knows the hearts of men and women and gives the Spirit according to His gracious will, and according to the humble desire of a believer to live more fully in His love, to enjoy an even more fulfilling relationship with Him. The sovereign Lord does His own work, giving His gifts to men and women as He will.

Simon had completely misunderstood Peter and John and Philip, and more importantly had evaluated the Holy Spirit in terms of money. Peter's rebuke was immediate. 'Your money perish with you', he said, 'your heart is not right with God. I see that you are in the gall of bitterness and the bond of iniquity. There is bitter poison within your heart'. (Acts 8:20-23).

Peter had given a direct, decisive and accurate diagnosis of Simon's problem. Psalm 78:37 speaks of those who are not straight, steadfast before God; someone who is not direct, honest, straightforward with Him. Simon is attempting to bribe God, to suit God to his purposes. The only course for Simon is to repent, (Acts 8:22), *metanoia,* to turn from his sin. And Peter insists that he must turn from this sin, to repent and 'to pray to the Lord that if possible, the intent of your heart may be forgiven you'.

Perhaps Simon felt that his own prayer for forgiveness would not be sufficient for the terrible sin he had committed. He asks Peter to pray for him, which Peter surely did, and Peter and John returned to Jerusalem, visiting many villages along the way and preaching the word. (Acts 8:25).

This is the last appearance of John in Acts, except for the mention of him as being the brother of James in Acts 12:2., though he is still mentioned as one of the pillars of the church in Paul's letter to the Galatians seventeen years later, men who together with James the Lord's brother and Peter, gave to Paul and Barnabas the right hand of fellowship. (Galatians 2:9).

But the mission to the Samaritans was not concluded. The leaders of the church in Jerusalem saw the need for the gospel to be preached in Antioch of Syria, and they sent Barnabas and Saul, as he then was, to Antoch. (Acts 11:22, 25). Later, when Paul and Barnabas were on their first missionary journey, they passed through Phoenicia and Samaria on their way to Jerusalem, reporting the conversion of the Gentiles to the worship of the Lord Jesus, completely outside the Jewish system, of circumcision and obedience to the law of Moses, the

joyful report of all that God had done for them. (Acts 15:3,4).
The work of the Holy Spirit begun under Philip's ministry was
still going on, as was also what was happening in the Jerusalem
church.

Paul's last visit to Jerusalem in Acts 21:17,18 was a mistake.
It was to appease the Jerusalem elders. God was never looking
for a superior hierarchy in His church, not even for any
prominence for the 'mother' church in Jerusalem, where God
first poured out His Holy Spirit upon them; for all are brothers
and sisters in Christ. He is a God of order, not of confusion,
(1 Corinthians 14:40) so He has appointed elders who are
shepherds over the flock of God, His church; not those who
domineer over them, but by being examples to the flock.
(1 Peter 5:2,3). We obey those who have the rule over us as
leaders who will have to give an account of themselves to God.
(Hebrews 13:17).

Jerusalem was chosen by God to be the birthplace of
Christianity, but as Stephen had rightly perceived and as was
evident in his speech, God is not limited to place or time; a
concept which Peter and John and Philip also came to understand.
The Holy Spirit was moving in Samaria just as He was moving in
Jerusalem. God is God and He will do His own work in His own
compassionate way, and sometimes, by His grace He will allow
men and women to cooperate with Him to bring about His desired
will and purpose. He is not confined to one place, or to one group
of people but is always moving forward in accordance with His
will; to move among them in new ways.

There is nothing static or stagnant about God. The Lord
our shepherd leads us on, His rod and His staff guiding us as
He comforts us, Psalm 23:4, and as we walk in the Spirit. And
being immersed in Him we receive His unmerited gifts of love,
joy, peace, and all the fruit of the Spirit. (Galatians 5:16,22).
Joyfully He leads us even into the valley of the shadow of
death, for we can fear no evil. He has promised to be with us
and it is personal, 'Thou art with *me*', personal to every one of
His beloved children.' Thou art with me'; perhaps some of the
most precious words in the whole Bible.

Acts 8:26-40. Philip and the Ethiopian eunuch

> But an angel of the Lord spoke to Philip saying 'Get up and go south to the road which descends from Jerusalem to Gaza. (this is a desert road). So he got up and went. And there was an Ethiopian eunuch, a court official of Candace, queen of the Ethipians who was in charge of all her treasure, and he had come to Jerusalem to worship. And he was returning and sitting in his chariot and was reading the prophet Isaiah. (Acts 8:26-28. New American Standard Bible)

Philip may have been tempted to go back with Peter and John to Jerusalem. After all, they had made a good team in Samaria. It would be sensible to carry on the good work which they had begun. But God's thoughts are not our thoughts nor His ways our ways. (Isaiah 55:8). He has something else in mind for Philip.

God sent an angel who said to him, 'Rise and go toward the south, to the road that goes down from Jerusalem to Gaza. (Acts 8:26). 'Rise up and go', the angel said. Philip was not allowed to rest back on all the wonderful things God had done in Samaria, as if it was a good job well done. 'Go' said the angel, and Philip went. Like Abraham he went, not knowing what God had in store for him, or for the person he was going to meet.

As Philip went along the desert road, (Acts 8;26). he espied a chariot, and seated in it a richly apparelled man of some importance, Many had come up to Jerusalem to worship, including this man who was a eunuch, an official at the court of Candace which means ruler, or queen, of the Ethiopians. The eunuch was in charge of all her treasure, her chancellor of the exchequer.

He was a man of authority and position, but also a man seeking after truth; and he thought he had found it in Judaism. He had travelled many miles from Ethiopia to Jerusalem because in Jerusalem he thought he found that which he could worship, the God of the Jewish people.

But somehow, he was not completely satisfied. While he was in Jerusalem he had managed to acquire a very rare object, a manuscript of the Book of Isaiah. Very few of these scrolls were privately owned. They were mostly kept in synagogues, where they were scrupulously and carefully preserved, for were they not the word of God?

Though the Ethiopian was anxious to get home, to find a place where he could sit quietly and read this treasured manuscript, he could not wait. Sitting in his chariot as the miles disappeared under the horses hooves, with the scroll in his hands, he found that he could not understand what the prophet had written, when he suddenly saw Philip on the desert road. And the Spirit said to Philip, 'Go and join yourself to this chariot' (Acts 8:29). Philip might have argued, 'Lord! I can't do that! He is an important man. Perhaps he wants to be alone to read his manuscript and I will be in his way! Besides, I am not a skilled rabbi, able to answer any question about the scriptures'.

But whether these objections occurred to him we do not know. We do know that he was obedient to the Spirit of God. He *ran* to the chariot and as he ran he heard the Ethiopian reading from the book of Isaiah the prophet. It was customary in those days to read out loud rather than silently.

Philip had a question for him, after he had got his breath back. He said, 'Do you understand what you are reading?' (Acts 8:30). Perhaps Philip recognized the chapter in Isaiah. The Ethiopian's immediate and welcome response was 'How can I unless someone guides me?' (Acts 8:31). And he invited Philip to come up into the chariot and sit with him.

Had the Ethiopian started at the beginning of Isaiah and now reached chapter 53, or was it just coincidence that the portion of Isaiah that he was reading, the verses which caught his attention were Isaiah 53, verses 7 and 8? As a sheep led to the slaughter, or a lamb which before its shearers is dumb, so He opened not His mouth. In His humiliation justice was denied Him. Who can declare His generation? For His life was taken up from the earth. (Isaiah 53:7,8. RSV. Acts 8:32,33).

And the eunuch said to Philip, 'About whom, pray, does the prophet say this. About himself or someone else? Please tell me'.

(Acts 8:34). Then Philip opened his mouth and beginning with this scripture, he told him the good news of Jesus.

Many down the centuries, since Isaiah had first written his prophecy, had concluded that Isaiah was speaking of himself, for what he had described could so easily have applied to many prophets of Israel in some measure, including himself. But Philip understood that this description of the servant of the Lord in the servant songs of Isaiah, including chapter 53, was speaking prophetically of the Lord Jesus, and was unique to Him. *He was like a sheep led to the slaughter. He was like a lamb that before its shearers was dumb. He was humiliated and justice denied Him.* Philip opened his mouth and told the Ethiopian the good news of Jesus.

Who was Philip in the eyes of this important Ethiopian man? Philip appeared to be just an itinerant preacher, yet as Philip spoke to him, his heart was stirred, his eyes were enlightened. At last, this important man could bear it no longer. They had come to a place in the desert where there was a most incredible and desirable feature, water. And the eunuch said to Philip, 'See, here is water. What hinders me, what prevents me from being baptized?' To be baptized into the Name of Jesus, this Lamb of God who takes away the sin of the world, and that included 'my' sin, was the most urgent and important thing for him to do at that moment. As Philip assented, he leapt out of the chariot and hurried over to the water. The horses were able to have a drink, and he and Philip went down into the water, and Philip baptized him. (Acts 8:32).

This was apparently enough. Philip had not even known his name, but only that he had become his brother in Christ. The Spirit of the Lord caught up Philip and the eunuch went on his way rejoicing (Acts 8:39). He was a new Christian, a babe in Christ, newly come to Him, travelling towards his home where they knew so little of God and possibly even less of Jesus. But he was a new man. He had found what he was looking for. He had found Jesus.

Philip was found at Azotus, with probably little idea of how he got there, only that he was transported by the Holy Spirit, the same Holy Spirit whom he had come to trust; and passing from Azotus, formerly Ashdod, one of the five Philistinian cities, he preached the gospel in all the towns till he came to Caesarea. (Acts 8:40).

He was still in Caesarea with his four daughters who prophesied, in Acts 21:9, when Paul and Luke arrived there at the time of Paul's third missionary journey. No further mention of him is made in Acts, but Luke described him as 'Philip the evangelist', (Acts 21:8), and we may legitimately assume that he never stopped preaching the gospel.

Evangelists, along with apostles, pastors and teachers were gifts of God to the church, according to Ephesians 4:11, 'to equip the saints for the work of ministry, for building up the Body of Christ, until we all attain to the unity of the faith, amd of the knowledge of the Son of God, to mature manhood, to the measure of the stature of the fulness of Christ'. Philip was a gift of God to His church, and also to the people of Caesarea, where he subsequently lived; a predominantly Gentile city, and chief Mediterranean port of Palestine. God's purposes for the Gentiles were being fulfilled through His obedient servant.

The eunuch who could not even become a proselyte of Judaism (Deuteronomy 23:1; Leviticus 21:16). had become a child of God.

Both the ministry of Philip and the ministry of Peter converge on Caesarea, (Acts 9:31-10:1), and indicate that there may have been a cosmopolitan church in Caesarea which included both Jews and Gentiles. Peter went here and there throughout Galilee and Samaria, possibly visiting the Samaritan villages of Acts 8:25, which Philip had also evangelized on his way from Ashdod to Caesarea. (Acts 8:40). (Bruce p 210), but neither the Ethiopian nor Cornelius (Acts 10:1) appeared to have been able to access the church community either in Jerusalem nor Caesarea.

But God is not dependent even on His people to seek out those who truly seek Him, but will raise up a Philip or Peter to bring about the salvation of one individual.

There is no evidence of a first century church in Ethiopia, though according to Irenaeus, (Adv Haer 4:23:2) and Eusebius

(H.E.2:1:13) the eunuch was the first missionary there. (Barrett p 422). Cornelius was one of those described as instrumental in establishing a necessary link, a relationship between the church in Caesarea and the church in Jerusalem, (Acs 11:18). God is still able to raise up men after His own heart who will do all His will. (Acts 13:22).

The Ethiopian eunuch had gone to Jerusalem to worship and found that God was actually waiting for Him in the desert. God had not met with him in Jerusalem even though his heart was set on finding Him, for He wanted to draw him to Himself in the desert. So the Ethiopian was searching for Him in the Hebrew scriptures, and God provided for him an interpreter of His word, for though he was reading he was not understanding.

'Do you understand?' said Philip. (Acts 8:30). The Hebrew Bible, the Old Testament, is not self explanatory. It requires a Christological interpretation. It makes sense only if one is able to begin with Jesus and Philip began with the Ethiopian's reference point, the Lamb of God who takes away the sin of the world and who is Identified completely in Jesus. (John 1:29).

Jesus fulfills all the prophecies of the servant of God, through whom God has acted. God has acted throughout all the sacrificial and humiliating death of Jesus and His witnessed resurrection, to achieve salvation to all who will accept Him in faith. In his first letter, Peter says that we are redeemed by the precious blood of Christ like those of a lamb without blemish and without spot, destined from before the foundation of the world but made manifest at the end of the times for our sake. (1 Peter 1:19).

This had been the message of John the Baptist from the very beginning of Jesus' ministry. God had revealed this wonderful truth to John, 'Behold the Lamb of God who takes away the sin of the world'. The Lamb of God, walking among them, was God's chosen sacrifice, God's chosen means of reconciling a people to Himself as an atonement for sin, a people who would be ransomed, healed, restored, forgiven, walking with Him in perfect harmony.

The image of Him portrayed by Isaiah and John was of the innocence and vulnerability of a lamb, or a sheep at an annual shearing time, and this image is transferred to One who allowed Himself, submitted Himself to those who despised and rejected Him, a Man of sorrows and acquainted with grief; and as one from whom men hide their faces, He was despised and we esteemed Him not, the One who became the sin bearer of the world, and the bearer away of our sin. (Isaiah 53:5). As Philip spoke of Him to the Ethiopian so Philip would speak of Him to whoever he was with, to whoever would listen to him, this great revelation of who Jesus was; as God opened up the scriptures to him which Jesus claimed, when speaking to the disciples on the road to Emmaus, had been written about Him, as He opened up their minds to understand. (Luke 24:45,46).

The Ethiopian went on his way rejoicing, (Acts 8:39), as Philip probably also did, rejoicing all the away to Azotus to which he was transported by the Holy Spirit, for God's miracles are not limited to healing and preaching, but even in the ordinary, trivial details of life, like travelling, He is prepared to act on behalf of His servants,

Philip had baptized the Ethiopian on the grounds of his acceptance of Jesus as the Lamb of God who had taken away his sin. Philip may also have benefited from his experience with Peter and John in Samaria and laid hands on him so that he might receive the Holy Spirit. The Ethiopian eunuch had become a follower of Jesus. He had become another servant of God.

At the end of Book 2 of the Psalms we have this wonderful doxology. Blessed be the Lord, the God of Israel, who *only* does wonderful things, and blessed be His Glorious Name for ever! (Psalm 72:18). He *only* does wonderful things!

Acts Chapter 9

Acts 9:1-18. The conversion of Saul

But Saul, still breathing threats and murder against the disciples of the Lord, went to the high priest and asked him for letters to the synagogue in Damascus so that if he found any belonging to the Way, men or women, he might bring them bound to Jerusalem. Now as he journeyed, he approached Damascus, and suddenly a light from heaven flashed about him, and he fell to the ground and heard a voice saying to him,' Saul, Saul, why do you persecute Me? And he said, 'Who are you Lord? And He said, 'I am Jesus, whom you are persecuting, but rise and enter the city'.
(Acts 9:1 -6).

Stephen had been buried, but his speech to the Jewish Sanhedrin had not been forgotten. This was subversive, revolutionary teaching, and was becoming more and more widespread in Jerusalem. It had even travelled as far as Galilee, Samaria, and even Damascus, the chief city in Syria, which had a thriving Jewish population. (Bruce p107). It must be stopped.

Fortunately there was a very able young man called Saul, who might be able to help in exterminating this heresy. Though it was possible that he had heard Stephen's preaching he had not been convinced by it. But he was convinced with the Sanhedrin of the unsettling influence which this movement which they called 'the Way' was having on the people. (Acts 9:2). Saul approached the high priest for permission to extirpate this unruly rabble. Breathing threats and murder against the disciples of the Lord, Saul went to the high priest, Caiaphas, who was probably still in office, (Acts 4:6), and obtained letters of authority to the synagogue of Damascus, so that if Saul found any belonging to 'the Way', men or women, he might bring them bound to Jerusalem to be severely punished. (Acts 9:2).

Together with his entourage, Saul set out for Damascus, a journey of about 150 miles from Jerusalem. (Marshall p 168). He was confident that as a righteous man and an observant Jew, and with a conviction that he ought to do many things contrary to the Name of Jesus of Nazareth, (Acts 26:9) he was doing the right thing. He was approaching Damascus when 'suddenly, a light from heaven flashed about him', (Acts 9:3), and he fell to the ground and heard a voice saying to him, 'Saul, Saul, (using his name twice for emphasis), 'why do you persecute Me?' And he said, 'Who are you Lord?' There was no mistaking the person for whom the words were intended, for the truth was beginning to dawn on him. And the voice said, 'I am Jesus whom you are persecuting. But rise and enter the city and you will be told what you are to do' (Acts 9:6).

Saul thought that he had been dealing with the adherents of a lost cause. He was beginning to realise that this was not the case. And that actually he was persecuting not just the followers of that person who had started the movement, but that the originator of that new movement was the Lord. The title 'Lord' in Saul's previous understanding had been the Lord God of Israel, the Sovereign Lord. This voice was introducing Himself, not only as Lord but as Jesus. It was the Lord, even Jesus, who had spoken to him, the Lord identified not only as the Lord God but as Jesus, and this same Lord Jesus identified Himself with His servants in their time of persecution.

Bruce quotes Augustine as saying, 'Caput pro membris clamabant'. The Head always suffers on behalf of His members. (Bruce p 198).

The men with Saul were overcome with amazement. They were speechless. They could not say 'Who are you Lord'? They were as fully committed to this terrible programme as Saul was. They saw the tremendous light, but they did not hear the words that the voice said or perceive a source from which a voice could come, yet the very glory of the light from heaven could have alerted them to the fact of something extraordinary happening.

God is very specific in His calling of human beings to be His witnesses and this was His calling of Saul. There may have been other opportunities for these men to have been presented with a challenge to their way of life, for the gospel is for all, but this challenge was directly aimed at Saul.

As Saul got up from the ground where he had fallen, he stumbled, for he had become blind, so the men took him by the hand and brought him to Damascus, where they hoped to find someone to care for him. They were not necessarily bad or unkind men, but deluded, deceived, persuaded by the chief priests to bind all who called on the Name of Jesus (Acts 9:14) and the council had made it clear that these believers must be wiped out, exterminated as blasphemers of God. This was what made these men dangerous. In addition it is probable that they had to submit a report to the high priest for the responsibility he had given them for the eradication of these members of 'the Way', the common name at that time for believers.

They had seen the light, they had heard something they could not understand so not knowing quite what to do, they brought Saul to the home of a man called Judas, who lived in a street called Straight. For three days, Saul was without sight and could neither eat or drink, (Acts 9:9), but he could pray and this he did (Acts 9:11). Was this a prayer of the kind he had prayed as a Pharisee? (Philippians 3:5). Or was it a prayer of thankfulness to God 'that He had revealed His Son in me?' (Galatians 1:16), that 'He had called him through His grace'? (Galatians 1:15).

In Damascus there was a man called Ananias. Ananias was a disciple of the Lord Jesus and it was quite possible that he would have been one of those destined to be carried off to Jerusalem for punishment with the other believers. But he was praying too, and as he was praying, the Lord gave him a vision. He said 'Ananias!' And Ananias said, 'Here I am Lord'. And the Lord said to him 'Arise and go to a street called Straight and inquire in the house of Judas for a man of Tarsus named Saul, for behold, he is praying and has seen a man named Ananias come in and lay his hands on him that he might receive his sight'. (Acts 9:12).

What was Ananias to do? He had heard of Tarsus in Cilicia, the third city in the region, together with Athens and Alexandria, known as a centre of learning, being devoted to rhetoric and philosophy and poetry. (Bruce p208). He had also heard of this man Saul, how successful he had been at rounding up the believers and carting them off to prison. He had heard how cruel he and his accomplices had been, even taking wives away from their husbands and mothers from their children because they had become followers of Jesus, suffering for His sake. (Acts 8:3; 9:2; 9:13).

If this man had become blind, this was surely a good way of preventing him from doing any more damage to the church, to the vulnerable members of this infant organization. What did the Lord mean by asking Ananias to go and lay hands on him that he might receive his sight?. He did not doubt that if he laid hands on him, the Holy Spirit would undoubtedly heal him, as He had healed so many.

Ananias was more concerned for the 'saints at Jerusalem'; (Acts 9:13,14). to whom Saul had already done much evil, and who were likely to be the predecessors of those to whom evil was about to be done in Damascus; those whom Saul had intended to persecute. But while Ananias thought about these things, and questioned the Lord about Saul, The Lord said to him 'Go Ananias, for he is a chosen vessel to Me, to carry My Name before the Gentiles and kings and the sons of Israel. For I will show him how much he must suffer for the sake of My Name'. (Acts 9:15,16).

So Ananias went, reassured by what the Lord had said to him, even if he had but a limited understanding of it. He departed and went to the house of Judas. There he found Saul, and laying hands on him he said 'Brother Saul'. This man who had so recently been persecuting the church, Ananias called 'Brother'. Though he did not fully understand what were the Lord's purposes concerning this man, he recognized that God had done something in him, that he was a brother in Christ, a believer.

How encouraging this must have been to Saul. Ananias was welcoming him into the family of God. Saul knew that something tremendous had happened to him on the Damascus road, but how significant that Ananias had been given a recognition of it too. And then Ananias said' Brother Saul, the Lord Jesus who appeared to you on your way here, has sent me to you so that you might regain your sight and be filled with the Holy Spirit. (Acts 9:17). And immediately scales fell from his eyes and he regained his sight. Then Saul arose, and was baptized and he took food and was strengthened. Acts 9:18,19).

Acts 9: 19-31. Saul begins to preach in Damascus

For several days, Saul was with the disciples at Damascus, And in the synagogues he immediately proclaimed Jesus, saying, 'He is the Son of God'. And all who heard him were amazed, and said, 'Is not this the man who made havoc in Jerusalem of those who called on this Name? And he has come here for this purpose, to bring them bound before the chief priests'. But Saul increased all the more in strength and confounded the Jews who lived in Damascus by proving that Jesus was the Christ. (Acts 9:19-22).

Filled with the Holy Spirit, the scales having fallen from his eyes both physically and spiritually, the eyes of his heart being enlightened, (Ephesians 1:18.), Saul/Paul spent some time with the disciples in Damascus (Acts 9:19).

But his great ambition was to proclaim Jesus, who had met him on the Damascus road, and immediately he became known as the one who preached that Jesus was the Christ, the Messiah, and the Son of God. The people were amazed. They said, 'Is not this the man who made havoc of the church in Jerusalem, of those who called on this Name? And he has come here for this purpose to bring them bound before the chief priests. (Acts 9:21). They could not believe that Saul was a changed man, but were concerned that he had an ulterior motive in view, an intention to find and persecute those Jews who had become believers, just as he had in Jerusalem, those Jews who had come to believe in Jesus as the Son of God.

As the Son of God, Jesus was the foreordained and prophesied Messiah. The high priest Caiaphas (18-36 A.D, Bruce p119), had said to Jesus at His trial, 'Are you the Christ, the son of the Blessed?' And Jesus had replied, 'I AM, and you will see the Son of Man seated at the right hand of power and coming with the clouds of Heaven. (Mark 14:61).

This is the One whom Saul is preaching, Jesus, the Son of God, enjoying that unique fellowship with God His Father, 'the Blessed' as so named by Caiaphas, which alone is His, (Matthew 11:27), in the Triune Godhead with the Holy Spirit. Saul had not come to trick them or cajole them; his original purpose in coming to Damascus no longer applied. All he wanted was to preach Jesus to them. And he increased in wisdom and strength and understanding (Acts 9:22), as he confounded the unbelieving Jews in Damascus, confounding all the previous knowledge that they had by proving that Jesus was the Christ, the anointed of God.

There appears now to be a hiatus in Luke's narrative. How long Saul was in Damascus with the disciples, and preaching Jesus in the synagogues we do not know, but in Galatians we have Paul's own account that at some point he went away to Arabia, the country east of Damascus, for three years. He need not have travelled far, for the distance from Damascus into the region of Petra the capital city of Arabia was not great, but it is probable that his intention was to spend some time alone, quietly waiting on the Lord for the revelation of those truths which he was afterwards to share with others on his missionary journeys, and especially in his letters. Arabia was for him an opportunity to receive the mysteries of the gospel, not the gospel according to man, perhaps handed down through the apostles teaching, but the gospel which came through the revelation of Jesus Christ to him personally. (Galatians 1:11,12)

Then he returned to Damascus, (Galatians 1:17). But when many days had passed he was compelled to leave Damascus because the Jews plotted to kill him. But their plot became known to Saul and the disciples; and his friends, knowing that the gates of the city were guarded day and night, let him down in a basket through a window in the wall, and so he escaped. (Acts 9:23-25; 2 Corinthians 11:32).

It appears that he then went to Jerusalem. (Galatians 1:18). Although it is now three years since the one who had persecuted them had returned, the disciples in Jerusalem were still a little afraid of him, for they did not believe that he was a disciple. (Acts 9:26). But here was a kindly compassionate man, Barnabas, 'son of consolation;. (Acts 4:26). Barnabas took Saul and brought him to the apostles (Acts 4:27), declaring his credentials as 'one who had seen the Lord' on the road to Damascus and how at Damascus he had preached boldly in the Name of Jesus.

This occasion, recorded in Acts, may have coincided with that of Saul going up to Jerusalem to visit Peter and staying with him for fifteen days. (Galatians 1:18), and also to see James the Lord's brother. Clearly, Saul was now accepted by the apostles, going in and out among them at Jerusalem and preaching boldly in the Name of the Lord. (Acts 9:28).

But he was not accepted by the Hellenists, Jews with their roots in the Greek speaking world. As Saul disputed with them, continuing to preach boldly in the Name of Jesus, so they sought to kill him. (Acts 9:29). Once again, Saul needed to be rescued, and when the 'brethren' (which together with 'the way' had become a name for this community); when the brethren knew of the intention of the Hellenists, they brought Saul down to Caesarea, a journey of some miles, to the port which was also the commercial and political centre of Judea under the Roman occupation. From Caesarea, Saul was able to procure passage on a boat which took him to Tarsus, his home city in the province of Syria-Cilicia. (Acts 9:30).

It was to be fourteen years before Saul was again in Jerusalem, accompanied by Barnabas and Titus. (Galatians 2:1). Having been only two weeks in Jerusalem on the previous occasion, and it having been fourteen years earlier, it was not surprising that 'Saul was unknown to the churches of Christ in Judea. (Galatians 1:22). They only heard it said that he who once persecuted us is now preaching the faith he once tried to destroy, and they glorified God in me' (Galatians 1:23,24).

We hear no more of Saul until Acts 11:25. We can only surmise that he went on preaching boldly in the Name of Jesus, (Acts 9:29), that is, by His authority, as His witness, His ambassador. He writes to the Corinthian church, 'we are ambassadors for Christ, God making His appeal through us. *We beseech you on behalf of Christ, be reconciled to God*'. (2 Corinthians 5:20). This was the whole of Paul's message, condensed into a few words.

Acts 9:31. The church enjoys peace and prosperity

So the church throughout all Judea and Galilee and Samaria had peace and was built up, and walking in the fear of the Lord and in the comfort of the Holy Spirit it was multiplied.

With the opposition raised against Saul declining, and his departure for Tarsus, the persecution of the church ceased and it enjoyed a period of peace. Luke speaks of 'the church' throughout all Judea and Galilee and Samaria, one church, not an organisation of many churches, but one church, one organism, a living reality.

The period of peace enabled the church to grow and be 'built up'. The church was 'walking in the fear of the Lord and in the comfort of the Holy Spirit', the Comforter, (John 14:!6, K.J.V), which is a sure recipe for being built up, and it is no wonder that the church was multiplied.

Paul refers to 'the *churches* of Judea which are in Christ', (Galatians 1:22) and also in 1 Thessalonians 2:14 as the *churches* of God in Christ Jesus which are in Judea. But in these references, Paul may be speaking in terms of geographical location, for these churches may well be the original church in Jerusalem now dispersed and scattered throughout Judea. This dispersion accomplished two things; obviously, firstly the spread of the gospel which was of paramount importance, but secondly, as we have seen, God is gradually moving the church away from any suggestion of hierarchy.

Though this new movement later to be called Christianity originated in Jerusalem, God never confined Himself to one place, or one nation, for His purposes extended to and included 'the ends of the earth'. (Acts 1:8; Genesis 12:3). Not only the church in Jerusalem, significant as it was, but all the churches in Judea formed one church, together with all the churches in Galilee and Samaria, together with all the large and small hubs of the faith, congregations of believers in every community. As we also learn from Ephesians 4:4,5, one body and one Spirit constitute the church; one faith; one baptism; one God and Father of all who is above all and through all and in all.

The characteristic of the church is not uniformity but unity. 'There is neither Jew nor Greek, there is neither bond nor free, there is neither male nor female, for you are all one in Christ Jesus. (Galatians 3:28).

Acts 9:32-43. Peter in Lydda and Joppa

Now as Peter went here and there among them all, he came down also to the saints that lived at Lydda. There he found a man named Aeneas who had been bedridden for eight years and was paralysed. And Peter said to him, 'Aeneas, Jesus Christ heals you. Rise and make your bed'. And immediately he rose. And all the residents of Lydda and Sharon saw him and they turned to the Lord. (Acts 9:32-34).

It came to pass, it so happened, *egeneto*, (Gk), that as Peter went here and there among them all he came to the saints at Lydda. We had left Peter in Jerusalem after he and John had been on trial before the Sanhedrin for 'speaking to the people the words of this life'. (Acts 5:20). After their aborted imprisonment and severe beating, they were allowed to go, rejoicing that they were counted worthy to suffer for the Name of Jesus. And every day, in the temple and at home, they did not cease teaching and preaching Jesus as the Christ. (Acts 5:42).

Now Peter is described as 'going here and there among them all', a reference to the church throughout Judea and Galilee and Samaria in Acts 9:31, an itinerant ministry through all the villages and towns between Jerusalem and Lydda. Though Lydda was about twenty five miles from Jerusalem and about twelve miles southeast of Joppa, modern Jaffa, Peter may have taken a circuitous route. It may be that these churches had come into existence through the ministry of Philip on his way from Azotus to Caesarea (Acts 8:40). The church in Jerusalem is still caring for the churches of the dispersion, and Peter has become part of its pastoral ministry.

This was how Peter came to be at Lydda, and almost casually it seems, he found a man there named Aeneas. Peter had travelled down the western coast of Palestine, not only as an evangelist, but also to encourage the saints who lived in Lydda. (Acts 9:32). Aeneas was evidently among them, this group of believers now known by another common name, 'the saints'. The saints lived in this locality whose chief trade was in purple dye, a very expensive dye used for the clothes of emperors; and where in Crusader times was founded the Christian tradition that this was where St George killed the dragon, possibly a huge sea creature captured in the harbour; and himself suffered martyrdom. (Bruce p 210).

Lydda was a town of considerable importance.

At Lydda there was care and concern for Aeneas, a man who was paralysed and had been bedridden for eight years. (Acts 9:33). Peter found him lying on his mattress and said to him 'Aeneas, Jesus Christ heals you. Rise and make your bed'. And immediately he rose. (Acts 9:34). And all the residents of Lydda and Sharon saw him and they turned to the Lord. (Acts 9:35).

These people who had so much prosperity, living in the beautiful fertile valley of Sharon, stretching from Lydda to Mount Carmel, yet needed to know about Jesus. Aeneas was a testimony to them that through Jesus, the healing of someone apparently insignificant, like Aeneas, who could contribute nothing to the prosperity of their city, had taken on a distinctive value. It emphasised that Jesus Christ was God, who had come down to them in human form, and was still concerned about the ones who needed His healing touch. It also emphasised the value of an individual to God, that through Jesus He is involved in the lives of ordinary men and women. They turned to the Lord who had done this wonderful thing. (Acts 9:35).

In this one short sentence, the life of Aeneas was transformed. Peter said 'Aeneas, Jesus Christ heals you'. (Acts 9:34). What had been for him a bed on which he could lie had now become a couch on which he could recline to share supper with his friends. (Marshall p 179). His recovery from paralysis was a visible sign of that new life which had become his when Peter spoke to him.

Peter is totally confident as he addresses Aeneas. 'Aeneas, Jesus Christ heals you!. It is none other than Jesus who effects the healing of this man. Peter is only the channel, the agent whom Jesus can use. His boldness and confidence is astounding. What if 'it didn't work?' That at his words the miracle had not taken place?

To Peter, such a situation was not even a remote possibility. He knew himself to be a humble agent of the Holy Spirit, totally given up to Him for the performance of those signs and wonders which were the outward sign of what He was doing in the human heart. (Acts 5:12). Immediately Aeneas rose, just as had the lame man at the beautiful gate of the temple. (Acts 3:9). When the Lord Jesus undertakes to do something through His servant, it is done. And not only Aeneas, but many others, seeing him, turned to the Lord.

Acts 9:36-43. The raising of Tabitha

Now there was at Joppa a disciple named Tabitha, which means Dorcas. She was full of good works and acts of charity. In those days she fell sick and died; and when they had washed her they laid her in an upper room. Since Lydda was near Joppa, the disciples, hearing that Peter was there, sent two men to him entreating him, 'Please come to us without delay'. So Peter rose and went with them. And when he had come, they took him to the upper room.

Whether the disciples at Joppa had heard news of what was happening at Lydda we do not know, but they did know that Peter was at Lydda. A terrible thing had happened at Joppa.

In those days, it came to pass, *egeneto,* (Acts 9:36), that a disciple whose name in Aramaic was Tabitha, and Dorcas in Greek, meaning 'gazelle' had been taken ill and had died. In a mixed society of Jews and Greeks she may well have responded to both names.

Tabitha was full of good works and acts of charity, abounding in them. And the community was devastated. What could they do but send for Peter? Meanwhile, they carefully washed her and laid her in an upper room. (Acts 9:37). This is an echo of the upper room where Jesus shared his last meal with His disciples. It leads us to consider whether the upper room in Joppa was part of a meeting house, one used for worship, as though the church was beginning to substitute the use of private homes for a house with an additional facility for worship, but we have no evidence for this. She may have just been laid in a bedroom.

The men were sent from Joppa to Lydda to look for Peter, a journey of about ten miles, and a journey full of haste and anxiety. When they found Peter, they entreated him, pleading with him, 'Please come to us without delay'. (Acts 9:38). So Peter rose and left what he was doing and went with them the ten miles back to Joppa. There was no time for rest or refreshment.

As soon as he had arrived the disciples took him to the upper room where the body of Tabitha lay, and where a full mourning vigil was in progress. The room was filled with widows, women who were weeping and wailing as they showed Peter the underclothes, tunics and other garments which Tabitha had made, ready to be distributed to the poor who were in such need of them, inspired as she was by the love of Jesus towards her, and her love towards them. It is possible that some of the widows were wearing garments which she had made.

Jesus the Healer had already healed Aeneas. Is it possible that He would go a step further and raise a woman to life who had now been dead for some days? Peter had come, but now he needed to pray, to talk to Jesus about what he should do. He gently put all the mourners outside; the saints, the widows, the messengers; so that he could be alone with his Lord and with Tabitha. He knelt down and prayed. (Acts 9:40). At last, assured of the will of the Lord for Tabitha and the little circle of believers, Peter rose from his knees and turning to the body he said 'Tabitha, arise'. At first, she just opened her eyes as though she had been enjoying a refreshing sleep. Then she saw Peter. How lovely to see him, she thought, but what was he doing in her bedroom? Then she sat up and Peter took her by the hand and lifted her up. (Acts 9:41). This wonderful miracle could not be enjoyed by themselves alone, and after a little while, Peter opened the door and 'calling the saints and widows, he presented her alive'. (Acts 9:41).

And what was becoming an inevitable conclusion was happening again. The raising of Tabitha 'became known throughout all Joppa, and *many* believed in the Lord'. (Acts 9:42). Luke calls them 'many'. These new believers were passing from death to life, not from physical death, that would come later, but from the death of being without Christ and without God in the world, to the life everlasting, only and always to be found in Him. (Ephesians 2:12).

Peter did not immediately leave Joppa. He found lodgings with Simon, a tanner, whose house was by the seaside for a reason, because the work he did as a tanner required a source of water. (Acts 9:43; 10:6). He stayed with Simon for many days. Simon was an Aramaic name, and Simon was probably a Jew but engaged in what was considered to be an unclean occupation, certainly one that was less than salubrious, turning the hides of slaughtered carcasses into leather, an odorous, smelly and difficult process.

The humble Peter, called by God to be a apostle, an evangelist and one whom God could use to bring not only healing to a paralysed man but new life to a dead woman, was happy and content to stay in Simon's home, until the Holy Spirit made it clear to him where he should go next. He was not looking for special treatment or luxurious accommodation but only to be available to the Holy Spirit for His leading and guiding.

Peter stayed for many days with Simon the tanner, helping him with his work. And as Peter was an ex-fisherman, and

Simon lived by the seaside, they were both happy and content, even though Simon had this unclean occupation.

Peter was well on the way to understanding salvation as a merciful provision for all, regardless of ethnic, religious or occupational status, irrespective of perceived eligibility. All have sinned and come short of the glory of God. (Romans 3:23). There is no distinction. But the righteousness of God through faith in Jesus Christ is also without distinction, available for all who believe, for they are made righteous by His grace as a free gift. This is salvation. The only qualification is that they seek God with all their heart, for if they seek Him He will surely be found of them and will be led to repentance and faith. (Romans 3:22-24; Jeremiah 29:13). If Jesus could make himself of no reputation, humble Himself, and take upon Himself the form of a servant, then it is certain that His servant Peter could do so too. (Philippians 2:6,7).

Acts Chapter 10

Acts 10:1:11-11:18. Peter at Caesarea with Cornelius

At Caesarea there was a man named Cornelius, a centurion of what was known as the Italian cohort, a devout man who feared God with all his household, gave alms liberally to the people and prayed constantly to God.

At about the ninth hour of the day he saw clearly in a vision an angel of God coming in and saying to him, 'Cornelius'. And he stared at him in terror and said, 'What is it Lord?' And he said to him, 'Your prayers and your alms have ascended as a 'memorial' before God. And now send men to Joppa and bring one Simon who is called Peter; he is lodging with Simon, a tanner, whose house is by the seaside. (Acts 10:1-6).

The lessons which Peter had been learning since Pentecost, recently reinforced in Lydda and Joppa, were now coming to a fruition of which Peter could never have dreamed. God was moving towards establishing certain serious principles in His church which had always been there, but had previously been nebulous and random in operation.

God was about to use Peter to confirm and ensure forever and for everyone that He was no respecter of persons, (Acts 10:34), but that He was prepared to give the gift of the Holy Spirit, not only to Jews, His chosen people but also to Gentiles. (Acts 10:45), even as He had to the gathered community in Acts 2:4 at the beginning. The gospel includes the outpouring of the Holy Spirit, and He has been given to the church which has within it both Jews and Gentiles without distinction and without partiality, and to individual members of it.

God had chosen Peter to initiate and inaugurate the inclusion of the Gentiles into the church. Though they lacked understanding of Jewish tradition and customs, and even possibly lacked scriptural knowledge, God was going to include them in the church which Jesus said He would build, and the gates of hell would not prevail against it. (Matthew 16:18).

Peter represented the earliest followers of the Lord Jesus. He represented one of the first recipients of the power of the Holy Spirit coming upon him. He was a disciple as well as an apostle, 'a learner' of Jesus as well as one of His 'sent ones'; sent to the lost sheep of the house of Israel as were all the apostles, (Mathtthew 10:6) and one who was constantly learning as all disciples are. And he was one of the pillars of the church in Jerusalem, (Galatians 2:9), although at this period he was an itinerant missionary preacher, journeying around the churches in western Palestine, prepared above all to follow the leading of the Holy Spirit. And wherever the Spirit told him to go, he went. (Acts 11:12).

This was the humble servant of God whom He had chosen to direct the growing church into a new understanding; a wonderful new stage of development in the life of the church, where neither circumcision, the seal of being within the covenant which God made with His people, nor uncircumcision, being outside the covenant, counted for anything, but only being a new creation in Christ. (Galatians 6:15). It will be many years before the principle is fully established in the church, but through Peter, God is beginning to implement it. (Acts 11:5-10; 15:6-12).

At Caesarea there was a man named Cornelius, a centurion of what was known as the Italian cohort, a military man. He was a devout man who feared God with all his household, gave alms liberally to the people, and prayed constantly to God. (Acts 1:1,2).

Cornelius was a Gentile, but also one who feared God; a devout man and yet a Roman soldier, a commissioned officer, a centurion in the Italian cohort. A cohort consisted of six hundred men, and Cornelius was in charge of one hundred of them. The description of him as being of the Italian cohort suggests that this event happened prior to A.D 41, for during the reign of Agrippa 1 (A.D 41-44), Roman troops were not stationed in Caesarea. Some expositors have suggested that Cornelius had retired and settled in Caesarea, but then he would not have had at his disposal a soldier to send to Joppa with his two servants (Acts 10:7), unless the soldier had also retired and was part of a security detail. (Barrett p499). Cornelius would have been a Roman citizen.

Though Cornelius was a Roman he had found no satisfaction in the pantheon of Roman gods and goddesses, in their alleged cruelty, their immorality and their indifference and distance from the ordinary human lives of men and women. In Judaism, Cornelius had found a God whom he could worship, a compassionate God who advocated piety and charitable giving to these people among whom he had come to live. He was constantly at prayer, (Acts 10:2), and his example encouraged the numerous members of his household to share the religious faith he had come to espouse and which had come to mean so much to him.

He was not a proselyte, that is, one who had taken the ultimate step of circumcision, but it is clear that he feared, reverenced God, and although not a proselyte, he was attached to the synagogue and its ethical principles and way of life. Such men and women were known as God fearers and were valued members of the synagogue community.

Cornelius was praying one day at the ninth hour (Acts 10:3), three o'clock in the afternoon, the time of the evening oblation or sacrifice (Acts 3:1), and Cornelius had a vision. At three in the afternoon this was not likely to be a nocturnal dream. Cornelius saw clearly, openly, manifestly in a vision, an angel of God coming in and saying 'Cornelius'.

Angels often appear in Acts as emissaries of God, and demonstrate divine intervention. (Acts 5:19; 8:26; 12:7; 27:23). Even as God had chosen Stephen, Philip, Peter and no doubt many others for a specific purpose, so God was now choosing Cornelius, calling him by name. This was God's initiative, His plan and purpose for His people, and He had chosen Cornelius to be a part of what He was doing. Nevertheless, Cornelius was terrified by the presence of the angel. With all his devotion to the One and Only True God, he had not expected this. He stared at the angel in terror, (Acts 10:4), but he recognized that behind the angel was the voice of God, and he said, 'What is it, Lord?' He did not address the angel as Lord but reacted naturally to the supernatural.

The voice was reassuring. He said to him 'Your prayers and your alms have ascended as a memorial before God', as a sacrifice before Him. (Acts 10:4). God was saying that Cornelius' devotion to Him was a *memorial offering* like the cereal offering in Leviticus 2:1-3, which speaks to God of the humanity of Christ, and is a pleasing odour to the Lord; a memorial, a remembrance of His Son, an aroma of Christ to God, as we read in Ephesians, Christ loved us, and gave Himself for us, a fragrant offering and sacrifice to God. (Epesians 5:2).

What God was doing at this time and what He was saying through the angel to Cornelius was so important. His message to Cornelius speaks of his prayers and almsgiving, arising to God as a memorial before Him. Unaware though he may have been of the sacrificial implications of the memorial offering of Leviticus 2:2, Cornelius was offering up to God the cereal offering, the 'bread' of his daily living, his prayer and almsgiving as the equivalent representation of the cereal offering. This memorial is the basis upon which God is not only going to reveal Himself to Cornelius, but also to do a new work for the whole of mankind, for the memorial spoke to God of 'the living Bread which came down from heaven', His Son. (John 6:33).

God had made a covenant with Abraham personally, to be not only his God but the God of his descendents. (Genesis 17:7), This covenant was extended to the whole people of Israel on Mount Sinai, that they should be His own possession among all peoples, and should be to God a kingdom of priests and a holy nation. (Exodus 19:4-6).

The sacrificial offerings which the people of Israel were commanded to bring before God established that relationship with Him, and each sacrifice had its own special purpose in providing God with a holy people. God's people had to be holy, for He is holy. They were to reflect His holiness which they could only do if God gave them the means to take away sin. Four of the five sacrifices they offered included the shedding of blood for the remission of sins, for without the shedding of blood there is no remission, no forgiveness. (Hebrews 9:22). This foreshadows of course the sacrifice of Christ, the shedding of His blood upon the cross, opening up for us a new and living way to God. (Hebrews 10:20).

But the cereal offering involved no shedding of blood, for the cereal offering spoke not of His redemptive sacrifice, but of His Humanity, for He was the cereal, the bread of life. (John 6:35). The cereal offering represented the Son of Man, the perfect spotless Son of God born as a human being, living His life as a Perfect Man. It is unsurprising that when this freewill, voluntary offering was made, it came up to God as a memorial, although as yet, Cornelius knew nothing of the Lord Jesus Christ or the Holy Spirit.

The offerer of the cereal offering came to the priest with his offering. We come to our great High Priest, who is holy, blameless and unstained, and separate from sinners, who offered Himself once for all when He offered up Himself. (Hebrews 7:26). He is both priest and victim at the eucharistic feast, when we break bread together in remembrance of Him, in memorial of Him, to remember Him, for He now has a resurrected Body though no human flesh in heaven.

He is the victim who is also the bread of life. We pray 'give us this day our daily bread' (Matthew 6:11), for how we need daily not only physical food, but above all, the bread of life, the Lord Jesus. The Israelites of old, even the poorest of the poor, could offer to the Lord a measure of grain, cereal, and frankincense, to symbolise the presence and work of the Holy Spirit and to symbolize prayer and commitment. It was an act of worship to God, (Leviticus 2:2), reminding Him of the offering of His Son and of the covenant He had made with His people, for the offering was also seasoned with salt, the salt of the covenant. (Leviticus 2:13).

This was the normal food of ordinary people, symbolizing their dedication and commitment to the Lord of their daily lives in dependence on Him, and their thankfulness for His provision. What a long queue there would have been each morning as they awaited their turn at the altar!. The crushed grain which sometimes became fine flour, and sometimes unleavened cakes of bread laid upon the altar as a symbol of a living sacrifice, a love gift to God in response to His love for them. (Leviticus 2:2, 4, 14).

God had recognised this quality of devotion and commitment in Cornelius, limited as it was by his understanding, and He was about to give Cornelius a more stable rationale for the truth which he had so dimly realized.

God was going to reveal to him Jesus. Through the ministry of Peter, God was doing a new thing in His church, and He was going to build it on the revelation given to Cornelius, *firstly,* that everything that was of any value in the life of a believer was based on the eternal, once-only sacrifice of Christ on the cross for our redemption; and *secondly,* that the continuation of that life in Him depended on feeding on Him daily; and *thirdly,* that this life, the intimate experience of knowing God personally was available to all who believe, whether Jew or Gentile, whether bond or free. All are one in Christ Jesus. (Galatians 3:28).

God will amplify this more fully as Peter speaks to Cornelius and his household of Jesus.

Acts 10:9-16. Peter's vision

The angel said to Cornelius, 'Now send men to Joppa and bring one Simon who is called Peter; he is lodging with Simon, a tanner, whose house is by the seaside. When the angel who spoke to him had departed, he called two of his servants and a devout soldier from among those who waited on him and having related everything to them, he sent them to Joppa. (Acts 10:5-8).

It was important for a tanner to live where there was a good supply of water for the tanning process. Simon had performed a small part in the divine plan but how essential that had been.

165

He would never forget those few days of fellowship with Peter, but now Peter was being given another task to do for God, and Simon could not stand in his way.

Unaware that men from Caesarea were on their way to see him, Peter had gone up onto Simon's roof top to pray in quiet contemplation. It was about the sixth hour, noon.

The Roman *prandium* or midday meal was normally taken at this time, though the Jews tended to have a light meal mid-morning and a more substantial meal in the late afternoon (Marshall p 183). But Peter became hungry and desired something to eat, but while *they* were preparing it, Peter fell into a trance. (Acts 10:10). 'They' may refer to Simon and his wife, or perhaps some other believers who had come to enjoy fellowship with Peter and Simon. But Peter fell into a trance.

'Trance' indicates more than vision. It indicates ecstasy, an ecstatic experience of standing outside of oneself, almost of watching something happening. Peter saw heaven opened. (Acts 10:11).

Heaven had opened on the occasion of the baptism of Jesus in the River Jordan, when there was a voice from heaven saying 'This is My beloved Son in whom I am well pleased'. (Luke 3:22). When Stephen was being stoned to death, full of the Holy Spirit, he gazed into heaven and said,' Behold I see heaven opened and the Son of Man standing at the right hand of God'. (Acts 7:56). Heaven is where God's will is perfectly realized and so we pray, 'Thy will be done on earth as it is done in heaven'. (Matthew 6:10).

In his trance, Peter is looking into an open heaven to see what the will of the Lord is. And to his surprise, he sees something descending like a great sheet, let down by four corners upon the earth. In it were all kinds of animals and reptiles and birds of the air, and there came a voice to him, 'Rise Peter, kill and eat. If you are hungry, here is food'. But Peter said, 'Not so Lord; for I have never eaten anything that is common or unclean. And the voice came to him a second time, 'What God has cleansed you must not call common'. This happened three times and the object was taken up at once into heaven.

Peter was in an attitude of prayer, either kneeling or prostrating himself upon the rooftop. To rise in obedience to the voice was possible, but to kill? How could he obey that command? How could he possibly go against the Word of God and eat something unclean? Leviticus distinguishes clearly between clean and unclean animals, those which could be eaten and those which could not. (Leviticus 20:25). And there was a long extended list in Leviticus 11:1-31, of food which was forbidden, part of what is known as the holiness code, for God intends that His people shall be holy even as He is holy. He has separated them from all other peoples so that they should be holy to Him, and wholly for Him. (Leviticus 20:26).

Peter is in a dilemma. Does he obey God's word, or does he obey God? As a disciple of the Lord Jesus he wants to obey God in all things, but can it possibly be that he is expected to eat that which is unclean? His first response is 'No, Lord, for I have never eaten anything that is common or unclean'. (Acts 10:14).

Twice before, Peter had said 'No' to Jesus; once when Jesus had explained to His disciples the necessity of His death and resurrection and Peter began to rebuke Him saying 'God forbid, Lord. This shall never happen to You'. (Matthew 16:22). On another occasion when Jesus began to wash His disciples feet before His crucifixion, Peter had said to Jesus, 'Lord, do you wash my feet? You shall never wash my feet!' (John 13:6,8).

On both occasions, Peter was absolutely ignorant of what Jesus was saying and doing. His categorical refusal to believe that Jesus could die such a dreadful death, or that he was worthy to have Jesus perform the act of a slave to him and wash his feet, hot and dusty from walking the roads of a Middle Eastern country, just because He loved him, (John 13:1), showed a complete lack of understanding of the divine purpose of God exemplified in His Son.

To say 'no' to the sheet containing the animals was no different, inasmuch as Peter still did not understand. This was in a sense, personal to Peter, but it had much wider, in fact, universal, cosmic implications. Peter heard the voice from heaven, 'what God has cleansed you must not call common'.

(Acts 10:15). This happened three times and then the sheet was taken up at once into heaven.

The important distinction which God had been making was between the clean and the unclean, between the sacred and the profane, between what was holy and what was unholy. And yet here, before Peter's eyes God was annulling the distinction. He was using what was familiar to Peter from his Jewish upbringing, the distinction between clean and unclean foods, to demolish the distinction between people. God is saying, there are not two groups of people, 'common' or 'special' people. All are special to Him, as Paul later writes, whether Jew or Greek, bond or free, male or female, all are one in Christ Jesus. (Galatians 3:28). Later Paul goes on to explain that food will not commend us to God, whether we eat or do not eat certain foods, (1 Corinthians 8:8). But Peter's vision was not immediately about food, but about people.

Peter's 'No, Lord!' was about to be changed into a whole hearted 'Yes, Lord!' for he was about to understand what the vision really meant. God says to him 'What God has cleansed you must not call common'. (Acts 10:15). This is imperative. He is not to go on doing what he has been doing. God had always been, and still is, concerned with cleansing. These defiled, profane people, for so the Jews regarded the Gentiles, were to be reckoned before God as righteous, justified, as they availed themselves of the cleansing blood of the Lord Jesus which cleanses from all sin, (1 John 1:7), providing cleansing for all men and women everywhere as they come to Him in faith.

God's people had been able to receive cleansing from sin through the Levitical sacrifices. But now, the ultimate sacrifice for sin, the blood shed by the Lord Jesus on the cross was available, not just for the Jews, but for everyone who called on the Name of the Lord for salvation. The word of God teaches us that we are redeemed by the blood of Jesus, justified by His blood, the blood pouring from His head, His hands, His feet, His side. (Romans 5:9). He died in pain and suffering and exsanguination as a living sacrifice, and He died for us, for me. This is the cost of our cleansing, provided for all men and women as they come to Him in faith. What God has cleansed, we may not call common either.

Peter gradually recovers from his trance, his mind full of what he has seen and heard, and what its significance could be for his future behaviour. He has received a mysterious revelation and he is 'inwardly perplexed', (Acts 10:17), and confused, wondering what the vision meant.

He was not kept waiting long, for 'behold, the men that were sent by Cornelius', having made inquiry for the house of Simon the tanner, 'stood before the gate and called out to ask whether Simon called Peter was lodging there'. (Acts 10:17,18). God had already prepared the way. These men who came from Caesarea, from Cornelius were undoubtedly pious men, and Cornelius had undoubtedly shared with them the vision which God had given him. He had related everything to them before they left Joppa. It was obvious that Cornelius could trust them with his most intimate concerns. He had told them about his vision and its impact on him, and the urgency of immediately sending for Peter.

Though the journey, presumably on horseback, was about thirty miles, they probably rode through the night, for they arrived at Simon's house at noon the next day, arriving just as Peter was pondering the vision. (Acts 10:19). And while they were standing at the door, the Spirit spoke to Peter and said to him, 'behold, these men are looking for you. Rise, go down and accompany them without hesitation, for I have sent them'. (Acts 10:20).

Leaving the rooftop, the place of prayer and vision, Peter went down to them, 'making no distinction, for the Spirit had sent them. He went down to the men and said, 'I am the one you are looking for. What is the reason for your coming?' (Acts 10:21). And they said, 'Cornelius, a centurion, an upright and God fearing man who is well spoken of by the whole Jewish nation, was directed by an angel to send for you to come to his house and to hear what you have to say'. (Acts 10:22).

There was no hesitation here either. Immediately Peter called them into the house as his guests. (Acts 10:23). Though he did not yet know what God had in mind, and though both his visitors and Cornelius were uncircumcised Gentiles, with whom Jews were forbidden to eat, Peter knew enough to invite them in, and the next day he rode off with them, and some of the brethren from Joppa accompanied them. (Acts 10:23). And on the following day, these ten men entered Caesarea (Acts 10:23). What a welcome they received! Cornelius had gathered together all his relatives and close intimate friends, completely certain that Peter would not refuse his invitation.

When Peter entered, Cornelius met him and fell down at his feet and worshipped him, a natural reaction from Cornelius who regarded Peter as a messenger from God, as indeed he was, but not God Himself. As a Judaized Roman citizen, Cornelius should have understood this, for what was known as the Shema', 'Hear, O Israel, the Lord our God is one Lord, and you shall love the Lord your God with all your heart and with all your soul and with all your strength'. (Deuteronomy 6:4,5), was usually abbreviated to the first phrase. 'Hear O Israel, the Lord our God, the Lord is One'. This was, and still is, the foundational truth of Judaism without exception. Yet Cornelius regarded Peter as more than a man and naturally accorded respect to him. He had recently seen an angel coming to him, and may have seen in Peter something of the supernatural, wanting to pay homage to him. But Peter refused to accept homage which should only be offered to God.

Dear Cornelius, he was on a steep learning curve, and as he will subsequently discover from experience, there is always so much more to learn. Peter recognized Cornelius' humility and hunger for spiritual enlightenment which he believed Peter had come to share with him. Peter raised Cornelius to his feet and lifted him up saying, 'Stand up. I too am a man'. (Acts 10:26). We share a common humanity, Cornelius. We are both seeking to know more of God and of His Son and to know the power of the Holy Spirit.

And as Peter spoke to Cornelius, putting an arm across his shoulder, they entered Cornelius' house together. They found many persons there, (Acts 10:27), and for a while had to suspend their private conversation, for Peter had something of great importance to say to them. He too, together with Cornelius, had learnt something of tremendous significance over the last few days.

Peter said to the gathered assembly, 'You yourselves know how unlawful it is for a Jew to associate with, or visit anyone of another nation. But God has shown me that I should not call any man common or unclean. So when I was sent for, I came without objection. I ask why you sent for me!' (Acts 10:28,29). Because of their association with Cornelius, and their attendance at the synagogue, the people assembled in his house were well aware that what was happening was not quite what they would have expected; and not only Cornelius' household, but also the men from Joppa, whom Peter had brought with him, probably felt the same.

They may have felt, what is Peter doing? He knows that association with Gentiles is against Jewish law, contrary not only to custom but actually forbidden on the grounds of defilement, rendering the Jewish person ritually unclean simply by entering the home of a Gentile. (Compare John 18:28). Peter's explanation lacks some element of assurance for the Joppa believers. 'God has shown me that I should not call anyone common or unclean', said Peter. But, they may have thought, what about those chapters in Leviticus? Alternatively, they may have thought, Peter is a man filled with the Holy Spirit and we can trust him not to lead us into forbidden ways.

Cornelius however was keen to interpose and give the reason for his request for Peter to come. He told them all what exactly had happened to him, how he had sent for Peter on the angel's instruction, and concluded, 'you were so kind as to come'. (Acts 10:33). 'So please Peter, we are all here present in the sight of God, to hear all that you have been commanded by the Lord'.

It was a remarkable speech, acknowledging the presence of God in their midst, acknowledging Peter, who in the estimation of a Roman centurion could be considered a person of no importance, to be one sent by God to give Cornelius an understanding which all his adherence to the Jewish way of life, and the teaching of the synagogue had been unable to supply. Cornelius longed for something more. He wanted to experience the reality of God in his life. He did not yet know that as Peter spoke, God would reveal to him Jesus, but like the disciples on the Emmaus road, his heart burned within him as Peter spoke of Jesus, who is Christ the Lord.

'And Peter opened his mouth', a phrase indicating that what Peter was about to say was to be taken in all seriousness.

Acts 10:34-43. Peter's speech in the house of Cornelius

And Peter opened his mouth and said, 'Truly. I perceive that God shows no partiality, but in every nation anyone who fears Him and does what is right is acceptable to Him. You know the word which He sent to Israel, preaching good news of peace by Jesus Christ, (He is Lord of all), the word which He proclaimed through all Judea, beginning from Galilee after the baptism which John preached; how God anointed Jesus of Nazareth with the Holy Spirit, how He went about doing good and healing all that were oppressed, for God was with Him. (Acts 10:34-35).

This is the basis on which Peter wants to speak to them. Because of what Cornelius had told him of the visit of the angel and the message of the voice which spoke to him, Peter knows that Cornelius is a righteous man, but of course, he had no means of knowing the spiritual status of the others. He just wants to make it clear to them from the beginning that God is no respecter of persons.

One who reverences God, honouring Him as God (Romans 1:21), and living a life of righteousness, righteousness in the broadest sense, loving and serving God and obeying the commandments, (Barrett p 520), is acceptable to God and accepted by Him, (Romans 2:6). This is the undeviating principle in divine judgement. (Bruce p 224).

This was the righteousness of the good life on the basis of Deuteronomy 10:12, amplified by the prophet Micah as 'what does the Lord require of you but to do justice and to love mercy and to walk humbly with your God? (Micah 6:8). And Peter adds, God shows no partiality, but 'in every nation, those who fear God are acceptable to Him'. The members of Cornelius' household had not been born into the privileged nation of Israel with all the many opportunities of being able to come to God through sacrificial offerings, and to live by all the commandments He had given. But they had a heart for God, a hunger and a thirst for righteousness which Jesus says is a blessing, for they will be satisfied. (Matthew 5:6).

Peter is explaining that God has something very much in His heart for Cornelius. Just as there was nothing vague or ephemeral about his righteousness, but a practical outworking of what he believed God desired of him, and as an example of his good works, giving alms liberally (Acts 10:2), so too God's inclusiveness was not a vague, pantheistic fuzzy feeling of warmth, but a practical recognition of where he and his household stood in relation to His Son. God wanted so much more for them. God wanted to clothe them in the robe of righteousness of the Lord Jesus, a robe promised long ago through Isaiah (Isaiah 61:10) and revealed to Paul as not having a righteousness of our own but that which is of faith in Christ, the righteousness which is of God through faith. (Philippians 3:9).

Peter continues to explain how this could be so. He goes right back to the beginning, to the earthly historical life of Jesus, of which they may have had some knowledge, for he says, 'You know that God sent His word to Israel, preaching good news by Jesus Christ; (Acts 10:36), the word which was proclaimed throughout all Judea, beginning from Galilee after the baptism which John preached; how God anointed Jesus of Nazareth with the Holy Spirit and with power; how He went about doing good and healing all that were oppressed by the devil, for God was with Him. (Acts 10:36-38).

Peter says to this group of potential believers, although you may not have realized the significance of all that He did, you know that at HIs baptism by John in the River Jordan, the Holy Spirit descended upon Him like a dove, God demonstrating that He was indeed the anointed of God, the Messiah who should come, God reinforcing the visual with the audible by a voice from heaven which said 'this is My beloved Son in whom I am well pleased'. (Matthew 3:17).

Under this anointing and this confirmation by His heavenly Father, Jesus went about doing good, healing all that were oppressed by the devil. *diabolus,* meaning 'the slanderer', for God was with Him. (Acts 10:38).

God did not leave us without witnesses, says Peter. Those whom Jesus had called to be with Him went about with Him both in the country of the Jews and Jerusalem, (Acts 10:39), and they witnessed the death which He died, hanging on a tree, taking upon Himself and reversing the curse laid on someone whose crime was punishable in this way, (Deuteronomy 21:22, 23), redeeming men and women from the curse of not being able to keep the law, becoming the curse for us, for it is written 'Cursed be everyone who hangs on a tree;. (Galatians 3:10-14). But God turned the curse into a blessing, because He loved you. (Deuteronomy 23:5).

But death could not hold Him. God raised Him from death on the third day and made Him manifest, not to all the people but to those whom He had chosen to be His witnesses (Acts 10:40,41, even eating and drinking with them after He rose from the dead. And as He was leaving to return to His Father, 'He gave us a commandment that we should preach to the people and testify that He is the One ordained by God to be Judge of the living and the dead'. (Acts 10:42). And Peter affirms, we are not alone. All the prophets bear witness to Him, all declare that 'everyone who believes in Him receives forgiveness of sins through His Name. (Acts 10:43).

Tremendous though these words of Peter were, he was not allowed to finish. While he was still speaking, the Holy Spirit fell on all those who heard the word and they spoke in tongues and extolled God. (Acts 10:46). The joy, the liberation, the goal to which they had been striving, they now experienced as they revelled in the power and presence of God for themselves, knowing the reality of who Jesus is, in their own experience.

How long this jubilation went on we do not know. The believers from Joppa were amazed, because the Holy Spirit had been poured out upon the Gentiles, but rejoicing with them too as brothers and sisters in Christ, rejoicing with them as Peter declared, 'Can anyone forbid water for baptizing these people, who have received the Holy Spirit just as we did? (Acts 10:47).

What a baptismal party that would have been as they were baptized one by one in the Name of Jesus Christ. (Acts 10:48). And we can imagine how unwilling to let Peter go. 'Stay with us', they would plead; we want to know more about Jesus'. And he remained with them for some days, (Acts 10:48), with these believers who had been baptized in the Name of Jesus Christ, bearing public testimony that they had become Christ's property, belonged to Him, in commercial terms, transferred to His account. (Barrett p 187).

Spending a happy time together, Jews and Gentiles were no longer identified under this terminology, but were all one in Christ Jesus. (Galatians 3:28). Peter and the men from Joppa spent some time in Caesarea with Cornelius and his household, those who had now become 'the brethren' of Acts 9:30, 'the saints' of Acts 9:32. We can imagine their joy as they broke bread together, listened to Peter's teaching and enjoyed such times of prayer and worship together as they had never known before.

But all these special times come to an end. It appears that Peter was summoned to Jerusalem to give an account of what had happened in Caesarea, summoned by the apostles in Judea, (Acts 11:1) for they realised that something of tremendous significance had been taking place in Caesarea. They wanted to understand this fresh revelation which had been given to Peter.

Acts Chapter 11

Acts 11:1-8. The debate in Jerusalem over circumcision

Now the apostles and the brethren who were in Judea heard that the Gentiles also had received the word of God. So when Peter went up to Jerusalem, the circumcision party criticised him saying, 'Why did you go to uncircumcised men and eat with them?

But Peter began and explained to them in order. 'I was in the city of Joppa praying, and in a trance I saw a vision, something descending like a great sheet let down from heaven by four corners, and it came down to me. Looking at it closely I observed animals and beasts of prey and reptiles and birds of the air. And I heard a voice saying to me 'Rise Peter. Kill and eat'. But I said 'No Lord, for nothing common or unclean has ever entered my mouth'. But the voice answered, 'What God has cleansed you must not call common'. (Acts 11:1-9)

At first, the apostles and brethren in Judea were inclined to be critical, to dispute Peter's actions in Caesarea, to debate with him the reasons for doing what he did, for they too, like the men from Joppa, understood the peril of becoming defiled by the 'uncircumcised', those who were not of the chosen people of God, who were not men and women of the covenant which God had made with Abraham (Genesis 17:10, 11). Not only was defilement possible by going to their homes, but especially when eating with them. (Acts 11:3).

Their criticism or concern was based on a genuine fear that Peter had been coerced, seduced into a false position. Had not the apostles been sent to the 'lost sheep of the house of Israel'? (Matthew 10: 6). Were the Jewish people now to be 'cast off, (Romans 11:1. K.J.V), denied their supreme calling as those to whom were given the law, and the promises, and the Shekinah glory, and to whom belonged the patriarchs and of their race according to the flesh was Jesus Christ? (Romans 9:4). Were they no longer to be God's chosen, special people?.

Circumcision was such a precious privilege to them. It spoke of the covenant which God had made with Abraham. It was to be an everlasting covenant. (Genesis 17:7). The covenant was that God was to be God to Abraham and to his descendents after him, and that they would be His own, exclusive, holy people. God is almighty, El Shaddai, God the Nurturer, (Genesis 17:1), for that is what El Shaddai has in its etymology, and He wanted a people who would walk before Him and be blameless, while He cared for them as a parent with His children.

But God had something addiional in mind, that through Abraham, *all* the families of the earth would be blessed. (Genesis 12:3). We read in Galatians that this amounted to God preaching the gospel beforehand to Abraham, saying 'in you shall all the families of the earth be blessed; that those who are men and women of faith will be blessed with faithful Abraham, the man whose faith was counted to him as righteousness'. (Galatians 3:6). This promise God intended to ratify, for His promises can never be annulled, and this promise of righteousness was to be fulfilled for all people who had faith in Jesus.

How could Peter convey this tremendous truth to his Jewish brothers and sisters in the faith, the saints in Jerusalem? Peter, they had said to him, these men are not of the circumcision They are uncircumcised. Why did you go and eat with them? (Acts 11:3). You must have had a very good reason for doing so. Please could you tell us what made you do something so extraordinary? It may be that God is showing us something of His will and purpose for the church, for we recognize that though we are circumcised it was not circumcision which gave us the gift of the Holy Spirit, but faith in Jesus. Please Peter, tell us what the Holy Spirit has been revealing to you.

So Peter began by telling them about his vision, of the sheet let down from heaven containing animals and beasts of prey and birds of the air, and of the voice which came to him and said 'Rise Peter, kill and eat.' He told them of his refusal to eat anything common or unclean, and that his 'No' to the voice and its command occurred three times, even though the voice had said, 'What God has cleansed, you must not call common'. (Acts 11:5-10).

At that very moment, said Peter, with absolutely perfect timing, three men arrived from Caesarea who were Gentiles, and the Spirit told me to go with them. (Acts 11:12), making no distinction. The six brethren from Joppa accompanied me and we entered the man's house, who told us that he too had seen a vision. He had seen an angel who standing in his house had said 'Send to Joppa for Peter. He has a message for you by which you will be saved, you and all your household'.

And as I began to speak, the Holy Spirit fell on them just as had on us in the beginning. Then I remembered the word of the Lord, how He said, 'John baptized with water but you shall be baptized with the Holy Spirit. (Acts 11:16) Peter concluded, 'If God gave the same gift to them as He gave to us, when we believed in the Lord Jesus Christ, who was I that I could withstand God? (Acts 11:17).

The apostles and brethren heard Peter's words and were temporarily silent. (Acts 11:18). Then the glorious truth dawned on them and they glorified God saying, 'To the Gentiles also then, God has granted repentance unto life'. Their opposition ceased, their praise began. (Bruce p 232). The great gift of salvation was not given to Cornelius and his household alone, but to all Gentiles, for God has accepted them. (Barrett p 543).

And a whole new mission to the Gentiles was begun as this remarkable episode shows as it draws to a close. How significant it was in the life and teaching of the church. The newly baptized men and women had previously been careful not to make waves in their community, especially in Jerusalem, regularly attending the temple as in Acts 3:1, and adhering strictly to the law of Moses.

Even the Hellenist Jews in Jerusalem, (Acts 6:1), those whose upbringing had been influenced by the Greek society in which they lived, together with those who were more strictly Jewish, were beginning to realise that where the Spirit of the Lord is, there is liberty! (2 Corinthians 3:17). Now they were no longer children, tossed to and fro with every wind of doctrine, but fellow citizens with *all* the saints, members of the household of God, a dwelling place of God in the Spirit. (Ephesians 4:14; 2:19,22). For freedom Christ had set them free, they were no longer in slavery to the law. (Galatians 5:13,14).

Stephen's speech had made the first breach in their position, and now Peter had compromised their carefully thought out plan of living comfortably with the religious authorities, for they had been well aware of the experience of Peter and John and their trials before the Sanhedrin.

But their thinking had now changed. There were many Jewish believers in Caesarea and Jerusalem. Did their newly discovered freedom, and especially their newfound freedom to share the gospel with the uncircumcised, render them liable to persecution? Was this to be the outcome of Peter's revelation and subsequent action? Reluctant though they may have been to admit it at first, Peter's account of his vision had made a huge impact upon them. It could involve a time of suffering for them and their families, which indeed became the case. (Acts 12:1)

Many Gentiles had indeed been brought to faith in Christ, due to believers having been dispersed in the persecution which arose after Stephen's death, (Acts 8:1). Now Peter was declaring that these new believers need not be circumcised in order to become part of the faith community.

But this was not just Peter telling them of a mystical experience which he had had, nor of the conclusion he had reached as a result of it; that with God there was no respecter of persons, none were common or unclean. The confirmation had come entirely from God. God had poured out upon these Gentiles the Holy Spirit, just as He had on Peter and the disciples at the beginning; (Acts 11:15); that wonderful experience they had received on the Day of Pentecost. This was a development and a confirmation which they could not refute. Peter himself had said, 'Who was I that I could withstand God'?

No doubt the apostles and brethren in Jerusalem valued their distinction as being indeed believers, but *circumcised* believers. God was showing by the outpouring of His Spirit that there was no longer any distinction. God was not interested in a two-tiered church. All have sinned and come short of the glory of God, (Romans 3:23), and all are justified, made righteous by His grace as a gift. (Romans 3:24).

As the mission to the Gentiles proceeds through Acts, this question may have arisen time after time. Is it necessary for those who have become Christians to be circumcised? It was not until the Council in Jerusalem in Acts 15 that the issue was completely dealt with by the Council where Peter, together with Paul and Barnabas were able to share their conviction as to the status of Gentiles who had become Christian.

Peter's vision was perhaps the first step along the way. God had made it very clear to Peter, and eventually to the church in Jerusalem, that God had a purpose for these Gentiles, and as Peter said, 'who was I that I could withstand, prevent, hinder, *forbid, kolein* (GK) God? Peter had neither the will nor the ability to prevent God from doing what He had set His heart on doing for the Gentiles, what He had purposed for them from the beginning. From henceforth, Jews and Gentiles could go to each other's houses, share table fellowship with them. God had accepted the Gentiles just as He had accepted the Jews, for there was no respecter of persons with Him. (Acts 11:18; 15:1).

Acts 11:19-30. The church in Antioch.
The first Gentile church

Now those who were scattered abroad because of the persecution that arose over Stephen travelled as far as Phoenicia and Cyprus and Antioch, speaking the word to none except Jews. But there were some of them, men of Cyprus and Cyrene who on coming to Antioch spoke to the Greeks also, preaching the Lord Jesus. And the hand of the Lord was with them and a great number that believed turned to the Lord. News of this came to the ears of the church in Jerusalem, and they sent Barnabas to Antioch. When he came and saw the grace of God he was glad. (Acts 11:19-23).

These verses mark the beginning of a new experience for many believers, The persecution arising from the death of that courageous man Stephen, had shattered their way of life. Beginning even from the day of his death, 'a great persecution arose against the church in Jerusalem, and they were scattered throughout the region of Judea and Samaria'. (Acts 8:1).

Under this persecution, Philip had gone down to Samaria and through his ministry, Samaria had received the word of God. (Acts 8:14), and another community of believers was established. The greatest persecutor of them all, Saul of Tarsus, had himself become a follower of the Lord Jesus. (Acts 9:1-39), and Peter had begun an itinerant ministry among the churches which had sprung up along the west coast of Palestine, including those at Lydda and Joppa. (Acts 9:32).

So the church throughout all Judea and Galilee and Samaria had peace, and was built up, and walking in the fear of the Lord and in the comfort of the Holy Spirit, was multiplied. (Acts 9:31).

This had been a rich time of expansion and growth, not only numerically but spiritually, But so far, those who were scattered abroad preached the word to none except Jews. (Acts 11:19). Jews alone were the recipients of the wonderful message of salvation. But it appears that there were some men of Cyprus, the island from which Barnabas came, and men of Cyrene on the North African coast, who on coming to Antioch, spoke to the Greeks also, preaching the Lord Jesus. (Acts 11:20). 'And the hand of the Lord was with them, and a great number that believed turned to the Lord'. There was a new church in Antioch, a new community of believers.

This newly established church is the focus of interest for the next section of Acts. (Acts 11:19-30) as it describes the evangelization and establishment of the church through Saul/Paul and Barnabas. This is followed by a description of the famine relief sent to Jerusalem and Judea by the hands of Barnabas and Saul, and after the episode of Peter's imprisonment, the first missionary journey undertaken by Barnabas and Saul, with its base at the church in Antioch from which they set sail to Cyprus. (Acts 11:22-13:4).

Antioch was a thriving commercial, cosmopolitan city on the banks of the river Orontes. It encompassed a numerous colony of Jews from the Diaspora, the dispersion of Jews from their homeland. Its port onto the Mediterranean or Great Sea was Seleucia, fifteen miles west along the navigable river, the port from which Saul and Barnabas sailed on their first missionary journey. (Acts 13:4). Antioch was the capital of the Roman province of Syria, having been founded by the Greek general Seleucus Nicanor 1 in 300 BC, the son of Antiochus, one of Alexander's generals and named after his father.

It was a beautiful city, full of beautiful buildings and boulevards, and according to Josephus, (Antiquities 12:119; Barrett p 549), the third most important city in the Roman world, the others being Rome and Alexandria; with a population of 500,000. About five miles away was the shrine of Daphne, the seat of the cult surrounding Artemis and Apollo, which became a byword for immoral behaviour.

In this city, believers were first called Christians. (Acts 11:26).

To this city and also to Phoenicia and Cyprus, the persecuted Christans had fled after the persecution which had arisen after the death of Stephen. (Acts 11:19). Phoenicia was the coastal plain which included Tyre and Sidon and is now known as Lebanon. It was about 120 miles long and 15 miles wide. The Phoenicians were largely merchants trading between the Mediterranean ports and were the founders of Carthage, now known as Tunis.

The island of Cyprus was a minor Roman province of about 3,000 square miles. Leaving the port of Seleucia, Paul and Barnabas first came to Cyprus where they preached the word of God. (Acts 13:4). Although it was their first missionary journey, commissioned by the praying, fasting church in Antioch, they were not the first believers to preach the gospel there. Paul and Barnabas were in a line of continuity with all who had gone before, taking the gospel with them as they were hounded from place to place, fulfilling God's plan of extending the kingdom as they faithfully followed His guidance; being obedient to His will as it was revealed to them by His Holy Spirit.

However, these persecuted servants of God, travelling through Phoenicia, Cyprus and Antioch, after the death of Stephen, preached the word to Jews only, (Acts 11:19), until the time came when in the Greek city of Antioch they also began to speak to Greeks, preaching the Lord Jesus. (Acts 11:20). The margin of the RSV indicates that these could have been Hellenists, that is, Greek speaking Jews as in Acts 6:1, but the word *elleisas* may also refer to non-Jewish Greek speaking people. Whatever their ethnicity, the hand of the Lord was with them, and a great number believed and turned to the Lord. (Acts 11:21).

Just as the apostles in Jerusalem had wanted to participate in what God was doing in Samaria under Philip's ministry, and had sent to them Peter and John, (Acts 8:14), so now, as the news reached Jerusalem about what was happening in Antioch, the church sent Barnabas to encourage them. In Acts 4:36, Barnabas's name had been given as 'son of encouragement', 'son of consolation', and in Acts 11:24, Barnabas is described as a 'good man, full of the Holy Spirit and of faith'. He was also a man of Cyprus, a Cypriot Jew, the right choice of someone who had been active in the evangelization of Greek speaking people.

When Barnabas arrived in Antioch, he was amazed at what was happening. He attributed it to the grace of God, and it filled him with joy. The encouraging son of encouragement exhorted the new believers to remain faithful to the Lord with steadfast purpose, (Acts 11:23 RSV), determined that with purpose of heart they would cleave to the Lord, (Acts 11:23 AV), and as Paul prays later for the Ephesians, that they might be rooted and grounded in love, continuing to follow Jesus. (Ephesians 3:17). To Barnabas, it was evident that a work of the Holy Spirit was in operation, the confirmation of His work being that many more, 'a large company 'was added to the Lord. (Acts 11:24).

It was obvious that Barnabas needed a brother in the Lord to help with the large numbers of believers anxious to learn about Jesus. So he went to Tarsus to look for Saul, and when he had found him, he brought him to Antioch. This new work of grace needed to be based on the original gospel, the affirmation of the earthly life, the death and the resurrection of Jesus and His ascension into heaven. This was the objective of the Jerusalem church in sending Barnabas to Antioch and Barnabas' objective in sending for Saul, for had not Saul heard the voice of Jesus on the Damascus road?. Had he not been called to be an apostle even though he persecuted the church? (1 Corinthians 15:8-10).

In Tarsus, Barnabas found Saul and persuaded him to come to Antioch. From Acts 9:27, we know that Barnabas had helped Saul when the believers in Jerusalem had been afraid that Saul in his role as persecutor would hand them over to the religious authorities. Barnabas had taken him and had brought him to the apostles, and declared to them how on the road to Damascus, Saul had seen the Lord, who had spoken to him, and how he had preached boldly in the Name of Jesus. This preaching had led to the Hellenists wanting to kill him, so they sent Saul off to Tarsus. (Acts 9:30). To those who had tried to kill him he was now about to preach the gospel, the word of God.

Saul's bold preaching in the Name of Jesus was a good reason for Barnabas wanting to seek Saul out, but a better reason was that there was a special relationship between them. They were both men of God with the spiritual insight to know that God was expanding and enlarging the outworking of the gospel north and east, beyond Judea and Samaria, to Phoenicia, Cyprus and Antioch on the North African coast but more significantly, to the Jew first but also to the Greek. (Romans 1:16). The gospel was the power of God to salvation for everyone, for all those who had faith.

Though it was the church in Jerusalem which had delegated Barnabas to visit Antioch, from now on the initiative in the mission to the Gentiles passed to the church in Antioch. But Jerusalem still retained its link with the historical Jesus and the commandment which He had given to His apostles, to be witnesses to Him. (Acts 1:8), and *both were aspects of the church's life lived in fellowship with Him.*

The church in Jerusalem had had the advantage from the beginning of listening to the apostles teaching, and worshipping together. (Acts 2:24). Now they were concerned for those being daily added to the Lord who had not had this privilege. So for a whole year, Barnabas and Saul met with the church and taught a large company of people, a community gathered together in the Name of Jesus. (Acts 11:26). In His name they were not Jews, they were not Hellenists, they were not pagan or Gentile. They needed a new designation. They were called Christians.

Professor Marshall suggests that the verb 'were called' Christians indicates that Christians may have been a nickname given by the populace of Antioch, and was perhaps derisory, as was the term 'Methodists' given to the members of the Holy Club of John and Charles Wesley. The Christians themselves appeared to prefer other terminology such as disciples; (Acts 6:1), saints; (Acts 9:13), brothers or brethren; (Acts 9:30). believers. (Acts 10:45). But all these terms were adequately covered by the word 'Christian', Christ's people.

When KIng Agripps said to Paul, 'Almost thou persuadest me to be a Christian' (Acts 26:28 AV), there may have been a touch of ridicule in his voice. The only other New Testament reference besides the two in Acts, (Acts 11:26; 26:28) is 1 Peter 4:16, where Peter writes 'If one suffers as a Christian let him not be ashamed, but let him glorify God in that Name'. But the term became widely used throughout the known world. Tertullian in the second century (160-220 A.D.) is reported as having said, 'See how these Christians love one another!. And in the conflagration in Rome it was' the Christians' who were wrongfully accused and punished by Nero for arson (60-64 A.D. Barrett p 556).

We are indeed believers, saints, disciples and brethren, but what an honour to be named and recognized as belonging to Christ, to be Christ's people! In Antioch the disciples were for the first time called Christians. (Acts 11:26).

Acts 11:27-30. Famine relief for the brethren in Judea

Now in those days, prophets came down from Jerusalem to Antioch. And one of them, named Agabus stood up and foretold by the Spirit that there would be a great famine over all the world; and this took place in the days of Claudius. And the disciples determined, every one according to his ability to send relief to the brethren who lived in Judea; and they did so, sending it to the elders by the hand of Barnabas and Saul. (Acts 11:27-30).

During this period, when the church in Antioch was growing daily in its knowledge and experience of Christian living under the teaching of Barnabas and Saul, Antioch was visited by prophets who came down from Jerusalem to Antioch. Among them was a prophet named Agabus. (Acts 11:28).

The church at Antioch had reached the stage where having been founded by the original believers fleeing from persecution, (Acts 11:19), and having been received with much joy by the church in Jerusalem, (Acts 11:22), it had now become an entity, a community of believers, a church in its own right, helped by the year long ministry of Barnabas and Saul.

Claudius was now the emperor in Rome. (41-54 A.D), and Agabus was a prophet from Jerusalem. This is the first mention of a Christian prophet in Acts, though we later find them in Acts 13:1, combined with teachers (Acts 13:1), and in Acts 15:32, combined with exhorting the brethren with many words and strengthening them. There is another mention of Agabus in Acts 21:10, and also in Acts 21: 9 a reference to Philip's four daughters who prophesied; perhaps a fulfilment of Joel's prophecy in Acts 2:17. 'I will pour out My Spirit upon all flesh, and your sons and daughters shall prophesy'.

A manifestation of the coming of the Holy Spirit upon the believers in Ephesus was that they spoke with tongues and prophesied. (Acts 19:6). In the Pauline letters, it appears that prophets worked alongside the apostles as leaders in the church, (1 Corinthians 12:28), and that, in fact, the household of God is built upon the foundation of the apostles and prophets, (Ephesians 2:20; 4:11). The use of the term 'apostle' in this verse in Ephesians is an indication that these were foundational *Christian* prophets and not those of the Old Testament.

Agabus had come down to Antioch with the other prophets specifically to use the gift of prophecy which had been given to

Him by the Holy Spirit to edify the church. (Acts 11:27; 1 Corinthians 12:7). During one of the times when the church met together, Agabus stood up. (Acts 11:28). In a seated company, it was usual for prophets to rise in order to speak. The prophets had come to bring the inspired word of the Lord to this new church in Syria, for their building up, edification and encouragement. (1 Corinthians 14:3).

Prophecy did not always or inevitably foretell the future, but on this occasion Agabus arose to prophesy something which was going to happen in the time of the reign of Claudius. God seldom gives us an insight into what is to happen in the immediate future. That He had done so in this case was an indication that it was something for which preparation had to be made. As Agabus speaks by the Spirit, he foretells that there will be a great famine throughout the (Roman) world, which happened in the days of Claudius. As Claudius was emperor from 41-54 AD, this gives us the dates during which the famine in Judea was expected to take place, and there are references to economic hardship in the time of Claudius in many ancient writers, including Eusebius and Josephus. (Bruce 240).

The church in Antioch took the prophecy of Agabus seriously. They were concerned for the disciples living in Judea, which became indeed one of the worst hit regions of famine. 'They determined, every one according to his ability, to send relief to the brethren who lived in Judea, (Acts 11:29), and they did so, sending it to the elders by the hand of Barnbas and Saul'. (Acts 11:30).

Following the Day of Pentecost, the new believers in Jerusalem were together and had all things in common, distributing to all, as any had need. (Acts 2:45). The church in Antioch had a different foundation, including many believers who had left everything when they were persecuted and fled to Syria and the Mediterranean coast. It is quite probable that although Antioch was a comparatively wealthy city, the prosperity of Antioch did not always filter down to newcomers, especially newcomers whom they considered to be practising a new and strange religion.

Nevertheless, the members of the church in Antioch were determined to give as much as was within their means, according to everyone's ability. There is no right or wrong way to share what we have with others. God may well have looked on the sacrificial giving of these believers, on their loving generous hearts, with infinite pleasure, for Jesus had said, 'For as much as you have done it to the least of My brethren, you have done it to Me'. (Matthew 25:40).

Impressed with the urgency of the approaching famine, the church in Antioch sent their gifts to the church in Jerusalem by the hand of Barnabas and Saul, commissioning them to take it to the elders. These elders, *presbyteros* could be identified as those in charge of poor relief and the social care of the believers as had the Seven of Acts 6, and here known as elders, The apostles are not mentioned because their ministry was the ministry of the word (Acts 6:2) rather than 'the ministry of tables', for caring for the weak and vulnerable members of the church such as widows and orphans had become the ministry of *diakonos*, deacons, or *presbyteros*, elders.

The government of the church is gradually emerging, for both are needed. Both are needed to be men of good report, full of the Holy Spirit and of wisdom, both contributing to the needs of the saints, loving one another with brotherly affection, (Romans 12:10,13).

Barnabas and Saul were entrusted with the gift of the church in Antioch to the church in Jerusalem, but having delivered the gift, they returned once more to Antioch when they had fulfilled their mission, bringing with them John whose surname was Mark. (Acts 12:25).

Acts Chapter 12

Acts 12:1-2. The death of James

About that time, Herod the king laid violent hands upon some who belonged to the church. He killed James the brother of John with the sword; and when he saw that it pleased the Jews, he proceeded to arrest Peter also. This was during the days of Unleavened Bread. (Acts 12:1-3)

There was a more immediate problem than famine for the church in Jerusalem, and his name was Herod Agrippa 1. A little unsure of his authority and wary of displeasing the Jewish leaders, preferring to accommodate them as much as possible, Herod laid violent hands upon some who belonged to the church

Members of the church must have wondered whether persecution would ever cease, whether they would ever be allowed to follow the Lord Jesus without suffering and hardship. And yet He had never promised that to follow Him would be easy. They would need to take up their cross of suffering and pain to follow Him; the cross which was a stumbling block to those around them, the cross of repudiation and criticism from those without understanding, but for them a total experience of the peace and joy of their salvation through the cross.

But now this terrible thing had happened. Herod had killed one of the apostles, with the sword, which usually meant decapitation. James had been one one of those who had been the first to respond to the call of Jesus to follow Him, one of the original Twelve. He was the brother of the apostle John. Dear James, who with Peter and John had been part of the 'inner circle' of the Lord's disciples, who was one of the sons of Zebedee, who had walked beside Jesus for three years and who had been there with Him at Gethsemane and Golgotha. Even though suffering and death were part of the experience of the early church, this was still a terrible blow, that one of its revered and trusted leaders should have been executed.

It was indeed the case that many believers had suffered for the Name of Jesus, but could God not have intervened in the case of James? Which of course He did in the case of Peter when Peter was released from prison.

Luke, writing in Acts, gives us no explanation of these phenomena, but we know and believe that everything turns upon God's compassionate purpose for each of His children. We have the words in the prophecy of Isaiah which tell us that God's thoughts are not our thoughts, nor His ways our ways. (Isaiah 55:8,9.). And He has given us His Holy Spirit to help us to understand. (1 Corinthians 2:12, 13). And though we may still not be totally aware of why our circumstances are as they are, we may remember His promise that 'when you pass through the waters, I will be with you; and through the rivers, they shall not overwhelm you. When you walk through the fire you shall not be burned and the flame shall not consume you, for I am the Lord your God, your Saviour'. (Isaiah 43:2,3.).

It is enough to know that He is with us; in the floods; in the fire.

Though opposition from the authorities whether Jewish or Roman had seemed from the beginning to be directed against believers, the martyrdom of James represented an attempt by the authorities at escalation; a determination to start with the leaders to exterminate altogether what they regarded as a rebel and rabble sect. They believed that this growing movement, growing numerically and therefore potentially powerfully, was becoming a real threat to national security, and was seen by Herod as threatening to his regime, as evidenced by James' execution.

Herod was the son of Aristobulus and the grandson of Herod the Great. He was not a Jew, but an Idumean. Idumea ws formerly known as Edom. It was probably because of the history of conflict between the Jews and the Idumeans or Edomites that Herod took great pains to cultivate the good opinion of the Jews as necessary to his power base. The prophecy of Obadiah focuses on the judgement of Edom.

Though Herod was an outsider and not a Jew, he nevertheless observed their customs and traditions so that the Pharisees were impressed by him. And when he saw that it pleased the Jews, that he had killed James, he proceeded to arrest Peter also. (Acts 12:3).

Acts 12:3-17. Peter's imprisonment and deliverance from prison

When Herod saw that it pleased the Jews, he proceeded to arrest Peter also. This was during the days of Unleavened Bread. And when he had seized him, he put him in prison and delivered him to four squads of soldiers to guard him, intending after Passover to bring him out to the people. So Peter was kept in prison; but earnest prayer for him was made to God by the church.

James had safely been disposed of, but what about the other leaders of the church, thought Herod? It had pleased the Jews when he got rid of James so he proceeded to arrest Peter also. To smite the shepherd and scatter the sheep had always been a good political ploy. (Matthew 26:31; Zechariah 13:7).

However, for the Jews it was now the feast of Unleavened Bread, that sacred time when the Jews remembered their deliverance from slavery at the hands of the Egyptians; how God had judged Pharoah because he would not let God's people go ino the wilderness to worship Him. And how on the night of the Passover the angel of death had 'passed over 'all the houses of the Hebrews because they had taken the blood of a lamb and put it on the lintels and doorposts of their houses, while on the houses of the Egyptians their was no lamb's blood, so all their firstborn died, according to the word of the Lord who said 'when I see the blood i will pass over you'. (Exodus 12:13). It may be that some of the Egyptians too, preserved the lives of their first born by putting blood on their doors according to the word of the Lord, and had become part of the mixed multitude which left Egypt, trusting in the God of the Israelites. (Exodus 12:38).

The Day of Passover was followed by the days of Unleavened Bread, for the children of Israel left the land of Egypt urgently and in haste, taking their dough with them before it was leavened. (Exodus 12:33). For forty years they journeyed through the wilderness to the land of Canaan, a land flowing with milk and honey, And God commanded that they keep this act of remembrance at its appointed time, from year to year. (Exodus 13:10).

Though there is no doubt that Herod intended for Peter the same fate which had befallen James, unfortunately for Herod, the Day of Passover got in the way. He had intended to bring Peter out before the people, either for some kind of show trial or public execution, but Passover intervened, the time when Jewish law permitted neither trial of prisoners nor the punishment of death. Herod had no alternative but to put him in prison, 'intending after Passover to bring him out to the people'. (Acts 12:4). 'And when he had seized him, he put him in prison, and delivered him to four quaternions of soldiers to guard him', (Acts 12:4), four groups of four soldiers. The four detachments of four soldiers were probably deployed on a watch to watch basis, changing the guard on Peter every four hours.

There could be no question that during the night watch the guards had fallen asleep, for was not Peter quite safe, bound with two chains and with sentries standing before the door of the prison? (Acts 12:6). Herod had spared no effort in securing the prisoner in his condemned cell, but had the guards been awake they would surely have prevented Peter's escape. We may assume that the angel who came to release Peter from prison had also caused a deep sleep to fall upon them, though the text does not tell us that.

Meanwhile, Herod was waiting impatiently for the days of Unleavened Bread to be over so that on that very night he could bring Peter out for public ridicule and humiliation. (Acts 12:6). But Herod had not reckoned with the power of a united church at prayer. Earnest prayer for him was made to God by the church, (Acts 12:5), and even as they were praying, the miracle was taking place. Uncomfortable though it may have been to sleep while being handcuffed to two soldiers, Peter was asleep and at peace. Full of concern though the church was, in earnestly praying for Peter's deliverance, they yet remembered the prayer of Jesus in Gethsemane as He prayed to His Father, 'Not My will but Yours be done'. (Matthew 26:39).

Peter was at peace because he was also praying that God's will might be done, not as a kind of fatalism but from a place of contentment. He was content to rest in the knowledge that nothing could happen to him outside of his Father's will; that whatever His heavenly Father had for him was best; that God knew what He was doing and Peter had absolute trust that nothing could happen to him without his Lord's permission.

Nevertheless, he was surprised to see a light shining suddenly in his cell, and to be struck quite heavily on his side as he heard a voice and saw an angel who said, 'Get up quickly'. (Acts 12:7). He may have struggled a little to get up but as he did so, the chains fell off his hands. The angel told him to dress himself and put on his sandals and then seemed to be aware that he would need his cloak. So, wrapped up in his cloak, he left the cell and went out with the angel and followed him, though 'he did not know that what was done by the angel was real, but thought he saw a vision'. (Acts 12:9).

There were three gates to be encountered, each one with a guard, the third being an iron gate leading into the city which opened to them of its own accord so that Peter and the angel could pass through. (Acts 12:10). But after one street, the angel left him. Peter was suddenly fully aware of what had happened. He came to himself and said 'Now I am sure that the Lord has sent His angel and rescued me from the hand of Herod, and from all the expectation of the Jews', (Acts 12:11 AV), 'all that the Jews were expecting. (Acts 12:11 RSV)

Where should he now go? He knew that the church would often meet in the home of Mary the mother of John Mark, who was the cousin of Barnabas. (Colossians 4:10). Though he did not know that the church had gathered together specifically to pray for him, he made his way to Mary's house and to his surprise, although it was night time, they were still at prayer. When he had knocked on the door, and called his name, a little servant girl called Rhoda ran to open it, but hearing his voice and recognizing it as Peter's, she was so full of joy that she did not open the door but ran back to the pray-ers saying 'It is Peter! It is Peter! He is standing at the door!'.

But they did not believe her. They said to her, 'You are mad!' (Acts 12:15). Rhoda, you are not thinking straight, don't be a silly girl!. And yet, strangely they could actually hear someone knocking at the door. Peter had continued knocking, and at last they opened the door. They were amazed! (Acts 12:16). They had been praying in faith for his release, yet could not believe that their prayer had been answered.

Rhoda's joy and their own incredulity are all absorbed into thankfulness at seeing Peter before them. We can imagine how they crowded around him for an explanation. Motioning with his hand for them to be silent, he described to them how the Lord had brought him out of prison. (Acts 12:7), and he requested that this news be passed on to the other James, James the Lord's brother, and to the brethren. It appears that from that time, James was recognised as the leader of the church in Jerusalem.

Peter now left them. With what sorrow they must have seen him go, but what a danger to them if he remained. He did not tell them where he was going. 'He departed and went to another place. (Acts 12:17). But we do know that he was in Antioch in Glatians 2:11, and in Jerusalem for the meeting of the Jerusalem Council, (Acts 15:7), by which time of course, Herod had died.

Acts 12:18,19. The execution of the soldiers

'Now when day came, there was no small stir among the soldiers over what had become of Peter. And when Herod had sought for him and could not find him, he examined the sentries and ordered that they should be put to death. Then he went down from Judea to Caesarea and remained there. (Acts 12:18,19).

When morning came, there was no small commotion among the soldiers as to what had become of Peter. Encouraged by Herod, they searched high and low, but could not find him. It appears that Herod was no less diligent in seeking him. He called the soldiers to him and interrogated them mercilessly. Why had they let Peter escape? Had they helped him to escape? Did they realize how dangerous he was to Herod's kingdom with his heretical views, undermining the political structure which Herod had so carefully built up under the Roman occupation? *Where was he?*

The soldiers had no answer to any of these questions, though they were fully aware of the consequences of allowing a prisoner to escape. Under their law, a guard who allowed this to happen was considered to be in collusion with the prisoner. He was therefore liable to the same penalty which would have awaited the prisoner.

Herod ordered that all the soldiers who had guarded Peter be put to death, proving that that had been his ultimate intention, and any kind of trial would indeed have been a show trial. In Herod's eyes, no trial was really necessary. Peter had already been condemned to death. Angry and humiliated, Herod left Jerusalem and went down to Caesarea. Caesarea was thoroughly Gentile. For a while, Herod wanted nothing to do with the Jews. (Acts 12:19).

Acts 12:20-23. The death of Herod Agrippa

Now Herod was angry with the people of Tyre and Sidon; and they came to him in a body, and having persuaded Blastus, the king's chamberlain, they asked for peace, because their country depended on the kIng's country for food. (Acts 12:20).

Herod now had something else to make him angry, furious, exasperated. (Bruce, p249). He was angry with the people of Tyre and Sidon, though why he was angry was unknown. However, there is a sense of desperation in the account.

Whatever had made Herod angry, it was important to the coastal inhabitants of Tyre and Sidon to have good relations with their hinterland, especially Galilee, for Galilee provided its food supply. They were free cities under Rome, but were economically dependent on territory which had been granted to Herod by the emperor Claudius.

In negotiating peace terms with Herod, the people of Tyre and Sidon obtained the good offices of Blastus, who was over the king's bedchamber, a position of great importance, enabling him to be familiar with the king's most personal and private affairs. This otherwise unknown person, for Blastus was a common name, was thought to be a good intermediary because of his close proximity to the king. Perhaps Blastus could help them to a more reasonable encounter with Herod.

The day arrived when they had permission to petition the king for his understanding of their plight. It may well have been that many of these people and their families were going hungry, if not actually starving. The situation was serious and could become worse. It also happened to be a day of festival. Bruce suggests that it could have been a day in honour of the emperor, perhaps the anniversary of his birth. It was always a judicious move to make it known that the emperor was beloved of his people. This was a propitious day for reconciliation. (Bruce p 259).

'On an appointed day, Herod put on his royal robes, took his seat upon the throne and made an oration to them', (Acts 12:21). Dazzling in his splendid robes, the people did not see Herod's heart of pride and vanity beneath, though they must have been aware of his tyranny over them. But what they did not see, God did. As they cried out 'the voice of a god and not of a man!', an angel of the Lord smote him, because he did not give God the glory, and he was eaten by worms and died. (A.D 44).

If Herod had rebuked them, remonstrated with them, repudiated their ascription of him; if he had shown any kind of humility at all, the outcome may have been different. As it was, he was suddenly aware of acute abdominal pain, which Luke attributes to being eaten by worms, and was carried out of the throne room and later died.

Tapeworms and liver fluke were common causes of death in Asia and in Africa still are, especially where drinking water is polluted. But Acts makes it clear that Herod was judged because he had fallen into the habit of so many of the Roman emperors. Herod was aspiring to be like them in his own limited but ambitious way, for they were regarded by their people as gods.

God did not apparently strike down everyone who magnified themselves in this way. But here, in the case of Herod, God was dealing with a man who on the one hand was seeking the approbation of the Jews, and on the other hand, wanting to be acknowledged as the Roman emperors were, as god-like or even as a god.

Herod sought to align himself with the Jews, a monotheistic people, attempting to please them by his regard for their festivals, customs and traditions, in other words, making himself acceptable to their God, while also trying to take on the pomp and circumstance and crucially, the pantheism, which belonged to Rome. James would have said of him, 'a double minded man, unstable in all his ways', (James 1:8), taking glory to himself which did not belong to him and thereby placing himself in the position of God. This was blasphemy; sin of the most outrageous kind, and God had to judge it. He was eaten by worms, not incrementally or gradually as happens in the majority of those affected, but 'immediately' (Acts 12:23), and he died.

Acts 12:34. The gospel continues to grow

But the word of the Lord continued to grow and to be multiplied. Barnabas and Saul returned from Jerusalem having fulfilled their mission, taking with them John, whose surname was Mark. (Acts 12:24,25).

But the word of God grew and multiplied, increased and spread; the *logos,* the gospel growing in proportion to the persecution. Acts 6:7 and Acts 9:21 tell the same story. In Acts 12, James had died and Peter had temporarily left them, but God was still at work, redeeming men and women from the power of Satan to God, (Acts 26:18) and empowering them by the infilling of the Holy Spirit. The tyrants, adversaries, opponents of the word of

God were learning what Peter had also come to understand. 'Who was I that I could withstand God?' (Acts 11:17), our sovereign, omnipotent, compassionate, merciful God.

Barnabas and Saul had fulfilled their mission of taking gifts from the church in Antioch to the church in Jerusalem in the expectation and advance of the famine to come. Had they been in Jerusalem at the time of James' martyrdom or Peter's deliverance from prison?. All we know is that the project for famine relief had been successful; the Jerusalem church will now be in a position to help those suffering from hunger, perhaps starvation, and that we are again given a glimpse by Luke of what was happening in Antioch.

Acts Chapter 13

Acts 13:1-4. The first missionary journey. A.D 47.
The beginning of the Gentile mission

Now in the church at Antioch there were prophets and teachers, Barnabas, Simeon who was called Niger, Lucius of Cyrene, Manaen a member of the court of Herod the tetrarch and Saul. While they were worshipping the Lord and fasting, the Holy Spirit said' Set apart for Me Barnabas and Saul for the work to which I have called them'. Then after fasting and praying, they laid their hands on them and sent them off. (Acts 13:1-3).

Many of those persecuted for their faith travelled to distant places taking the gospel with them, but the church in Antioch was convinced that there were still many places where until now the gospel had not been preached, They were convinced of the necessity of sending experienced teachers of the word of God to those places, so they met together to pray and fast, and to ask the Holy Spirit to choose from among them those whom He would send.

There were many to choose from. Antioch is now an established church with prophets and teachers, (verse 1) including Barnabas, Simeon called Niger who may have been from Africa, Lucius of Cyrene in North Africa, Manaen who had been brought up in the court of Herod Antipas the son of Herod the Great who became the tetrarch, and Saul. These were the leaders of the church in Antioch, a church given to prayer and fasting whenever they wanted to know the mind of the Lord.

Happy and blessed as they were to be together as a church, rejoicing in the Lord and in the power of the Holy Spirit, they still had a concern for those who had never heard the gospel, had never had a personal encounter with the Lord Jesus Chriat.

The laying on of hands had been the means whereby the Levites had been ordained to their ministry in the tabernacle at the time of Moses (Numbers 8:10). It was a demonstration to the people of Israel that the tribe of Levi had been called by God to serve Him in the place of His dwelling with His people, the place where they met with God. By the laying on of hands, the Levites were recognised as those who were 'separated unto God', wholly given to Him. This may have been the precedent for the church to act in this way, for they realised how important was the work to which the Holy Spirit was calling these men, as He said to them, 'Separate unto Me Barnabas and Saul for the work to which I have called them. (Acts 13:2).

Then, after fasting and prayer, they laid their hands on them and sent them off. (Acts 13:3). Barnabas and Saul had already been doing the work of an apostle, a 'sent one'. Now their apostleship was confirmed, and the laying on of hands also confirmed their identification with the believers in Antioch. Though it was Barnabas and Saul who were being 'sent', the whole church was committed to standing with them in prayer and fellowship, participation in the gospel.

It is possible that they were the most gifted of the teachers in the church. The church was going to be deprived of them while they were on missionary service, but others would become equally outstanding teachers in their absence. Thankfully, the choice of who should be appointed to this ministry rested with the Holy Spirit as the church waited on Him. Barnabas and Saul had been chosen by Him. All that the church had to do was to be obedient to Him; to acknowledge what the Holy Spirit was doing amongst them.

The whole church fasted and prayed, and it was the whole church which sent them off to the work to which the Holy Spirit had called them. In Acts 14:26 we learn that they returned to Antioch and reported to the church all that God had done, and how He had opened a door of faith to the Gentiles. The obedience of the church in Antioch to the leading of the Holy Spirit was vindicated.

Being sent out by the Holy Spirit, they went.

Acts 13:4-12. Barnabas and Saul in Cyprus

So, being sent out by the Holy Spirit, they went down from Antioch to Seleucia, the port at the mouth of the river Orontes, and from there they sailed to Cyprus.

Cyprus is known in the Old Testament as Kittim. Cyprus refers to its extensive copper mines, for which it had been annexed by the Romans. Cyprus was well known to Barnabas; it was his homeland; and perhaps this was why they were sent by the Holy Spirit to Cyprus first. His knowledge of the geography of Cyprus would also prove invaluable.

Barnabas and Saul began their ministry at Salamis, at the eastern end of the island, where there were synagogues of the Jews, and where they proclaimed the word of God; having been invited to do so by the ruler of the synagogue as was the normal procedure. Though Paul describes himself as an apostle to the Gentiles in Galatians 2:7-9, he never ceases to be concerned for the salvation of the Jews and Galatians 2:7-9 does not mean that he would never preach to the Jews. (Barrett p 625), Peter too, though described as an apostle to the Jews in Galatians, did not believe his ministry was exclusively to the Jews but had been happy to share in what God was doing in Caesarea in the house of the Gentile Cornelius. Peter declares that God made choice among the Twelve that by his mouth, the Gentiles should hear the word of the gospel and believe. (Acts 12:2, 13:5).

Salamis was their starting point, but they did not stop there. They travelled through the whole island until they came to Paphos on the western side; and Luke Implies that they proclaimed the gospel throughout their journey.

Paphos was the administrative centre of the island. It had become a Roman senatorial province and was therefore entitled to be governed by a proconsul. At this time, the proconsul was Sergius Paulus, who had gathered around him an entourage of advisors, one of whom was called Bar-Jesus, a Semitic name which means son of Joshua or Jesus. He was also called Elymas. He was not an astrologer, for astrologers, Magi, came from the east, and as his name discloses, his origins were in Palestine, though his family may have migrated to Cyprus from Palestine.

Like Simon in Acts 8:9, he appeared to have some magical expertise, and was called a magician. (Acts 13:6). He also had an ability to prophesy, even though his prophecy was false, for he pretended to divine revelation which he did not have.

Sergius Paulus had heard of the apostles and their proclamation of the word of God and wanted to hear for himself. 'He summoned Barnabas and Saul and sought to hear the word of God'. (Acts 13:7).

Elymas perceived that he was in a difficult position. If Sergius Paulus was more than just intrigued by the message of the apostles, if he actually accepted it, then he would be like all those other people who had become believers. He would no longer be interested in what Elymas had to say. All his magician's tricks and wiles, all his so-called ability to prophesy would not prevent him from losing his employment, his status and position at the proconsul's right hand. What could he do but try to withstand Barnabas and Saul and seek to turn away the proconsul from becoming a believer, seek to pervert the truth?

'But Saul, who is also called Paul', (Acts 13:9), (the first time we read of the name by which Paul was always afterwards known), understood what Elymas was trying to do. This was an important moment. A man's eternal destiny was at stake.

It is a serious thing to put a stumbling block in the way of anyone who is seeking the truth, whether they are children, or humble ordinary people, or people in authority like Sergius Paulus; anything which would prevent them from coming to Jesus, to receiving Him into their lives, as Jesus Himself authoritatively said. (Matthew 18:5; Luke 17:1). Once a child, or a man or a woman has heard the gospel, there are two ways open to them. *Either* they can accept the teaching of the gospel, understand their condition before God as having sinned and come short of His glory, (Romans 3:23), and been assured that by repenting and believing in Him, on His redemptive power through the blood which He shed on the cross, they could enter into the kingdom of God and receive eternal life and become sons and daughters of their heavenly Father, and become part of His Family; *or* they could reject the gospel, recognising the cost of following Jesus.

This was the turning point in the life of Sergius Paulus. Would he respond to the message of the apostles, or to the words of Elymas who was seeking to turn him aside from the faith? (Acts 13:8)?

'But Saul, who is also called Paul, filled with the Holy Spirit, looked intently at him and said, 'You son, not of Joshua or Jesus but son of the devil; you enemy of all righteousness, full of deceit and villainy, will you not stop making crooked the straight paths of the Lord? And now, behold, the hand of the Lord is upon you and you shall be blind and unable to see the sun for a season'. (Acts 13:10,11).

Immediately, mist and darkness fell upon him, and he went about seeking people to lead him by the hand. *Then the proconsul believed when he saw what had occurred,* for he was astonished at the teaching of the Lord. (Acts 13:12).

Though Paul's diagnosis of Elymas's condition was accurate, it must have come as a great shock to Sergius Paulus. This was a man whom he had trusted. Was he really guilty of all those dreadful things of which Paul had accused him and enumerated? How did Paul know? Was it really the case that being filled with the Holy Spirit could give a mere man an insight into another's status before God? Yes, but only when such an insight was truly from God and was vitally necessary, as is evident from the conclusion of the narrative.

Paul had pronounced judgement on Elymas because he had sought to turn Sergius Paulus from the truth. This was why he had to endure the terrible experience of losing his sight, and having to find others to lead him by the hand. But this was not to be a permanent condition for Elymas. It was only to be for a short time, for a season. (Acts 13:11). Its chief purpose was to demonstrate and confirm to the proconsul that Paul and Barnabas were indeed messengers of the word of God; that these were genuine alternatives of life and death; life lived in the abundant life given by Jesus, or the death that is separation from Him, not knowing Him and having no hope in the future.

These were not acceptable alternatives to Elymas. Elymas was completely at odds with all that Barnabas and Paul had been saying. Sergius Paulus was convinced and convicted and he believed for he was astonished, not only at the judgement upon Elymas, but more especially at the teaching of the Lord. (Acts 13:12).

The episode of Sergius Paulus and Elymas somewhat overshadows the mission of Barnabas and Paul to Cyprus, but there are distinctive emphases and theological principles to be observed.

Sent out by the church of Antioch, Paul and Barnabas were in truth sent out by the Holy Spirit. (Acts 13:2). Their whole mission was under the control of the Holy Spirit, under His direct guidance.

Cyprus had a large Jewish population and it was prudent to begin their ministry to Cyprus in a synagogue, for this was a principle which the Holy Spirit was early seeking to inculcate in the apostles, teaching them this principle as His missionary strategy. A theological principle was emerging, *to the Jew first and also to the Greeks.* (Romans 1:16), for God did not cast off his people whom He foreknew. (Romans 11:2).

This principle Paul always hereafter follows. (Acts 13:4; 14:1; 17:1,10, 17; 18:4,19 and 19:8). This was not just a technique, but a conviction that the new covenant had its roots in the old; that what God had said in His word, which for them at that time was the Hebrew scriptures, was settled in heaven. (Psalm 119:89), His word. Forever settled. Forever firm and unchanging like God Himself. (Malachi 3:6). The old covenant was designed by Him to bring them near to Himself. (Deuteronomy 7:6-9). Through His new covenant in the death, resurrection and ascension of Jesus, God was doing a new thing, but paradoxically, it was not a new thing, it was the total fulfilment of the old, for it had always been His intention to have sons like His own dear Son, many sons brought to glory through His suffering, (Hebrews 2:10), a people for His own possession.

Now that the Spirit had come, it would have been easy to cast off the old as having no relevance; the old former ways of understanding the purposes of God as being no longer necessary to this new movement of God. Do these new Christans really need to read the law, the prophets, the Psalms? Did they need to know about the Levitical sacrifices? Or the experiences of patriarchs and prophets from a different era, from hundreds of years ago?

But Jesus had specifically stated and Luke records, that beginning with Moses and all the prophets, Jesus interpreted to the two disciples on the road to Emmaus, all the scriptures concerning Himself. (Luke 24:27), for they were all fulfilled in Him. (Luke 24:44). It was so important for them to realise this wonderful truth, and to know that the God of this new movement was also the God of the law and the prophets; the same unchanging God; that all the promises of God in the old are fulfilled in the new, and are still available to those who are walking with God. And that the Gentiles have been given a share in what was given to Israel by God and all fulfilled in Jesus. (Jewell pp 14,40. Marshall The theology of Acts. pp 45, 70-76).

Even though the synagogues represented the old order of things, they were (and still are) places where the scriptures of the Jewish people were loved and cherished. Paul says, 'to the Jew first and also to the Greek' for the Jews had been custodians of the precious truth, unknown in the ancient world, that God is One. (Deuteronomy 6:4). Other nations had multiple gods and goddesses. Isaiah said of Egypt, 'they carry about their wooden idols and keep on praying to a god that cannot save' (Isaiah 45:20).

Psalm 135:15-18. is scathing about any abilities these gods may have. It says, 'eyes they have but they see not, ears they have but they hear not, nor is there any breath in their mouths. And those who make them and trust them are like them'. They are utterly incapable of any relationship with their god. But how tempting for those without the knowledge of the One eternal, invisible and true God; who have no knowledge of Him; to make an external figure or figurine to which they could turn in any one of the exigencies of life. It is an innate desire of human beings to have something outside of themselves to worship.

The other important aspect of the mission to Paphos was that Sergius Paulus was a Gentile with no previous acquaintance with Judaism, unlike Cornelius. There may of course have been many 'ordinary' people without any religious connections who responded to the message of the gospel. Although Sergius Paulus was proconsul, he had responded to the gospel in the same way as they had, in penitence and faith.

But Sergius Paulus was a proconsul, a man of political power. To see the gospel spreading among the people was tremendous, but though Paul was aware that 'not many wise according to human standards, not many powerful, not many of noble birth were called (1 Corinthians 1:24), there were some. The gospel message was not just for the slaves and lower members of society, though how desperately they needed to know the joy of sins forgiven, the deep love of the Lord who had given His life so that they might have a purpose in their lives, to serve Him and love Him in return. But all who respond to that love, who come into that relationship with Him, whether rich or poor, slave or free, man or woman, may happily claim to be a follower of Jesus. And they did not need to become a Jew, or have access to the precious teaching and promises of the Hebrew scriptures in order to come to God.

It had been Paul's special privilege to speak the word of God to a Gentile without any prior knowledge of God and to see him turn to the Lord. From a believer's point of view the division in society between Jew and Gentile no longer existed. The gospel message was of salvation for all, Jews and Gentiles alike. All have sinned and fall short of the glory of God, but all may be justified, made righteous, by faith in Christ. (Romans 3:23-25). And all are brothers and sisters in Him, as they encourage one another and encourage others to put their trust in Him.

Now Paul and Barnabas set sail north, for Perga in Pamphylia.

Acts 13:13-50. Paul and Barnabas in Pisidian Antioch

Now Paul and his company set sail from Paphos and came to Perga in Pamphylia. And John left them and returned to Jerisalem, but they passed on from there and came to Antioch in Pisidia. And on the Sabbath day they went into the synagogue and sat down. After the reading of the law and the prophets, the rulers of the synagogue sent to them saying, 'Brethren, if you have any word of exhortation for the people, say it. So Paul stood up, saying........

These verses suggest that Paul has now become the leader of the company. Previously, Luke has used the expression 'Barnabas and Saul'. This new expression is an indication of Barnabas's willingness to take second place to Paul. It throws a light on what is to come in the future of Paul's Spirit- given ability to engage with the needs of both recent converts to the faith, and also more established believers as they struggle to find new ways of understanding the purposes of God. It also gives us a glimpse into the character of Barnabas, and his Spirit- filled humility; described as he is as a good man, full of the Holy Spirit and of faith in Acts 11:24.

Paul and his company came to Perga in Pamphylia. Bruce explains that they probably landed at the port of Attalia and travelled by land to Perga, a distance of twelve miles. Pamphylia was a district of Asia Minor south of the central region of Galatia, which was a Roman province. Perga was the regional capital. (Broce p 259).

From Perga they went to Pisidia, an area also within the province of Galatia and one of the regions into which Galatia was divided, to the city of Antioch of Pisidia, the civil and military centre of this Roman province, where many turned to the Lord as a result of the preaching of the gospel by Paul. Driven out of Antioch of Pisidia, they went to Iconium, where after preaching the gospel, they learned of an attempt to stone them, so they fled to Lystra and Derbe, cities of Lycaonia, also a district of Galatia.

Lystra, Derbe and Iconium were all places in Galatia. Lystra was a Roman colony inhabited by Roman army veterans since 26 B.C. and twenty five miles southwest of Iconium, the modern Konyo. Derbe was fifteen miles southeast of Lydda and these cities of central Asia Minor were revisited by Paul and Barnabas on their return to Antioch in Syria, from where 'they had been commended by the grace of God for the work which they had fulfilled' (Acts 14:26).

This brief geographical excursus on the first missionary journey of Paul and Barnabas enables us to understand the background to chapters 13:1-14:28, and the hardships they must have endured. The reference in the letter to the Galatians to the 'bodily ailment' which afflicted Paul as he preached to them, (Galatians 4:13), reminding them that such was their care of him that they would have plucked out their own eyes and given them to him, (Galatians 4:15), is an indication that the journey had taken its physical toll on him and possibly Barnabas too.

They had left Paphos and Sergius Paulus, and had now reached Perga in Pamphylia, (Acts13:13), and it was at this point that John Mark left them and returned to Jerusalem. Perhaps it was his care for his friends which prompted him to leave them, hoping that they might follow and find some respite from the rigours they had been facing. Or there may have been strong family reasons for returning to the home of Mary, his mother. (Acts 12:12). It may even have been that he was conscious that he had not received from the church in Antioch the commissioning from the Holy Spirit which He had given to Paiul and Barnabas, and was reluctant to continue to do that work without the seal of the Holy Spirit, for such work would be invalid. Or simply that his cousin Barnabas had invited him along (Colossians 4:10), and he now needed to go home.

Whatever the reason, Paul was disappointed that one who had shared the work with them in Pamphylia had later withdrawn, and this caused a temporary rift between Paul and Barnabas as to who should accompany them on their second missionary journey later (Acts 15:37-39). However, we read in Philemon 23 of Mark being a fellow worker with Paul and 'useful' to Paul while he was in prison in Rome, and also when he was at the point of 'being sacrificed, for the time of his departure had come', in 2 Timothy 4:11.

There was forgiveness and restoration for John Mark, another opportunity for him to be of service to God's precious servant, a special time of fellowship together at the end of Paul's life, which both Paul and Mark embraced wholeheartedly.

But Paul and his company had now reached Antioch of Pisidia. (Acts 13:14). As it had now become their custom to do, they went into the synagogue on the sabbath day and sat down.

Acts 13:15-47. Paul's sermon in Pisidian Antioch

The synagogue service would have consisted of the Shema, 'Hear O Israel, the Lord our God, the Lord is one', followed by a prayer from the leader or ruler of the synagogue; the reading of the law and the prophets on sabbath and feast days, and lastly an exposition by a person chosen by the ruler. In Luke 4:13, Jesus had been selected to speak in the synagogue in Nazareth, and had chosen to speak from the prophecy of Isaiah 61 concerning His Spirit anointed ministry, and the total fulfilment of that prophecy in Himself. Paul's sermon to the congregation in Pisidian Antioch had the same purpose: to show the congregation that Jesus was the fulfilment of all the scriptures.

After the reading of the law and the prophets, the ruler of the synagogue sent to Paul and Barnabas saying 'Brethren, if you have any word of exhortation for the people, say it'. (Acts 13:15). The ruler recognized that they were fellow Jews, perhaps even recognizing Paul's rabbinical status. (Phillipians 3:5). So Paul stood up and motioned with his hands to them, (Acts 13:16), requesting their silence and attention while they listened to the life transforming message he was about to give them; and began to speak.

Paul begins, 'Men of Israel', a term which does not exclude women but includes them as among the privileged people of God, counting himself among them, as indeed he was. (Philippians 3:5,6.) 'Men of Israel and you that fear God, listen'.

There may have been God-fearers among them like Cornelius, who were attracted to Jewish teaching and the Jewish way of life but had not become proselytes, committed enough to have been circumcised.

As Stephen had done in his defence of himself against the charge of blasphemy, so Paul begins by reminding them of their heritage. He begins, however, not as Stephen did with Abraham but with the exodus from Egypt. He says, 'the God of this people Israel chose our fathers and made the people great during their stay in Egypt; and with an uplifted arm, He led them out of it, (Acts 13:17), according to His promise to Moses, 'now you will see what I will do to Pharaoh. (Exodus 6:1).

Paul continues, 'for about forty years, He bore with them in the wilderness, (Acts 13:18, or an alternative reading, He cared for them in the wilderness (R.S.V. margin). Deuteronomy describes it as, 'In the wilderness you have seen how the Lord your God bore you, as a man bears his son'. (Deuteronomy 1:31), a description of God's overwhelming, overshadowing love for His people.

Paul continues to quote from Deuteronomy, 'And when He had destroyed seven nations in the land of Canaan, He gave them their land as an inheritance for about one hundred and fifty years'. (Deuteronomy 7:1). This was the inheritance which He had promised to Abraham in Genesis 12:7, and fulfilled through Joshua. (Joshua 16:1; 18:1). The land was subdued before them, for the Lord had confirmed His promise to Joshua, saying to him, 'Be strong and of a good courage for you shall cause this people to inherit the land which I swore to their fathers to give them'. (Joshua 1:6). This had been a period of about four hundred and fifty years. Bruce explains this period of time as referring to the beginning of the sojourn in Egypt through Joseph, and the entry into Canaan and the distribution of the land to the eleven tribes through Joshua; Ephraim and Manasseh counting as one tribe as the sons of Joseph, and Levi given no inheritance for they were given the special task of serving the Lord in the tabernacle. (Bruce p 264). This period of four hundred and fifty years ranged therefore from the time of Joseph, lasted through the time of the judges and concluded with the time of Samuel.

Samuel was regarded as the last of the judges, and also a prophet, (1 Samuel 3:20), the one through whom God appointed Israel's first king, Saul, the son of Kish of the tribe of Benjamin. This may have been a personal reference to himself, for Paul too was of the tribe of Benjamin, and had also previously been known as Saul. (Phippians 3:5). And he too, like Saul, had signally failed his God, until God, his God, had spoken to him on the road to Damascus with the tender voice of Jesus, leading him to penitence and faith.

King Saul was succeeded by David, a man after God's own heart who would do all His will. (Acts 13:22). As Paul continues his sermon, he describes David as having been 'raised up' by God to be their king. This may be a reference to David's humble origins as a shepherd boy. Psalm 78 records that God chose David His servant and took him from the sheepfold, from tending the ewes that were with young and brought him to be the shepherd of Jacob, and Israel His inheritance. 'With upright heart he tended them, and guided them with skillful hand'. (Psalm 78:70-72).

This history was well known to these 'men of Israel', so what was Paul trying to convey to them? 'Raised up', Paul's description of David' could imply a gradual recognition on David's part that God had been teaching him how to be a king over His people. Step by upward step, over much time and many experiences, David learned about trusting God, looking to Him for forgiveness when things went wrong and guidance from Him as to how he could best govern His people. He was the one chosen by God to lead His people, and this was the most satisfying life that anyone could have. This is expressed in so many of the psalms of David. God could in reality say of David, 'I have found David the son of Jesse, a man after My own heart who will do all My will'. (Acts 13:22).

This was God's testimony to David. That this accolade could be given to an ordinary human being was a tremendous testimony, but Paul is seeing in David a likeness to the Lord Jesus.

He too was a Man after God's own heart, but how differently He accomplished all His Father's will. From before time began His will was one with His heavenly Father. He came to a broken humanity, saying 'Lo, I come to do your will, O God' and by that will we have been sanctified. (Hebrews 10:7,10).

No wonder that Paul 'leaped over the centuries', (Barrett p 636), from David to Jesus. Paul is informing his hearers of what they may already have known, that of this man, David's posterity, God had brought a Saviour, Jesus, as He had promised.

Paul continues by explaining that God had sent a forerunner to Jesus in the form of John the Baptist, to prepare the way for Jesus. Was it possible that there were disciples of John in Pisidian Antioch, just as there were in Ephesus when Paul arrived there? and was that the reason for Paull's inclusion of John's emphasis on baptism and repentance?

Paul was sure of one thing, that John made no claim to be the Messiah and in fact repudiated any suggestion that he might be the One who should come. Paul quotes John as saying 'What do you suppose that I am? I am not He, no, but after me One is coming, the sandals of whose feet I am unworthy to untie'. (Acts 13:25).

Disciples of a rabbi were to be as slaves to him, as to a great teacher, and willing to do everything for him that a slave would do, but even then were not worthy to untie his sandals. John did not count himself worthy even to untie the sandals of Jesus, the One whom he knew to be so much greater than himself. John describes Him as the Lamb of God, who takes away the sin of the world, the sacrificial animal who is actually God Himself, sacrificing Himself not on an altar, but on a cross, once and for all, unlike the sacrifices made daily in the temple, sacrificing Himself 'to take away sin by the sacrifice of Himself'. (Hebrews 9:26).

John spoke truly when he said 'He who is coming after me is greater, mightier than I' (Matthew 3:11). John was indeed the forerunner of whom Malachi, Isaiah and Jesus Himself had spoken (Malachi 4:5; Isaiah 40:3; Matthew 11:14). Jesus had said of him, 'among those born of women, there had arisen no-one greater than John the Baptist'.

But these Jews gathered together in the synagogue in Antioch of Pisidia were also greatly privileged. They knew themselves to be the sons of the family of Abraham. (Acts 13:26). Paul knew himself to be of the family of Abraham, so he could call them 'Brethren'.

'Brethren', he says 'and also you that fear God'. He is unwilling to exclude men and women who had become known as God fearers, who had been so manifestly attracted to the worship of the One True God, 'to whom has been sent the message of this salvation'. (Acts 13:27).

For Paul, this message goes right back to the time of Abraham. Although he had not started there but with Moses in the wilderness, he saw in the covenant which God had made with Abraham the whole purpose of salvation history, God's desire for a people near to Him, (Deuteronomy 4:7), the descendents of Abraham whom He could bless and who would be a blessing to the whole inhabited earth, (Genesis 12:2).

God was not slack concerning His promise that in Abraham all the families of the earth would be blessed. He blessed all those who had the faith of faithful Abraham, the righteousness reckoned to them through faith; and these people in Pisidian Antioch are blessed with the blessing of Abraham if they are people of faith, complete and unquestioning faith in the God of Abraham. Galatians 3:7 says that it is the people of faith who are the sons of Abraham; not those who have his ethnicity but the faith of faithful Abraham.

But God had something more for them.

How privileged they are to be receiving this message of salvation, that Christ was the fulfilment of the purposes of God from as far back in human history as the time of Abraham. This message had been given to them as children of Abraham, and Paul as also a descendant of Abraham had called them 'Brothers', *adelphoi*. His tone is beseeching, inclusive, because he really wants them to understand the absolute, life-transforming message which he is bringing to them. And his theme is fulfilment, the fulfilment of all Old Testament history, all the Old Testament prophecy, in Jesus, in His life, trial and death at the hands of those in Jerusalem who with all their scriptural knowledge and expertise in the law, failed to see in Him all the promises of God fulfilled.

Paul says, 'those who live in Jerusalem and their rulers, because they did not recognize Him nor understand the utterances of the prophets which are read every sabbath, fulfilled them by condemning Him. Though they could charge Him with nothing worthy of death, yet they asked Pilate to have Him killed. And when they had fulfilled all that was written of Him, they took Him down from the Tree and laid Him in a tomb. But God raised Him from the dead and for many days He appeared to those who came up with Him from Galilee to Jerusalem, who are now witnesses to the people. (Acts 13:27-31).

This summary of the gospel Paul announces and emphasises to his listeners as good news. Paul says, `We bring you good news that what God promised to the fathers, this He has fulfilled to us their children by raising Jesus; as also it is written in the second psalm, 'You are My Son, today I have begotten You'; and Paul follows it up with a quotation from Isaiah where God says 'I will give you the sure mercies of David', Isaiah 55:3, and Psalm 16:10 'You will not give your Holy One to see corruption'.

With this corroboration from the Hebrew scriptures, Paul is asserting that the resurrected Jesus is truly the Son of God, that these verses of scripture refer to Him and are fulfilled in Him. David died, and his flesh did see corruption, but the body of Jesus never saw corruption. In fact God could not allow His Holy One to see corruption. He is the only one who has ever risen from the dead to die no more. Only in Jesus could these scriptures be fulfilled; they could never be fulfilled in a human being, even one like David, who, Paul says, served the counsel of God in his generation and then fell asleep and was laid with his fathers and saw corruption. But He whom God raised up saw no corruption. (Acts 13:37).

If then Paul concludes, Jesus is the risen and exalted Son of God, He has the right, and the only one who has the right, to forgive sins. And forgiveness of sins is what is proclaimed to these Jews in Pisidian Antioch, followed by complete freedom from which they could not be freed by the law of Moses. (Acts 13:39).

Paul could later write to the churches of the Galatians, 'For freedom Christ has set you free!' (Galatians 5:1). Paul is preaching justification by faith, being made righteous by faith in Christ. Precious though the Abrahamic covenant was, God was providing them with a new covenant, of which the mediator is Jesus who through the Eternal Spirit offered Himself without blemish to God, (Hebrews 9:14,15). Paul says 'By Him, everyone that believes is freed from everything from which you could not be freed by the law of Moses'. (Acts 13:39). Jesus is redeeming them from transgressions under the old covenant so that they might receive the promised eternal inheritance, not a promised land but a promised Person, as Jesus Himself prayed to His Father, 'I in them and You in Me, that they may be one, even as We are one', the last recorded prayer of Jesus before He went to the cross. (John 17:22,23).

Paul is making his Galatian hearers in Pisidian Antioch aware of the choice they have to make. He quotes again from their Old Testament scriptures, this time from Habakkuk. If they disagree with him, they cannot go against the word of God. Habakkuk carefully warns the people of his day not to scoff or mock at what God is doing. 'Behold you scoffers and wonder and perish, for I do a deed in your day, a deed you will not believe if one declares it to you'. (Habakkuk 1:5).

Acts 13:42-52. Paul and Barnabas leave the synagogue

As Paul and Barnabs were going out, the people kept begging them that these things might be spoken to them the next sabbath. And when the meeting of the synagogue broke up, many Jews and devout converts to Judaism followed Paul and Barnabas, who spoke to them, and urged them to continue in the grace of God. (Acts 13:42).

Having given this last warning, Paul and Barnabas went out of the synagogue, and as they went, the people begged that these things might be told them on the next sabbath. (Acts 13:42). They had heard the word of the gospel. They had also received a warning to beware of not appreciating Paul's message for what it truly was, a matter of life or death. For having heard it they now had to make their decision, their choice, to believe it or reject it.

Perhaps they felt they needed a little time to think it over, to consider carefully what Paul had said and its implications for their lives. Paul had been emphatic. God was doing a new thing in their days. They were being given the opportunity of believing God, of being prepared to have some share in what He was doing, or let it all go by them, to continue with their own customs and traditions. Many Jews and devout converts to Judaism followed Paul and Barnabas as they left the synagogue, and Paul and Barnabas encouraged them, urging them to continue in the grace of God. (Acts 132:43).

On the next sabbath, almost all the whole city gathered together to hear the word of God. There was great anticipation. The people were roused by what had happened the previous sabbath, and anxious to know what further truth Paul would share with them. (Acts 13:44).

But as always, there were those who were not pleased by what was happening, probably seeing it as a threat to their own position and influence. When they saw the multitudes gathered together to hear the word of God, they were filled with jealousy and contradicted what was spoken by Paul and reviled him. (Acts 13:45).

There was only one possible outcome. Paul and Barnabas spoke out boldly and said, 'it was necessary that the word of God should be spoken first to you, as Jews, as God's covenant people. But since you thrust it from you and you have rejected it, you have judged yourselves unworthy of eternal life and therefore we must turn to the Gentiles. God has called us to be a light to the Gentiles, to bring salvation to them, as it says in Isaiah 49:6, and to the Gentiles we must now go.

When the Gentiles heard this, they were glad and glorified the word of God. They were grateful and rejoiced, glad to hear the words of Paul, and 'as many as were ordained to eternal life believed'. (Acts 13:48). This is not a word of predestination. They believed, and by doing so, it was correctly assumed that by doing so, they were ordained to, and received eternal life. If they had not believed, if they had rejected the salvation offered to them through Jesus they would also have rejected the gift of eternal life, for eternal life is given to those who believe.

The word of the Lord was not bound; it was being spread throughout the whole region. (Acts 13:49). But together with the spreading of the gospel came almost inevitably the persecution which followed. The Jews incited the devout women of high standing and the leading men of the city and stirred up the persecution, and drove them out of their district. (Acts 13:50). Sadly, they involved some of the leading families in the city.

So Paul and Barnabas shook off the dust from their feet against them, as Jesus had recommended in Matthew 10:14, and went to Iconium in the Roman province of Galatia, known today as Konya.

Paul's first reported sermon in Pisidian Antioch had bridged the gap between the early 'primitive' chapters of Acts and the mature doctrine of the letters later written by Paul, according to Bruce, p272. The mission to Pisidian Antioch had strengthened the theological principle that the gospel was preached first to the Jews and then to the Gentiles. (Romans 1:16). To the Jews would have been given the privilege of evangelizing the world, bringing the good news of the gospel to the Gentiles, if they had believed the gospel. For the gospel of the kingdom, the gift of resurrection life in the heart of the believer was available to all, whether Jews or Gentiles, and those who came to know Christ as Saviour from their sin could experience the joy of the age to come in anticipation, as well as in their day to day living.

Christ had come into the world as a light for the Gentiles. (Acts 13:47), and His intention was that His covenant people should be that light to the Gentiles. But this privilege the Jews of Pisidian Antioch had rejected. Of course they were not alone in this. Though the Pisidian Jews had not been the means, having heard the gospel, of bringing that gospel to the Gentiles in Galatia so that they could receive the grace of God, God had not left Himself without witness. He had appointed many of His servants, including His servants Paul and Barnabas, to be that light, as together with the disciples they were filled with joy and with the Holy Spirit, (Acts 13:52), for many who were ordained to eternal life believed. (Acts 132:48).

In writing to Timothy, Paul recalled this persecution, his sufferings which had befallen him at Antioch, Iconium and Lystra. (2 Timothy 3:11). Yet his abiding impression of that particular missionary journey was that from the persecution, the Lord delivered him, together with the joy which he and Barnabas shared as they were filled with the Holy Spirit and continued to rely on His presence with them, and His guidance as they continued to Iconium. (Acts 13:52).

Acts Chapter 14

Acts 14:1-7. Paul and Barnabas at Iconium

Now at Iconium, they entered together into the Jewish synagogue and so spoke that a great company believed, both of Jews and Greeks. But the unbelieving Jews stirred up the Gentiles, and poisoned their minds against the brethren. So they remained for a long time, speaking boldly for the Lord who bore witness to the word of His grace, granting signs and wonders to be done by their hands.

The partnership of Paul and Barnabas continued as they entered the synagogue, for this was a scriptural principle that at the mouths of two or three witnesses every word should be established. (Deuteronomy 17:6; 19:5; Matthew 18:16; 2 Corinthians 13:1; 1 Timothy 5:19; Hebrews 10:28). Entering into the synagogue, they were again given the opportunity to speak to those gathered together, so that a great company believed, both of Jews and Greeks. As it is improbable that the synagogue was normally a meeting place for Greeks, it appears that what Paul and Barnabas said may have overflowed to those who were listening on the perimeter, or even outside the building.

But here again a pattern emerged of what had become an important theological principle, 'to the Jew first and also to the Greek' had the gospel been given. (Romans 1:16). It also seemed to be the case that whenever the gospel was preached there was an adverse reaction on the part of both Jews and Greeks. The unbelieving Jews stirred up the Greeks and poisoned their minds against the brethren (Acts 14:2).

John the Baptist made it quite clear that there is an equivalence between unbelief and disobedience, and between faith and obedience. Speaking of Jesus as the Son of God to some Jews who came to him, John said,' He who believes in the Son has eternal life. He who does not obey the Son shall not see life, but the wrath of God rests on him'. (John 3:36).

Unbelief and disobedience are both involved in the rejection of the gospel. At Iconium, there were many both Jews and Greeks who believed, but there were also unbelieving Jews, disobedient to the gospel, who poisoned the Gentiles against the brethren, literally, made the minds of the Gentiles evil against the brethren (Bruce p 277). The sense of evil is strong and God's anointed messengers are the object of maleficence against them.

We might have expected that in the face of such evil opposition, in which even the rulers of the city took part, (Acts 14:5), Paul and Barnabas would have left the city. But they had no liberty in their spirits to do so. God had not given them permission to go, so they stayed, remaining there for a long time, speaking boldly for the Lord who bore witness to His grace, granting signs and wonders to be done by their hands. (Acts 14:3).

God obviously had more for them to do and as always, His witness to their proclamation of the gospel had practical and physical outcomes as well as spiritual. Signs and wonders were evidence of divine power at work through His servants right from the beginning, when the Holy Spirit had been outpoured at Pentecost.; (Acts 2:22); evidence of the breaking into this world of the other world where God reigns, 'the powers of the age to come'. (Hebrews 6:5). This was a powerful witness by God to the word of His grace.

Nevertheless, the people of the city were divided. (Acts 14:4) There were those who were neither obedient to the gospel nor persuaded by the signs and wonders which God wrought by the hands of Paul and Barnabas. Those Jews and Greeks who did believe were united, but those who did not believe were divided, some siding with the Jews and some with '*the apostles*'. (Acts 14:4).

Acts 14:4. Paul's apostleship

This is the first use of the term 'apostle' in Acts for anyone other than the twelve disciples who were called apostles, sent ones, by Jesus, (Matthew 10:2), and it deserves some consideration.

Paul and Barnabas had been called, 'the brethren' in verse 2, *adelphoi,* and so far throughout these chapters of Acts, the term brethren had also been used as a way of referring to believers. (Acts 6:3; 11:1). To refer to Paul and Barnabas as apostles, 'sent ones' is an acknowledgement of their total reliance on the Holy Spirit, the Sending One, who knew precisely where and at what time to send them. He was the One who had sent them out, separated them out from the church at Antioch in Syria for the work to which He had called them. (Acts 13:2). To be an apostle was not an ecclesiastical title, like elder, but a description of what the Holy Spirit was doing in the lives of these men, a description which distinguished them from other roles in the church, like prophets and teachers, (Acts 13:1) although of course they could fulfil those roles too.

To be an apostle was to be sent out by God, just as the Lord Jesus had sent out His disciples as apostles 'to the lost sheep of the house of Israel'. (Matthew 10:2,5). To Paul this was a very precious gift, that he who had once persecuted the church, was now called to be an apostle to the Gentiles. (1 Corinthians 15:9; Romans 16:7; I Thessalonians 2:6).

In Galatians 1:1, Paul described himself as an apostle, not someone highly important, like the elders of the church in Jerusalem, (Acts 15:4,6) and those who were commissioned as apostles before him, but simply as one who had been chosen by God,'an apostle not from man, nor through men, but through Jesus Christ and God the Father who raised Him from the dead;. (Galatians 1:1)

Iconium, Derbe and Lystra were all part of the province of Galatia, and Paul's letter to the Glatians was written to those believers whom he had ministered to on his first missionary journey, (Acts 13:4-14:28); second missionary journey (Acts 16:6), and third. (Acts 18:23). The time spent in Galatia during this first missionary journey was a significant time for Paul, for Paul knew himself to be an apostle to the Galatians. (Galatians 1:1) and as such had much to write to them as they wrestled with the concept of obedience to the law from which they had been delivered by their faith in Christ.

Paul had of course also been chosen to be an apostle to the Romans, 'set apart for the gospel of God which He promised beforehand through the prophets in the holy scriptures'. (Romans 1:12). To the church in Corinth, he had also been called by the will of God to be an apostle of Christ Jesus, (1 Corinthians 1:1 and similarly in 2 Corinthians 1:1, Ephesians 1:1; Colossians 1:1 and 1 Timothy 1:1, where Paul writes of being an apostle of Christ Jesus 'by command of God our Saviour and of Christ Jesus our hope'. In Titus also, Paul writes of being a servant of God and an apostle of Jesus Christ, as though these self referential tiles amounted to the same thing; that to be an apostle was to be a servant, or more accurately, a bond slave of God and of the Lord Jesus Christ, a bond slave whose whole life is concerned only with doing the will of another.

There were men in the church at Corinth who prided themselves on being apostles; false apostles, Paul called them, deceitful workmen, disguising themselves as apostles of Christ. (2 Corinthians 11:13). He even calls them superlative apostles, for this was what they claimed to be, (2 Corinthians 12:11).

This is an indication that although Paul himself was, and remained, a humble follower of Jesus, apostleship had already taken on a more authoritative role in church leadership in the church at Corinth, and possibly in other churches too. Far from being separated out from the church for work to which the Holy Spirit had called them as Paul and Barnabas had been, (Acts 13:2), these superlative apostles take advantage of the believers, even putting on airs and striking them in the face! How different from the first apostles to whom Jesus said, 'If anyone strikes you on the right cheek, turn to him the other cheek also, and if anyone would sue you and take your coat, let him have your cloak also, (Matthew 5:39,40). Freely you have received, freely give. (Matthew 10:8 AV)

Paul's apostleship was of a very different character from theirs. It was not a claim to being someone special in the church, but simply an acknowledgement that the hand of God was on his life, the Holy Spirit bearing witness to both Paul and Barnabas during this time in Iconium, confirming the word with signs following which to Paul were the signs of a true apostle. (Mark 16:20; Acts 5:12). There is a suggestion in 2 Corinthians 8:23 that there was even a group of those who were not of the Twelve but yet were apostles,'messengers', literally 'apostles', (Greek) of the churches. Epaphroditus is also described in this way in Philippians 2:25, and possibly Junius and Andronicus in Romans 16:7.

Is Paul's estimation of apostleship important?

Paul was only too aware of his previous persecution of the church to claim any kind of position within it for himself. All he could do was thank God that His grace toward him had not been in vain. (2 Corinthians 6:1). He clearly states his conviction that he is the least of the apostles, not fit to be called an apostle because he persecuted the church of God (1 Corinthians 15:9).

To claim that being an apostle gave him position in the church would have been anathema to Paul, but subsequently, both in Paul's lifetime and as the church moved on into the second century, apostleship became a designation of authority. Unlike Paul's humble estimation of himself as primarily a servant of God, apostleship had become a title, indicative of a special kind of Christian, which Paul would have repudiated if applied to himself.

It appears that human beings are prone to put people on pedestals not designed for them.

This assessment of Paul's apostleship is by no means to disparage Paul's ministry. Where would the church be without the inspired letters he wrote? But to recognize that there is a tendency, perhaps even sometimes in the church, to value some people above others. This is the only place in Acts where Paul and Barnabas are called apostles, perhaps because of the subsequent use of the concept of *apostoloi*, sent out ones, first by the Lord Jesus as we have seen in Matthew 10:2,5 and then by the Holy Spirit in Acts 13:2. to describe part of the leadership of the church, leaders whose claim to apostleship provided them with authority. Luke is very careful over his use of terminology.

Acts 14: 5-20. Persecution in Iconium, Lystra and Derbe

There is a pattern emerging in Acts. After the preaching of the word, the proclamation of the gospel, comes opposition from those who would not, or could not accept it. This was the case in Acts 4:2, after Peter and John had been instrumental in the healing of the lame man at the beautiful gate of the temple; in Acts 5:12, after many signs and wonders were done among the people by the hands of the apostles; in Acts 6:12 and 7:54 after the death of Stephen; in Acts 9:1 by Saul who later became Paul; in Acts 11:19, the persecution which arose over Stephen; in Acts 12 1-28, the death of James and the imprisonment of Peter; in Acts 13:45 against Paul and Barnabas in Antioch of Pisidia, and now here in Iconium, Acts 14:5.

Paul and Barnabas had remained for some time in Iconium, (Acts 14:3), speaking boldly for the Lord, but now an attempt was made to molest them and stone them. (Acts 14:5). This was not the legal stoning, the punishment for idolatry according to the law of Moses, (Deuteronomy 17:5) but lynching, mob violence, a crowd both of Jews and Greeks who also enlisted the help or connivance of their rulers (Acts 14:5). Luke here uses the word 'to injure, to insult', translated here as 'molest and then the word 'to stone'.

It is possible that some of the opposition was intended only to hurt them but not to kill them. But when Paul and Barnabas heard of it, they fled. They made haste to leave Iconium and take refuge in Lystra and Derbe, cities of Lycaonia, which together with Phrygia and Pamphlia were regions of the province of Galatia. According to Acts 16:1, Lystra was also the home of Timothy. He may have met Paul at this time.

Having fled to Lystra, Paul and Barnabas did not confine themselves to the cities of Lystra and Derbe, but also to the surrounding countryside (Acts 14:6) where in spite of a plot to kill them they continued to preach the gospel.

Acts 14:8-18. Paul and Barnabas at Lystra

Now at Lystra, there was a man sitting who could not use his feet; he was a cripple from birth who had never walked. He listened to Paul speaking; and Paul looking intently at him and seeing that he had faith to be made whole, said in a loud voice, 'Stand upright upon your feet.' And he sprang up and walked. (Acts 14:8-10)

Returning to Lystra, Paul and Barnabas were immediately confronted by this poor lame man. Unlike their previous pattern of evangelism when entering a new city with the gospel, Paul and Barnabas did not on this occasion go straight to the synagogue in Lystra although Acts 14:19 suggests that there may have been a considerable Jewish population in the city with whom the Jews from Antioch of Pisidia and Iconium were in communication. (Acts 14:19)

There may well have been some conflict between these Jews, who worshipped the OneTrue God and those of the population who worshipped the imported gods of the Greeks and the Romans. Did they really need somebody coming among them and telling them about yet another religion concerning someone called Jesus who was supposed to have risen from the dead?

But there were some, like the previously lame man of Lystra, who had heard Paul preaching and had become men and women of faith. Just as in the gospels, there is often a reason why a general time of healing by the Lord Jesus is followed by a more specific allusion to a single person of faith, or who relies on the faith of a friend, to enable a miracle to take place; so it appears to be the case here.

It is probable that many signs and wonders had been done by the hands of the apostles in Iconium. (Acts 14:3). Here in Lystra one powerless, helpless individual who nevertheless had faith received healing from Paul. He had heard Paul preaching for Paul had already preached the gospel in Lystra and Derbe and the surrounding countryside, and when Paul fixed his eyes on him he saw that he had faith to be made well. (Acts 14:9). And like the lame man at the beautiful gate of the temple in Jerusalem, His Name, through faith in His Name, had made this other man well also. (Acts 3:16). For there is no other Name under heaven given among men whereby we must be saved. (Acts 4:12).

Though Paul makes no mention of the name of Jesus on this occasion to this man, it is evident that his faith is in Jesus, and to Him he attributed the wonderful miracle of being able to jump up and stand on his feet and walk.

This was of course very significant in the life of the man, but also significant for the events which followed. There was an immediate reaction from the crowds who saw the formerly lame man leap up. Using their own Lycaonian language, they lifted up their voices saying 'the gods have come down to us in the likeness of men!' (Acts 14:11), identifying Barnabas as Zeus, in Greek mythology, the supreme god, also known as Jupiter in the Roman mythology, and Paul as Hermes, the Greek god known as Mercury the son of Jupiter in Roman religious tradition because Hermes was the messenger of the gods and Paul was the chief speaker. (Acts 14:12).

The use of the Lycaonian language rather than the Greek normally used by Paul may have caused some delay in their understanding of what the people of Lystra were intending to do. How surprised they must have been to see the priest of Zeus approaching them from the temple in front of the city, leading oxen decorated with garlands of flowers to offer sacrifices to them with the people. (Acts 14:13).

When the apostles understood what was happening, (Luke's only other allusion to them as apostles), they tore their garments and rushed among the multitude crying 'Men, why are you doing this?' (Acts 14:14,15). They had come to Lystra to proclaim the preeminence of the Lord Jesus; He who was Son of God and Son of Man, who was the only One who could give them new life, to give them a purpose for living, to give them hope for the future and a personal, present day-day relationship with Him.

How terrible if their proclamation of the gospel had been misunderstood, or misinterpreted! Rushing into the multitude, they tore their garments to indicate their distress at the blasphemy of regarding men as divine beings, and cried out, 'Men why are you doing this? We also are men of like nature with you and bring you good news that you should turn from these vain things to the living God who made heaven and earth and the sea and all that is in them!'. Paul may have been thinking of Psalm 19, where the psalmist says, 'The heavens declare the glory of God and the firmament shows His handiwork'. There is no excuse. Men and women may look around them and see the handiwork of the One True God, the Creator. And in these last days, He has spoken to us in His Son. (Hebrews 1:1).

Paul wass trying to explain to these people that Zeus and Hermes, or Jupiter and Mercury had no ultimate reality. They are no living gods but figments of someone's imagination, for everyone needs someone or something to worship, some explanation as to why the world is as it is, with its sorrows and its joys, its good and evil; there is always a need for some external supernatural power who could change circumstances for them if sufficiently appeased when things go wrong.

But Paul says, you must abandon this polytheism. You must turn to God from idols to serve a living and true God and to wait for His Son from heaven whom He raised from the dead, Jesus, who delivers us from the wrath to come. (1 Thessalonians 1:9).

Until now, many of the people of Lystra may not have heard of Jesus, though Paul and Barnbas had preached the gospel in their community (Acts 14:7). Now Paul was assuring them that that the true God, the Creator of heaven and earth and the sea, had always been there as a witness to them, for who could supply to them the rain and the weather which gave them fruitful seasons, satisfying their hearts with food and gladness? Only the One True God whose providential care is for all men and women everywhere.

Paul had preached the word of His grace (Acts 14:3), the loving favour of God to them, and God had confirmed His word with signs following. (Mark 16:20). Healing the lame man of Lystra was an example of God's favour towards them.

The people still wanted to do sacrifice to them, (Acts 14:18), but Jews came to Lystra from Antioch of Pisidia and Iconium. The oxen were reprieved, but not Paul. These were the unbelieving Jews who had already tried to exterminate the apostles, and with the connivance of the rulers, sought to stone them to death. (Acts 14:2,5). This was their second attempt. The Jews persuaded the people that Paul was a charlatan; that his message of peace and love and grace were completely untenable and together with the people, the Jews stoned Paul and dragged him out of the city, supposing that he was dead. (Acts 14:19; 2 Corinthians 11:25; 2 Timothy 3:11).

Those in the city who had come to love Paul and greatly appreciated his ministry, and had become disciples of the Lord Jesus, gathered around Paul. Perhaps they prayed to the Lord for his healing or laid hands on him as Ananias had done. (Acts 9:12). To their great joy, Paul rose up and entered the city, and to their sorrow, left them the next day and went on with Barnabas to Derbe where many others became disciples on hearing the preaching of the gospel (Acts 14:20).

Was their work now finished? No, for those who had recently become believers in Lystra, Iconium and Antioch In Pisidia, were still young in the faith. Paul and Barnabas made a return journey to these cities, despite the recent hostility towards them, 'strengthening the souls of the disciples, exhorting them to continue in the faith', and saying what had become so obvious, 'that through many tribulations we must enter the kingdom of God. (Acts 14:22).

Neither were these fleeting visits to these new Christian communities. Paul and Barnabas spent time in prayer and fasting with them as they appointed elders in every church, men who would encourage them and look after them as shepherds over the flock (Acts 20:28,29), committing them to the Lord in whom they had believed. (Acts 14:23).

It was a long way back to Antioch in Syria. They passed through parts of Galatia, through Pisidia and Pamphilia and preached the word in Perga. Then they went down to Attalia and from there they sailed to Antioch, across the sea from the port of Attalia, to the church from which they had been commended to the grace of God for the work which they had fulfilled (Acts 14:26).

What a homecoming that would be as Paul and Barnabas gathered the church together and declared all that God had done with them. But It was not them but what God had done through them, and what He had done was to open a door of faith to the Gentiles. (Acts 14:27).

Luke writes, 'they remained no little time with the disciples', (Acts 14:28), for even the church in Antioch needed their encouragement in the faith, the rehearsal of what great things God had done. These were for them all, seasons of refreshing from the presence of the Lord. (Acts 3:19).

Acts Chapter 15

Acts 14:1-29. The council of Jerusalem

But some men came down from Judea and were teaching the brethren 'unless you are circumcised according to the custom of Moses, you cannot be saved'. And Paul and Barnabas had no small dissension and debate with them. (Acts 15:1,2).

These precious times of prayer and fellowship at Antioch did not last long. The church at Jerusalem was nominally the mother church, the home of the apostles whom the Lord Jesus had sent forth, the original Twelve. (Matthew 10:2,5). But a terrible thing had happened. Men from Judea, the region surrounding Jerusalem, had come down to Antioch and were teaching the brethren, 'unless you are circumcised according to the custom of Moses, you cannot be saved'. (Acts 15:1).

This teaching implied two things. It implied that this new movement called Christianity was a group or sect within the larger group of Jewish people, the people of God, who had their own sacred laws, written in their holy scriptures, and their own initiation ceremony or ritual of circumcision. It implied that without that ceremony, these people could not become Christians, or be part of the Jewish faith, so the second implication was that in order to become Christians, a person had to be circumcised.

After all, the argument ran, people had always adopted the Jewish faith as proselytes and had submitted themselves to circumcision. Was there any point in changing what had worked so well for so long?

It was clear that there were many God-fearers, pious and God worshipping people who were monotheistic, believing in the one true God, who avoided idol worship, and who were attached to a synagogue. They observed the Sabbath and the law regarding clean and unclean foods, but had not been circumcised, so were therefore not completed Jews. The term God-fearers was applied to them, but though this was a massively commendable term especially in view of the culture of alien gods in which they lived, it fell short of a total commitment to the Jewish faith, and therefore concluded that they were somehow second class Jews.

This distinction was beginning to be applied in the church. Gentiles who had become Christians were distinguished from Jews who had also become Christians. After all, Christianity had its roots in Judaism. It did not yet have its own scripture but of course relied heavily on the Hebrew scriptures, the law and the prophets. It could be said to have its origins in Judaism because Jesus Himself was a Jew, as were also His disciples.

But what if some of the things Jesus said had to be taken literally? Did it not mean that God had no further use for the Jewish people or the Jewish way of life? His teaching seemed to imply that His was a new revelation from God, that God wanted all people everywhere, both Jews and Gentiles to be part of what He was doing on the earth; creating a new family, an extended and inclusive people of God. The Jews would not lose their status as God's chosen people but would be part of a huge increase of God's activity in His world.

But the men from Judea had another problem, echoed by people of the Pharisaic party. (Acts 15:5). Could these circumcised Gentiles be trusted to keep the intricacies of the law of Moses? For as Barrett comments, p698, there would be no point in being circumcised and yet not keeping the law.

The Jews from Judea were concerned, probably quite legitimately, that neither Jews nor Gentiles who had become Christians were aware of the spiritual significance of circumcision, the sign of the covenant between Abraham and his descendents, and God; and were afraid that this precious outward sign of the covenant could be overlooked, neglected, or even annihilated.

It was obviously time for a full and frank discussion of the problem, for unless its implications were dealt with, there was going to be a potential division or split between those churches like the one in Antioch which did not insist on new Christians being circumcised, (Acts 11:19-25), and the church in Jerusalem which was in danger of adopting a legalistic position.

The problem had been exacerbated by those who had come down from Judea to Antioch, debating the question with the brethren and insisting that unless they were circumcised they could not be saved. (Acts 15:1). They were from Judea, where Jerusalm was situated, but had not been authorised by the church in Jerusalem to persist in this teaching.

At Antioch, Paul and Barnabas took it upon themselves to enter into debate with them, and 'had no small dissension and debate with them', (Acts 15:2), for the whole church at Antioch was troubled about the outcome for the whole church if this teaching were universally accepted.

The church in Antioch determined to send Paul and Barnabas and 'some others', (perhaps including Titus? Galatians 2:3, 2 Corinthians 2:13, 7:6, 13), to Jerusalem, to the apostles and elders about this question, (Acts 15:2); to restore fellowship between Jewish and Gentile believers and establish the fundamentals of this new faith.

These included the question, was it possible to become a Christian without also becoming a Jew? Could there be conversion without circumcision? Faith in the Lord Jesus Christ without attention to the Mosaic law? For Christianity was not an attempt to restore Judaism to its original purpose and destiny as the people who would be the means of bringing the whole world into a place 'where all the families of the earth would be blessed (Genesis 12:3), initiating them into all the privileges which Israel, the people of God enjoyed; but the source of that Shoot, who was the Lord Jesus Christ, who came from the root of israel's greatest king, David, and yet was superior to it, for the Spirit of the Lord rested upon Him, the Spirit of wisdom and understanding, the Spirit of counsel and might, the Spirit of knowledge and of the fear of the Lord. (Isaiah 11:1-3).

This One, the Son of God, foreordained from before the world was, was incarnated as a Man, and was called Jesus for He came to save people of all races from their sins. (Matthew 1:21). It was His Name, through faith in His Name, that had drawn so many to Him, both Jews and Gentiles. The church had ro be seen as operating not as a Jewish sect, but as a worldwide fellowship of all believers.

Chapter 15 of Acts is the fulcrum, the focus of the whole book of Acts. These are the two major problems facing the developing church, the problem of circumcision and the problem of Jews and Gentiles eating together. for it was forbidden for Jews to eat with Gentiles. Paul writes to the Galatians of 'those who would trouble you and want to pervert the gospel of Christ; false brethren secretly brought in, who slipped in to spy out our freedom which we have in Christ Jesus, that they might bring us into bondage'. (Galatians 1:7).

Paul may have been writing of an earlier visitation by these troubling men from Judea, but the issues remained the same; the issue of entry into the church and the issue of fellowship within the church.

Paul makes this very clear in his letter to the Galatians. These were not simple, easily dealt with issues. They required not compromise but complete understanding of what God had ordained as far back as Abraham, in Genesis 12:3, and as recently as the ministry and teaching of the Lord Jesus who commissioned His disciples to go into all the world and preach the gospel to every creature; (Mark 16:15), to be witnesses to Him in Judea, and Samaria and to the uttermost parts of the earth; (Acts 1:8) and to 'go therefore and make disciples of all nations, baptizing them in the name of the Father, and of the Son and of the Holy Spirit, teaching them to observe whatever I command you'. (Matthew 28:19)

All are included in the gospel message. Paul writes again 'for as many of you as were baptized in Christ have put on Christ. There is neither Jew nor Greek, there is neither bond nor free, there is neither male or female, for you are all one in Christ Jesus'. Galatians 3:27,28).

Paul is quoted again here because this is of such fundamental importance to the early church, and worthy of more than can be considered here. Luke is not here offering an enlightened theological investigation into primitive Christianity. He gives us the salient facts with little commentary, but enough to see how simple and yet how profound was the conclusion reached by the church gathered together under the overshadowing wisdom of the Holy Spirit.

These examples of Paul's later grave concerns about controversies and even more importantly, heresies, creeping into the church, are reflected in the area of table fellowship, breaking bread together, sharing in the Lord's Table. Gentiles and Jews had been unable to take meals together for Gentiles were regarded as unclean. The Gentiles may also have eaten food sacrificed to idols, (1 Corinthians 8 and 10) or may have eaten meat from which the blood had not adequately been drained. Even were this not so, the mere possibility of offending against the law of Moses forbad Jews and Gentiles from eating together.

Paul utterly repudiates this position as applying to Jewish and Gentile Christians from eating together, that as idols have no real existence, no reality, behind them, food offered to them has no real spiritual significance. However, if you know that your fellow Christian who has a Jewish background is concerned about food which had previously been offered to idols and then sold in the marketplace, then do not eat it, because you have no right to wound another's conscience. Paul says, 'if food is a cause of my brother's stumbling, then I will never eat meat again lest I cause my brother to fall'. (1 Corinthians 8:12,13).

Paul continues, 'all things are lawful, but not all things are expedient, or helpful, or beneficial'. (1 Corinthians 10:23), 'so whether you eat or drink or whatever you do, do all to the glory of God'. (1 Corinthians 10:31). 'And give no offence to Jews or Gentiles or to the church of God'. (1 Corinthians 10:31).

These are, of course, Paul's future comments on the problem of eating together. But in Galatians 2:11, Paul rebukes Peter because before 'certain men came from James', the Lord's brother, Peter did eat with his Gentile brothers and sisters, (Acts 11;3), but after the visit of these men, 'Peter drew back and separated himself', (Galatians 2;12), possibly in submission of himself to James as the acknowledged leader of the church, and therefore as he believed, possessing the mind of the Lord.

Though Paul understood Peter's reasons for doing what he did, he was quite blunt in saying to him, 'Peter, you know that we are not justified by what we do, by obeying the works of the law. You above all know that we are only justified by faith in Christ. There are no other grounds for our ministry. If justification was by the law, then Christ died to no purpose, but this is the grace of God to us. (Galatians 21:21)

Dear Peter, says Paul, through whom God has done so much, do not get carried away by their dissimulation, by going against your own conviction. This is such an important principle. Which is more important, some kind of ritual purity, or justification by faith, being made righteous through faith? For that is the issue here. Justification, being made righteous can only come by faith in Christ and the redemption which He purchased for us on the cross. There is no justification for any of us in obeying the law of Moses.

Paul is following his own advice here. 'Brethren, If any man be overtaken in a fault, restore such a one in a spirit of meekness, of gentleness lest you too be tempted'. (Galatians 6:1). But he is absolutely of the conviction that the whole of God's plan and purpose for a worldwide company of people of faith was at stake here, and Paul was given the discernment to understand and to oppose any diminution of what God was doing.

Meanwhile, in Jerusalem, the men of Judea, of the Pharisaic party, had not moderated their position and their expression of what was demanded of Gentiles who became Christians and now reinforced the suggestion that only by the keeping of the law of Moses that men and women could be saved, which of course included circumcision. (Acts 15:1,5).

Paul and Barnabas had much to think and pray about as they travelled to Jerusalem through Phoenicia and Samaria, while at the same time encouraging the Christians whom they visited, reporting the conversion of the Gentiles and giving great joy to all the brethren. (Acts 15:3). This was in response to the agitation being caused by these men from Judea; and having been sent out by the church in Antioch, they used the opportunity of the journey to speak to people about the Lord Jesus and how to enter and live in, His kingdom. (Acts 15:3).

Arriving at Jerusalem, they were warmly welcomed by the church and the apostles and elders, (Acts 15:4), but it was not long before the question of the authenticity of the Gentile Christian experience was again raised by believers of the Pharisaic party. (Acts 15:5).

These former members of the Jerusalem synagogue were spiritual descendents of 'the Devout', or 'the Hasidim', Jews who did not forgo their loyalty to God or to the Torah, the Law of Moses, in spite of the persecution by Antiochus Epiphanes IV, (175-163 B.C), who was attempting to enforce Hellenization on the Jews and throughout his empire, forbidding Jews to observe the Sabbath or circumcision, or own a copy of the Torah; and looting the temple in Jerusalem of all its treasures to finance his army while setting up a pagan sacrifice in the temple and sacrificing a pig on it, 'the abomination that makes desolate'. (Daniel 11:31).

The Pharisees of the New Testament were keenly aware of what their courageous ancestors had done in resisting this terrible persecution, and of course were all the more determined to maintain the Jewish practices of circumcision and Sabbath observance. For them it was not just history, but their own devotion to what they believed to be the only way to God, and the only way to be faithful to Him.

The Pharisees were a minority group in the Sanhedrin at the time of Jesus, but a significant minority, the Sadducees being the ruling party. The Sadducees, represented by the High Priests Annas and Caiaphas, were aware of the importance of political influence, especially under the dominance of the Roman occupation of their country. The Pharisees were more concerned with obedience to the law of Moses, especially as interpreted by the scholars, the lawyers known as Scribes, lawyers committed to the understanding of the law. (Matthew 9:14; 15:2, 23; Mark 7:1-5; Luke 18:11,12).

Acts 4:1 and 5:17 carry the implication that the Sadducees were less inclined than the Pharisees to accept the new faith.

There was a Pharisaic party in the Jerusalem church who had come to faith in Christ, and how wonderful was that! But they were unwilling to let go all that had been of such vital importance to them as devoted servants of God. This was a very hard thing to do, to leave all in order to follow Jesus.

It is to their credit that although they were making a last ditch attempt to resist the laxity of a conversion without circumcision, insisting on circumcision as an entry requirement into this new faith, and maintaining the law of Moses as a way of life, they listened in silence as Paul and Barnabas and Peter spoke of what they had seen and heard of the grace of God to unbelievers. (Acts 15:12). By Acts 15:22, they were part of the whole church, with the apostles and elders, determining to send a letter to Antioch, Syria and Cilicia, annulling the burden of circumcision, and the burden of not being able to eat together, especially around the Lord's table.

The Pharisaic party were not the only ones with a view on how the gospel should proceed.'The apostles and the elders were gathered together to consider the matter', (Acts 15:6). And after much debate and deliberation, Peter rose to speak to them. Paul and Barnabas had already declared all that God had done with them, (Acts 15:4), how He had demonstrated His confirmation of their evangelical teaching with signs following; (Mark 16:20); but now after much debate, it was Peter's turn to speak. (Acts 15:7).

We had noted that on a previous occasion, when Peter came to Antioch, (Galatians 2L:11), Paul had rebuked Peter for freely enjoying food with Gentile Christians, although he was a Jew, until 'certain men came down from James', when he had drawn back and separ\ated himself. (Galatians 2:12).

Now Peter had the opportunity to share what he believed to be the undeniable truth in this situation. Since Paul does not write of the council of Jerusalem in Galatians, it is legitimate to assume that Paul's confrontation with Peter had occurred on an earlier occasion.

Now Peter said, 'Brethren, you know that in the early days, God made choice among you that by my mouth the Gentiles should hear the word of the gospel and believe. And God, who knows the heart, bore witness to them, giving to them the Holy Spirit just as He did us, and He made no distinction between us and them, but cleansed their hearts by faith. Now therefore, why do you make trial of God by putting a yoke upon the neck of these disciples which neither our fathers nor we were able to bear? But we believe that we shall be saved through the grace of the Lord Jesus, just as they will. (Acts 15:7-11)

Paul and Barnabas had not been summoned to Jerusalem to provide evidence for their lax behaviour in eating with Gentiles. This was a conference, a consultation, not a trial and Peter was able to give his views forcefully knowing that they would be backed up by Paul and Barnabas as they related again what signs and wonders God had wrought through them among the Gentiles, thereby proving that the conversion of the Gentiles was His work. (Acts 15:12).

Now it is the turn of James to speak. First, he refers to Peter as 'Simeon'. Simeon or Simon was Peter's Semitic name. Was James referring to Peter by an affectionate nickname, a remembrance of his early days in company with Jesus as Simon Peter? Or was it a way of reinforcing Peter's viewpoint, he who had been the first to follow Jesus, the first disciple among the disciples though equal with them? (Matthew 4:18; 10:2).

This is James the Lord's brother, for James the brother of John had been killed by Herod. (Acts 12:2) and Peter imprisoned until released by the angel, and it was to James the Lord's brother that Peter wanted the incident to be reported. (Mark 6:3; Acts 1:14) attributing the status of apostleship to James although he was not one of the Twelve. James is described as an apostle and as a pillar of the church in Galatians 1:19 and 2:9. He also saw the resurrected Christ who appeared to him and then to all the apostles, a further testimony to his apostleship. (1 Corinthians 15:7; Acts 1:22).

James, the leader of the church in Jerusalem and therefore *ipso facto*, the moderator of the council, may have used Peter's

Semitic name as an indication that though now a servant of Jesus Christ, (James 1:1), James still valued his origin as being a Jew. How gracious then was his opening comment. 'Brethren, listen to me. Simeon has related how God first visited the Gentiles to take out of them a people for His Name'.

James was conceding that God obviously had a greater and fuller plan which He was now revealing to them. From now on, the Jews were not to be the only people whom God would call His, but people from all the nations, Gentiles from all around the world could call on the Name of the Lord and be saved. All the privileges enjoyed by His chosen people could be theirs and more so, as they repented and believed the gospel, as they received eternal life from the Lord Jesus through the Holy Spirit, as Peter had already intimated.

And if God made no distinction between Jew and Gentile, cleansing their hearts by faith and giving them the gift of the Holy Spirit, who was James that he could withstand God? He could only acknowledge that this was indeed what had been promised throughout the writings of the prophets and he quotes Amos 9:11,12, Jeremiah 12:15 and Isaiah 45:21.

Amos, though only a herdsman, who claimed that he was neither a prophet nor a prophet's son but only a herdsman whom God took from following the flock; yet had this amazing vision of what God would do at the end of time, besides what He was doing in Amos' own time.

'In that day', says Amos prophetically, 'I, God, will raise up the booth of David that is fallen, repair it and raise it up, and rebuild it, that the rest of men may seek the Lord and all the Gentiles who are called by My Name, says the Lord who has made these things known from of old'

And Jeremiah and Isaiah concur with the message of Amos. The booth or dwelling place of David is the house of the Lord, for David says, 'I will dwell in the house of the Lord forever'. (Psalm 23:6). In David's time, the tabernacle was a place where people could go to meet with God and later in Solomon's time, there was the temple. Though God is present everywhere,

His presence would be most powerfully felt in those places where He had put His Name. (1 Kings 8:29)

But Jeremiah and Ezekiel speak of a new dwelling place of God, where His law is written in the hearts of those who love Him, where they will know Him and be known of Him. (Jeremiah 31:33,34). Ezekiel is even more specific. 'God says, a new heart will I give you and a new spirit will I put within you and I will take out of your flesh the heart of stone and give you a heart of flesh. And I will put My Spirit within you' (Ezekiel 36:24).

This is God's ultimate design for His people, that He should dwell in their hearts by faith. (Ephesians 4:17). His purpose for them is ratified, not in the old covenant, not in the covenant of circumcision and obedience to the Mosaic law, but in the new covenant, the new covenant ratified in the blood of Jesus. (Hebrews 9:15-22) which is available to all who avail themselves of it, whether Jew or Gentile, whether bond of free, whether male or female. (Galatians 3:28). Jesus said, this is the blood of the new covenant which is poured out for many for the forgiveness of sins. (Matthew 26:28).

Therefore, says Jmes, my judgement is that we should not trouble the Gentiles who turn to God. He was acutely troubled by the suggestion that through the teaching of the importance of circumcision, some may have felt unable to commit themselves to Christ. Others, though prepared to obey what they believed were the requirements approved by the apostles and elders in Jerusalem, yet regarded themselves as second class Christians because they were not allowed to eat with their Christian brothers and sisters, even at the celebration of the Lord's supper.

How could he have been so blind? thought James. They often remembered and spoke together of how when Jesus went out among them, crowds came to Him and He turned no-one away but had compassion on all, willingly ministering to people like the Roman centurion and the Syro-Phoenician woman who were not Jewish. His word to everyone without distinction was, 'Come to Me and I will give you rest'. (Matthew 11:28).

James, as far as we know, had not been involved in any evangelical activity, but as a shepherd he had tended the flock in

Jerusalem; and as a shepherd he now spoke to them. He was amazed at what Paul and Barnabas had been sharing with the council about what the Holy Spirit had done through them; about not only their teaching and preaching but also that people had been healed and demons cast out. (Acts 15:12). He was amazed at the clarity of Peter's conviction that God who knows the heart had given the Holy Spirit to the Gentiles, just as He had given Him to them on the day of Pentecost. The Holy Spirit had evidently, before their eyes, visited the Gentiles in the same way as He had visited them.

And though Peter had wonderfully observed this visitation in the household of Cornelius, we may believe that, unrecorded by Luke, such an episode may have been re-enacted time and again as Peter, Paul and Barnabas and others sent forth by the Holy Spirit with the gospel, discovered the Lord confirming the word with signs following, (Mark:16:20) and 'sending His Holy Spirit on them even as He did on us'. (Acts 15:8). Peter had appealed to what he believed to be common knowledge among the apostles and elders in Jerusalem. 'Brethren, *you know*, I don't need to tell you, that from the early days, God has been in control, and it was He who chose me that by me the Gentiles should hear the word of God and believe'. (Acts 15:7).

Barrett comments, God chose the unchosen people to hear the gospel. He had clean=ned their hearts by faith, and what He has cleansed we may not call common. (Barrett p714; Acts 10:15).

James' capitulation is complete. He says 'My judgement is that we should not trouble the Gentiles who turn to God, but should write to them to abstain from the pollution of idols and from unchastity and from what is strangled and from blood (Acts 15:19).

He had obviously come to recognize that the present situation was extremely troubling to the Gentiles. They were troubled by many questions. They wanted to come to faith in Jesus. How sufficient did their faith have to be? Did they need to do something extra to be accepted by Him? How powerful was His grace toward them? Was it powerful enough to redeem them from their sin even though they had not been circumcised?

It was troubling indeed on so many levels, affecting their ultimate destiny, and their present relationship with God through the Lord Jesus Christ. It also affected their relationship with those people whom they so wanted to acknowledge as their brothers and sisters in Christ, but who stood aloof from them because they were not Jews.

James realized that such a situation could not be allowed to continue. With diplomatic skill, he recommends that a letter be written to these Gentile believers urging them to abstain from the pollution of idols, unchastity or immorality, from what is strangled and from blood.

And that was all. Nothing else.

Under the covenant that God had made with His people through Moses, these four principles, outlined in Leviticus 18:6-18, were intended to enable the people of God to resist and neglect all that they had learned, though not necessarily experienced, in the land oF Egypt where they had been slaves, and to protect them from the idolatry in the land of Canaan towards which Mosess was leading them.

God's people had a spiritual heritage. They also had a moral and ethical one, to be faithful to one's husband or wife, and to make sure that the food they ate was drained of blood, for the life was in the blood, (Leviticus 17:11). These four moral principles would enable them to avoid any contact with what could defile them. (Leviticus 18:30).

For the Jews, these were the most abhorrent sins, idolatry, fornication and murder, but regarded lightly by the Greeks and Romans. (Bruce pp299, 230)

And, James adds, if you need to discover any more about that which defiles you, you can go tho any synagogue in any city, where Moses is read every Sabbath day. (Acts 15:21).

This letter is intended to lift the burden from believing Gentiles, but it also stresses the fact that from now on, God is doing something new. He is calling out a people for His Name from all the nations. What James is doing is including Gentiles in the purpose of God that He had for His peopleI Israel from the very beginning, that they should be holy as He is holy. (Leviticus 19:2; 20:26).

It had been His intention that Israel should be to Him a kingdom of priests and a holy nation, God's own possession among all people. (Exodus 19:5,6). The revelation to Peter was that though believers were scattered throughout Asia Minor, the people to whom he was writing in his first letter, there is a new people of God, (I Peter 1:1). Once they were no people, but now they are God's people. Once they had not received mercy. Now they had received mercy. They had become God's chosen race, a royal priesthood, to declare the wonderful deeds of Him who had called them out of darkness into His marvellous light. (1 Peter 2:9,10)

Peter recognized that God had expanded His vision to include them, revealing His glorious purpose to include all those who had come to His Son (1 Peter 1:3,4), all those for whom He had become precious, (1 Peter 1:7), whether by birth they were Jews or Gentiles.

This proposal by James was willingly accepted by the apostles and the elders and the whole church (Acts 15:22), and it appears that it was the decision of the whole church to send this projected letter to Antioch, Syria and Cilicia, not only with Paul and Barnabas but other men also, among them Judas Barsabbas and Silas, leading men among the brethren. (ACts 15:22, 23).

Judas Barsabbas is not otherwise mentioned in Acts, but Silas, a Roman citizen also known by his Latin name Silvanus, becomes an important companion to Paul. (Acts 15:40; 1 Thessalonians 1:1; 2 Corinthians 1:19; 1 Peter 5:12).

This new and believing community of the church will now and forever be home to both Jews and Gentiles, the legitimate continuation of God's purpose for all mankind, fulfilling the prophetic scriptures.

This was no ordinary letter. It had seemed good to the church in Jerusalem to send it to Antioch, the chief city of the united province of Syria and Cilicia, (Bruce p302) by these chosen men, Judas Brsabbas and Silas. And by 'our beloved

Barnabas and Paul who have risked their lives for the sake of our Lord Jesus Christ'. (Acts 15:26). Not only would they bring the letter, they would be able to share 'the same things, by word of mouth' (Acts 15:27). No longer would the church in Antioch consider itself to be ploughing a lonely furrow apart from what was happening in Jerusalem. They were now on the same page.

It had seemed good to the church to implement this decision but more importantly, it seemed good to the Holy Spirit not to lay upon the Gentiles any greater burden than a moral and ethical responsibility of not living as did the the Greeks and Romans, who lived lightly to any kind of morality, eating food offered to idols, or indulging in fornication. For those who had committed to following the Lord Jesus and His teaching, these were of course activities from which they wanted to abstain. And the Holy Spirit inspired letter ends with the word in translation, 'farewell', *valete, be strong.*

This is the last mention of Peter in the book of the Acts.

Acts 15:30-35. The church at Antioch receives the letter

So, when they were sent off, Paul and Barnabas went down to Antioch, and having gathered the church together, they delivered the letter. And when they read it, they rejoiced at the exhortation, the parakleous, (Gk: the encouragement and comfort of the Holy Spirit is implied).

Luke does not tell us whether Paul and Barnabas followed the same route back to Antioch through Phoenicia and Samaria, but we can speculate that those who had come to faith the last time they saw the apostles would have been doubly glad to see them again, and learn of the decree of the Jerusalem church.

We can imagine too the extreme excitement and eagerness to see the letter when Paul and Barnabas arrived home in Antioch, and 'having gathered the congregation together, they delivered the letter, and when they read it they rejoiced at the exhortation', (Acts 15:31), the encouragement to continue as they had been doing, receiving Gentiles into their midst without insisting on circumcision as entry into the fellowship, or excluding anyone from eating with others. Their previous policy of welcoming all without any kind of initiation ceremony, (for even baptism did not grant believers salvation but only witnessed to their absolute commitment to Christ in His death and resurrection), had been totally ratified. And the complication of division between the churches avoided.

Judas and Silas, who had the spiritual gift of prophecy, which not only gave the church guidance about the future, but also gave them a brother whose gift enabled him to speak to believers for their upbuilding and encouragement and consolation (1 Corinthians 14:3), were also on hand, strengthening the faith of the brethren (Acts 15:32). Judas and Silas, and possibly others (Acts 15:22,23), were with the Christians in Antioch for some time, but eventually decide to return to Jerusalem, and were sent off in peace by the brethren to those who had sent them. (Acts 15:33)

Some ancient manuscripts insert verse 34 here: 'but it seemed good to Silas to remain there', to accord with verse 40: 'Paul chose Silas and departed' on the second missionary journey. An alternative suggestion is that Silas, with Judas and the others who had accompanied them from Jerusalem to Antioch were indeed 'sent off', sent back in peace by the brethren to those in Jerusalem who had sent them. (Acts 15:33), but that Silas returned at some point to Antioch to be with Paul and Barnabas who had remained in Antioch, teaching and preaching the word of the Lord, with many others also. (Acts 15:35).

Having spent some time with Paul, whether or not he had returned to Antioch in the interim, what more likely than that Silas should want to continue to be with Paul, a man full of courage and determination, with a heart full of compassion for those outside the gospel, and a great desire for the establishment and enlightenment of those within the church. How glad and grateful Silas would have been when Paul asked him to accompany him on the second missionary journey.

Acts 15:36-44. The second missionary journey. The mission to Asia Minor and its aftermath

After some days, Paul said to Barnabas, 'Come, let us return and visit the brethren in every city where we proclaimed the word of the Lord and see how they are. (Acts 15:36).

Paul never ceased to be concerned for those believers who had become Christians through his ministry. Paul had a very high regard for the church, again and again denouncing himself as one who had once persecuted it. (Galatians 1:13; Philippians 3:6; 1 Corinthians 15:9). He sees the church as Christ did, for Christ so loved the church that He gave Himself for her. (Ephesians 5:25). So Paul also loved the church, not of course in a redemptive way as Christ did, but like a father caring for his children, (1 Corinthians 4:14,15). Paul daily carried upon himself the burden of the care of all the churches, (2 Corinthians 11:28), and the pressure of his anxiety for all the churches.

In writing to Timothy, Paul is eager to advise him that leadership in the church is like fatherhood in the family. Just as a father manages his home and his children, keeping them safe, assuring them at all times of his love for them, so should the leader of a church be, for the church is unique. It is the church of the living God, and nothing has a higher destiny than that. It is the church of the living God, the pillar and ground of the truth. (1 Timothy 4:15).

Paul, fully aware of his responsibility for the churches of Syria and Cilicia, now proposes to go through to them, strengthening them (Acts 15:41). The church at Antioch had received and read the letter from the Jerusalem council. Now Paul wanted to revisit the brethren in every city 'where we proclaimed the word of the Lord, and see how they are' (Acts 15:36). In addition, the churches in Syria and Cilicia would be glad to know of the Jerusalem decree. Certainly they would be glad of his coming, for it always had the effect of strengthening the churches, (Acts 15:32, 41).

The time in Antioch was fast coming to an end. Barnabas was fully in agreement with Paul that the proposed visit to those cities was necessary. He was eager to return to Cyprus where their first missionary journey had begun and to take John Mark, his cousin, with them, perhaps replicating some of the blessings which they had previously enjoyed.

John Mark was the cousin of Barnabas, (Colossians 4:10), a Cypriot Jew who had lived for some time in Jerusalem with his mother Mary (Acts 12:12,25) and had come with Barnabas and Saul, as he was then known, from Jerusalem to Antioch. Barnabas and Saul had been set apart by the Holy Spirit 'for the work to which [I have] called them', (Acts 13:2), and had set sail for Cyprus. And John Mark had gone with them through Cyprus, Paphos and Perga in Pamphlia. John had then left them and returned to Jerusalem.

Barnabas wanted to take John Mark with them. But Paul thought best not to take with them one who had withdrawn from them in Pamphylia, and had not gone with them to the work. (Acts 15:37).

It is unclear exactly what were Paul's reasons for excluding John Mark on this occasion. Perhaps Barnabas had dismissed John's decision to leave them in Pamphylia and return to Jerusalem as excusable, on what grounds we do not know, But Paul thought it best not to take John with them With his typical kindness, Barnabas may have wanted to give John an opportunity to prove himself. Paul's concern was for the mission and the reliability of the messengers of the gospel. Having once left the mission for probably very good reasons, could John be trusted not to do so again?

Paul knew from experience that taking the gospel to various cities of Asia Minor had resulted in opposition, in aggression both from the people and their rulers, even to attempts on their lives. Paul was not sure that John Mark would have the stamina to cope with all that and more. It was in all seriousness that Paul had told the churches in Lystra, Iconium and Antioch that it is through many tribulations that we enter the kingdom of God. (Acts 14:21.22).

Barnabas' concern was for one beloved brother. Paul's concern was always and preeminently for the gospel, for those outside of Christ who needed to hear and believe. Sometimes both concerns can be mutually provided for. On this occasion however, a sharp contention arose between Paul and Barnabas (Acts 15:39). Barnabas took John Mark with him and sailed away to Cyprus, but Paul chose Silas and departed, being commended by the brethren to the grace of the Lord. (Acts 15:40). They departed northwards, through Syria and Cilicia, strengthening the churches (Acts 15:41), even though they were temporarily heartsick at losing the companionship of Barnabas. John Mark had separated from Paul and Barnabas in Perga in Pamphylia. Now Paul and Barnabas had separated from each other. (Barrett, p756).

But the story of John Mark does not end there. Colossians 4:10; 2 Timothy 4:11; and Philemon 24, all suggest that John Mark continued to be a close friend to Paul, especially when he was in the prison in Rome. He is described as a comfort to Paul, useful in serving him, and a fellow worker.

Barnabas is also referred to as a close colleague of Paul's in 1 Corinthians 9:6., a passage where it is assumed that Paul and Barnabas have a strong relationship as fellow apostles, (1 Corinthians 9:2); having a further opportunity of working together in Ephesus, from which church Paul is writing to the Corinthians. (1 Corinthians 16:9). This letter is dated as 54/55 A.D. only three or four years after their disagreement in Antioch. Reconciliation had evidently been achieved between them.

Meanwhile, in the interim, Paul and Silas go overland through Syria and Cilicia which was one administrative province; strengthening the churches. It may be that this was their only intention at this time, although they also had to fulfil the commission impressed on them by the Jerusalem council to take the letter to the brethren who are in Antioch, which they already done, Syria and Cilicia (Acts 15:23).

Acts Chapter 16

Acts 16:1-4. In the province of Galatia.
Timothy joins them.

And Paul came also to Derbe and Lystra. A disciple was there named Timothy, the son of a Jewish woman who was a believer; but his father was a Greek. He was well spoken of by the brethren at Lystra and Iconium. Paul wanted Timothy to accompany him and he took him and circumcised him because of the Jews that were in those places, for they knew that his father was a Greek. (Acts 16:1-3).

Timothy was the son of a mixed marriage. HIs mother Eunice was a Jew but his father was a Greek, (2 Timothy 1:5). The verb 'was' in verse 1 may indicate that his father had now died.

Paul was aware of Timothy's reputation. He was well spoken of by the brethren at Lystra and Iconium. Having been brought up in the Jewish faith, he had become a disciple earlier, perhaps through one of Paul's earlier visits, together with his mother Eunice and his grandmother Lois. (2 Timothy 1:4). But although he had been brought up as a Jew, he had never been circumcised, perhaps because his father had forbidden it.

Mixed marriages were common among the Jews of the Dispersion, the Diaspora, though discouraged among the Jews of Palestine for whom it was not allowed.

Timothy had become very dear to Paul. He calls Timothy 'my beloved child', (2 Timothy 1:2), 'my beloved and faithful child in the Lord', (1 Corinthians 4:17). But Timothy ws neither a true Jew, nor a true Gentile, because he had a Jewish mother.

Paul wanted to legitimise Timothy's status because he could see in Timothy an ability for strong Christian leadership, and he wanted to take Timothy on this journey both spiritually and geographically. His status as an illegitimate child under Jewish law because his father was Greek, the fact that he had not been circumcised on the eighth day after his birth, although he had been brought up as a Jew, rendered his status problematic to the Jews.

Timothy needed to be circumcised, not because circumcision was an entry requirement into the Jewish faith, prior to becoming a Christian, as some men in Judea had claimed, (Acts 15:1), but to legitimate him as a Jew for the sake of the Jews that were in those places, 'for they all knew that his father was a Greek'. (Acts 16:3).

For Paul to be able to present Timothy as a Jew if he had not been circumcised would have been dishonest. The Jews were God's chosen people. Paul was unwilling to do anything that would prejudice them against accepting the gospel through a Jew. He was always ready to conciliate them. (Acts 21:26). He writes to the Galatians, 'to the Jews I became as a Jew in order to win Jews. to those under the law, I became as under the law that I might win those that were under the law. (1 Corinthians 9:20). He was following Ezekiel the pastoral prophet, watching over those entrusted to him, sitting where they sat. (Ezekiel 3:15). Paul says, 'I have become all things to all men that I might by all means save some. I do it for the sake of the gospel. (1 Corinthians 9:22).

He was encouraging his 'true child in the faith', Timothy (1 Timothy 1:2), to do the same, to be circumcised not as a means to his salvation but as a legal act, to remove a stigma from Timothy. (Barrett p260).

Paul is not recommending circumcision, nor repudiating it, except as an entry requirement into the church, for he is adamant that the gospel gives only one status, that of being a new creature in Christ. (2 Corinthians 5;17). Paul writes again, neither circumcision avails for anything nor uncircumcision, but a new creation, (Galatians 6:15). There is nothing contradictory or controversial about Paul's decision to take Timothy and circumcise him. It was appropriate and justifiable on this specific occasion. Other situations would need to be looked at along the same individual line, and all for the sake of the gospel. (1 Corinthians 9:22).

This was all part of Paul's strategy to establish the churches as they went through the cities of Derbe and Lystra, and Timothy was a willing participant in Paul's strategy.

At the same time, Paul and Silas and Timothy delivered to the churches the decisions, the '*dogmatoi*' (from which we get our word dogma, Bruce p308) reached by the apostles and elders in Jerusalem. (Acts 16:4). So the churches were strengthened in the faith, and they increased in number daily. (Acts 16:5). The church in Jerusalem was the first community raised up through the outpouring of the Holy Spirit to witness to the gospel; repentance towards God and faith towards our Lord Jesus Christ, (Acts 2: 4,21). And its recommendations were still highly respected by later groups of believers. As time went on, the strengthening power of fellowship between Jerusalem and the satellite churches became less didactic, but nevertheless cannot be overestimated.

Acts 16:6-10. Guided by the Holy Spirit to Troas

And they went through the region of Phrygia and Galatia, having been forbidden by the Spirit to speak the word in Asia. And when they had come opposite Mysia they attempted to go into Bithynia, bot the Spirit did not allow them. So passing by Mysia, they went down to Troas. (Acts 16:6-8).

What kind of missionary journey was this? In all sincerity, Paul, Silas and Timothy had taken a route through the region of Phrygia and Galatia which they wanted to pursue in the interest of sharing the gospel.

But the Holy Spirit said 'No'. You may not speak the word in Asia. So, being obedient to Him, they came to a place opposite Mysia.

But again, the Spirit of Jesus, the Holy Spirit said 'No'. So passing by or through Mysia, they went down to Troas.

We are impressed by the geographical knowledge of Luke as he meticulously describes the route taken by the travellers, but even more impressed by their having such a close relationship with the Holy Spirit, who is the Spirit of Jesus, that they are constantly aware of His whispered instruction in their hearts; of when He says 'No', and when He says 'Yes'.

On leaving Antioch, Paul and Silas had gone through Syria and Cilicia, and then to Derbe and Lystra where Paul had recruited Timothy to be with them. They had chosen this route because they had been charged by the Jerusalem church to take the decisions regarding circumcision and table fellowship to the churches in the region of Galatia. Since now they were relieved of any obligation, they intended to go on to Asia. The province of Asia was a wealthy and highly civilized part of Asia Minor. Having passed through Phrygia and Galatia, Phrigia being a province of Glatia of which Pisidian Antioch was the most important city, they were close to the border with Asia.

In Stott's view, (p259), it was now natural that the eyes of the missionaries should now look southwest along the road that led to Colossae, and then along the coast to Ephesus. Instead, prevented and guided by the Holy Spirit, they turned north until they reached the border of Mysia, northwest Asia. They wanted to continue north and enter Bithynia, near the southern shores of the Black or Euxine Sea, but the Spirit of Jesus would not allow them to. The only route open to them was north west. So they passed through Mysia, the northern part of the province of Asia, and came to Troas, a city on the Aegean coast. (Barrett p770).

It had been a long and perplexing journey, all the way from Antioch and Seleucia in southwest Asia Minor to the north west, to Troas. What did God have in mind? What was His purpose in bringing them so far?

At least part of the answer came to Paul in a vision of the night. He saw a man of Macedonia, standing and beseeching him, and saying, 'Come over to Macedonia and help us'. (Acts 16:9)

Macedonia was on the other side of the Aegean Sea, an association of Hellenistic cities which had become a Roman province. (Barrett p 772). It was a part of Greece made famous by Alexander the Great, a Macedonian. Macedonia was part of

Greece *and in Europe*. They were on the brink of bringing the gospel to Europe. Campbell Morgan is quoted as saying 'the invasion of Europe was not in the mind of Paul, but it was evidently in the mind of the Spirit'. (Stott p258).

Great as Macedonia had been in the time of Alexander, nothing could be greater than the 'help' Paul and his companions could give the Macedonians than to hear the gospel message.

Some commentators, for example, Barrett, (p766, 772), see little significance in the cry of the man of Macedonia to 'come over to Macedonia and help us' as paving the way to the evangelization of Europe. But Stott (p258) sees it as a positive indication that God had the nations of Europe in His plan and purpose for the world.

Stott acknowledges that for Paul and his fellow travellers, there was no demarcation between Asia and Europe at that time, for both western and eastern shores of the Aegean Sea were part of the Roman empire. But Europe was the first continent to engage in world wide missionary activity; as Jesus said, to the ends of the earth. This was surely in the purpose of the Holy Spirit as He nudged Paul and his companions in the right direction.

When Paul had seen the vision, he immediately sought to go on into Macedonia, concluding that 'God had called us to preach the gospel to them'. (Acts 16:10). Now the narrative becomes not 'they' but 'we'. Luke is including himself as a companion to Paul. It appears that he had already been in Troas when Paul, Silas and Timothy arrived, Troas being his hometown. But we have no information as to when Luke became a Christian, only that he had become a fellow worker with Paul, (Philemon 24), a beloved physician (Colossians 4:14) and a beloved friend, according to 2 Timothy 4:11 where Paul writes, 'only Luke is with me', when in prison in Rome.

It has been suggested that while in Troas, Paul had a recurrence of the infirmity which he had suffered in Galatia, (Galatians 5:13), and that Luke was on hand to help him. (Stott p260). But Luke is self effacing, drawing no attention to himself beyond the use of the pronoun 'we'. All that Luke knows is that

God has called Paul, Silas and Timothy to evangelize the Macedonians, and he is happy to go along with them.

Acts 16:11-12. From Troas to Philippi

Setting sail therefore from Troas, we made a direct voyage to Samothrace, and the following day to Neapolis, and from there to Philippi, which is the leading city of the district of Macedonia and a Roman colony. (Acts 16:11,12)

We are amazed at the many miles on foot made by Paul, Silas, Timothy and later Luke, but the Pax Romana which operated throughout the Roman empire made border controls unnecessary, and no doubt the travellers found Christian friends along the way who were only too glad to offer them hospitality.

God was again doing a new thing, and Paul and his companions were chosen to be His instruments in what He was doing. Paul was executed during the reign of Nero, (54-68 AD). The Acts of the Apostles can therefore be said to cover three decades from the ascension of the Lord Jesus, and to have a sure basis historically. (Marshall p47).

Once the church at Antioch had been established, Paul played a leading role in Acts. Until then, Peter had been the leader of the church. First established in Jerusalem, from its early days after Pentecost, until the time came when the gospel was acknowledged to be for everyone, including Gentiles, Peter, together with James the Lord's brother and John were described as pillars of the church in Jerusalem. (Galatians 2:9). With two established Christian communities, in Jerusalem and Antioch, it was now time for Paul, led by the Holy Spirit, to proceed to Asia Minor and Greece proclaiming the good news of the gospel on his first and second missionary journeys. By Acts 20, the gospel had been effectively preached throughout the eastern Mediterranean world. (Marshall p26).

This second missionary journey, which began in Antioch, had led them, through the guidance of the Holy Spirit, to the

Aegean coast. Paul's vision of the man of Macedonia is taking him further, taking the gospel further, than it had previously been allowed to go. Because of the obedience of one man and his companions to the leading of the Holy Spirit, many men and women who had lived in spiritual darkness all their lives, will now come under the grace of the Lord Jesus and the power of the Holy Spirit and have their lives transformed.

Together with Silas, Timothy and Luke, Paul set sail from Troas, first making for the island of Samothrace 'and the following day to Neapolis, and from Neapolis to Philippi, which is the leading city of Macedonia'. (Acts 16:11).

In his letters, Paul is always careful to name his fellow workers, those whom God had supplied to be with him as part of a team, not only as evangelists but often those with a ministry of encouragement and comfort to local believers; or those with a ministry of hospitality, with whom he often stayed some considerable time, These were men and women with spiritual qualities, who relied on the guidance of the Holy Spirit.

Luke was now part of the team, fully immersed in Paul's ministry.

But it cannot be denied that from Acts 16:10 onwards, Paul is the major protagonist in Acts. Paul is now seen to work independently as an evangelist, pastor and teacher, no longer reporting back to Antioch as in Acts 14:26. Paul was a truly apostolic figure, appointed by the Holy Spirit and totally guided by Him.

Acts 16:11-40. Paul and Silas in Philippi

Paul, Silas, Timothy and Luke have now accomplished the voyage across the Aegean Sea to Philippi from Troas, probably in a couple of days before a favourable wind, though the return journey in Acts 20:6 from Philippi to Troas took them five days.

Neapolis was the port of Philippi, which was about ten miles inland. Philippi was made a Roman colony in 42 BC, 'colony' being a term used of a city and its environs which replaced Rome itself, a kind of facsimile of Rome, with Roman law and important privileges for its leading families, maintaining a military presence as an outpost of empire. (Bruce p313).

Acts 16:12-16. The conversion of Lydia

We remained in this city some days and on the Sabbath day we went outside the gate to the riverside where we supposed there was a place of prayer; and we sat down and spoke to the women who had come together. One who heard us was Lydia from the city of Thyatira, a seller of purple goods who was a worshipper of God. The Lord opened her heart to give heed to what was said by Paul. (Acts 16:12-14).

Philippi was the leading city of Macedonia and a Roman colony. Yet though it was a leading city, it had no synagogue. Paul's usual practice was to go to the synagogue on the Sabbath day when entering a city which he had not previously visited, but deprived of this opportunity, Paul went down 'outside the gate to the riverside where he supposed there was a place of prayer', 'a place where prayer was wont to be made'. (Acts 16:13. RSV; AV).

There *we* (including Luke), sat down and spoke to the women who had come together. They were either Jewish women by birth or proselytes who were all that this leading city could produce of worship to God on a Sabbath morning, but how precious to God that this was what these women wanted to do. In his gospel Luke is always interested in the attitude of Jesus towards women, and His compassion for them. This concern he shows also in Acts.

Synagogue service required a quorum, (minyam), of ten men. Because of the lack of men, and probably also because of anti-semitism in the city, the women could not meet together as a synagogue. But that did not deter them from meeting together to pray.

Among them was a woman named Lydia. She was a business woman from Thyatira, a garrison city in the province of Asia, famous for its purple dye. She may have been a dealer in purple cloth, or the dye itself, for both of which there was a ready market amongst the nobility, and may explain why the place of prayer had not been disbanded but had been allowed to continue and not abandoned.

As she is the person responsible for a 'household', (Acts 16:15) there is a likelihood that she was a widow, running the business after her husband's death, or unmarried. Her household would have included servants and other dependents. But above all, she was 'a worshipper of God' (Acts 16:14). She lost no time in asking that she might be baptized, for the river was close by. And she was baptized, with her household.

This may have included children as some have argued who seek for scriptural evidence for the baptism of children. But there is no warrant for that assumption, as children are not mentioned. Marshall writes (p268), that neither adult nor infant baptism can be proved or disproved from this passage and similar ones. (Acts 11:14, 16:33; 18:8; 1 Corinthians 1:16), even though there was a strong possibility that the household included children. We do not know whether Lydia had children among her dependents.

After taking this important step, Lydia longed for Paul and his companions to come to her house, a house full of newly baptized people. 'She besought us saying, "If you have judged me to be faithful to the Lord, come to my home and stay".' (Acts 16:13). And she prevailed upon us; the first woman in Europe to be baptized, and a confirmation to the missionaries that they had truly been guided by the Holy Spirit to cross the Aegean Sea.

Acts 16:16-18. The slave girl with a spirit of divination

As we were going to the place of prayer, we were met by a slave girl who had a spirit of divination and brought her owners much gain by soothsaying. She followed Paul and us, saying, 'These men are servants of the Most High God who proclaim to you the way of salvation'. And this she did for many days.

Luke uses the word *egeneto, it came to pass,* as they were going to the place of prayer. Luke often uses this phrase in his gospel (e.g. Luke 9:18;14:1;20:1), as an indication that what is about to happen is all under the sovereign control of God. It is coming to pass as His ordained will in the present circumstance. This is not a perfunctory or casual setting of a scene by Luke, but a conviction that the purpose of God in this situation is about to be realised.

We do not know how often Paul, Silas and Luke traversed the path which led to the riverside for prayer with the women, but this poor slave girl seemed always to be there, following them. (Acts 16:17) calling out, 'these men are the servants of the most high God who proclaim to you the way of salvation!'

Eventually, after many days, (Acts 16:18) Paul, being grieved, turned and said to the spirit which controlled her, 'I charge you in the Name of Jesus Christ to come out of her!' And it came out that very hour.

It was obvious to Paul that the poor girl had been possessed by 'a spirit of divination', the spirit of a snake or python, which were thought to inhabit 'pythonesses', young women who served the Delphic shrine and delivered the oracles to it.

This pythonic spirit enabled the slave girl to speak oracularly, as in clairvoyance, or foretelling the future, and she had brought her owners much profit by using this spiritual agency.

The spirit of Python, this evil spirit, was under no illusions as to the function and activity of these men who had come to Philippi. It causes the girl to say, 'these men are servants, slaves of the most high God who proclaim to you the way of salvation'. (Acts 16:17). In the Roman pantheon, Jupiter was the most high god. The evil spirit is suggesting that just as it inhabits the girl, who is a slave, a servant to both it and her masters, so 'these men are servants, slaves of another god and have his spirit inhabiting them'.

While acknowledging that there is only one most high God, and that He alone is the way to salvation, the python spirit is deliberately confusing the meaning of the slave girl's utterance, mingling the use of a term used of a Roman god with God, and the false Roman way of salvation with the true salvation which can only come from God. Confusion, compromise, distraction, have always been ways by which the truth is obscured and made of no effect.

It appears that for a considerable time, the declaration from the slave girl had been repeated. Finally, Paul, understanding the phenomenon for what it was, turned to the girl possessed by the evil spirit and said, 'I order you to come out of her in the Name of Jesus Christ'. (Acts 16:18). Paul did not assign to himself the ability to cast out evil spirits. All his trust was in the Name of Jesus Christ, for there is no other Name under heaven given among men whereby we must be saved. (Acts 4:12).

The evil spirit was not engaged in publicity for the gospel but was seeking to convince a potentially aggressive and violent crowd that these people who had come as unwelcome Jews among them were using the occult to further the worship of a different God, unlike the worship of Zeus or Jupiter, and aimed to gain dominance over the citizens of Philippi by the promise of a false salvation.

The owners of the girl were using her ability under the evil spirit for soothsaying to get much gain, much profit, from her. She was deeply disturbed and Paul was deeply troubled by her condition. At last, his distress at her condition had caused him to command the evil spirit to come out of her. Perhaps, being no longer of any use to her owners, she came to faith in Jesus and became a member of the infant church in Philippi.

But when her owners saw that their hope of gain was gone, they seized Paul and Silas and dragged them into the market place before the rulers. (Acts 16:19).

Acts 16:19-40. Paul and Silas in prison

When they had brought Paul and Silas to the magistrates, they said, 'These men are Jews and they are disturbing our city. They advocate customs which it is not lawful for us Romans to accept or practise. The crowd joined in attacking them; and the magistrates tore the garments off them and gave orders to beat them with rods. And when they had inflicted many blows upon them, they threw them into prison charging the jailer to keep them safely. (Acts 16:20-23).

Until now, it has been the Jewish authorities who have taken exception to the apostle's preaching. From chapter 16 it is the Roman authorities also. While Christianity had been regarded as a sect within Judaism, this was of little importance to the Roman officials, unless it caused a riot. Now however, Christianity is perceived as coming outside the closet of Judaism. There were now more Gentile Christians than Jewish ones and this new religious movement was threatening to take on the whole world. It had even got as far as Greece and was in no sense confined to the synagogues. Rome had a fairly healthy tolerance of other religions, as witnessed by the latitude given to the high priests in Jerusalem, but there was a limit to their forbearance.

Understanding this, the owners of the slave girl took the case of Paul and Silas to the Roman magistrates (Acts 16:20). When they saw that their hope of gain was gone, they dragged Paul and Silas before the rulers. The evil spirit had gone, and for the next few passages, until Acts 20:3, Luke, though not Timothy, (Acts18:5), had also gone. (Bruce p316).

It was obviously Paul and Silas whom the masters of the slave girl regarded as responsible for their loss of profit. Timothy and Luke may have remained at Philippi to encourage the church, the new church, the new believers, but Luke makes no mention of this, concentrating as he does on on what happened next in the establishing of the church in Philippi, a group of Christians under the leadership of Lydia and an anonymous former jailer as the story unfolds.

Paul's later letter to the Philippian church when he was in prison in Rome, is full of his encouragement for them, and his longing to see them. (Philippians 1:7; 13;14;16). They apparently had no problems such, for example, as those experienced by the church in Corinth. Paul's only rebuke in the Philippian letter was for two women, Euodia and Syntyche, who were in disagreement with each other. (Philippians 4:2). The Philippian letter includes one of the most beautiful and enlightening passages in the whole Bible. (Philippians 2:5-11). The Holy Spirit had begun a wonderful work of salvation in Philippi. The church was born in much adversity, but also in much joy, so Paul could write to them, 'Rejoice in the Lord always and again I say rejoice! (Philippians 4:4).

In Philippi, Paul and Silas had been dragged before the magistrates by the owners of the slave girl, who said, 'These men are Jews, and they are disturbing our city. They advocate customs which it is not lawful for Romans to accept or practise'.

The loss of profit was their motive; the charge they brought against Paul and Silas was a falsehood. There was anti-Jewish sentiment in Philippi, but was that enough to have their garments torn from them and to be subjected to be beaten with rods? Was it that the magistrates were afraid of any breach of the peace as being evidence of their inability, as Roman officials, to control a diverse community? Jews especially, with what they regarded as their dubious religious customs, were regarded with deep suspicion, refusing to accept the Roman worship of many and sometimes immoral deities.

The Roman authorities were determined to emphasize their superiority to these Greeks who surrounded them, to say nothing of the Jews also.

Paul and Silas were condemned to be beaten with rods by *lictors,* whose function this was, a cruel and humiliating punishment. Paul never forgot the pain of being beaten with rods, a Roman punishment he endured three times. (2 Corinthians 11:25). The five times he received forty lashes save one, with a whip for scourging, was at the hands of the Jews. Paul was a man who suffered for his faith, and on this occasion, Silas suffered too.

And when they had inflicted many blows on them, they threw them into prison, charging the jailer to keep them safely. Having received this charge, he put them into the inner prison and fastened their feet in the stocks. (Acts 16:23,24).

This was the inmost prison and the stocks themselves were instruments of torture, forcing the legs wide apart, causing great discomfort and pain to men whose backs were already bleeding from the beating they had received. (Bruce p318). The jailer was doing his job, and he was good at it. It was not for him to question the justice of those in authority over him. Barrett suggests that the stocks may only have been used as a means of security, and then simply as confinement (Acts 16:24). (Barrett p792). The same instruments were used for both purposes and it is possible that the context suggests security rather than torture. (Barrett 793).

Nevertheless Paul and Silas were rejoicing that they had been counted worthy to suffer for the Name of Jesus. But about midnight, Paul and Silas were praying and singing hymns to God, and the other prisoners were listening to them'. (Acts 16:25). Tertullian says, neither did they feel the torture, for their souls were in heaven. (Bruce p319).

The jailer had been charged to keep them safely, but God was about to set them free. The slave girl had been in terrible bondage, but the Name of Jesus had set her free. Paul and Slas were in human bondage but their spirits were free. In the midst of the pain and the wounds on their backs, and the possible dislocation of their hip joints by the use of the stocks, they were found praying and singing hymns to God and praising Him, and the other prisoners were listening to them. (Acts 16:25).

Perhaps the explosion of joy from the inner prison kept the other prisoners awake. It was more than matched by the sudden explosion of a great earthquake, so that the foundations of the prison were shaken. And immediately, all the doors were opened, and everyone's fetters were loosed, unfastened. (Acts 16:26).

In the Mediterranean, earthquakes were familiar occurrences, as indeed they are today. But this earthquake was not simply fortuitous, just happening at the right time. It was designed by God for His glory and the salvation of many, and for the protection of His servants.

Immediately all the doors were opened, and every one's fetters were loosed. What a relief to aching, painful backs and legs that would have been!. Why did the prisoners not escape?

The jailer evidently expected them to have done so, when he was woken from his sleep by the earthquake and saw that the prison doors were opened. (Acts 16:27). His employment, his income, the disgrace to his family and probable punishment for dereliction of duty were all at the risk of loss and immediate prosecution. He and his family had no future. All this conspired him to draw his sword, and he was about to kill himself when he heard Paul's voice, 'Do yourself no harm, for we are all here'. (Acts 16:28).

It caused him to drop his sword arm for a moment and call his servant to bring lights so that he could assess the situation for himself. When he saw that Paul was indeed correct, that none of the prisoners had escaped, 'he rushed in and trembling with fear, he fell down before Paul and Silas, and brought them out and said, 'Men, what must I do to be saved? And they said, 'Believe on the Lord Jesus Christ and you will be saved and your household'. (Acts 1629-31). Paul and Silas were not concerned with their own physical condition. Here was a man who needed God, and here was an opportunity to preach the gospel.

From springing into the prison cell where Paul and Silas were confined, to falling before them in trembling and fear, to calling for lights so that he could see that what Paul was saying was true, to seeing in the supernatural earthquake a connection with Paul and Silas and what the slave had said about salvation, the jailer immediately came to a crisis of faith. He brought them out of the cell, saying, 'What must I do to be saved?'

Perhaps he only intended at first to find a way out of the consequences of his present dilemma. But God had considerably more in view for him and his family. He needed more than just the assurance of keeping his job, maintaining his way of living. He needed Jesus.

So Paul says, 'Believe on the Lord Jesus Christ and you will be saved, and your household'. (Acts 16:31). This short sentence sums up the whole gospel. He is the Lord, the Lord Jesus Christ and the way to come to Him and receive salvation, eternal life, is through faith. Believe and receive. This was all the man needed to know just then. More, so much more would come later. But to accept Him as Lord is the beginning, a Lord powerful enough to activate earthquakes when required to liberate His servants when they had been publicly humiliated.

It would be reasonable to speculate that since the other prisoners had heard Paul and Silas praying and singing hymns to God at midnight, they also may have heard Paul saying to the jailer, 'Believe on the Lord Jesus Christ and you will be saved', and their own spiritual journey of faith could have begun.

The jailer, now a saved and changed man, living in the good of the salvation promised to those with faith in Jesus, listened to Paul and Silas as they spoke the word of the Lord to him and to all that were in his house. (Acts 16:32). And he took them that same hour of the night and washed their wounded and injured bodies from the many blows they had been given. (Acts 16:23). Then he was baptized with all his family, the whole family rejoicing in what God had done for them.

The jailer brought Paul and Silas into his house and set food before them, and he rejoiced with all his household that he had believed in God. (Acts 16:34).

'But when it was day, the magistrates sent the police, probably the lictors who had beaten Paul and Silas, saying 'Let those men go!'

Their night's rest had also been interrupted by the earthquake and they assumed that it had something to do with those men whom they had committed to prison the day before without a trial and without any evidence of wrongdoing. The lictors were men who carried bundles of rods as staves or as a badge of office, called 'fasces' from which we get our word 'fascist' and had the responsibility of carrying out arrests and punishments.

This was the message which the magistrates wanted the lictors to transmit to the jailer. 'Let those men go'. It was within the magistrates power to authorize the release of prisoners, presumably regarding a beating and a night in the stocks as sufficient exercise of their authority. (Marshall p274).

The lictors brought the message to the jailer who reported it to Paul saying, 'The magistrates have sent to let you go. Now therefore, come out and go in peace. (Acts 16:36).

In a period of continual surprises, this surprise may have been the greatest of all to the jailer. Paul and Silas refused to leave: they found this curt dismissal anything but satisfactory. They knew that the authorities had committed a grave offence. Paul and Silas were Jews, but they were also Roman citizens. (Acts 16:38). They had only to say, 'civis Romanus sum', and then Roman law came into play. They could only be punished under Roman law if they had done something wrong, and only that on evidence.

How this statement of their Roman citizenship could be checked and verified, is unclear, but even the claim could be enough to cause a magistrate to pause, in anticipation of an unfortunate outcome if the claim was true. Roman citizens could not be publicly disgraced, especially uncondemned and without a fair trial. They had considerable immunity from the law, and could seek legal aid if their rights were infringed.

Paul said to the jailer, 'They have beaten us publicly uncondemned, men who are Roman citizens, and have thrown us into prison, and do they now cast us out secretly? No! Let them come themselves and take us out!' (Acts 16:37). He is impressing upon the authorities the enormity of what they have done.

Would it have been possible for Paul to have disclosed their citizenship earlier? Or was the arrest of Paul and Silas so expedited that no opportunity for a statement had been given to them by the magistrates?. But hearing that they were Roman citizens, the magistrates came and apologized to them, (Acts 16:39) probably grateful that nothing worse had happened to them for not protecting Roman citizens. They had got off lightly, and asking, urging Paul and Silas to leave the city, they were careful in future when dealing with these unpredictable Christians. The official apology may have helped to protect Christans in Philippi from the persecution all too often experienced in other parts of the Roman empire. The magistrates in Philippi had left themselves open to severe retribution and would not do so again.

Paul and Silas had returned to the prison from the jailer's house, to receive the official apology; to underline their unlawful incarceration and to save him from opprobrium. They now went out of of the prison, and visited Lydia, who together with 'the brethren', those who had already come to Christ through Paul's preaching and the women's praying, had no doubt been praying during this difficult time. And when they had seen the brethren, the members of this infant church, they encouraged them, exhorted them and departed. (Acts 16:40).

It may be that Luke was left behind in Philippi to care for the church, where he is mentioned as having been again present in Acts 20:5.

Acts Chapter 17

From Thessalonica to Athens

Acts 17:1-9. The uproar in Thessalonica

Now when they had passed through Amphipolis and Apollonia, they came to Thessalonica, where there was a synagogue of the Jews. And Paul went in, as was his custom, and for three weeks he argued with them from the scriptures, explaining and proving that it was necessary for the Christ to suffer and to rise from the dead and saying 'This Jesus whom I proclaim to you, is the Christ! (Acts 17:1-3).

Paul, Silas (verse 10) and possibly Timothy (verse 14), have now left Philippi, taking the road, the Via Egnatia, which ran west from Neapolis the port of Philippi on the Aegean coast to Dyrrhicum, through Philippi, Thessalonica, Beroea and Athens. Amphipolis was a town about 30 miles west southwest of Philippi, and Apollonia about 27 miles west southwest of Amphipolis and the Egnatian way. (Bruce p324. Barrett p 808).

Thessalonica was an important city in Roman times. It would have taken many days to reach Thessalonica from Philippi and Bruce suggests that at least part of the journey may have been taken on horseback.

Since Luke gives no indication of incidents happening in Amphipolis and Apollonia, we conclude that Paul and Silas did not stay there but moved on to Thessalonica. Here they stayed for at least the following three weeks (Acts 17:2), going into the synagogue every sabbath and reasoning, debating with them from the Old Testament scriptures, explaining and proving to those gathered together that it was necessary for the Christ to suffer and die and to rise from the dead, and saying as emphatically and persuasively as possible, 'This Jesus, whom I proclaim to you, is the Christ'. (Acts 17:3).

The three weeks of the R.S.V have been substituted for the three days of the K.J.V, and may indicate other occasions in addition to the Sabbath when Paul and Silas were to be found in the synagogue; covering a more extended period of time, and not necessarily consecutive Sabbaths. In Philippians 4:15, Paul describes how he left Macedonia and Philippi for Thessalonica and how the Philippian church entered into partnership with him in giving and receiving, even when he was in Thessalonica sending Paul help once and again. The tenor of the first chapter of 1 Thessalonians suggests a longer stay than three weeks.

Paul spoke in the synagogue in terms they could understand, opening up the Old Testament scriptures to them, biblically based exposition, identifying the long foretold and prophesied Messiah with Jesus, the only One to have died and to have risen from the dead.

To this teaching there was a positive response. Some were persuaded and joined Paul and Silas, as did a great many of the devout Greeks and not a few of the leading women. (Acts 17:4). We note Luke's signature use of litotes, and his perennial care for lesser people in society such as women, even 'leading' women in a patriarchal society, just as he had in his gospel.

The future church in Thessalonica was going to include Jews such as Jason, (Acts 17:6), Aristarchus and Secundus, (Acts 20:4), from the synagogue, and devout Greeks, pious men who had become involved in the Jewish religion through the synagogue worship, and leading women who on their own or their husband's account had some position in the city. This was the nucleus of the church in Thessalonica.

But there were Jews who were jealous. (Acts 17:5). Their religious practices were good and their doctrine unexceptionable. They wondered, what were Paul and Silas trying to do? Were they about to destroy all the work they had been doing to encourage the worship of the one true God, as an alternative to the majority of the Greek and Roman pagan populace who worshipped other gods?

They needed to do something about the subversive teaching of Paul and Silas before it got out of hand. They found some 'wicked fellows of the rabble', (Acts 17:5) rabble rousers, who gathered a crowd together and set the city in an uproar and attacked the house of Jason, (Acts 17:5), probably surmising that Paul and Silas were hidden in his house.

Those who had been 'persuaded by the gospel' (Acts 17:4), had joined Paul and Silas, and it was possible that they were meeting together in Jason's house, away from and apart from the synagogue. This may well have contributed to the jealousy of the Jews, (Acts 17:5), and even more to their frustration when Paul and Silas could not be found. Instead, they dragged Jason and some of the believers before the city authorities crying 'These men who have turned the world upside down have come here also and Jason has received them, and they are all acting against the decree of Caesar, saying that there is another king, Jesus. (Acts 17:7).

These are seditious acts in a Roman city. There were two charges against the Christians. First, that they had turned the world upside down, and secondly, that there is an alternative set of decrees, belonging to another ruler; not Caesar but Jesus.

The first claim suggests that knowledge of the activity of Paul and Silas, possibly even that of Paul and Barnabas had preceded them and was beginning to have a significant impact on the Roman empire. The second claim rests on the assertion of Jesus' teaching concerning the kingdom of God. HIs first recorded words in Matthew;s gospel are 'Repent, for the kingdom of heaven is at hand'. (Matthew 4:17). And where there is a kingdom there must of necessity be a king. 'Jesus is Lord' is a very early credal statement in the church, (1 Corinthians 12:3).

This claim is at the very centre, and the focus of every sermon recorded in Acts. Its importance cannot be overestimated. But for that very reason, it could well be interpreted as treasonable against Caesar, even though Jesus had explicitly stated on trial before Pontius Pilate, 'My kingdom is not of this world. If My kingdom was of this world, then would My servants fight'. (John 18:36).

There is no doubt that the city authorities and the people of the city were disturbed when they heard these accusations.

(Acts 17:8). But the main perpetrators of these disturbing doctrines, Paul and Silas, could not be found. All they could do was to take security from Jason, a court order in effect, which he was probably more than happy to accept, for his love for his brethren, and their future safety. This involved not allowing Paul and Silas to take up residence in his house again. They presumed that the apostles had left Thessalonica, but Jason was bound by his court order not to allow them to return to Thessalonica.

After this, all the city authorities could do was to let Jason and the other brethren go. (Acts 17:9).

Acts 17:10-15. Paul and Silas in Beroea

The brethren immediately sent Paul and Silas away by night to Beroea, and when they arrived, they went into the Jewish synagogue. Now these Jews were more noble than those in Thessalonica, for they received the word with all eagerness, examining the scriptures daily to see if these things were so.

Many of them therefore believed, with not a few Greek women of high standing, as well as men. (Acts 17:10-12).

There is such a sense of urgency here, as though there was no time to lose. Paul and Silas knew that the Jews would not take long in pursuing them to Beroea. They wanted to approach the Beroean Jews as quickly as possible with the gospel.

The journey from Thessalonica was long, about forty five miles on foot, but the imperative was strong. Here was another city, another synagogue where people needed to hear about Jesus.

The imperative of jealousy was also strong for the Jews of Thessalonica, (Acts 17:5), for they saw in what Paul and Silas were preaching an antinomian form of Judaism, a Judaism without the law of Moses, but having some kind of internal rationale of its own, concentrating on the person of a man called Jesus, who they claimed had been crucified and had risen from the dead.

All nonsense, they thought. Who could ever believe that someone had died, someone who was nobody, just a carpenter from Nazareth, who had become an itinerant preacher, and had come alive again and moreover was still alive and claimed to be active in this new sect which had been created in His Name? No wonder they were jealous of this perceived rival to their own way of worshipping God.

Paul and Silas had been sent away by night to Beroea, under cover of darkness by the brethren, the newly established church in Thessalonica. And losing no time, they had quickly made themselves known to the Jews of Beroea. Nobly, without prejudice or bias towards their own evaluation of the scriptures, they had listened to what Paul and Silas had to say, and examined it carefully, comparing their message to what was written in the word of God. And they did this daily, to see if these things were so which Paul and Silas were sharing with them. (Acts 17:11).

It becomes almost inevitable that Luke should write, 'many of them believed, with not a few women of high standing', women who had leisure to spend time listening to Paul and Silas; (a privilege not often given to women), 'as well as to men'. Luke again, as in his gospel, is not unaware of the subservient position of women in a patriarchal society, but wanted to demonstrate that the early church comprised women as well as men who had turned to the Lord in repentance and faith.

This happy state of affairs was not to last. The Jews of Thessalonica were on their way. When they learned that the word of the Lord was proclaimed by Paul at Beroea also, they came there too, stirring up and inciting the crowd. (Acts 17:13). This was the method they had used before, to try to bring the whole movement before the authorities so that Paul and Silas could be adequately punished and their teaching of no effect. What the authorities, deriving their authority from Rome, were really afraid of, were riots and unlawful assembly, for that indicated an inability on their part to control the populace.

Something had to be done and done quickly. The brethren, these new, beloved Beroean believers, immediately sent Paul off on his way to the sea, for the voyage to Athens, (Acts 17:14), sending with him some of the brethren to look after him and conduct him on his way. (Acts 17:15). This may have included Sopater of Beroea, the son of Pyrrhus. (Acts 20:4). Paul was sorry not to have with him Silas and Timothy who remained in Beroea, and asked them to come to him as soon as possible. Then the little group departed for Athens. (Acts 17:15).

Acts 17:16-34. Paul at Athens

Now while Paul was waiting for Silas and Timothy at Athens, his spirit was provoked within him as he saw that the city was full of idols. So he argued in the synagogue with the Jews and the devout persons, and in the Agora, the marketplace, every day with those who chanced to be there. (Act 17:16,17).

Paul was left alone in Athens, waiting for his friends to join him, but he could not help noting the proliferation of idols in the city as he travelled about. This was Athens, the city famous for its intellectual and academic learning. It had been the place where many philosophers like Socrates had had their home, and it was the adopted home of Aristotle, Epicurus and Zeno, the founder of Stoic philosophy.

As early as the fifth century it had become a democratic city where everyone, excluding slaves and women, could take part in its governance, and when it came under the control of Rome in 146 BC, it was still allowed to be a free and liberated city, *civitas libera et foederata*. The cultural influence of Athens in the early centuries was tremendous. At the time of Paul's visit, there was a famous university, although it was the synagogue and then the Agora to which Paul directed his attention. (Acts 17:17 Bruce p 331).

Paul's spirit was provoked within him while he waited for Silas and Timothy. Beautiful though many of the artefacts were, the statues and images of gods and goddesses which he saw as he traversed the city, they aroused in him a strong antipathy for he knew them to be idols, that which is worshipped in a fundamental aversion and opposition to God, the only God, the only God who should be worshipped.

His spirit was troubled because he saw that in spite of their great wisdom, these men had become fools, for they had exchanged the glory of the immortal, invisible God for images resembling mortal men, men who looked just like themselves. (Romans 1:23). What Paul longed for, and what he tried to show them was they should turn to God from idols as they had in Thessalonica, to serve the living and true God and to wait for His Son from heaven. (1 Thessalonians 1:9,10).

So he argued every day in the synagogue with not only the Jews but devout people who really wanted to know the truth, (Acts 17:17), as his custom had become. (Acts 17:2). And he also spent time in the marketplace, discussing moral philosophy with the Epicurean and Stoic philosophers.

The Epicureans whose teacher was Epicurus, 341-270 BC were hedonists. They regarded pleasure as the chief aim in life, and to be achieved by avoiding pain. Hedonism comes from the Greek word for pleasure, *hedone*. It was a life free from pain, untroubled by passion of any kind on their own behalf or on the behalf of others. Though they believed in gods, their gods were indistinct beings, unconcerned with the ordinary lives of men and women. So there was no restraint on whatever action they wanted to perform in order to achieve complete tranquility and peacefulness. Theirs was not an uncontrolled hedonism, but the absence of pain.

Epicureans held an atomic theory, the theory that everything in the universe is made up of atoms which are moving in empty space. An earlier philosopher Democritus, also thought that the universe was composed of atoms, but his atoms came down in a predetermined way colliding every so often in order to bring about change. Epicurus thought that these atoms actually swerved for no apparent reason, that they had free will, and that therefore the world is due to chance, a random course of atoms. There is no survival after death and no judgement, so why not pursue pleasure?

The Stoics were founded by Zeno of Citium, 333-262 BC, and met together at the Stoa Poikile, or Painted Stoa, a beautiful colonnade in Athens, hence their name. They regarded nature, 'natural' or 'creation' theology, not theology as we know it, but as the standard to which they should aspire; the '*logos*', 'reason', or the design of nature as the principle which created the universe and the highest expression of nature. (Marshall p282). They were indifferent to pleasure or pain, believing that the only thing completely within an individual's control was the ability to acquire the correct moral attitude, which could be equated with virtue and grounded in knowledge. These ideas were taken up later by Seneca, 4 B.C-65 A.D and Marcus Aurelius, 121-80 A.D. (Lesley Levene. I think therefore I am. 2020).

These Stoic philosophers had a concept of God as of an ultimate Being who was the world soul; a devolved kind of pantheism; that this world soul inhabited everything and every individual soul. But like the Epicureans, they were materialistic, emphasizing the rational over the emotional and being completely self-sufficient, to the extent of taking their own life if necessary when it could not tolerably be supported. (Bruce p 332).

There was a sense in which they had a glimmer of truth. The logos or word or reason, the creator of the universe was in the world. The logos who was the light that lightens every man who comes into the world, had come. (John 1:4,9). But He came as a gift to be received not as an impersonal, automatic force. Yet to all who received that gift, who believed in His Name, He gave the right, the authority to become a child of God. (John 1:12). There was nothing automatic about it. No one automatically became one with the word, the logos. It required faith.

While Stoicism enabled men, especially men, to live with dignity and a high moral sense, Paul would have been revolted by their pride. His spirit was revolted (Acts 17:16), by their attitude, so contrary to, and antagonistic to the spirit of Christianity, indeed to the spirit of Christ Himself. They thought they had achieved what was actually impossible, the correct way to live by virtue of their own reason and logical training.

Of course, people had to be wealthy to live in such a way. No thought was given to the lives lived by working men and women on whom their life of leisure depended. They were of no account. Paul himself had known poverty. He spoke of himself as having nothing and yet possessing all things. (2 Corinthians 6:10). But what a contrast to these philosophers who lived in plenty, relying on their own wisdom and conviction as to what makes a good life. Paul is concerned for them. He is fearful for their salvation, abhorring as he does their complete indifference to any other viewpoint but their own, while at the same time asking Paul to expound his theories to them. (Acts 17:20).

These were the men with whom Paul was conducting debates in the Agora, the marketplace. They were not impressed by Paul. Some said, 'what would this babbler say?' Others said, 'He seems to be a preacher of foreign divinities', because he preached Jesus and the resurrection. And they took him and brought him to the Areopagus, or Mars Hill, saying 'May we know what this new teaching is which you present? For you bring some strange things to our ears. We wish to know therefore what these things mean'.

Rev. John Stott envisages a problem here, for he notes that in our own day there are many religions, many schools of thought, and we are commended for not disturbing their convictions, to which of course they are entitled, as we are to ours. But this is the rejection of any kind of evangelism. Students are encouraged to study comparative religion, to try to understand why Hindus, Muslims and others believe as they do, and to respect their views. This is obviously a good thing until it means that Christians are forbidden to encourage them to understand the gospel of Christ.

Paul understands that these men were on the way to perdition without knowing the uniqueness of Jesus, of His saving love and compassion for them, of His agony on the cross for them, of His resurrection and His glory at His Father's right hand. Stott's concern is that in our day, though men and women may be 'lost', alienated from God, 'dead through their trespasses and sins in which they walked, (Ephesians2:2). until the light of the glorious gospel of God in the face of Jesus Christ has shined upon them, (2 Corinthians 4:4), it is often regarded as inappropriate to speak to them of Christ and Him crucified. (1 Corinthians 2:2).

So, why did Paul disturb their well thought out and happy lives with talk about Jesus? Because only Jesus could save them from their sin and give them new life in Him.

There are faithful Christians and communities however, which still persist in preaching the gospel, where men and women still respond to the good news of salvation, where the Holy Spirit is still doing His work of convicting men and women of sin and righteousness and judgement, (John 16:8), of glorifying Jesus, of guiding men and women into all truth. (John 16:12). It is not a question of changing one's religion, but of coming to the living God, the one who loved us so much that He gave His only Son to save us from our sins, from ourselves.

God is still seeking the lost, bringing them to Himself.

Paul did not leave the Athenians to their own devices but gave them a challenge. The alternatives were Jesus, or some representation of a god in the likeness of a human being, or even the choice of no god at all, but an intellectual and moral construct of how men ought to live. Isaiah reports God as saying, 'I am the first and the last, *besides Me there is no god.* (Isaiah 44:9-20). No doubt Paul remembered the word of the Lord spoken to Isaiah.

Paul's presence in the Agora attracted the attention of the Epicurean and Stoic philosophers, for this had long been their modus operandi; debate, asking questions, and trying to supply answers.

They were disappointed in Paul. Some called him a babbler. Others thought he was preaching some foreign divinities because he preached Jesus and the resurrection which they may have thought of as two divinities. To accuse him of being a babbler is to accuse him of picking up ideas from others and claiming them as his own. To accuse him of preaching foreign divinities is to accuse him of proclaiming a new but lesser god, Jesus.

The Greek construction could imply a personification of the Greek word for resurrection '*anastasia*', perhaps another female deity. But Barrett, p831, thinks that unlikely. He says 'Jesus and the resurrection' is straightforward enough and corresponds to all that we know of Paul's teaching. And in this instance, Paul is adapting his observations to that of the Athenians, discussing moral questions in the Agora, but in the light of the gospel of Jesus and His resurrection, and according to the promise of Jesus, being given what to say by the Holy Spirit. (Matthew 10:19,20).

A greater, much greater, than Epicurus or Zeno was here.

Acts 17:19-31. Paul before the Areopagus

And they took hold of Paul and brought him to the Areopagus, saying, May we know what this new teaching is which you present? For you bring some strange things to our ears; we wish to know therefore what these things mean.

Now all the Athenians and the foreigners who lived there spent their time in nothing except telling and hearing something new. (Acts 17:19-21).

In the New Testament, Achaia is paired with Macedonia, Achaia referring to the southern half of Greece, particularly Thessaly and the northern part of the Peloponnesus; and Macedonia the northern half of Greece, as in Acts 19:21; Romans 15:26 and 1 Thessalonians 1:7-8. Together they refer to Greece as a whole.

Achaia became a Roman senatorial province, that is, governed by a proconsul of Rome, including not only the mainland but several islands. In the time of Paul, this was Gallio. (Acts 18:12). The most important of its cities was Corinth.

Athens on the whole proved unresponsive to Paul's teaching, but Achaia in general was moved by it to come to faith. The household of Stephanas were said to be the first converts in Achaia, and his household probably an early Christian meeting place. (1 Corinthians 16:15). And 2 Corinthians is also addressed to the church in Achaia. (2 Corinthians 1:1). The Achaian church also helped to send aid to the church in Jerusalem (2 Corinthians 9:2; Romans 15:26).

The Areopagus

The name Areopagus denotes both a low hill north of the Acropolis in Athens, and also the court of the Areopagites, the ancient Athenian council. Areopagus means 'the will of Ares'. Ares was the god of war in Greek mythology, but Mars was the Roman god of war, so the hill was also known as Mars Hill. There is also archaeological evidence which located the court in the Stoa Basileios, or royal colonnade or portico and this may be the court of the Areopagites before whom Paul appeared. (Acts 17:19, 22) This was a court, however, not of trial, but an unofficial, almost improvised, informal discussion with Greek philosophers. The Parthenon, a temple dedicated to the goddess Athena, was located on the Acropolis in Athens.

In Paul's time, Athens was still the intellectual centre of the world, yet he did not succeed in establishing a church there as he had in Corinth, Colossae and Ephesus. Dionysius, an Areopagite, and Damaris and 'some men', however, joined him and believed, and may well have formed the nucleus of a Christian community. (Acts 17:34).

It was to the court of the Areopagus that Paul was taken. 'They took hold of him and brought him to the Areopagus saying 'May we know what this teaching is which you present? For you bring strange things to our ears; we wish to know therefore what these things mean'. (Acts 17:19). Now all the Athenians and the foreigners who lived there spent their time in nothing except telling and hearing some new thing, (Acts 17:21).

The Epicurean and Stoic philosophers had itching ears. Paul later writing to Timothy speaks of a future when people will not endure sound teaching but having itching ears they will accumulate to themselves teachers to suit their own likings, and will turn away from the truth and wander into myths. (2 Timothy 4:3). Paul was right. This is surely the case with our own generation. But the Athenians had lived like that long before Paul wrote to Timothy. Their whole lives were filled with wanting to know something new, although some of them at least may have genuinely wanted to explore other ideas in order to come to the truth.

But when Paul stands in the midst of the Areopagus, (Acts 17:22), his concern is not with their philosophical exploration. He says. 'Men of Athens, I perceive that in every way you are very *religious*. For as I passed along and observed the objects of your worship, I also found an altar with this inscription "to an unknown god". What therefore you worship as unknown, this I proclaim to you'. (Acts 17:23).

Paul had seen many statues and sculptures beautifully executed and extensively worshipped in Athens, but he concentrated on speaking of an altar he had seen, for an altar represented sacrificial worship, where the worshipper is identified with the animal being sacrificed. This altar was to an unknown god, signifying that the worshipper wanted to know him.

How do we know God? What is the relationship between God and the creatures He has made? Ecclesiates 8:8 looks upon God as the one who has the power to retain the spirit of man, and authority over the day of his death. Ecceesiastes says, 'there is no discharge from that war'.

Paul says to the Athenians rather less morbidly that there is a Fatherhood of God, available to all men and women everywhere and at all times, for God is the Creator of life and we are His offspring. (Acts 17:28). He it is who gives life to the child in the womb, and He it is who determines the day of our death, 'since He Himself gives to all men life and breath and everything'. (Acts 17:25).

God has the ultimate word. His decision is final. In His infinite love and mercy, He has it all under control. He does not live in shrines made by man as though He needed anything, but has so arranged for mankind their allotted period and the boundaries of their habitation that He has made it possible for men and women to seek after Him; though He is not far from each one of us, for in Him we live and move and have our being. And we are indeed His offspring.

Paul says, for 'the Deity is not like gold or silver or stone, as are the idols in Athens, but the times of ignorance God has overlooked, and now commands all men everywhere to repent, because He has fixed a day when He will judge the world by the Judge whom He has appointed, Jesus Christ, and of this He has given assurance to all men by raising Him from the dead.' (Acts 17:29-31)

In creation terms, God is the Father of all mankind and all are His offspring, receiving their life from Him. (Stott p287). It is in redemption that He is the Father only of those who are in Christ.

God is the Father of all men and women because He gives them life. He is the Father of those who have been redeemed by the blood of His Son because He gives them Himself, not as the world soul of the Stoics entering our soul on a universal basis, but as a personal intimate knowledge of Him, for He is known as Father by the person who has been redeemed by Him, the repentant sinner who has had his sins forgiven, making way for the Holy Spirit to come and dwell within him with no barrier of sin between (Stott p287).

Paul knew that these men and women needed to come to a new understanding of God, and who they were and what they could become in Him. The Athenians were ignorant. Paul says, so 'what you worship in ignorance I proclaim to you', (Acts 17:23), because he wanted them to come to a place of repentance and redemption, of understanding that God had a purpose for their lives in creating them, giving them life on a physical level, but longing for them to understand Him on a spiritual level. God wanted to give them life eternal, life which never dies.

Paul continues, God does not live in a shrine. How can He live in a shrine when He is the Lord of heaven and earth, and gives to all men and women life and breath and everything? (Acts 17:25). Paul regards it almost as an insult to God to provide Him with a shrine. How can He be confined in that way, dependent on being served by human beings who are no doubt well intentioned but ill informed and mistaken, having to rely on Him for the very breath they breathe?

Bruce writes, (p336), the Epicureans and the Stoics were believers in an impersonal divine essence pantheistically conceived. Paul leads them to the living God, revealed however not only as Creator but Judge.

The Greeks considered themselves to be a superior race, all other races being barbarians. Paul says they are nothing of the sort. All human beings derive from one man, (that is, Adam), and are part of the whole human race in divinely determined periods of time and location. (Acts 17:26).

God's purpose in this was that they should seek God, in the hope that they might find Him. (Acts 17:27). Yet He is not from each one of us for in Him we live and move and have our being. (Acts 17:28).

As Creator, God is naturally Lord of that which He has created, but He wants more than that. He wants men and women to seek after Him. He knows that they are ignorant, like blind people stumbling around in the dark, in the hope that in feeling after God they might find Him. But He is not far from any of us. As God breathed His life into the man whom He had created and man became a living soul, so the Holy Spirit, the Breath of God, can equally intimately breathe into a human being the spiritual life of God because of the sacrifice of Jesus, who makes all things new. (Revelation 21:5).

The problem is that people have been seeking God but seeking Him in the wrong way. We are God's offspring, Paul says. We have bodies that move, think, work, sleep. We think and feel, and yet make images of wood or stone, gold or silver, and confine them to a box, or a building, images that represent deity and yet cannot do any of the things which we can do. If we do not confine ourselves like that, why should we seek to confine that which we worship in that way?

The God we are seeking is a living, purposeful still creating God who is making Himself available to us, for He is not far from any of us, (Acts 17:27). He may be invisible, inaccessible to our sight, but He is real, so real, so present with us, so kind and compassionate, merciful wise and loving. We already exist in Him, for in Him we live and move and have our being. (Acts 17:28). He is not remote from us but accessible. He says 'draw near to Me and I will draw near to you'. He is so near.

But here Paul issues a word of warning to the Athenians: 'the times of ignorance God overlooked, but now He commands all men and women everywhere to repent because He has fixed a day on which He will judge the world in righteousness by a Man whom He has appointed, and of this He has given proof, assurance, by raising Him from the dead.' (Acts 17:30,31).

For a long time, the Greeks had concentrated on their view of natural theology, that is, a god of nature, a god as Creator. For many Greeks however, there had evolved a different kind of theological outlook, a pantheon of so many gods and goddesses, for all occasions and for all circumstances, that these Greeks were concerned in case they were in danger of forgetting one of them, and so had built an altar to an 'unknown god'. It is to these confused and probably troubled souls that Paul is saying, these were times of ignorance, but God is a God of forbearance and mercy. Though it was a time of ignorant, idolatrous worship, those times of ignorance He has overlooked.

But now the time has come for all men and women everywhere to repent, for unless they come to Him in repentance, and come to a knowledge of the truth, they will continue permanently in this state of Ignorance and darkness, perhaps even having a form of godliness but denying its power. (2 Timothy 3:5).

This leads inevitably to what Paul says about the outcome of their non-repentance. God has determined on a day when He will sit as Judge. God is a God of righteousness. He will have to judge the worship of idols. The very proliferation of idols in the city demonstrates how important worship is to them. There were so many expressions of a compromised deity in the form of idols, but even so, they were afraid of having missed one out. But God is calling them through Paul's words, to repent from worshipping idols, to turn from them, for they were being worshipped in unrighteousness.

And as they turn from idols and turn to Him, they will discover the Man whom God has appointed to judge the world, a Man who is also God's own Son, who had been alive but who had died and had now been raised from the dead. Paul had already spoken to the Athenians in the Agora of Jesus and the resurrection. (Acts 17:18). Now he amplifies his message.

The Man was of course Jesus, but Paul does not say so in this hearing before the Areopagus. His emphasis is on the fact that this Man was unique To begin with He was living, alive, not like those idols which represented the gods whom they worshipped. And then this Man died, as only a living man could do. And then He lived again, raised from the dead as proof that He was a righteous, sinless man whom death could not hold.

This was the Man whom God had chosen to be the Judge at the end of time, for there was no unrighteousness in Him. However hard the Epicureans and the Stoics struggled, tried to live a blameless life, all their efforts failed. There was only One who was completely righteous and without sin, and only the one who was totally righteous could have the privilege of judging the unrighteous. Paul says, 'He will judge the world in righteousness, this Man whom God has appointed. (Acts 17:31). This is why Paul faithfully explains to the Athenians that they must repent and turn to Him who will take away their unrighteousness and fill them with His righteousness.

The reaction of some of those who were listening to Paul was predictable. How could anyone believe that a man could rise from the dead? they mocked. But there were others who thoughtfully said, we would kike to hear more about this, 'we will hear you again about this'. (Acts 17:32).

So Paul went from among them, down the hill from the Areopagus, thinking and praying that these men would turn from idols to serve the Lord, the living and true God. (Acts 17:33).

There were some who believed and who joined him, including Dionysius the Areopagite, who would have been part of the council of the Areopagus, and a woman named Damaris, and others with them (Acts 17:34).

God had overlooked the times of ignorance, (Acts 17:30) until the day of the resurrection of His Son. Now God has His perfect righteous Servant, the Lord Jesus, and judgement could no longer be suspended. A new era has begun. God loved the world so much that He sent His only begotten Son that whoever believes in Him will not perish but have everlasting life (John 3:16). His Son is the Man appointed to judge the world, this righteous One.

And God wants the men and women of Athens to see Jesus as He sees Him, and to turn from their idolatry and sin to find in Him the salvation He came to give. He is full of joy when one sinner repents, and full of sadness if they turn away from Him, for in a sense they have passed judgement on themselves by rejecting Him.

God had sent His faithful servant Paul to share the good news with the Athenians, that they might receive eternal life in Jesus. Many will have rejoiced in this good news. Others will have rejected it. Paul must move on to Corinth for so God had ordained.

Acts Chapter 18

Acts 18:1-4. Paul arrives at Corinth

After this Paul left Athens and went to Corinth. And he found a Jew named Aquila, a native of Pontus, lately come from Italy with his wife Priscilla, because Clauduis had commanded all the Jews to leave Rome.

And Paul went to see them; and because he was of the same trade he stayed with them and they worked, for by trade they were tentmakers. And he argued in the synagogue every Sabbath, and persuaded Jews and Greeks.

Athens was the intellectual and cultural centre of the known world. Corinth was a famous commercial centre. And together with Ephesus these were the three most important cities outside Rome. Yet they all had the same reputation for immorality, especially Corinth, and Corinth was the city to which Paul had now been brought through the guiding of the Holy Spirit, that through the gospel, he might become a father in Christ to those who would become his children in the faith. (1 Corinthians 4:15).

Corinth was about thirty seven miles from Athens. It had been a famous city in classical times, but had been destroyed when Rome conquered Greece in 146 BC. Under Julius Caesar it was rebuilt and became a Roman colony. In 27 BC it became the capital city of Achaia, the southern part of Greece. Because it was a maritime city, occupying a position on the isthmus of Corinth on the Aegean sea, it became a great commercial centre, lying as it did on the great trade route between the Greek mainland and the Peloponnesian peninsula.

It also had a reputation for sexual immorality. On the summit of a rocky eminence behind the city stood the temple of Aphrodite, the Greek goddess of love, also known in the Roman pantheon as Venus. The temple of Aphrodite was served by a thousand female slaves. (Stott p 296). It also cultivated a Hellenized version of the worship of Astarte, a Syrian goddess sometimes identified as the female consort of Baal in the Old Testament, (Judges 2:11, 13; 3:7) Asherah being the plural of Astarte. (Barrett pp 256,342). Astarte was also worshipped as the queen of heaven by the people of Judah before they were carried away captive to Babylon. (Jeremiah 44:17,25).

These details help to explain many of the warnings given to the church in Corinth in Paul's letters. The Corinthian believers had much to overcome culturally as they embraced Christianity, and Pau's letters reflect some of their problems, including their internal divisions and their relationships to each other and to idols. These problems were more destructive of their witness to the Lord Jesus than outward persecution, but have made the Corinthian letters especially precious to later believers.

To Paul's joy, he found in Corinth a Jew named Aquila, a native of Pontus, who had recently come from Italy with his wife Priscilla, because the emperor Claudius had commanded all the Jews to leave Rome. (Acts 18:2). We can surely see here an example of the mysterious working of God. Because of the edict of Claudius, Aquila and Priscilla were in Corinth at exactly the right time to befriend Paul, God's servant. Claudius meant it for evil, but God meant it for good. (Genesis 50:20; Romans 8:28).

There is evidence that Claudius tried on several occasions to remove the Jews from Rome. The time recorded in Acts 18 was probably in 49/50 AD. In Acts 11:28 mention has already been made of Claudius in connection with a famine during his time as the fourth emperor, which gave the Christians in Antioch an opportunity to send relief to the churches in Judea and Jerusalem.

Claudius ruled Rome from 41-54 AD, and during that time, Britain was conquered and became a Roman province. (Barrett p 240).

We have noted that the edict went out, causing Jews to leave Rome just at the right time for Priscilla and Aquila to meet with

Paul and offer him Christian companionship. When Paul had gone to Athens, he had left Silas and Timothy in Beroea, sending them a message to join him as soon as possible. From 1Thessalonians 3:1 it appears that Timothy had joined him in Athens, but had then been sent by Paul to Thessalonica to establish the Thessalonians in the faith, although it meant that Paul was in Athens alone.

Timothy then went to Macedonia, northern Greece, probably Philippi, where he met up with Silas again; and Paul went to Corinth, Acts 18:1, Silas and Timothy returning from Macedonia to be with Paul in Corinth. (Acts 18:5; 1 Thessalonians 3:6). It is from Corinth that Paul writes to the Thessalonians. (Bruce p 330).

Aquila had originally come from Pontus, a region which was part of Bithynia, near the Euxine or Black Sea. (Acts 18:2). He had travelled to Rome and had now come to Corinth with his wife Priscilla. (The diminutive of Prisca. Romans 16:3; 1 Corinthians 16:19).

Paul was delighted to discover that they were not only Christians, but were also tentmakers, a trade to which he had been apprenticed as a rabbinic student, for the rabbis considered it important that a teaching rabbi should have a means of supporting himself while engaged with teaching his students freely, gratuitously. In Paul's farewell speech to the Ephesian elders, he reminded them that 'these hands ministered to my necessities and to those who were with me' (Acts 20:34). He also mentions this in 1 Thessalonians 1:9; 2 Thessalonians 3:8; and 1 Corinthians 9:1-7. For Paul, this was a principle of his ministry as an apostle, that he should not be a burden to anyone, least of all to these men and women who had become believers under his proclamation of the gospel.

Paul's home was in Tarsus, in Cilicia. He was a citizen of no mean city. (Acts 21:39). The province of Cilicia was famous for its manufacture of a kind of cloth using goat's hair. This rough cloth was ideal for the making of tents and this was such a necessary commodity in an age when soldiers were on the move all the time, and when travellers often preferred to use their own tents rather than stay in inns which were not always clean and sometimes verminous.

Paul and Aquila and Priscilla worked happily together, working at their trade and arguing in the synagogue every Sabbath, persuading Jews and also Greeks, those known as God fearers, men and women who had become such a feature of synagogue life as a result of the diaspora, the dispersion of Jews throughout the empire. These men and women were attracted by the ethical teaching of the Old Testament, the Jewish way of life, and the worship of the only true God.

A further encouragement to Paul was the arrival of Silas and Timothy from Macedonia, bringing news of Phillipi and Thessalonica. Paul was 'occupied with preaching, testifying to the Jews that the Christ, the Messiah was Jesus', (Acts 18:5) a message which Paul had constantly and consistently preached in all the synagogues wherever he had been invited to preach. It may be that Silas and Timothy brought supplies from Macedonia, enabling Paul to cease from his tentmaking for a while in order to give himself up to the preaching of the gospel, proclaiming to the Jews that the one whom they considered to be a prophet, the Messiah of whom they read in their scriptures was Jesus, the one foretold so long ago, but now the one who had been crucified, had died and had been raised from the dead to sit at His Father's right hand.

We do not know how long these five Christian believers lived in close harmony with one another, working and praying together, having an opportunity to testify to the Jews that Jesus was the Messiah, rejoicing in those who on hearing the word became believers.

But at some point, the inevitable happened. The Jews rose up, opposed Paul and reviled him. (Acts 18:6), Paul was no longer free to use the synagogue. He shook out his garments against them, signifying that from now on he no longer had any part with them and said, 'Your blood be upon your own heads. I am innocent. From now on I will go to the Gentiles'. (Acts 18:6). It was necessary for him to make them understand the consequences of rejecting, not only the interpretation of their scriptures in the light of the Lord Jesus entering the world, but that the One of whom the scriptures spoke so clearly, was indeed the Lord Jesus Christ.

This appears to have become the pattern of Paul's ministry; an initial attempt in the synagogue to persuade the Jews of the Messiahship of Jesus, followed by opposition by the Jews, then a determination by Paul to go to the Gentiles. Acts 13:46; 28:28 confirm this.

In Galatians, Paul makes much of his apostleship to the Gentiles. He says that he had been entrusted with the gospel to the Gentiles, while Peter had been entrusted with the gospel to the Jews. (Galatians 2:7). But this did not mean that Paul never preached to the Jews, only that it happened as a frequent pattern that his preaching was almost continually opposed by the Jews so that it appeared that his ministry was outside the synagogue and amongst the Gentiles, This was not a deliberate ploy on his part, but the result of the Jewish rejection of his message.

Paul says, (Acts 18:6), 'I am innocent, clear of neglecting to declare to you that Jesus, for whom you have been searching, and longing and waiting, has come. He has come in the flesh and has died and has risen again from the dead and is at God's right hand in glory. You have heard the gospel at my mouth, that this same Jesus has come to give you forgiveness of sins and eternal life in Him. But you have rejected it. I must continue to preach the gospel for to that I have been called by God. Since you will not or cannot receive the gospel, I must go to the Gentiles. I have no choice'.

And leaving the synagogue, he went to the house of Titius Justus, a worshipper of God, whose house was next to the synagogue. (Acts 18:7). This may have been overflow accommodation for the numbers of people who wanted to come and hear the gospel message. Barrett suggests, not that Paul left the home of Aquila and Priscilla, but that Titius Justus used his home as a preaching centre as it was so close to the synagogue, (Barrett p 867).

It is quite likely that Paul had already used the home of Titius Justus for this purpose, and it had become an alternative venue for those Corinthians who would not have wanted to go to the synagogue and identify themselves as God fearers but were eager to find out more of what Paul was preaching. Titius Justus was a Roman name, and not to be identified with the Titus of whom Paul often writes. (e.g 2 Corinthians 2:13). He was a Gentile believer, and like Cornelius, in Acts 10:2, was a man who reverenced God. (Acts 18:7).

Perhaps it was in the home of this man that Crispus, the ruler of the synagogue, believed on the Lord with all his household, and many Corinthians hearing Paul, believed and were baptized. (Acts 18:8). The baptism of Crispus was mentioned by Paul in his first letter to the Corinthians, together with Gaius, which may have been the Latin name of Justus, (Barrett p345), while many others were baptized, though not by Paul. (1 Corinthians 1: 14).

Once again, men and women were coming to know the truth concerning Jesus and were persuaded that He was indeed the Saviour of the world, and that through Him they could have eternal life, life in the Holy Spirit, life that cannot die but goes on forever, new life in Jesus.

It encourages us to know that even Paul's ministry among the Corinthians was in weakness and fear and much trembling, and that nevertheless God was able to use him. In fact God used these aspects of his ministry to be the means whereby the faith of those who believed rested not in the wisdom of man but in the power of God. (1 Corinthians 2:3; 5). 'And the Lord said to Paul one night in a vision, "do not be afraid, but speak and do not be silent, for I am with you and no man shall attack you to harm you, for I have many people in this city"'. (Acts 18:9,10).

On this word to him, Paul could gladly go on. Knowing that God was with him was all he needed to know. So often the servants of the Lord have been encouraged to pursue the way set for them by their loving heavenly Father, knowing that He recognizes their human limitations yet uses even those to glorify Him.

God always encourages and comforts His servants, and on God's word to him, Paul stayed in Corinth a year and six months, teaching the word of God among them; (Acts 18:11), probably from late summer 50 A.D to early spring 52 A.D, and during this period, also writing comforting letters to the Thessalonians. (Bruce p346).

Acts 18:12-17. Paul before Gallio

But when Gallio was proconsul of Achaia, the Jews made a united attack upon Paul and brought him before the tribunal saying, 'This man is persuading men to worship God contrary to the law'.

But when Paul was about to open his mouth, Gallio said to the Jews, 'If it were a matter of wrongdoing or vicious crime, I should have reason to bear with you, O Jews. But since it is a matter of questions about words and names and your own law, see to it yourselves. I refuse to be a judge of these things. And he drove them from the tribunal. (Acts 18:12-16).

According to the Roman historian Pliny, Gallio became proconsul of Achaia under Claudius in July 51 A.D. Achaia was an important province and Corinth was the chief city of Achaia. It contained the residence of the proconsul, in front of which was the tribunal.

To Gallio, the Jews of Corinth now brought an accusation against Paul. The Jews were allowed some licence in the ordering of their own community, but some areas of perceived lawlessness had to be subject to Roman law. So the accusation which the Jews brought against Paul had to be subject to Roman law, saying, 'this man is persuading men to worship contrary to the law', that is contrary to Roman law.

There may have been more than one synagogue in Corinth, and on this occasion at least, they were united. (Acts 18:12). It was a united atack on Paul by the Jews as they brought him before the tribunal. This tribunal *bema*, was possibly a kind of rostrum or raised platform from which the judge decided whether a charge against a Corinthian citizen was of legal importance (Barrett p 871, 872), for domestic law could conflict with that of the mighty Roman legal system.

Gallio was not taken in by the Jew's duplicity. He recognized that their real objective was Paul's teaching which was causing some disturbance among the Jews. Paul was preaching not the annulment but the fulfilment of the Mosaic law by Jesus. In effect, the Jews had totally misunderstood what Paul was saying. Their perception was that Paul was preaching contrary to the *Mosaic* law, but their perception was erroneous. Their way of life was not threatened but would be enhanced by faith in Jesus. But they were troubled enough to want to bring Paul before Gallio.

Were they expecting that Gallio would give them protection against such teaching by forbidding it as being opposed to *Roman* law? Did they truly believe that such teaching would undermine their whole religious perspective and way of life? Claudius had published edicts against interference of the Jewish religion by non- Jews and the Jews of Corinth wanted to prove that Paul was a Jewish heretic and the faith which he was preaching was an illegal religion. Standing in front of the tribunal, Paul was about to open his mouth, but Gallio prevented him. It was not necessary for him to provide a defence of his teaching for Gallio, for he was aware that there was some misrepresentation here, some deception. The Jews were claiming that what Paul preached was contrary to Roman law, but in fact they were only concerned with their own law.

Gallio was commissioned by his office as proconsul to investigate any infraction of Roman law, but he had no interest in sorting out squabbles over Jewish law, especially as theoretically it was important only to the Jews, a troublesome group of people at the best of times. Gallio said to the Jews, 'If it were a matter of wrongdoing or vicious crime, I should have reason to bear with you, O Jews. But since it is a matter of questions about words and names and your own law, see to it yourselves. I refuse to be a judge of these things'. And he drove them from the tribunal. (Acts 18:14-16).

In their anger and frustration, the Jews seized Sosthenes, the ruler of the synagogue who had become a believer (1 Corinthians 1:1), and beat him in front of the tribunal. Why did Gallio not interfere and stop this cruel treatment of this man who had been one of the leaders of the synagogue? Luke tells us that Gallio 'paid no attention to this', or in the AV, 'Gallio cared for none of these things'. Paul had committed no offence according to Roman law and Gallio was not interested in Jewish law or how the Jews applied it.

Sosthenes took the beating which the Jews had intended for Paul. Sosthenes was either the successor to Crispus or had been a ruler of the synagogue in conjunction with Crispus. (Acts 18:8). In 1 Corinthians 1:1 he is acknowledged as sharing with Paul his ministry to the Corinthian church, evidently not dissuaded from the truth of the gospel by his undeserved punishment.

Gallio's refusal to interfere with the Jewish law, and his impartiality towards the complaint against Paul which he had exercised, and his indifference towards the Jews, may have encouraged Paul to overestimate the liberality of the Roman law, and to believe that he could appeal to the supreme tribunal in Rome when he later affirmed his demand to appeal to Caesar. (Acts 25:11).

Acts 18:18-23. Paul's return journey to Antioch in Syria

After this, Paul stayed many days longer and then took leave of the brethren and sailed for Syria, and with him, Priscilla and Aquila. At Cenchreae, he cut his hair, for he had a vow. And they came to Ephesus and he left them there, but he himself went into the synagogue and argued with the Jews. When they asked him to stay for a longer period, he declined but on taking leave of them he said, 'I will return to you if God wills'. And he set sail from Ephesus. (Acts 18:18:21)

Since Gallio did not choose to pass judgement on him, Paul had the option of staying longer in Corinth, possibly for an additional period of about six months. (Acts 18:11) Gallio's attitude had been that Paul was no danger to the Roman empire, that the charge against him had not been relevant, and Paul was therefore a free man, free to stay in Corinth. Eventually however,

Paul took leave of the brethren, the church community, and sailed for Syria together with Priscilla and Aquila.

Paul, Priscilla and Aquila started on this further journey back to Antioch which has become for some exegetes the end of the second missionary journey which began in Acts 15:35. These scholars understand Paul's first missionary journey as being from Acts 13:4 to Acts 14:26, with Barnabas, then the council in Jerusalem, then the second missionary journey of Paul from Acts 15:36 to Acts 18:22, with Silas and also Timothy intermittently, and then Paul's third missionary journey from Acts 18:23 to Acts 20:38. Other scholars regard all Paul's journeyings as one continuous journey.

On their way to Syria, Paul, Priscilla and Aquila stopped off for a short time in the port of Corinth, Cenchreae, in order to fulfil a vow which Paul had taken.

His vow is usually presumed to be a Nazarite vow. According to Numbers 6:1-21, a Nazarite vow was taken by a man or a woman who wanted to separate him or herself to the Lord, entirely and completely devoted to Him, usually for a season. (Numbers 6:2). During the period of the vow, the Nazarite may drink no wine or strong drink, not even the juice of the grape, its seeds or its skin, (Numbers 6:4). If he is a man, no razor shall come upon his head. He may not cut his hair but let the locks of his hair grow long; for all the days of his separation he is holy to the Lord; his head is consecrated to the Lord. (Numbers 6: 5,8,9). At the end of his separation, which was usually thirty days but could be longer, he may shave his head and offer a sacrifice to the Lord. (Numbers 6:13).

This was a precious time of separation to the Lord for those performing the vow. But what the Lord really wanted for His people was a constant state, so that they never ceased to be holy and wholly to Him. Because of their frailty, God recognized that this special time of separation to Him was limited, but He wanted His people always to be separated, sanctified to Him, their being 'Holy to the Lord' always a constant in their lives. He wanted them always to be under His blessing, and His keeping power; that His Face would always shine upon them.

He promised that He would always be gracious to them, that they would dwell in His peace.

This was the Lord's blessing for them. The Lord bless you and keep you. The Lord make His Face to shine upon you and be gracious to you. The Lord lift up His countenance upon you and give you peace. (Numbers 6:24-26). God's intention is always to bless His people.

This blessing has become known as the Aaronic blessing, because the Lord said to Moses 'Say to Aaron and his sons "thus shall you bless the people of Israel". (Numbers 6:22), but the context suggests that it could also be known as the Nazarite blessing, the blessing upon all those who had, and have, consecrated their lives to the Lord.

Marshall suggests that Paul made this vow either in thankfulness for past blessings, such as Paul's safekeeping in Corinth, or as part of a petition for future blessings such as safekeeping on Paul's impending journey. (Marshall p 300).

Stott adds the comment that once Paul had been liberated from the attempt to be justified by the Mosaic law, his conscience was free to take part in practices which, though being cultural or ceremonial, belonged to 'matters indifferent', that is, neither particularly Jewish nor particularly Christian, for God is the God of both the old and new covenants. Stott ponders whether on this occasion, Paul performed the vow in order to conciliate the Jewish Christian leaders he was going to see in Jerusalem. (Acts 21:23). (Stott p 301). Paul's taking of a Jewish vow and his subsequent sharing in the purification of a group of Jewish men in Jerusalem at that time, demonstrates that as a Jew, Paul keeps the law, not for justification by the law, but as evidence that he does not dissuade other Jewish Christians from keeping theLaw. (Marshall p 73). Paul was prepared to be as a Jew to the Jews. (1 Corinthians 9:20).

An alternative view is that the Jews who had attempted to undermine Paul's ministry were still in Corinth, even as Paul continued to be after Gallio had refused to take the Jews seriously. These were the people whom Paul was seeking to conciliate, demonstrating by his performing of a Nazarite vow that he was set on consecrating himself to God however his conduct appeared to them, and that his whole desire was that they should also find fulfilment in doing the same, through being consecrated to, and sanctified by, the Lord, and separated to Him, for they would have known their scriptures. And of course coming into a relationship with Him through Jesus. Paul could never forget that preeminent truth. On leaving Corinth, he was able to remove the marks of his vow, and shaved his head.

It is possible that there was already a church in Cenchreae. Paul speaks of Phoebe, a deaconess of the church in Cenchreae, describing her as a help of many and of Paul himself. (Romans 16:1). But leaving Cenchreae, Paul, Aquila and Priscilla arrive at Ephesus. Paul had missed Ephesus earlier because he and Timothy had been prevented by the Holy Spirit from preaching in Asia. (Acts 16:6).

Ephesus was the chief city of the province of Asia Minor, and was the home of the present governor. It was a large and important city, famous both for its commercial status and its culture, for it contained one of the seven wonders of the ancient world, the temple of Artemis, a goddess in the Greek pantheon, also known as Diana in the Roman, who was also assimilated to the goddess Astrarte in the syncretized religious culture of the period. Astarte had originally been a goddess of war and fertility among many of the Semitic peoples, as was also Artemis. But the Artemis of Ephesus was distinct from the Greek virgin goddess of the same name. (Bruce p363).

The Ephesian Artemis was the great mother goddess of Asia Minor whose worship dated back to earlier times. Many needed the presence, or imputed presence of a mother figure in their lives. Artemis was protector, sustainer and donor of fertility. No wonder their cry was 'Great is Artemis of the Ephesians!' (Acts 19:34).

In addition to its pagan religion, Ephesus was also a centre for magical practices. (Acts 19:13,14).

Paul came to Ephesus with Priscilla and Aquila, and left them there when he moved on to Phrygia and Galatia,

(Acts 18:23), though he did spend a little time in the synagogue in Ephesus, reasoning with the Jews. But when they asked him to stay for a longer time, he did not consent. Setting sail from Ephesus, he landed at Caesarea, went up and greeted the church, and then went down to Antioch. (Acts 18:21,22).

Aquila and Priscilla remained in Ephesus until the end of 55 A.D, holding meetings at their house. (1 Corinthians 16:19). But in 56 A.D they returned to Rome where they remained until 57 A.D (Romans 16:3). Paul describes them as his fellow workers with much affection, sending greetings again to the church in their house. (Bruce p 340).

In a very few verses, Luke has outlined Paul's journey from Corinth to Ephesus, from Ephesus to Caesarea, from Caesarea to Anioch in Syria and back through Galatia to Ephesus again. (Acts 18:18-23). By including the two years Paul spent in Corinth (Acts 18:11,18) and the three years he spent in Ephesus, (Acts 20:31), together with the intervening periods of travel by land and sea, Luke is here condensing quite a period of Paul's life into a few verses, perhaps unaware of quite what Paul was doing and having to rely on oral sources for his information.

But such details as Luke gives us, reinforced by sometimes apparently casual references in Paul's letters, place not only the Acts of the Apostles but also the letters, in an historical context. These are not just references in a holy book, but part of the living testimony of many lives, including Paul's, lived in total obedience to God, inspired by the Holy Spirit, devoted to the Lord Jesus Christ, in far from politically ideal historical circumstances.

Luke never tells us what he does not know. Stott believes that Luke was in Philippi at this time, from the 'we' passage in Acts 16:16 to the 'they' passage in Acts 17:1. (Stott p 300).

Paul's destination was Antioch in Syria, (Acts 18:18), for that was the church from which he and Barnabas had been commissioned for their missionary service, (Acts 13:2; 14:26; 15:35) and Paul wanted to report back to the church all the wonderful works that God had done. But first he spent some time in Ephesus, where he left Priscilla and Aquila and 'he himself went into the synagogue where he reasoned, argued, with the Jews'. (Acts 18:19). The Jews of Ephesus were like those of Beroea. They wanted to learn more from him, and beseeched him to stay for a longer period. But he declined, promising however that he would return to them 'if God permits'; *ton theon thelontes,* if it is God's will.

So Paul set sail from Ephesus, (Acts 18:19), and came to Caesarea, (Acts 18:22), a few words to encompass a very long sea journey. Caesarea was the chief port of Palestine, but it may not have been the church in Caesarea but the church in Jerusalem to which he went 'up'. (Acts 18:22).

Bruce estimates that the journey outlined in verses 19-23 compressed a journey of 1500 miles (Bruce p 350), including from Corinth to Antioch to which Paul now went, thus completing his second missionary journey, and beginning his third. Luke tells us nothing of his time in Antioch, except that 'he spent some time there'. (Acts 18:23) and then left Antioch to visit all the places in Galatia and Phrygia, from the east to the west, where he had left disciples, 'strengthening them', encouraging them in their Christian faith.

According to his promise to them, Paul was on his way back to Ephesus, but during that time, he may have had the opportunity to visit the churches in Colossae and Laodicea in southern Galatia. (Colossians 2:1), though he may not have been personally known to all the saints and faithful brethren at Colossae. (Colossians 1:2,4). Certainly there were those at Colossae and Laodicea 'who had not seen my face' (Colossians 2:1), and perhaps many in Pisidian Antioch, Iconium, Lystra and Derbe who had become Christians subsequently to his former time among them, who had never actually seen Paul.

But these were churches for which Paul had a deep affection. (Romans 16:24). Under the necessity of preaching the gospel, for he says, 'Woe is me if I preach not the gospel', (1 Corinthians 9:16), Paul had established these churches in his first missionary journey. (Acts 13:4-16:6) followed by churches like Philippi springing up as Paul and his companions went through Macedonia in northern Greece, and then through Achaia, in southern Greece. (Acts 16:10-18:18).

Acts 18:24-28. Apollos at Ephesus

Meanwhile, a Jew named Apollos, a native of Alexandria, came to Ephesus. He was an eloquent man, well versed in the scriptures. He had been instructed in the way of the Lord and being fervent in spirit, he spoke and taught accurately the things concerning Jesus, though he knew only the baptism of John. (Acts 18:24,25).

We may say, what a man! What a devoted servant of Jesus Chrfst! How we would love to have such a leader in our church! But there was something missing.

Apollos had come to Ephesus from Alexandria, for what reason we do not know. But in Ephesus he began to speak boldly in the synagogue (Acts 18:26). What a blessing to him that Aquila and Priscilla were also in the synagogue at that time. They heard him speak and they took him aside and began to expound the way of God to him more perfectly, more accurately.

Was there a church in Alexandria from which Apollos had been sent? He was accurately aware of the life and teaching of Jesus, but had apparently missed out on the baptism of the Holy Spirit which Jesus had promised to those who followed him. (Acts 1:8).

Alexandria had a substantial Jewish population. Its library, founded by Ptolemy in 322 B.C after the death of Alexander the Great, was the literary envy of the Hellenistic world. In Alexandria the Greek version of the Old Testament known as the Septuagint, had been translated from the Hebrew in 270 BC, by seventy scholars, (hence the term, Septuagint'). It was a version used extensively by New Testament writers.

Apollos was a 'learned' man, an alternative meaning to the word translated 'eloquent'. He had perhaps made use of the famous Alexandrian library. He was a cultured person. It has been suggested that Alexandria had been reached by Christianity in 50 A.D, (Bruce p 371) fewer than 20 years after Pentecost. But Apollos had not heard the words which the Lord Jesus had spoken to His disciples before his ascension back to His Father. Jesus had said, 'You shall receive power after the Holy Spirit has come upon you and you will be witness to Me in Jerusalem and in all Judea and in Samaria and to the uttermost parts of the earth'. (Acts 1:8).

Apollos was certainly witnessing to the Lord Jesus, but imperfectly, knowing only the baptism of John. (Acts 18:25). He needed Priscilla and Aquila to explain and expound the way of God to him more perfectly. The way of God was to be baptized, immersed in the Holy Spirit, so that he could speak boldly under the anointing of the Holy Spirit, under the Holy Spirit's power.

Just as Paul did later to the twelve disciples in Ephesus in chapter 19:5,6, so we must assume that Priscilla and Aquila laid hands on Apollos so that he might receive the Holy Spirit. For without the personal experience of receiving and being filled with the Holy Spirit, much of the doctrine espoused by the writers of the New Testament, especially those of Paul, would be difficult to understand. The future ministry of Apollos seems to suggest this. (1 Corinthians 3:5; 4:6).

Encouraged by these faithful servants of God, and all the believers in Ephesus, Apollos knew that he was commissioned to go to Corinth, to the church there, and the brethren wrote a letter of commendation to the disciples in Corinth, that they might receive him.

When Apollos arrived in Corinth, he greatly helped those who through grace had believed, for he powerfully confuted the Jews in public, showing by the scriptures that the Christ was Jesus. (Acts 18:27,28). And 1 Corinthians 1:2 and 3:4, demonstrate how greatly God used him in Corinth. Paul acknowledges his ministry. He says, I planted, Apollos watered, but God gave the increase. So neither he who plants nor he that waters is anything, but God who gives the growth.... for we are fellow workers. You are God's field, God's building. (1 Corinthians 3:6-9).

Apollos was eloquent and well versed in the scriptures but he needed the Holy Spirit for the enlargement of his ministry. Paul appears to include Apollos with himself and Peter as an apostle (1 Corinthians 3:22) and certainly as a servant of Christ and a steward of the mysteries of God, undergoing great hardship for the sake of the gospel; (1 Corinthians 4:19-13); becoming the refuse of the world and scum of the earth, the off scouring of all things, together with Paul and Peter, fellow apostles.

Later in his letter to the Corinthians, Paul tells the believers that he has urged Apollos to visit them again, a second visit to Corinth which he could not have done if he had any doubts about the ministry of Apollos. (1 Corinthians 16:12). This man was now indeed expounding the word of God more perfectly, just as Priscilla and Aquila had done and showed him how to do, a man who had known only the baptism of John, the baptism of repentance, but who had now come into the good of all that Jesus had promises when he said that his disciples would receive power after the Holy Spirit had come upon them.

How could it be possible that the baptism of John, though so evidently valuable in itself, could provide the followers of Jesus with all that they needed if they were to endure the hardships attendant on preaching the gospel? They needed the Holy Spirit to enable them to witness to Him and to suffer for His Name's sake.

Acts Chapter 19

Acts 19:1-7. Paul and the twelve disciples at Ephesus

While Apollos was at Corinth, Paul passed through the upper country and came to Ephesus. There he found some disciples. And he said to them, Did you receive the Holy Spirit when you believed? And they said, 'No, we have not heard that there is a Holy Spirit'. And he said, 'into what then were you baptized?' And they said, 'into John's baptism'. Paul said, John baptized with the baptism of repentance, telling the people to to believe in Him who was coming after him, that is, in Jesus.

When they heard this, they were baptized in the Name of Jesus. And when Paul had laid his hands on them the Holy Spirit came upon them, and they began to speak with tongues and prophesy. They were in all about twelve men. (Acts 19:1-7).

After Apollos had left and gone to Corinth, Paul came to Ephesus where he had left Aquila and Priscilla. (Acts 18:19). He was surprised to find a small group of disciples who had only received the baptism of John, the baptism of repentance. It may be that they had some connection with Apollos, who had also only received the baptism of John, or they may have been part of the audience which had heard him speak of the things concerning Jesus. (Acts 18:25). Apollos had now left them and gone to Corinth, but here was Paul who had recently come to Ephesus. Perhaps he could help them, for like Apollos, they too had known only the baptism of John.

Alternatively, it may have been a deliberate choice on Paul's part to seek them out, for he 'found' them and without hesitation or any apparent introduction presumably because of their association with Apollos, asked them this direct question. 'Did you receive the Holy Spirit when you believed?' (Acts 19:2). Astonished, they said to him, 'No, we have never even heard that there is a Holy Spirit'. Even more astonished, Paul then said to them, 'Into what then were you baptized? They said, 'Into John's baptism'.

'Well', Paul may have said, that's a good start anyway, for without repentance, there can be no forgiveness of sins. But God has something more for you. As you are aware, John's ministry was telling the people to believe in the One coming after him, that is, Jesus. (Acts 19:4)

On hearing this, (Acts 19:5), they could wait no longer, but gladly asked if they could be baptized in the Name of the Lord Jesus. And as Paul laid his hands on them the Holy Spirit came upon them and they spoke with tongues and prophesied. (Acts 19:6). The promise which Jesus had made to His disciples before His ascension into heaven to be with His heavenly Father had been fulfilled once again. 'You shall receive power after the Holy Spirit has come upon you and you will be witnesses to Me. (Acts 1:8).

Our chief difficulty with this account lies with the assertion made by these twelve earnest and well taught disciples that they had never heard of the Holy Spirit, for this had been a significant part of John's message. Speaking of Jesus, John said, 'He will baptize you with the Holy Spirit and with fire. (Matthew 3:11).

But John's emphasis in speaking of repentance, and the visual activity of baptism had maybe clouded their understanding. Now that Paul had come, and like Priscilla and Aquila had expounded the way of God more perfectly to them, how glad they were to enter into the fullness of the baptism of the Holy Spirit in the Name of the Lord Jesus.

Their understanding of their experience was ratified by their Spirit-given ability to speak in tongues, just as the disciples had done on the day of Pentecost; and to prophesy. From now on, these disciples will be part of the church in Ephesus, which like the church in Corinth, which when the Corinthian believers came together, each one had a hymn, or a teaching or a revelation or a tongue or an interpretation (1 Corinthians 14:26) as part of their normal worship. We cannot believe that these gifts and privileges were given only to the church in Corinth.

Acts 19:8-10. Paul leaves the synagogue for the school of Tyrannus

And Paul entered the synagogue in Ephesus and for three months spoke boldly, arguing and pleading about the kingdom of God. But when some were stubborn and disbelieved, speaking evil of the way before the congregation, he withdrew from them, taking the disciples with him and argued daily in the hall of Tyrannus. This continued for two years so that all the residents of Asia heard the word of the Lord, both Jews and Gentiles. (Acts 19:8-10)

Paul did not abandon the Christians in Ephesus, including its twelve new believers, but as his custom had become, he entered the synagogue of the Jews and for three months spoke boldly, arguing and pleading about the kingdom of God. These Ephesian Jews however, were not like the Jews of Beroea, and the Ephesian Jews to whom he had formerly preached. (Acts 18:9). They were 'stubborn and disbelieved', speaking evil of 'the way', one of the terms by which this new religious movement was known.

The use of this term, 'the way', had been used before as a description of the Christian movement, and would be again, especially by Paul. (Acts 9:2; 19:23; 22:4; 24:14,22). Marshall notes that the use of the term is peculiar to Acts, and believes its use was due to the concept of the way of the Lord as being the way of salvation, (Acts 18:25), a way which God had appointed for people to follow if they wished to be saved. (Acts 16:17; cp Mark 12:14). (Marshall p168).

Other non-Christian groups also used the concept in various ways, but according to the words of Jesus, He is the only way to come to the Father. (John 14:6), thus for Christians displacing the Hebrew *halakhah*, the walk or way of life which had been understood by the Jews as the most strict observance of the Mosaic law in addition to the Hebrew scriptures. The exact performance of the Hebrew 'way' was understood as living in the entire will of God, and describes not only the behaviour of those who adopted it, but themselves. Those who chose the way were themselves the way. (Bruce p197. Barrett p 448).

Paul appears to have found the Christian equivalent, not in a set of ideas and extreme self discipline, not in the Jewish *halakhah*, not even in the teaching of Jesus except that He spoke always those things which His heavenly Father gave Him to speak; but in considerably greater form, in Jesus Himself, for Jesus himself is the way and allows this title to be used of all those of his followers who know Him as 'the way', and the truth and the life. (John 14:6).

This is the way against which the congregation of the Jews spoke evil. (Acts 19:9). In disparaging the way of life of the believers, they were disparaging Jesus Himself. Paul had no choice but to withdraw from them (Acts 19:9). He had given them the opportunity of learning about Jesus, of coming to a place of repentance as 'he spoke boldly, arguing and pleading about the kingdom of God', and they had rejected it. (Acts 19:8).

But some did respond, and taking these disciples with him, he withdrew to the school or lecture hall of Tyrannus. Paul could no longer resort to the synagogue. Paul continued his ministry in the school of Tyrannus for two years, so that all the residents of the province of Asia heard the word of the Lord, both Jews and Greeks. The Holy Spirit had previously forbidden Paul, Silas and Timothy to preach the word in Asia. (Acts 16:6). Now Paul was given ample time and opportunity to do so, probably from the autumn of 52 AD to the summer of 55 AD. (Bruce p 356).

This may not however have been a quiet and tranquil time, idyllically preaching every day in the school of Tyrannus. In 1 Corinthians 15:32, Paul writes of fighting with beasts at Ephesus and in 2 Corinthians 1:8-10 of 'affliction we experienced in Asia, for we were so utterly, unbearably crushed that we despaired of life itself'.

'Asia' probably refers to the area surrounding Ephesus in Acts 16:6, which also encompassed Colossae and Laodicea. It became one of the chief centres of Christianity and Bruce suggests that the seven churches of Revelation in Revelation chapters 2 and 3 were founded during those years, though not necessarily by Paul. (Bruce p 356).

Colossae may have been evangelized by Epaphras, (Colossians 1:7; 2;1; 4:12,13). Colossians was obviously written when Paul was in captivity, but not necessarily in prison, in Rome. He writes to the Christians in Colossae, 'Remember my fetters' (Colossians 4:18), and in 2 Corinthians 11:23, speaks of his many imprisonments. It may have been during one of these that he had written to the Colossians the letter which he wanted them to share with the church in Laodicea. (Colossians 4:15).

Acts 19:11-19. Signs and wonders at Ephesus

And God did extraordinary miracles by the hands of Paul so that handkerchiefs and aprons were carried away from his body to the sick, and diseases left them and the evil spirits came out of them. (Acts 19:11,12).

In addition to all this activity, Paul did many miracles by the hands of Paul. Something similar had happened in Jerusalem, the sick being carried into the street so that as Peter passed by, his shadow might fall on some of them, and they were all healed. (Acts 5:12-14). These were extraordinary miracles, for there was no direct contact between Paul or Peter and those who were healed, only in Paul's case, through the handkerchiefs and aprons.

What is here described as handkerchiefs were probably a kind of sweat band or kerchief used on the head while working, indicating that it is possible that Paul was still engaged in tentmaking.

These God given miracles did not either have the purpose or give the impression that Paul was a great man, but on the contrary, were simply a sign that God was with him and through Him was at work in the lives of men and women. God really wanted to bless men and women, and here is a man through whom His blessing can be poured out. God is using His servant to bless others. For Paul these are the signs of his apostleship, proof that he and his companions are truly God's 'sent ones', for that is what 'apostle' means.

Paul writes in the second letter to the Corinthians that 'the signs of an apostle were performed among you in all patience, with signs and wonders and mighty works'. (2 Corinthians 12:12). It was not only in Ephesus that the Holy Spirit witnessed to him and his teaching in this way. How grateful Paul was that God was allowing these signs, these signatures from God which were setting the seal on his ministry, endorsing and legitimating all that Paul was engaged in, the outward signs of his calling as an apostle as he remarks in Romans 15:16. He says it was the grace of God given to him to be a minister of Christ Jesus to the Gentiles In the priestly service of the gospel of God so that the offering of the Gentiles may be acceptable, sanctified by the Holy Spirit.

But of course, such activity is always under the scrutiny of the forces of opposition, of challenge to this ministry. It was inevitable that some itinerant Jewish exorcists, travelling from place to place, should come upon the this huge enigma of what was going on in Ephesus; that evil spirits were being cast out, not as they attempted to do, by speaking to the evil spirit or using magic, but simply by touching aprons and kerchiefs which had belonged to Paul.

This power, attributed by Paul to the Holy Spirit, was believed by these exorcists to reside in the Name of Jesus, strangely, for it would appear that the threat to evil spirits would come from 'the' Holy Spirit, rather than the Name of Jesus. How would they know that the whole purpose of the Holy Spirit is to glorify Jesus? (John 16:14) They undertook to pronounce the Name of Jesus over those who had evil spirits, saying, 'I adjure you by the Jesus whom Paul preaches'. (Acts 19:13).

Acts 19:11:19. The seven sons of Sceva

There was a Jewish high priest or chief priest who had seven sons, and they were using the formula, 'I adjure you by the Jesus whom Paul preaches. (Acts 19:14).

But the evil spirit answered them and said, 'Jesus I know and Paul I know, but who are you? And the man in whom the evil spirit was, leaped on them, mastered all of them and overpowered them so that they fled out of that house naked and wounded. (Acts 19:15,16).

Exorcism was not unknown in Palestine. It was presupposed by the Pharisees in the time of Jesus, who accused Him of exorcism under the power of Beelzebub, the prince of demons, the lord of the flies. (Matthew 12:24. Luke 11:19). The sons of Sceva however, believed that they had discovered a new incantational formula, 'in the Name of Jesus', which appeared to be successful when used by Paul. But because they were not quite sure that that was enough, they added to the formula,' I adjure you by the Jesus whom Paul preaches'.

It is particularly distressing that these men were from a priestly family, sons of a chief priest, and could perhaps have had the right to become priests themselves. Priests were those who served God in temple worship, who were shepherds of the people of God, His flock, an occupation so much more fulfilling than exorcism.

What could have happened to them to have turned them away from the worship of the true God to concern themselves with evil spirits? At that time, disease was considered to be evidence of evil spiritual activity. Perhaps their original motivation had been to relieve the suffering of those with whom they came into contact, but this had developed into an exercise of power, power which they were reluctant to relinquish to an itinerant preacher like Paul.

How easy it would be, just to pronounce the Name of Jesus over someone possessed by an evil spirit and to claim that the evil spirit had been dismissed. But there was an awful reality about the work in which they were engaged, of which it seemed they had previously been unaware. It is always dangerous to tamper with what is alien to, antagonistic to, what is of God. There is a spiritual battle going on, a battle between good and evil, between light and darkness, and not to be trifled with.

Here is a person who is inhabited by something altogether alien to Jesus. We do not know how or when at some point in his life he had been taken over by the evil spirit, this evil thing within him. But it was real, aggressive, threatening and made him abhorrent to himself. How could he escape?

There were groups of exorcists in Ephesus. Surely they would help him to get rid of this evil thing. The sons of Sceva were willing to help him, but recognized that pronouncing the Name of Jesus over the possessed man would be more effective than their usual incantations. So they say over this man the new formula they have learned, pronouncing the Name of the Lord Jesus, 'I adjure you by Jesus whom Paul preaches'. And the man said to them.' Jesus I know and Paul I know, *but who are you?* Overtaken by the spirit which controlled him, he leaped on the sons of Sceva, and mastered them and overpowered them so that they fled out of that house wounded and naked. (Acts 19:16).

The Name of Jesus may not be used in this desultory, irreverential fashion. There is power in the Name of Jesus because it expresses the whole authority of God behind it, and His purpose that through it men and women are saved. The angel said to Joseph 'you shall call His Name Jesus, for He will save His people from their sins'. (Matthew 1:21). It is the name of salvation and dear to the Father's heart, and the one who bore that name carried it up to the throne of the majesty on high completely spotless; the name of one who had never sinned in thought, word or deed and was therefore qualified to take upon Himself the sin of the whole world. And the day is coming when at the Name of Jesus, every knee shall bow and every tongue confess that He is Lord, to the glory of God the Father. (Philippians 2:10,11).

This remarkable incident of the sons of Sceva 'became known to all the residents of Ephesus, both Jews and Gentiles and fear fell upon them all, and the Name of Jesus was extolled'. (Acts 19:17). Fear fell upon them, lest what had happened to the sons of Sceva might also visit some kind of repercussion on them if they took the Name of Jesus lightly or unworthily, for they had come to appreciate that there was indeed power, mighty power in that Name. It was deserving of being used, if at all, carefully and worshipfully.

In addition, the incident had the effect of causing some to become believers, (Acts 19:18) and a long line of people came to confess and divulge their arcane secrets. And as they came, they brought with them their scrolls and parchments of magic, and threw them on the fire so that everybody could see that they had relinquished their former way of life.' And they counted the value of them, and found it came to fifty thousand pieces of silver. So mightily grew the word of God and prevailed'. (Acts 19:20).

Those who had watched the conflagration were so impressed that they estimated the financial value of the manuscripts. It is difficult to compute exactly how comparable this is to any modern currency. But the sum mentioned reflects a strong rejection of the magic on which these new believers had been relying, and emphasises the greater value of that which is truly spiritual, life affirming, and draws its focus and importance from the Holy Spirit as He glorifies Jesus.

Luke concludes, the word of the Lord grew and prevailed mightily. (Acts 19:20). Though Paul's ministry in Ephesus Is not yet concluded there is already a powerful sense of the Holy Spirit being at work in that city, just as He had been throughout Acts. (Acts 6:7; 9:31; 12:24; 16:5; 28:31) These events do not just punctuate the narrative, but give evidence that the church is growing and expanding throughout the Roman empire which will one day fall. But the word of the Lord endures for ever, (Isaiah 40:8. Bruce p 254).

Acts 19:21-40. Riot in Ephesus

Now after these events, Paul resolved in the Spirit to pass through Macedonia and Achaia and go to Jerusalem saying, 'After I have been there I must also see Rome'. And having sent into Macedonia two of his helpers, Timothy and Erastus, he himself stayed in Asia for a while. (Acts 19:21-22).

Paul had spent two years in Ephesus, (Acts 19:10), and now knew from the Holy Spirit that it was time to move on. He sent two of his helpers, Timothy and Erastus to Macedonia but he himself stayed in Asia for a while. There was more work to be done before he left Asia for good. He wanted the stay in Ephesus at least 'until Pentecost, for a wide door for effective work has opened for me and there are many adversaries'. (1 Corinthians 16:8,9), an impression which proved all too accurate.

When the time came to leave Ephesus, Paul's purpose was to take the money collected by the generosity of the churches in Macedonia and Achaia to the poorer members of the church in Jerusalem. (Romans 15:26). So he sent Timothy and Erastus ahead of him to Macedonia to advise them of his coming. But he had an ultimate plan too, to visit Jerusalem and then to see Rome. (Acts 19:21). Though Rome was not a city which he himself had evangelized, he longed to see the Christians there, as is clearly shown by the letter he wrote to them from Corinth. (Romans 16; I Corinthians 16:1,4).

Acts 23:11 and Acts 27:24 confirm that Paul's vision of seeing Rome was within the purpose of God for him. He also longed to use Rome as an embarkation point for a proposed visit to Spain. (Romans 15:24, 28). If God had allowed His word to be preached as far as Rome, why not the furthest reaches of the Roman empire? But this was not to be within Paul's remit.

Though the proposed journey had begun with the needs of some members of the church in Jerusalem being acute, and the churches in Macedonia and Achaia wanting to express their fellowship with the church in Jerusalem with a generous and self sacrificial gift, the journey had been extended to include so much more, for wherever Paul went, he wanted to preach the gospel and bring encouragement to the disciples.

Opposition to Paul's teaching had taken a little longer to erupt in Ephesus than in other cities where he had preached the gospel, for he had now been in Ephesus for two years, (Acts 19:8,10), openly teaching, first in the synagogue and then in the school of Tyrannus about the kingdom of God. (Acts 19:8).

But eventually, perhaps partly due to Paiul's confrontation with the exorcists, Paul's preaching had filtered through to the silversmiths who made images of the goddess Artemis, or Diana.

It is possible that Aquila and Priscilla were still with Paul, and by this time many of the Ephesians had become disciples. But he had sent Timothy and Erastus off to Macedonia to strengthen the disciples in Philippi, Beroea and Thessalonica, and he is now in Ephesus with a reduced number of helpers. It was inevitable that when he was most vulnerable, as he was at that time, 'there arose no little stir concerning the Way', the Christian movement. (Acts 19:23).

It had belatedly occurred to Demetrius that Paul's teaching about God being the only true God and the Lord Jesus being the Son of God could seriously undermine his silversmith business, together with the other silversmiths, craftsmen who made shrines to Artemis. The religious aspect of the worship of the goddess did not worry him unduly. What he foresaw was that his lucrative business was in danger of slipping away. He gathered together his companions, the men of like occupation as himself and began to harangue them.

He said, 'Men, you know that from this business we have our wealth. And you see and hear that not only at Ephesus, but almost throughout all Asia, this Paul has persuaded and turned away a considerable company of people, saying that gods made with hands are not gods. And there is danger, not only that this trade of ours may come into disrepute, but also that the temple of the great goddess Artemis, may count for nothing and that she may be deposed from her magnificence, whom all Asia and the world worship. (Acts 19:25-27).

If the latter part of Demetrius' speech were true, it was high time that 'Asia and the world' heard the gospel. This however was not the chief point he was making. He was not really interested in what Paul had to say, but only that 'there is danger that this trade of ours may come into disrepute', (Acts 19:27) that if people really began to believe that gods made with hands were no gods, the magnificent temple of Artemis might count for nothing, and people would no longer want to buy and own for themselves the silver shrines of Artemis.

The other craftsmen had not apparently worked this out for themselves, but when they heard Demetrius, 'they were enraged and cried out, "Great is Artemis of the Ephesians!" (Acts 19:28). The city was filled with confusion. It was in an uproar and the citizens rushed together into the theatre dragging with them Gaius and Aristarchus, two of Paul's companions in travel who were Macedonians. (Acts 19:29). Gaius was from Derbe and Aristarchus from Thessalonica. (Acts 20:4).

Rushing together, running together into the theatre, the largest possible site in Ephesus, the makers of the silver shrines dragged Gaius and Aristarchus. Archaeologists have discovered in Ephesus a theatre or amphitheatre capable of accommodating 25,000 people. It was the most convenient place for the whole of the citizenry to assemble.

Paul wanted to join them, to go in among the crowd, (Acts 19:30), but was restrained by the disciples. Some of the Asiarchs too, who were his friends, the foremost men of the cities of Asia sent to him and begged him not to venture into the theatre. (Acts 19:31). For now, utter confusion reigned, some people not even knowing why they had come together. (Acts 19:32).

There were however many Jews among them, and they prompted Alexander, a respected member of the community and a Jew, to try and quell the riot. Alexander did his best. He motioned with his hand in an effort to plead for silence so that he could make a defence to the people (Acts 19:33), but the crowd appeared to be as violently anti-Jewish as anti-Christian. Far from responding to Alexander's call for silence, 'they all with one voice cried out, "Great is Artemis of the Ephesians!"' (Acts 19:34).

They did this for two hours.

It was time for the town clerk to intervene. He was an Ephesian, an important official in Ephesus and in the whole province of Asia because of the importance of Ephesus. He was responsible to the Roman authorities for the maintenance of law and order, and for what went on in the city. Concerned that the news of what was happening in Ephesus could be reported to Rome, he began to speak to the Ephesians in a conciliatory tone.

'Men of Ephesus', he said, 'what man of you is there who does not know that the city of the Ephesians is the temple keeper of the great Artemis, and of the sacred stone which fell down from the sky? Seeing that these things cannot be contradicted, you ought to be quiet and do nothing rash'. (Acts 19:35).

To be the temple keeper to Artemis was considered to be a great honour, not only to the individual citizens of Ephesus, but to the city as a whole. The Ephesians were also guardians of the 'sacred stone which fell from the sky', which they believed came down to them from Zeus, their most powerful god. It was a meteorite, like the one which is revered as the Black Stone in Mecca, incorporated into the Ka'ba, the house of worship for Muslims.

The town clerk was reminding them of their own great heritage, which was not to be disparaged by an itinerant preacher like Paul, though he acknowledges that Paul was neither sacrilegious nor a blasphemer. (Acts 19:37). He was unwilling to put Paul on a charge until he had been investigated further, but advised the crowd that the courts were open and they had the right to bring a complaint against Paul; or indeed against anyone. Such trials were regularly held by the proconsuls and were open to all to attend.

These were lawful assemblies. (Acts 19:35). Unlawful assemblies were not tolerated by Rome, and were likely to cause considerable damage to the city's privileged status as the chief city of the province.

The town clerk was reminding the people that they could be accused of being guilty of insurrection against Rome by continuing their present aggression against Paul, and concluded by dismissing the assembly. (Acts 19:40). It took some time for the uproar to cease but Paul felt it was now time to leave Ephesus and return to Macedonia.

Acts Chapter 20

Acts 20:1-6. Paul's journey back to Palestine through Macedonia, Greece and Troas

After the uproar ceased, Paul sent for the disciples and having exhorted them took leave of them and departed for Macedonia. When he had gone through those parts and had given them much encouragement, he came to Greece. There he spent three months, and when a plot was made against him by the Jews as he was about to sail for Syria, he determined to return through Macedonia. (Acts 20:1-3).

This is now the summer of 55 A.D. The riot in Ephesus is over and Paul's intended visit to Jerusalem to take the contribution from the churches of Macedonia and Achaia can now be realized. (Acts 19:21; 1 Corinthians 16:1; 2 Corinthians 8:1-9:15; Romans 15:25).

Paul is now urgent that he must be on his way from Ephesus to Jerusalem, so he gathers together the Ephesian disciples, encouraging them to continue in the faith. They had of course been expecting that he could not stay with them indefinitely, but how sorry they were that these two happy, fruitful years had come to an end. There would be many tears as they said goodbye to their faithful pastor and teacher, not knowing when they would see him again.

So Paul begins the long overland journey north, through Asia Minor to Macedonia, in northern Greece. (Acts 20:1). The next few words cover quite an extended period of time. Luke writes, 'when he had gone through these parts, and had given them much encouragement, he came to Greece', that is, to southern Greece, Achaia. 'These parts' probably included Philippi, Beroea and Thessalonica, cities of Macedonia, where there were of course Christian communities. (Acts 16:40; 17:4,12), and may have taken as long as a year. (Bruce p369).

Marshall assumes that the visit through Macedonia, northern Greece is the journey referred to in 2 Corinthians 2:12 when Paul went north to Troas (Marshall p 322). Paul had sent Titus to Corinth in the south with a letter (now lost), (2 Corinthians 7:8; 2:3,4), to prepare the way for his own impending visit, and had hoped to meet Titus half way in Troas, but something had happened to prevent that meeting. Paul's worries about the Corinthian church were resolved when Titus finally arrived in Macedonia with good news about the church. (2 Corinthians 7:6; 14,15).

And Paul, when he had gone through these parts of Macedonia, came to Corinth himself; Corinth, the chief city of the province of Achaia, and to his beloved but sometimes difficult brothers and sisters in Christ. He says, 'I wrote to you ... to let you know the abundant love I have for you in Christ'. (2 Corinthians 2:4)

In Romans 15: 19, Paul writes that he had preached the gospel as far as Illyricum, the region north of Macedonia, present day Yugoslavia. It may have been on this journey that he attempted the mission to Illyricum. Then, passing through Troas and the aborted rendezvous with Titus, he made the journey down through Macedonia until he came to Greece, to Corinth.

The reference to Corinth may be the second recorded visit to Corinth, the 'painful visit' Paul made to them between writing 1 and 2 Corinthians. (2 Corinthians 2:1). It was at this time that Paul wrote the letter to the Romans. (Romans 16:1,23; 15:25). It could now be winter and the three months Paul spent at Corinth may have covered the winter period when sea travel was not encouraged. But at the end of those months, the winter of 56/57 A.D, when sailing conditions had improved, (like that in Acts 27:12 when Paul was on his way to Italy, and Titus 3:12, when Paul decided to spend the winter in Nicopolis), there was a plot made against Paul by the Jews as he was about to sail for Syria. (Acts 20:3)

The plot may have centered on the fact that confined to a ship, Paul may easily have been at risk of assassination, so having learned of the intention of the Jews, Paul decided to go overland on his way to Jerusalem, and to make the return journey to Macedonia.

Luke has described this journey in a few words, but we have valuable references in Paul's letters to some of his activity over this fairly lengthy period of time. From Ephesus in Asia he travelled north through Asia to northern Greece, Macedonia where were Philippi, Thessalonica and Beroea, then south to southern Greece, Achaia and on to Corinth, then the reverse journey back through Achaia to Macedonia and Troas, a journey of many months.

During this time, a group of men had come to join him, representatives of the Macedonian churches, with their gifts for the church in Jerusalem. They included Sopater of Beroea, the son of Pyrrus; Aristarchus and Secundus from Thessalonica; Gauis of Derbe; Timothy; and from the province of Asia, possibly Ephesus, Tychicus and Trophimus. (Acts 20:4).

This group of men who had been Paul's travelling companions (Acts 20:4), now went on to Troas to wait for Paul there, leaving Paul and his unnamed companion, who we know to be Luke, to follow. Luke and Paul were able to find a ship going toTroas from Philippi *after Passover*, which had become for Christans the celebration of the resurrection of Christ from the dead, so an important time to be together with others.

But though this was now spring weather, the journey still took them five days, unlike the two days from Troas to Philippi in Acts 16:11,12. Luke is flagging up in advance how unpredictable and in fact dangerous, sea journeys could be, for there will be others before Paul arrives in Rome.

We conclude from the use of the first person plural by Luke that 'we' in verse 6 and 'us' in verse 5 indicate that it was indeed Luke who accompanied Paul. It is possible that Luke had stayed on in Philippi, after Paul and Silas had left to arrive eventually in Thessalonica, (Acts 16:40), helping to form a new Christian community which included Lydia, the woman who prayed by the riverside, the young woman from whom a spirit of divination had been cast out, and the Phillipian jailer and his household. Now Luke had discovered that this was all part of God's plan, and he had the privilege of accompanying Paul to Jerusalem, for no doubt the church in Philippi had made their contribution for the church in Jerusalem.

In Colossians 4:14, Luke is described as the beloved physician; in 2 Timothy 4:11 as the only one who is with Paul in the prison and in Philemon 24 as Paul's fellow worker. It is obvious that Luke is very important to Paul, as indeed Paul was to Luke as these final chapters of Acts demonstrate.

So Paul and Luke arrive at Troas in five days, after five days of precious fellowship together on board ship, and they stay there for seven days, meeting up with those who had travelled before them, but also with the Christians whose home this was.

Acts 20:7-12. Paul at Troas. The fall and recovery of Eutychus

The brethren went on and were waiting for us at Troas, but we sailed away from Philippi after the days of Unleavened Bread, Passover, and in five days we came to them at Troas where we stayed for seven days. On the first day of the week when we were gathered together to break bread, Paul talked with them, intending to depart on the morrow; and he prolonged his speech until midnight. There were many lights in the upper chamber where we were gathered. And a young man named Eutychus was sitting in the window. He sank into a deep sleep as Paul talked still longer, and being overcome by sleep, he fell down from the third story and was taken up dead.

There was in Troas a reasonably large house, large enough for the church to meet in, with a lage upper room, necessarily large to contain a further nine guests, those who had accompanied Paul and of course Paul himself.

The church had become accustomed to meeting together on the first day of the week, Sunday, to worship, to listen to the teaching and to break bread together, remembering the Lord Jesus and proclaiming his death 'until He come'. (1 Corinthians 12:26). This often took place in the context of a 'love feast', *agape*, a sharing together of food and fellowship, a 'participation in the Body of Christ'. (1 Corinthians 11:16).

Paul was glad to have an opportunity of sharing this time with the believers in Troas, for he had much to say to them, although he and Luke had now been in Troas for a week, and no doubt he had had many opportunities for teaching. But he was due to depart on the following day, (Acts 20:7), and he still had so much to share with them of the wonderful life into which they had been immersed by the life, death and resurrection of the Lord Jesus.

Paul prolonged his speech until midnight. The room was warm, and the light from the oil lamps around the room added to the heat. People were sitting on benches, on the floor, wherever they could find a space, for Paul's words were so gripping that they were totally engaged, and they noticed neither the discomfort nor the time.

One young man, *pais*, lad, (Acts 29:9,12), a term usually denoting a lad between eight and fourteen, had found a perch in the window. (Acts 20:9). There was of course no glass, and the shutters had been left open for the purpose of ventilation. As Paul continued preaching, the young man, Eutychus, felt his eyes grow heavy and being overcome by sleep, he fell down from the third storey and was taken up dead.

We do not read of panic, only concern from the disciples as Paul went down the stairs and out into the courtyard where the lad lay. Paul bent over him, saying to the disciples, 'do not be alarmed for his life is in him', (Acts 20:10). And giving him a final little hug, Paul went back upstairs and broke bread with the believers, carrying on conversing with them until the dawn came and he had to leave them to go to the ship.

As the time of being together came to an end, the believers took Eutychus away, 'took him alive and were not a little comforted'; (Acts 20:12) an experience which neither he nor they were ever likely to forget.

The name Eutychus means 'fortunate'; but it was not fortune but the mercy of God and the love of the brethren which restored Eutychus on that day.

Acts 20:13-16. From Troas to Miletus

But going ahead to the ship, 'we' set sail for Assos, intending to take Paul aboard there, for so he had arranged, intending himself to go by land. And when he met us at Assos we took him on board and came to Mitylene. And sailing from there we came the following day opposite Chios; the next day we touched at Samos and the day after came to Miletus. For Paul had decided to sail past Ephesus so that he might not have to spend time in Asia, for he was hastening to be at Jerusalem, if possible, on the day of Pentecost. (Acts 20:13-16).

The journey from Ephesus to Jerusalm was taking longer than expected, but Paul and Luke were still hoping to meet with the church in Jerusalem at the time of Pentecost. (Acts 20:16). The church in Jerusalem rejoiced to remember their beginnings when the Holy Spirit came, and Paul wanted to celebrate with them.

After the meeting together in the house in Troas, and the wonderful miracle of raising Eutychus from the dead, Paul and Luke departed from Troas, Luke going ahead to the ship which was to take them to Assos, while Paul preferred to go to Assos overland, (Acts 20:13), having an arrangement with Luke that the ship would take him on board at Assos. It is possible, as Bruce suggests, that Paul stayed in Troas till the last moment, to be assured of Eutychus' recovery. The journey by ship took longer than the overland journey to Assos, thus giving Paul a little extra time. (Bruce p 374).

This arrangement worked out well. Paul joined the ship at Assos and they sailed to Mitylene. (Acts 20:14). Mitylene was the chief town of the island of Lesbos, the home of much lyrical poetry. And sailing from there they sailed the following day to Chios, another large island off the coast of Asia Minor.

(Acts 20:15). The next day they came to Samos, yet another large island, slightly south of Ephesus, and the day after that they came to Melitus, where there was a Jewish settlement. (Bruce p 375).

The decision to take ship was probab;y taken by Paul and his companions at Troas, for although it stopped at various places along the way, it was still the surest and quickest way of getting to Jerusalem in time for Pentecost. And Paul 'was hastening to be at Jerusalem in time for Pentecost'. (Acts 20:16).

Although Paul was now on a whirlwind journey, comparatively speaking, he realized that when they reached Miletus, they would be only about thirty miles from Ephesus. Although he wanted to get to Jerusalem as quickly as possible, and they had sailed past Ephesus, he wanted to see the Ephesian elders in Ephesus for what he believed would be the last time. (Acts 20:38). It might be possible to spend some time with them before going on to Jerusalem. Quickly he sent a message to Ephesus and was overjoyed when they arrived at Miletus, for he had much to say to them.

This speech, as recorded by Luke, is different from all others made by Paul in Acts, for all the others had an evangelistic purpose in view. On this occasion, Paul is also proclaiming the gospel, but in a sense reiterating it to the Ephesian elders as the whole ground, focus and foundation of all his ministry to them in the past, and as the focus of all *their* ministry as they take heed to themselves and to all the flock in which the Holy Spirit hade made them overseers, to care for the church of God which He had obtained with the blood of His own Son. (Acts 20:28).

In Acts 20:17, the leaders of the church are called 'elders', *presbyteros,* a term previously applied to the rulers of the synagogue. In Acts 20:28 Paul calls them 'overseers', *episkopoi,* bishops, guardians, and also, in verse 28, he refers to them as those who care for the flock, pastors or shepherds. The leaders must be all of these to God's people; those who lead them, guide them, guard them, care for them.

If, as seems possible, a hierarchy is developing in the church, it is important to notice that all these terms; elder, bishop, pastor, all refer to the same men, and point significantly to what Christian leadership implies.

It makes clear what is at stake here. Leaders in the church may not be those in the church who are ambitious for the position of leadership over God's own people or who consider themselves worthy of such a position. But alternatively, It may be that others recognize that responding to such a call upon their lives is likely to involve a considerable cost, and that such a position carries with it enormous privilege but also, great responsibility, the inevitable cost of caring for the flock, loving them, supporting them, coming alongside them as they sacrifice themselves for them, faithfully speaking to them of the grace of God and encouraging them to walk with the Lord, turning their eyes upon Jesus.

A hierarchy did need to develop, as Paul explains to both Timothy and Titus. There needed to be leadership in the church, but it had to be the right kind of leadership. (1 Timothy 3:1-15; 2 Timothy 4:1-5o; Titus 1:5-9; 2:1,15). Peter exhorts the elders among them to shepherd the flock which is among them, exercising oversight not under compulsion but voluntarily, according to the will of God. (1 Peter 5:1,2) NASV.

Paul never describes himself in those terms, but only as an apostle, together with others who are apostles, like Peter and Apollos, (1 Corinthians 3:22; 4:9; 15:8), whom he also describes as servants of Christ and stewards of the mysteries of God. (1 Corinthians 4:1). This may have been because Paul had never stayed long in one place but was always moving on to 'preach the gospel, not where Chist had already been named, lest I build on another man's foundation'. (Romans 15:20).

It is obvious how little the title 'apostle' means to Paul as a designation of the respect due to him. Though now an apostle, he had once devastated the church of God until Christ met him on the Damascus road. He can only wonder at the grace of God to him and his determination to suffer anything that brings him nearer to Him. (Philippians 3:6-10). However, the title apostle demonstrates how concerned he is that he had the right to be regarded as such by those who had responded to his teaching as that which comes to them, through him, but from God. He can honestly say to the Ephesian elders, 'I did not shrink from declaring to you the whole counsel of God', (Acts 20:27). He says to the Corinthian believers 'you are the seal of my apostleship in the Lord' (1 Corinthians 9:2), because they were questioning his authority. But he also calls them his beloved children, those who have come to faith through his ministry; for whom he has become their father in Christ. (1 Corinthians 4:14,15). That probably says it all.

Paul acknowledges that some title is necessary so that all may know who is taking responsibility for the people of God, a solo leadership, or better still, a group of those called by God to look after His flock, the flock of God which is so precious to Him because He obtained it with the blood of His Son, His dear son (Acts 20:28).

Acts 20:17-38. Paul's speech to the Ephesian elders

And from Miletus, Paul sent to Ephesus and called to him the elders of the church. And when they came to him he said to them, 'You know how I lived among you all the time from the first day that I set foot in Asia, serving the Lord with all humility and with tears and with trials which befell me through the plots of the Jews; how I did not shrink from declaring to you anything that was profitable and teaching you in public and from house to house, testifying both to Jews and Greeks of repentance towards God, and faith towards our Lord Jesus Christ. And now, behold, I am going to Jerusalem, bound in the Spirit, not knowing what shall befall me there'. (Acts 20:17-22).

These Ephesian elders were very dear to Paul. He reminds them how he had lived among them from the first day he had arrived in Ephesus, 'from the first day that I set foot in Asia'. (Acts 20:18). He had not come with a fanfare, with fellow workers going ahead of him to proclaim what an accomplished, distinguished speaker it was who was coming to visit them. This had never been Paul's way. Instead, he had come to them with all humility, and with tears and with trials which befell him through the plots of the Jews (Acts 20:19).

We are aware of the trials which befell him in chapter 19. But the tears? Tears indicate deep emotion. He repeats the phrase in verse 31, 'That for three years I did not cease night or day to admonish every one with tears'. His was the emotional cost of giving everything he had as he spoke to them of Jesus, of His claim upon their lives, for he decided to know nothing among them but Jesus Christ and Him crucified. (1 Corinthians 2:2).

To the church in Rome, Paul writes of the great sorrow and unceasing anguish in his heart if the gospel he preaches is not received by the Jews to whom Jesus came as a Jew, sent by God to the lost sheep of the house of Israel, (Matthew 10:6; 15:24); but whose message was also to Gentiles, to every creature, to all nations. (Mark 16:15; Luke 24:27; Matthew 28:19). Even when writing to the Corinthian believers, Paul says he wrote to them 'out of much affliction and anguish of heart and with many tears, not to cause you pain but to let you know the abundant love I have for you'. (2 Corinthians 2:4).

Paul felt deeply the tremendous responsibility given to him to set before these precious people, life and death. Life if they believed on the Lord Jesus, death if they rejected Him. They were not only dead while they lived, but there was the prospect of judgement to come. (1 Timothy 5:6; Ephesians 2:1,2).

It is doubtful if the Jews and Gentiles who listened to Paul so carefully (Acts 17:2,10; 19:10) would have been so responsive to his message had he been cold, clinical, calculating. This was 'just' teaching, the imparting of some doctrine, however inspired. But Paul poured out his heart to them, made no secret of his unbounded love for them (2 Corinthians 2:4), and for all who are without God and without hope in the world. (Ephesians 2:12).

He may not have been the only one. He writes in 1 Corinthians about the seed that was sown in Corinth, where Paul sowed, Apollos watered and God gave the increase. It is not inconceivable that Apollos watered the seed of the word of God with his tears also. Together, he and Paul had brought the gospel to Corinth (Acts 18:1; 19:1, 27), but all the glory went to God without whom there would have been no increase, no growth. But God had commissioned them to be His fellow workers, and that was a tremendous privilege. (1 Corinthians 3:9)

At the other end of the scale, Paul could write to the Philippians, 'Rejoice in the Lord always! And again I say, rejoice! (Philippians 4:4). There was nothing half hearted about Paul.

Acts 20:18-28. Paul's final word to his beloved Ephesians

Behold, I go to Jerusalem, bound in the Spirit, not knowing what shall befall me, except that the Holy Spirit testifies to me in every city that imprisonment and afflictions await me. But I do not account my life of any value nor as precious to myself, if only I may accomplish my course and the ministry which I received from the Lord Jesus, to testify to the gospel of the grace of God. (Acts 20:22-25).

And now behold, I know that all of you among whom I have gone preaching the kingdom will see my face no more.

Paul had reminded the Ephesian elders of how he came to them the first time, serving the Lord with all humility and with tears; and the trials which befell him through the plots of the Jews; how he did not shrink from declaring to them anything that was profitable, and teaching them in private and from house to house.

He had a full programme, yet still remembered and reminded them, further on in his speech that 'these hands ministered to my wants and to those who were with me'. (Acts 20:34), a reference to his tent making skills. He needed no superfluous luxuries, coveted no man's gold or silver or apparel, for his sole purpose in being with them was to testify to both Jews and Greeks, repentance towards God and faith towards our Lord Jesus Christ. (Acts 20:21).

Now Paul knew what the next phase of his life was going to be, for the Holy Spirit had revealed it to him. He is going to Jerusalem, bound in the Spirit, the Holy Spirit testifying to Him that in every place, every city, imprisonment and afflictions await him. (Acts 20:22,23). His experience in Ephesus had been hard, as they knew. In 1 Corinthians 15:32, Paul writes 'I fought with beasts at Ephesus', and in 1 Corinthians 16:9, he tells the Corinthian believers that 'a wide door and effective work has opened to me, and there are many adversaries'. He goes even further in 2 Corinthians 1:8-10 when he writes of the affliction which 'we' (possibly when he was with Apollos) experienced in Asia (that is, Ephesus); for we were so utterly unbearably crushed that we despaired of life itself'.

In Luke's account of Paul's time in Ephesus, these sufferings are not described. Perhaps Luke did not need to, for these events may have already been widely known, for Paul constantly had to evade the Jews who tried to kill him. (Acts 20:3). It appeared to be a consistent reaction to his preaching and Luke had therefore no need to comment on what had happened in Ephesus.

Paul had limited time at his disposal to spend time on minutely recalling past events in Ephesus for he was hastening to be at Jerusalem for Pentecost. (Act 20:16). Paul just wanted the Ephesian elders to be aware of what the Holy Spirit was saying to him of the future. He had spoken briefly of the past, but the Holy Spirit was always moving on, always indicating a future ministry which He had for Paul.

Paul is in effect saying to the Ephesian elders 'I am going to Jerusalem. I am on my way there for this is what I believe the Lord wants me to do. I go bound in the Spirit, under His constraint, according to His will. (Acts 16:6; 19:21). I know that this is what I am meant to do and that imprisonment and afflictions await me, just as they have in every city, for that is what the Holy Spirit has shown me, and I do not know what may befall me in Jerusalem but I do not account my life to be of any value so long as I may be permitted to pursue my course, the course which God has laid out for me, and to accomplish my ministry which I received from the Lord Jesus, to testify to the gospel of the grace of God, His unmerited favour'.

Paul's trinitarian experience of God the Father, the Lord Jesus Christ and the Holy Spirit, has enabled him thus far to preach the kingdom of God throughout the known world. But he has a sense that this is coming to an end.

Not only the Ehesian church but all the other churches with which he is associated will see his face no more. |(Acts 20:25). And in this his farewell speech he wants their assurance that he is innocent of the blood of all of them. (Acts 20:26). He is emphatic. He says, I testify to you this day that I am innocent of the blood of all of you for I did not shrink from declaring to you the whole counsel of God' (Acts 20:27).

The implication is clear. Paul is responsible for no-one's eternal death through neglecting to preach the gospel to all, and he delivers it in all its fullness. (Barrett p 973). He had declared to them *the whole counsel of God,* (Acts 20:27), which is impressive as a huge undertaking, unlimited, totally conclusive; the whole counsel of God summed up as the mystery, the open secret of God's will, (Ephesians 1:9), that which is only known through revelation, through faith and by grace, that God should have a people united under One Head, the Lord Jesus Christ, who should bring praise to His glory as He is glorified in the church, in His people, a people chosen by Him since before the foundation of the world. (Ephesians 1:4).

With such teaching, and the recognition of the finality of what he is saying that they will see his face no more, how could these elders do anything other than embrace Paul and kiss him, 'sorrowing most of all because of the word which he had spoken that they should see his face no more'. (Acts 20:36).

But he had one more thing to say to them, for his teaching was very pragmatic. He says, you are pastors, shepherds of the flock of God, guardians of His flock when wolves come in among them, as they will, not sparing the flock. Even among yourselves will men arise who will speak perverse things, distorting the truth, speaking heresy, and they will seek to draw disciples after them creating schism in the church.

So Paul says, Take heed to yourselves and to all the flock, for God has made you overseers and guardians of the flock and it is very precious to Him. It is His church. It is the church of God and it became His through the blood of His own dear Son. (Acts 20:28).

Paul had laid a foundation in Ephesus, for the church, the household of God was built upon the foundation of the apostles and prophets, Jesus Christ Himself being the chief cornerstone. (Ephesians 2:20,21). It was necessary for Paul to warn them that this foundation would be contested in the future, just as it had been in the past.

But now, having spoken to them faithfully of all that was on his heart, Paul must now depart, not just with a farewell but with a time of prayer as they committed one another to the Lord, weeping and embracing Paul and no doubt each other too, for they knew they would see his face no more. (Acts 20:36,37).

And they brought him to the ship.

This is the finale of Paul's third missionary journey, but not the end of his ministry. Even when he is an 'ambassador in chains' in prison, (Epesians 6:20) Paul writes to the Ephesian Christians to pray for him, that utterance may be given to him in opening his mouth boldly to proclaim the mystery of the gospel. (Ephesians 6:18).

But first, he must make that final journey to Jerusalem.

Acts Chapter 21

Acts 21:1-16. Paul's last journey to Jerusalem. Arrival at Tyre

And when we had parted from them and set sail, we came by a straight course to Cos, and the next day to Rhodes, and from there to Patara. And having found a ship crossing to Phoenicia, we went aboard and set sail. When we had come in sight of Cyprus, leaving it on the left, we sailed to Syria and landed at Tyre, for there the ship was to unload its cargo. And having sought out the disciples, there we stayed seven days. (Acts 21:1-6)

Clinging to him, not wanting to let him go, the Ephesian elders brought Paul to the ship. This ship brought Paul and Luke to Cos, an island off the coast of the province of Asia. The next stop made by the ship was at Rhodes, Rhodes being the name of the island and also the city. Then on to Patara. Here Paul and Luke changed ships and took a ship which was going to Phoenicia. It set sail from Cyprus though it did not stop here but sailed past, making for Syria and the ancient port of Tyre.

Though Paul was hastening to Jerusalem, they were compelled to stay in Tyre for seven days while the ship unloaded its cargo and took on another shipment. This was an opportunity for Paul and Luke to seek out the disciples in Tyre.

There had been a persecution of Christians after the death of Stephen in Jerusalem, and 'those who were scattered abroad because of the persecution travelled as far as Phoenicia and Cyprus and Antioch'. (Acts 11:19). Some of them came to the Phoenician coastland bringing the gospel with them. This may have been the origin of the church in Tyre, and how glad they were to see Paul and Luke.

For seven days, they enjoyed fellowship with each other, but there was one disturbing feature of this special time. One or more of the disciples was given a word of prophecy from the Holy Spirit, that Paul would suffer many things in Jerusalem, and told him 'not to go on to Jerusalem'. (Acts 21:4).

The prophecy was true. Paul did suffer many things in Jerusalem but for Paul that was not reason enough for him to change his mind, for he had received from the Holy Spirit the same revelation, (Acts 20:22), and through the prophecy given through the disciples in Tyre, the Lord was confirming that this was indeed the will of the Lord for him.

The disciples had, in obedience to the Holy Spirit received the prophecy, but their human concern for Paul had taken over and would have interfered with what the Holy Spirit was about to do in Jerusalem, if Paul had listened to them rather than Him. Their concern for Paul was more than adequately demonstrated by their farewell leave-taking of him on the beach, where the whole church, including the women and children, gathered together to pray for Paul and commit him to the Lord. The scene is reminiscent of what happened at Miletus with the Ephesian elders. Paul was undoubtedly highly regarded by the many communities of believers which were growing up throughout the empire, but the cost to him personally was very great.

Then Paul and Luke went on board the newly laden ship, for the voyage to Ptolemais, and the Tyrian believers returned home. (Acts 21:6). There is a sense of completeness about Paul's time in Tyre, even though it was only seven days. Acts 21:5 says, 'when these days were ended, fulfilled, complete, we departed and went on our journey.'

There had obviously been a special reason why it was necessary for Paul and Luke to spend time with them, and significant that the sea voyage to Jerusalem had enabled Paul and Luke to have this extended time in Tyre, and to receive the prophecy which strengthened Paul's determination to go to Jerusalem whatever the cost.

In such apparently unimportant ways, such as the lading of a ship, God is able to meet the needs of His people both physically and above all, spiritually. God is able to accomplish all things after the counsel of His own will. (Ephesians 1:11).

Acts 21:7-9. Arrival at Caesarea

When we had finished the voyage from Tyre, we arrived at Ptolemais, and we greeted the brethren and stayed with them one day. (Acts 21:7).

On the morrow we departed and came to Caesarea and we entered the house of Philip the evangelist who was one of the Seven and stayed with him; and he had four unmarried daughters who prophesied. (Acts 21:8,9).

The voyage from Tyre to Ptolemais, within the region of Syria which included Damascus, completed, Paul and Luke sought out the disciples in Ptolemais and stayed with them for just one day. Ptolemais is now known as Akka, but was the famous Acre of the time of the Crusades. Ptolemais had also received the gospel after the persecution which arose after the death of Stephen. (Acts 9:19). From this short journey from Tyre to Ptolemais by sea, Paul and Luke made their way to Caesarea.

This was the beginning of Paul's journey to Rome, although we only observe this in hindsight, for his immediate purpose was to bring the money collection from the churches in Macedonia and Achaia to the church in Jerusalem; and Jerusalem had been the object of this journey, not only because of the gift to the Jerusalem church, but also to meet with James and the other apostles who remained in Jerusalem.

Caesarea was the home of Philip the evangelist, who had been one of the Seven in Acts 6:3, appointed by the church to minister to the physical and material needs of believers, to care for them and support them and comfort them while the apostles performed the ministry given to them to preach the word and devote themselves to prayer. (Acts 6:4).

These distinctions however, appeared in practice to be quite fluid. Stephen had been one of the seven and was stoned to death for preaching to the Sanhedrin. (Acts 6:15). Philip was another of the seven whose ministry included preaching the gospel, and as a result had been greatly used of the Lord in the evangelization of Samaria (Acts 8:1,4), when the church in Jerusalem had been scattered after the death of Stephen.

After the episode in Acts 8:38 when Philip had an opportunity to explain to the Ethiopian eunuch the significance of Isaiah 53, a scroll of which he had purchased at great cost in Jerusalem, and which he was at pains to understand until Philip preached to him Jesus; Philip had gone to Caesarea (Acts 8:40), where he now lived with his four daughters, about twenty years later. We know nothing of his ministry in Caesarea except that the church had been a loving fellowship of Spirit filled believers, enabling even children to grow up with the gift of prophecy.

Paul and Luke were there 'for some days' (Acts 21:10), and Philip and Luke may have spent time together talking over the the early experiences of the church, and this may have been an oral source for Luke for at least some of the material which he was later able to incorporate into this volume, especially some of the early chapters of Acts. (Barrett p 993).

Philip is described as an evangelist. Bultmann sys this is to make the distinction between the role of the evangelist from that of an apostle, the term apostle being confined to the Twelve at that time. Calvin regards evangelists as being halfway between apostles and teachers, (Bultmann. *Theology* p458; Calvin, Barrett p 993). These assessments appear to denigrate somewhat the work of the evangelist.

Apostles and teachers are also proclaimers of the gospel, but to be called to be an evangelist is to be a person after God's own heart, to seek and save those who are lost, even as Jesus did. (Luke 19:10). Paul is urgent when writing to Timothy. He writes, 'do the work of an evangelist, fulfil your ministry'. (1 Timothy 4:5). Philip was called to evangelize. His daughters were called to prophesy and being thus gifted by the Holy Spirit were able to bring the word of the Lord when the church gathered together. (I Corinthians 11:5). Paul writes to the Ephesian believers that Chtist's gifts to the church were apostles, prophets, evangelists, pastors and teachers, for building up the body of Christ, until all attain to maturity, to the measure of the stature of the fullness of Christ. (Ephesians 4:7-13).

Philip and his daughters were doing just that and God was blessing the church in Caesarea which included the home of Cornelius (Acts 10:1) and the home of Philip and his daughters.

Acts 21:10-14. The prophecy of Agabus

While we were staying for some days, a prophet named Agabus came down from Judea. And coming to us, he took Paul's girdle and bound his own hands and feet and said, 'Thus says the Holy Spirit. So shall the Jews at Jerusalem bind the man who owns this girdle and deliver him into the hands of the Gentiles'. When we heard this, we begged him not to go up to Jerusalem.

It was however by the prophet Agabus, and not by the daughters of Philip, that a prophecy was given to Paul about his intended visit to Jerusalem.

Luke had mentioned Agabus before in Acts 11:28, when Agabus had prophesied that a famine would take place over all the known world; and this took place in the time of Claudius, an emperor who reigned from 41-54 A.D. His prophecy was the impetus that prompted the collection for the 'brethren who lived in Judea, sending it to the elders by the hands of Barnabas and Saul'. (Acts 11:29, 30).

Now Agabus has come down to Caesarea from Judea, the region which included Jerusalem. This was some journey to make to deliver a prophecy. It can only have been the Holy Spirit who prompted Agabus to come down to Caesarea, to confront Paul once again with the warning that to go to Jerusalem was to deliver himself into the hands of the Gentiles.

Until now, it had been the Jews who plotted to kill him. Gentiles like Gallio appeared to have no interest in charging Paul with insurrection, as the Jews had urged him to do. To have the Gentiles also arraigning him was another step along the way and would eventually lead to his imprisonment in Rome.

Agabus was very bold and forthright in his prophecy. Approaching Paul, he removed the girdle from Paul's waist and tied it around his own feet and hands saying, 'Thus says the Holy Spirit; so shall the Jews at Jerusalem bind the man who owns this girdle, and deliver him into the hands of the Gentiles'. (Acts 21:11).

The prophecy of Agabus concerning the famine had been realized. There was nothing to suggest that this further prophecy should not equally be fulfilled. The Holy Spirit was again giving Paul the option of relinquishing the visit to Jerusalem and no-one would have blamed him, especially considering all he had already suffered as a result of his determination to preach the gospel, and bring the good news of sins forgiven and new life in Christ to the lost souls he saw around him wherever he looked.

Paul believed that whatever the personal cost to himself, it was still God's perfect will for him that he should go to Jerusalem.

But this was not made easier for him by the loving reaction of Luke and his companions, who begged him not to go up to Jerusalem. (Acts 21:12). And Paul said to them, 'What are you doing, weeping and breaking my heart? For I am ready not only to be imprisoned but even to die at Jerusalem for the Name of the Lord Jesus'. (Acts 21:13). Luke comments, And when he would not be persuaded, we ceased and said, 'the will of the Lord be done'. (cts 21:14).

This was always the safest thing to say, the safest place to be, in the will of the Lord. We can imagine the shed and unshed tears of the believers as Paul and Luke prepared during the next few days for the journey to Jerusalem. How confident was Paul in the will of God. His will surpassed any eventuality that might overtake him, for above all and in spite of all, God was in control. There had been a memorable occasion when God had spoken to him one night in a dream, assuring Paul of his presence with him. 'Do not be afraid', God had said, 'for I am with you'. (Acts 18:9). That was all Paul needed to know, that God was with him, and would not fail him nor forsake him.

Was this what Paul was contemplating as he and Luke prepared to leave Caesarea? The plots of the Jews had so far come to nothing. Though Paul had suffered at their hands, many men and women had come to faith through his proclamation of the gospel in the power of the Holy Spirit. But now it was more than probable that the prophecy of Agabus would be fulfilled and that Paul was walking into real danger.

Nevertheless, Luke says, 'after these days, we made ready and went up to Jerusalem. And some of the disciples from Caesarea went with us, bringing us to the house of Mnason of Cyprus, an early disciple with whom we should lodge'. (Acts 21:15,16).

Acts 21:15-16. Arrival at Jerusalem

The journey to Jerusalem from Caesarea to Jerusalem was about 64 miles, a considerable overland journey, requiring a degree of preparation. But at last, the journey was complete, and Paul and Luke, together with some of the disciples who had accompanied them from Caesarea, found lodging at the home of a disciple named Mnason.

Mnason was called an early disciple. (Acts 21:16). He may have become a believer as a result of Peter's evangelistic activity in the early church. He was originally from Cyprus, but he may well have been in Jerusalem during those early, heady days of the church. (Acts 5:14). Nevertheless, it seems strange that lodgings for Paul and his companions had to be organized by the disciples from Caesarea (Acts 21:16), when hospitality could have been extended to Paul by James and the other elders. (Acts 21:18).

Perhaps the largeness of the company was a factor, for Luke does write that in Jerusalem, that is, in the church, they were received gladly, (Acts 21:17), and we remember that it was because of the poverty of the church in Jerusalem that Paul was conveying this gift to them.

Mnason may have known Barnabas who was also a Cypriot (Acts 4:36) and may have been one of those men from Cyprus who went to Antioch, preaching the Lord Jesus after Stephen had been martyred. (Acts 11:20). Whatever his background, he was glad to share his home with Paul and his companions.

Acts 21:17-26. Paul at Jerusalem. The meeting with James and the elders

When we had come to Jerusalem, the brethren received us gladly. On the following day, Paul went in with us to James, and all the elders were present. After greeting them, he related one by one the things that God had done among the Gentiles through his ministry, and when they heard it, they glorified God. (Acts 21: 17-20).

Paul's aim had been to be at Jerusalem by Pentecost, (Acts 20:16). We are given no assurance that this aim was accomplished, but conclude that it was so. Paul's visit to the temple does not imply this, for he went to the temple for completely different reasons, and though Pentecost was a Jewish feast it had become for Christians a special time, as the anniversary of the occasion of the outpouring of the Holy Spirit and the birth of the church; (Acts 2:1) and was not associated with the Temple festival.

Paul is still accompanied by Luke as the pronouns 'we' and 'us' confirm, (Acts 21:17), but in verse 19, the pronoun is 'he' referring to Paul, and 'we' is not resumed until Acts 27:1. This is not to presume that Luke had left Jerusalem. Indeed, his immaculate description of subsequent events suggest the opposite and imply his presence.

On the day following their arrival in Jerusalem, Paul and his companions 'went in with us to James and all the elders were present'. (Acts 21:17). It is obvious that James occupies a leading position in the Jerusalem church, as he had in Acts 15:13. But in Acts 15 there appeared to be other apostles and elders present. (Acts 15:22). The other apostles appear to be no longer in Jerusalem since the Apostolic decree of chapter 15, or at least are not mentioned by Luke. In Acts 21:18 Luke writes, 'James and all the elders', not 'all the apostles and elders'.

Until this moment, the church in Jerusalem had been in the forefront of the Christian movement, able to issue the decree that Christians should abstain from what had been sacrificed to idols; from blood; and from what had been strangled; and from unchastity. (Acts 15:25). This decree was respected and expected to be obeyed by the new churches springing up, especially by those new Christians who were being influenced by Judaizers, men who wanted the church to retain Jewish customs.

The authority of the Jerusalem church now appears to be greatly diminished, and perhaps this was a source of regret to James, and prompted his suggestion to Paul that he join the four Jewish men who had been experiencing all the thirty days or so, and the restrictions of the Nazarite vow which for them had now come to an end.

The meeting with James and the elders gave Paul an opportunity to recount to them all that God had been doing among the *Gentiles,* through his ministry. (Acts 21:19). And when they heard it, they glorified God, (Acts 21:20), probably also asking Paul to convey their thanks to those Gentiles as well as Jews who had contributed to the gift sent to the Jerusalem church, although Luke does not mention this.

But paradoxically, other Jews in the city had a completely different understanding of what Paul had been preaching, not only among the Gentiles but among the Jews as well. They had received reports that Paul had been teaching that the law no longer applied to Christians, the law in this case understood as the Mosaic law. They claimed that there were thousands of Christian Jews who were still 'zealous for the law'. (Acts 21:20). They still wanted to circumcise their children. They still wanted to observe Jewish customs, but they understood that Paul was telling them to 'forsake Moses', and everything concerned with the old dispensation.

How little they understood of Paul's teaching. Paul's message was that believers are justified, made righteous, not by works, but by faith. No matter how hard men and women try to please God by observing every jot and tittle of the law, those who rely on the works of the law are under a curse. (Galatians 2:16, 3:10;

Deuteronomy 27:26). But Christ has redeemed us from the curse of the law, having become a curse for us, for it is written, 'cursed is everyone who hangs on a tree'. (Galatians 3:13). Whether Jew or Greek, bond or free, none of these distinctions matter when a believer comes to Christ in faith, for that which unites all believers is faith in Him. They have received Him not by works of the law but by the hearing of faith. (Galatians 3:2). For freedom Christ has set believers free, free from the law to which he or she was in bondage, for the law is bondage, it is a yoke of slavery. (Galatians 5:1). The law was indeed given by Moses under the hand of God, but grace and truth came by Jesus Christ. (John 1:17).

Men and women may now be free from the bondage of the law. They are free not to sin. Sin will no longer have dominion over them, for they are not under law but under grace. (Romans 6:14). For the wages of sin, disobedience to the law, is death, separation from the life of God, but the free gift of God is eternal life in Christ Jesus our Lord. (Romans 6:23). And if they are led by the Spirit, they are not under the law. (Galatians 5:8).

This is the substance of Paul's preaching. He is not instituting another set of rules and regulations to be obeyed. He is declaring to both Jews and Gentiles.' You are free!' Free from the yoke of bondage which was the Mosaic law. 'Only use not your liberty as a reason for licentiousness, but be filled with the Holy Spirit. (Galatians 5:13), and by love serve one another'. This is Paul's loving concern for the Galatian Christians, and for all to whom God has called him to be an apostle.

For Jews who had now become Christians, the temptation was great. There is comfort in holding on to long held customs, family traditions; and to step out in faith can be challenging. But the rewards are also great. These Jews, so beloved by Paul, (Romans 9:1-5) needed to live in a different way, according to the life of Christ within them; to learn to trust and be fully committed, not to a set of rules but to a Person, and to the abundant life which He promised. (John 10:10).

James and the elders of the church in Jerusalem had the responsibility of proclaiming this new and wonderful life lived in the Spirit to the Jewish believers. But we see human concern creeping in to frustrate the purposes of God, just as happened in Tyre after the prophecy to Paul and later, that given through Agabus; a tendency to reinterpret what has been prophesied, 'Are you sure? Has God said? Can we really trust what we think He is saying to us?' It is as old as the garden of Eden. (Genesis 3:1).

James is legitimately concerned for these four men who have come to the end of their time as Nazarites. He is also unwilling that Paul should, in his view, abrogate all that the law stood for in relation to the Jews, all that was culturally comfortable for them, but also what they genuinely believed to be necessary to them as observant Jews. For these Jews who thought this way, becoming a Christian could be described bluntly as an extra though important dimension to their original faith position. But surely James could not have accepted such a diminution of the revolutionary power of the gospel, even to accommodate those who were finding the transition to whole hearted commitment to grace rather than law, to freedom rather than slavery, a difficult challenge to accept. James appeared not to have realised that these Jews were foregoing the joy of being dead to sin and alive to God through our Lord Jesus Christ. (Romans 6:11).

But James had a plan. And we wonder why, in the light of all that Paul had written in his letters to the churches, did Paul go along with it? Was it out of deference to James' authority? On a previous occasion when he and Barnabas had visited Jerusalem Paul had been pleased to receive from James and Peter and John the right hand of fellowship, a recognition from these apostles which Paul greatly valued, as these men were 'pillars of the church' in Jerusalem, and this sign of fellowship was a recognition of his ministry to the Gentiles, although he did not confine himself to the Gentiles. He was equally committed to the Jews who came to know the power of the Holy Spirit in their lives. (Galatians 2:9).

But here was James, suggesting that in order to conciliate those Jewish Christians who were 'zealous for the law',

(Acts 21:20) Paul should accompany four men who had completed their Nazarite vow into the temple. From the description in Acts 21:24, it appears that at the end of seven days, these four men would shave their heads, indicating that this was a Nazarite vow such as Paul himself had completed at Cenchreae. (Acts 18:18).

This was a vow based on Numbers 6 and focussed on separation from anything that defiles a person, or is even a distraction, from complete submission to God, a complete separation to the Lord. This is commendable in itself. It was especially necessary for anyone defiled by sin in any way for it affirmed an intention that the person involved wanted to live his or her life in future, free from anything that would come between them and their devotion to God.

Of course, in essence, this was the objective of every observant Jew, though not everyone was expected or indeed was able, to take the Nazarite vow. But these four men were Christian Jews, and from Paul's own experience he could truthfully say that such a vow was now obsolete.

Every believer, whether Jew or Gentile could know, *did* know, the forgiveness of sins through the efficacy of the blood of the Lord Jesus shed on the cross for them. In addition, the apostle John recognized that forgiveness of sin may not be a one-off experience only, but if we walk in the light, as He is in the light, we have fellowship with one another and the blood of Jesus cleanses us and goes on cleansing us, from all sin. (1 John 1:7). Every believer can know the joy of the altar life, presenting his or her body as a living sacrifice, holy and acceptable to God, which is their spiritual worship; a constant offering of oneself to God, a transformed, transfigured life. (Romans 12:1).

Paul however complied with the suggestion made by James that he should go to the temple with the four (unidentified) men and purify himself along with them. In this way, as James understood it, Paul would conciliate all those believers who were still 'zealous for the law'. (Acts 21:20), 'that all will know that there is nothing in what they have been told about you, but that you yourself live in observance of the law'. (Acts 21:24).

Paul was willing for this. It was adaptation, not compromise, for he was free, and free to limit himself because he was free. He himself writes that he was free from all men, yet made himself a slave to all that he might win the more. He had become all things to all men, that he might by all means save some. He did it for the sake of the gospel. (1 Corinthians 9:19-23).

Then Paul took the men and the next day he purified himself with them and went into the temple to give notice when the days of purification would be fulfilled and the offering presented for every one of them. (Acts 21:26).

Gentiles of course did not need to act in this way. The Apostolic Decree which James had just reiterated, (Acts 21:25), only required that Christians should abstain from food sacrificed to idols, and from blood, and from what had been strangled, and from unchastity. (Acts 21:25). Was this request from James that Paul should align himself with these Jewish Christians, inadvertently designed to make a distinction between Jewish and Gentile believers to the detriment of the Gentiles? Paul had resisted such a distinction with all his might. His emphatic statement, 'There is neither Jew nor Greek, there is neither bond nor free, there is neither male nor female, for all are one in Christ Jesus', was a trademark conviction of his. (Galatians 3:28).

And yet he accepted James' request. Perhaps James intended that the position of Jewish Christains should be unambiguously superior. Perhaps he wanted to ensure that Paul, whose ministry had provided the knowledge of the way of salvation for so many of the Gentile converts, should be reined in a little, lest he be given too large a place in the hierarchy of the church. James may have been conscious that this action too would provide an instance of the fact that Paul was a Jew and that seeing Paul take this step would remind Jewish Christians of his origins, that he was 'one of them'.

Paul had so recently reminded the Ephesian elders of the dangers of division and schism in the church, (Acts 20:30), yet it seems as though he is himself being drawn into schismatic action, though having no perception of any motivation behind it except conciliation. It is possible that neither did James, and in seeking to provide motivation for this action of James, who may have had no such incentives for his behaviour, it may be that James has been seriously maligned. Nevertheless, this was the beginning of a course of events which had a disastrous outcome for Paul.

The gathering together of the money from the many and various Christian communities scattered throughout Macedonia and Achaia had been a generous and praiseworthy attempt to bring all the churches together with one another in a practical way, whether Jewish or Gentile believers, and for this reason Paul had come to Jerusalem. (Acts 24:17). But in spite of this, Paul allowed himself to be subject to James' authority, and when Paul accepted the discipline imposed on him by James, he discovered that he had been trapped in an impossible position. Acceding to James' request, Paul found himself at the centre of a putative revolt on the part of the Christian Jews.

When the seven days of purification were almost completed, the Jews from Asia, who had seen him in the temple, stirred up all the crowd and laid hands on him. (Acts 21:27).

The temple was a sacred place for the Jews. It was the place where God could be approached, for although He was the creator and sustainer of the universe He could be found in the innermost part of the temple, the Holy of Holies, to which only the high priest had access once a year on the Day of Atonement.

There was, happily, a court of the Gentiles, but the Holy Place, the penultimate place of worship before the Holy of Holies, was reserved for Jews.

These Jews had seen Paul going into the temple. This was a man who in their eyes had a reputation for speaking against the temple, and the people of God, and the Mosaic law. (Acts 21:28). Not only that, but he had taken four men into the temple with him whom they assumed to be Gentiles, and that was an act of defilement. This last atrocity had become a charge against him and was based on the fact that they had previously seen Paul with Trophimus, a Gentile believer from Ephesus, and had assumed that Trophimus had accompanied Paul when he went into the temple.

Like other instances such as had occurred at Iconium, Corinth and Ephesus, (Acts 14:2,19; 18:12; 19:26-28), experience had taught Paul that it could all happen again, including that the charges against him were not consistent with the facts. Paul had himself reminded the Ephesians of the trials which befell him through the plots of the Jews, (Acts 20:19), but that even so he did not shrink from declaring to them what was profitable, teaching them publicly and from house to house, solemnly testifying both to Jews and Greeks repentance towards God and faith towards our Lord Jesus Christ.

But these Jews had done their worst. They had aroused the whole city and the people ran together. They seized Paul and dragged him out of the temple and at once the gates of the temple were shut, (Acts 21:30), probably by the captain of the temple, who would have the task of purifying the temple against defilement and desecration caused by something which had not actually happened, its incursion by Paul and Trophimus. (Acts 6:1).

The shutting of the gates may have a symbolic as well as a practical meaning, not only for Paul, but for all people everywhere. The veil of the temple, the curtain which hung between the Holy place and the Holy of Holies had been rent from the top to the bottom as Jesus hung on the cross. (Matthew 27:51). God was no longer to be found in a particular place. From now on, He was to found through a new and living way, the way of repentance and faith in the sacrifice of Christ, forgiveness of sins through His death on the cross. The veil was rent and all mankind could enter into the Holy of Holies, through the curtain, that is to say, His flesh. (Hebrews 10:20). 'So let us draw near with a true heart and in full assurance of faith, with our hearts sprinkled clean'. (Hebrews 10:22), exclaims the writer to the Hebrews.

The temple gates were shut, but the way to God was gloriously open. But inevitably, the tradition of the cleansing of the temple after its supposed desecration ground on as the captain of the temple re-consecrated it.

Meanwhile, outside the temple, the Jews were trying to kill Paul. (Acts 21:31). Word came to the military tribune of the cohort that all Jerusalem was in confusion. This tribune we later discover to be Claudius Lysias. (Acts 23:26).

We have no information as to what James and the elders of the church were doing at this time of utter confusion. (Acts 21:30,31). There was presumably little that they could do, but perhaps someone had sent word to the tribune. He was the Roman official in charge of security and especially at the times of the feasts of the Jews when numbers came up to Jerusalem from the Diaspora, the dispersion of Jews throughout the Roman empire, and would keep the courts of the temple under constant surveillance. This was apparently the feast of Pentecost and Claudius Lysias would be on constant alert. It is not inconceivable that someone from the church had been able to get a message through to him.

Claudius Lysias took soldiers and centurions and ran down to them. And when they saw the tribune, they stopped beating Paul. Then the tribune came up and arrested him and ordered him to be bound with two chains. (Acts 21:32,33). As more than one centurion was present, we may conclude that there were at least two hundred men, one centurion being in charge of a hundred soldiers, though numbers were sometimes flexible.

Paul's life was saved through the intervention of the Roman soldiers. Without it, we may not have had some of Paul's more acute writings, though of course, the soldiers were not aware of that. They did what they had to do, fastening chains around Paul's wrists, linking him to two soldiers. The tribune, having arrested him, then inquired of the Jews who he was and what he had done (Acts 21:33), for he was certain that he must be a person of some importance to have been the cause of all the uproar.

If he was expecting some sort of coherent explanation from Paul, as to why the crowd was behaving in this way, he was disappointed. Some people were shouting one thing and some another and the tribune could not learn the facts because of the uproar. (Acts 21:34). So the tribune had no choice but to bring Paul into the barracks (which Bruce identifies as the fortress of Antonia, p 396). Paul actually had to be carried up the steps to the barracks by the soldiers, because of the violence of the crowd. (Acts 21:35). He may also have been weak from the beating he had received. The prophecy of Agabus had been fulfilled. Paul was now in the hands of Rome, delivered into the hands of the Gentiles. (Acts 21:11), for the mob of the people, the Jewish people followed, crying 'Away with him! (Acts 21:36).

Paul never rescinded or revoked his Jewish heritage, (Acts 21:39), but it seems that with this rejection of him, the Jews were making every attempt to do it for him.

Claudius Lysias was in for another surprise. As Paul was brought into the barracks, he said to the tribune, 'May I say something to you?' (Acts 21:37) And the tribune said, 'Do you know Greek? Are you not that Egyptian then? Who really stirred up a revolt and led four thousand men of the Assyrians out into the wilderness? (Acts 21:38). The tribune had assumed that because Paul was a Jew, he spoke Aramaic. For Paul to be able to converse in Greek was an indication that he was an educated man and not the rough Egyptian which Claudius had suspected him of being.

Paul replied, 'I am a Jew, from Tarsus in Cilicia, a citizen of no mean city. I beg you, let me speak to the people'. (Act 21:39).

This Egyptian was a false prophet who had led a revolt, commanding a company of four thousand men, known as Assassins, into the wilderness, forming them into a guerilla force which he had subsequently led to the Mount of Olives in order to take Jerusalem.

The governor of Jerusalem at that time was Felix. He had killed or captured many of the Egyptian's followers but not the Egyptian himself, (identified as a person named ben Strada by Josephus in 'The Jewish wars', according to Bruce p 398), who had subsequently escaped. The tribune had obviously concluded that the person named ben Strada was standing before him, and that he had now reappeared. He was the cause of the revolt which the tribune was in the process of extinguishing.

Marshall helpfully explains that there were many such men at the time. Aggrieved at the Roman occupation of their country, clinging to Messianic expectations, they believed that through their devotion to God, He would undertake for them the expulsion of the Roman authorities. (Marshall p 351). Jesus had warned that this would happen, that many false Christs and many false prophets would arise and show great signs and wonders so as to lead astray if possible, even the elect. Then if anyone says to you, 'Lo, He is here', or 'Lo, He is there', do not believe it. (Matthew 24:23,24). And there have been many false prophets since the time of Jesus; some even in Paul's lifetime, who would lead many astray.

But this is not how God works.

Even discounting the fact that the Lord Jesus, the Messiah, the Anointed One had already come, they were not going to hasten the coming of the Messiah by ardent though misplaced activity in His name. They were looking for release from the oppression of the Romans, and giving it the justification of hastening the coming of the Messiah according to their scriptures, when He had already come. Neither does God work through the methods employed by such groups as the Assassins or Sicarii; as they were also known because they carried a short word or dagger known as a 'sica'.

From his name, Judas *Iscariot,* it is possible to deduce that Judas had been one of them before becoming a disciple of Jesus. We remember how, when Jesus was being arrested in the Garden of Gethsemane, someone had tried to defend Him with a sword and Jesus had said to him, 'put away your sword, for all who take the sword will perish with the sword'. (Matthew 26:52).

Claudius Lysias had asked the question, 'Do you know Greek? Are you not that Egyptian?' Paul's reply was not to give him a list of qualifications, of which he had many. He does enumerate them on another occasion, in order to compare their worth unfavourably with 'the surpassing worth of knowing Christ Jesus my Lord'. (Philippians 3:8). Paul had been making a different point when writing to the believers in Philippi. To Claudius Lysias he simply said, 'I am a Jew from Tarsus in Cilicia, a citizen of no mean city'.

Tarsus was a university city, and would explain to Cladius why Paul was an educated man. But then came this unusual request from Paul. 'I beg you, give me leave to speak to the people'. (Acts 21:39).

It was a very risky thing to do after the beating they had given Paul, and Claudius may have wondered why Paul did not prefer the safety of the barracks. But something in Paul's demeanour encouraged Claudius to do as Paul had pleaded with him to be allowed to do. So Paul, though still bound by his chains to a soldier either side of him, stood on the steps of the barracks and motioned with his bound hands to the people to gain their attention. When there was a great hush Paul began his defence, speaking to them in the Hebrew or Aramaic language. (Acts 21:40).

Acts Chapter 22

Acts 22:1-21. Paul's defence to the crowd

And when there was a great hush, Paul spoke to them in the Hebrew language saying, 'Brethren and fathers, hear the defence which I now make before you'. And when they heard that he addressed them in the Hebrew language, they were the more quiet. And he said: 'I am a Jew, born at Tarsus in Cilicia, but brought up in this city of Jerusalem at the feet of Gamaliel, educated according to the strict manner of the law of our fathers, being zealous for God as you all are this day. (Acts 21:40- 22:3).

Claudius Lysias had intended to take Paul into the barracks where he could be examined more closely, but was content to allow Paul some leeway, giving him permission to stand on the steps of Antonia and speak to the Jews who had so recently tried to kill him. Paul's defence was his testimony to what he had been and what he had now become. He spoke a little of his past history, but at greater length of the appearance of the Lord Jesus to him on the road to Damascus.

It is interesting to read Luke's account of this experience of Paul's in Acts 9 and to compare it with Paul's own memory of what had occurred as he recounts it in Acts 22 and Acts 26. There are slight omissions and additions but it is substantially the same.

Paul's own accounts were largely adapted to his audience, but intentionally speaking of Jesus, not as of someone of whom they may have heard. If they had heard, they may have understood Him as someone with revolutionary ideas who had appeared on the political scene for a short time, but who had been crucified as a result of His activity, on the authority of Rome. Some may even have heard that He had been raised from the dead and was alive for evermore, but that was surely unlikely, and probably mere propaganda. Paul wanted them to know the reality of who Jesus is.

This was the Jesus whom Paul had encountered on the Damascus road. There was indeed a revolutionary aspect to His teaching. He *had* been crucified, but He had been gloriously raised from the dead and He was now *alive*. The One whom Paul had seen on the road to Damascus was not an angel or a spirit being but Jesus Himself, glorified to such an extent that the light coming from Him had blinded Paul.

Paul had begun his defence by addressing them as 'Brethren and fathers'. (Acts 22:1), This was not just politic, or a term of respect, but a declaration that what he had to say to them was not controversial or in any way an attempt to destroy the precious gift they had of being the chosen people of God. It was not to destroy that precious destiny, but to fulfil it that Jesus came, and this what Paul wanted them to understand. They were his brethren, his fathers because they were bound together in that great truth of having received the covenant, initiated by Abraham, confirmed through Moses, anointed by David and totally fulfilled in the New Covenant ratified by Jesus.

All this implied history was understood by the people being addressed as brothers and fathers. Their problem was associating it with Jesus.

Having made his position clear, Paul could now go on to say that he was a Jew, born at Tarsus in Cilicia but that his religious training had been at the feet of Gamaliel in Jerusalem. Gamaliel was a well known and respected rabbi and of a tolerant disposition. Luke wrote of him in regard to the trial of Peter before the Sanhedrin, describing him as a Pharisee and a teacher of the law and held in honour by all the people, (Acts 5:34), and it was though his advice to the council that Peter and the apostles (Acts 5:40 had been beaten but then allowed to leave the prison, rather than being given an indeterminate sentence, 'rejoicing that they were considered worthy to suffer for the Name of Jesus'.

Paul's education at the feet of Gamiliel had been earlier than this incident, but it confirmed to his hearers that he had been educated to the highest standard, 'educated according to the strict manner of the law of our fathers, being zealous for God as you all are this day', (Acts 22:3) for though Paul had suffered greatly at their hands, he had some sympathy with their reasons for doing it. Paul had quite literally sat at the feet of Gamaliel, for that was the position taken by the student, at the feet of, or on the ground before, their teacher, so that their master was literally elevated both actually and symbolically.

Nevertheless, the tolerant attitude of the master had not been assumed by his pupil. Paul was a firebrand, zealous for the law, so zealous in fact that when he had become aware of the new movement called 'the way', and especially when he had heard Stephen's defence of it in his dying speech, his ire was aroused. Stephen had spoken of Jesus in Messianic terms, quoting the Old Testament texts at some length as of One who had fulfilled all the prophecies, all the types and figures, but was now being rejected by the leaders of God's people. When these leaders rose up against Stephen, intending to kill him for blasphemy, Paul was consenting to his death. (Acts 8:1).

Paul confesses that he had persecuted this 'way' to the death, binding and delivering both men and women to prison, 'as the high priest and the whole council of elders bear me witness'. (Acts 22:4). He hoped that this would convince his hearers how very zealous he had been, but also how very wrong. Though he had letters, documents from the high priest and the elders to root out these people whom they regarded as transgressors of the law, Paul now realised that they were men and women who had seen Jesus as the fulfilment of the law and believing in Him as their Lord and Savior were prepared to give their lives for their faith in Him. But Paul was prepared to go to Damascus 'to bring them bound to Jerusalem' to be punished. (Acts 22:5).

As Paul made his journey and drew near to Damascus, about noon, when the sun was at its height, an even greater light than the light of the sun shone about him (Acts 22:6). He fell to the ground. (Acts 22:7).

Some early artistic impressions show Paul falling from a horse and it is the case that it was quite a journey from Jerusalem in Judea, to Damascus in Syria. This perhaps necessitated being mounted, but Paul does not tell us this in his speech, only that in the presence of such light, all he could do was fall to the ground. As he did so, he heard a voice speaking to him, 'Saul, Saul, why do you persecute Me?' And he answered 'Who are you Lord?'

In Luke's account, the answer from the Lord came as 'I am Jesus whom you are persecuting'. But in Paul's own account, he recalls Jesus as saying, 'I am Jesus *of Nazareth* whom you are persecuting'. Though of course there is absolutely no doubt about who is speaking to Paul, Paul remembers this detail particularly as it applies to his present hearers, for they will have heard of Him as the Person known as Jesus of Nazareth. This was the title which had been placed over His head as he hung on the cross, by Pilate; Jesus of Nazareth the king of the Jews.

In his speech, Paul emphasises that those who were with him saw the light but did not hear the voice which spoke to him. It was Paul alone who became blind, and he alone who heard the voice, the voice which said to him what he may have already guessed, 'I am Jesus whom you are persecuting'. (Acts 22:8).

Luke's next question is also not in Luke's account, but very significant both of course for him, but also for his hearers, for it was confirmation that the ministry upon which he had now been engagedfor many years, upon which he had spent all the following years in pursuing, had been a commissioning from the voice from heaven; the voice which could only have been that of Jesus, but of Jesus as risen, ascended, glorified Lord.

Paul said to Him, 'What shall I do, Lord?' And the Lord said to him, 'Arise and go to Damascus, and *there you will be told all that is appointed for you to do'*. (Acts 22:10). At first sight, this does not appear to be a very comprehensive commission, but the Lord was testing his obedience to what he had seen and heard. He could at this point have turned his back on the vision that had been vouchsafed to him and refused to go to Damascus. But he could not see because of the brightness of that light which had blinded him, and he sought someone to lead him by the hand and so came to Damascus.

This experience was for Paul both conversion and commission, but an experience within Judaism. He had not ceased to be a Jew, he was still as he had been, but he was seeking to make relevant to these people in the crowd that he was justified in bringing to the attention of Jews everywhere as well as Gentiles, what God had shown him, that Jesus, though a Jew from an insignificant little town called Nazareth, was truly the Messiah figure for whom they had waited so long, and that He had come, not for the Jews only but for the Gentiles too.

After such an experience, Paul could only be obedient to what God had given him, made clearer to him as he was led to a man in Damascus named Ananias. They probably chose to go to Ananias because he was a devout man according to the law, well spoken of by all the jews who lived there. (Acts 22:12).

Ananias' first task in this version of Paul's conversion was to restore Paul's sight to him. He stood by Paul and said to him, 'Brother Saul, receive your sight'. (Acts 22:13). How wonderful, how grateful Paul must have been to hear that word, 'Brother'. It was a word of love, a word of acceptance, of welcome for someone who had not only persecuted the followers of the Lord Jesus, but Jesus Himself through them. Yet here was Ananias recognizing the tremendous event which had transformed Paul from a persecutor into a humble servant of Jesus Christ, one who would follow Him in glad obedience to the ends of the earth, as indeed, Ananias began to explain.

'In that very hour', Paul had seen Ananias and received his sight. (Acts 22:13). Now Ananias had something of great importance to say to him, something which Paul also wanted to convey to his hearers.

Ananias said, 'The God of our fathers appointed you to know His will, to see the Just One and to hear a voice from His mouth. For you will be a witness for Him to all men of that which you have seen and heard. And now, why do you wait? Rise and be baptized and wash away your sins, calling on the Name of the Lord'. (Acts 22:14-16).

According to Acts 9:15, this was a summary of what Ananias had said to Paul. The act of being baptized testified to Paul's having become a follower of the Lord Jesus and identified him with all those whom he had formerly persecuted. It signified a 180 degree turn around, going in the opposite direction. HIs former victims had become his brothers and sisters in the family of God.

But Paul had still to return to Jerusalem, having spent several days with the disciples in Damascus and preaching in their synagogues (Acts 9:19). This was a difficult decision for a former persecutor for he had become a suspect. Would not both Jew and Gentile believers view him with suspicion? Nevertheless, he not only went back to Jerusalem but while he was there he went into the temple and fell into a trance. (Acts 22:17).

This is not recorded by Luke in Acts 9, but there is no real discrepancy but only the difference in Paul's approach to these Jews who had so lately accused him of desecrating the temple, and tried to kill him.

Paul had gone to the temple seeking confirmation from the Lord of his commissioning, for there was a plot of the Jews in Jerusalem to kill him (Acts 9:23), an all too familiar outcome of his preaching, both then and now in this later episode. He was emphasising to his present audience that he had not rejected his Jewish roots on becoming a follower of Jesus. He still had access to the temple and had gone there to pray, (Acts 22:17) sincerely seeking the will of 'the God of our fathers'. (Acts 22:14), for so had Ananias spoken to him, that he was appointed to know His will and to be witness to Him. (Acts 22:14,15).

Acts 22:17-21. Paul's vision in the temple

When I had returned to Jerusalem and was praying in the temple, I fell into a trance and saw Him saying to me, 'Make haste and get quickly out of Jerusalem because they will not accept your testimony about Me'.

And I said, 'Lord, they themselves know that in every synagogue
I imprisoned and beat those who believed in You. And when the
blood of Stephen your witness was shed, I also was standing by
and approving and keeping the garments of those who killed
him'. And He said to me, 'Depart, for I will send you far away
to the Gentiles'. (Acts 22:17-21).

Paul has now returned to Jerusalem from Damascus full of
wonder and joy at what has happened to him, and soon paid a
visit to the temple. Paul's visit to, and subsequent trance in the
temple became a significant aspect of his life. Though Paul uses
quite ordinary terminology, it obviously meant a great deal to
him. Sometimes It is difficult for believers to speak to others
about their most precious experiences, in case they appear to be
boastful or self glorifying, or simply because the experience has
been such a personal time with their Lord.

Paul may have had similar thoughts, but there was another
aspect to this too. He was concerned for these Jews to whom he
was speaking. He wanted them to know the claim of Jesus on
their lives, this One whom they had rejected. He wanted them to
receive the eternal life and forgiveness of sin which He had
come to give to all who follow Him. So he describes how on
entering the temple he had fallen into a trance, and had spoken
with Jesus.

While he had been with Ananias in Damascus, three things
had been promised to him through Ananias. Firstly, that the God
of *our fathers* had appointed him to know His will, providing a
continuity between his love of God under the old regime, the old
covenant and his love of the Lord Jesus, the Son of God, under the
new covenant. Then Ananias had promised that he would see the
just One, the righteous One, who could be no other than Jesus
Himself, for this is also a Messianic title, and could well explain
Paul's undoubted obsession with the difference between the
righteousness of the law and the righteousness which comes by
faith. And thirdly, that Paul would hear a voice from His mouth.

These promises had already been fulfilled for Paul in some
measure. There would be other occasions when Paul had a

vision of the Lord, (2 Corinthians 12:1,2) and when he heard the Lord speaking to him. (Acts 23:11). God had also spoken to him through Ananias informing him that he was to be a witness for Him to all men, of what he had seen and heard. (Acts 22:14).

But now, in the temple, Jesus had spoken to him without the mediation even from Ananias, that obedient servant of the Lord. And what he said was full of urgency. It was not some great theological truth or revelation but very practical. 'Get quickly out of Jerusalem, make haste for they will not accept your testimony about Me. Depart, for I will send you to the Gentiles'. (Acts 22:21).

Paul was astounded. He had thought that the Jews might receive his word to them and understand that his was a commission from God, their God, his God, and that although he was a Jew, he must go to the Gentiles for that was the will of God concerning him. But his audience, the crowd of Jews, were not impressed by this. They had little expectation of the Messianic prophecies being fulfilled, of becoming a reality, in their lifetime. They were not committed to those scriptures but to the keeping of those commandments which made them distinctively Jewish in a culturally diverse world. Paul wanted to introduce them to Jesus, the key to all the scriptures.

Up to this point in Paul's speech, the Jews had listened to him. There may have been some who had second thoughts about wanting to kill him. Others may have wanted to hear more of what he was saying. But at the mention of the Gentiles, the Jews 'lifted up their voices and said "Away with such a fellow from the earth! For he ought not to live!" '

Paul had no illusions about his antecedents. He knew that he was not fit to be called an apostle because he persecuted the church of God. (1 Corinthians 15:9). But he also knew the grace of God in his life and he wanted to share with these Jewish people what he had seen and heard from the Lord, and especially what he had heard from the Lord in his trance, for he thought it would explain his actions.

The Lord had said to him, 'Make haste and get quickly out of Jerusalem because they will not accept your testimony about

Me'. (Acts 22:18). Paul had been astounded. Surely Lord, he said, they would believe what I have just told them about my persecution of those who believed in You. How in every synagogue I imprisoned and beat them. And when the blood of your witness Stephen was shed, I was standing by and approving and keeping the garments of those who killed him, executed him for blasphemy. (Acts 22:19,20).

Paul himself was to be a martyr later, even as Stephen had been. But not yet. God still had work for him to do. Disappointed though he may have been that his word to his beloved Jews had not been received, (Romans 9:2), he was not slow in responding to the repeated command of the Lord to him, 'Depart, for I will send you far away to the Gentiles'.

In Acts 9:30, we read that a similar revolt among the Jews had caused the disciples in Jerusalem to take Paul and bring him down to Caesarea, sending him off to Tarsus where he undoubtedly had many opportunities to speak to the Gentiles about the Lord Jesus.

Paul had no opportunity of continuing his testimony on this occasion. Acts 22:22 brings to an abrupt end all that Paul had wanted to say. At the mention of the Gentiles the whole crowd interrupted Paul and prevented him from continuing his speech.

He had attempted to convey to his listeners that on at least two occasions, on the road to Damascus and in the temple in Jerusalem Jesus had personally confirmed to him his destiny as a servant of His, and a witness to His saving power; direct, divine revelation. He wanted to persuade them that he was not a charlatan, or an apostate Jew, but only one who wanted to do the will of God as it had been revealed to him, just as they did, for he was confident that that too was their desire, their object and intention, and that on that understanding he could call them 'Brethren and fathers'. (Acts 22:1).

He had hoped that his acknowledgement of his persecution of those who called themselves 'the way' would help them to understand that he had come out from under the cloud of rejection of Jesus as the Messiah into the light of knowing Him personally; a personal relationship with Him that was open to them too, something that all could experience whatever their background, whether Jew or Gentile.

Surely these people would listen to such a testimony. But Paul now realizes that the word of the Lord had a dual purpose. Of course it was primarily to enable him to escape from the murderous intentions of the Jews, but in addition, and specifically, to commission him as an apostle to the Gentiles.

This was enough. The Jews not only did not want to hear any more, but displayed their acrimony against Paul by throwing off their garments and tossing dust into the air, and shouting, crying out, 'Away with him!'

Both Stott and Bruce suggest that in the eyes of the Jews, proselytism was acceptable, that is, Gentiles accepting Judaism. What was not acceptable was allowing Gentiles to become Christians without first becoming Jews, without requiring them to submit to the obligations of the Jewish law. What Paul was offering to Gentiles was equal privileges with the Jews, which was tantamount to saying that Jews and Gentiles were equal. (Stott p 348; Bruce p 406).

This was indeed what Paul was saying. Jews and Gentiles were equal for they both needed to come to God through Christ and that on identical terms. (Stott ibid). Paul had not broken away from his ancestral faith. He had not apostatized but he had changed. He had met with Jesus, had a personal encounter with Him and had been completely transformed by the divine revelation.

Now he was intent on sharing that faith with others, but not with Jews only, but also with Gentiles, as Jesus had commanded him.

This was the stumbling block for the Jews.

Crowds, mobs of protesters are not famed for being rational, but there must have been some rationality behind what they were doing, at least in the minds of the leaders of the revolt. They were sufficiently hostile to Paul to want him dealt with, preferably by death. The attempt to lynch him had failed. Perhaps the demonstration of throwing dust in the air and waving their clothes in front of the barracks would inspire the

Roman authorities to take over and do what they had been unable to do.

Acts 22:22-29. The riot continued. Paul reveals his Roman citizenship

They listened to him up to this statement and then they raised their voices and said, 'Away with such a fellow from the earth! He should not be allowed to live!'

And as they were crying out and throwing off their clothes and tossing them into the air, the commander ordered him to be brought from the barracks, stating that he should be examined by scourging so that he might find out the reason why they were shouting against him in that way.

It was the mention of the Gentiles that determined the overreaction of the crowd. They had accused Paul of defiling the temple, their most sacred space. They have also heard the rumours about his teaching that the law of Mosess was obsolete. For them, it was perfectly legitimate that he should not be permitted to live. They were frantic enough in their opposition to throw their garments in the air. They cried out in anger and great distress that such a person should not be permitted to live. They were used to Gentiles becoming proselytes, or God fearers, but not to offer them all that the Jews had with regard to the law, for they were God's chosen people and proud of their identity, of which they feared Paul would deprive them. They threw dust in the air. This would quickly be followed by stones.

The tribune had been standing by, probably wondering what all the excitement was about, when the crowd erupted. The only course open to him was to stop the riot by removing the man at the centre of it. So he commanded that Paul should be brought into the barracks and examined by scourging.

There was a quite erroneous idea that torture by means of scourging would elicit the truth and enable it to be brought into the light. In the barracks, Paul would be safe from the murderous intent of the crowd outside, but would the end result be any different? The scourge or flagellum was just as likely to cause a man's death. It was a series of leather strips attached to a wooden handle, the strips being supplied at intervals with pieces of bone or metal.

As Paul was being laid upon or stretched upon the frame used for tying up the prisoner with leather thongs, Paul asked the centurion, 'Is it lawful for you to scourge a man who is a Roman citizen and uncondemned?' (Acts 22:25).

Paul had been careful to claim his right as a Roman citizen on another occasion when he and Silas had been publicly beaten and thrown into prison in Philippi, men who were also Roman citizens and uncondemned, that is, denied a legal trial. (Acts 16:37). But the beating by the lictors, the rod bearers of Philippi would have been with rods which the lictors carried as the executive arm of the higher Roman magistrates. The situation in Jerusalem was different in that the punishment was not to be by rods, in itself a very painful punishment, but with the murderous scourge.

Even if condemned, Roman citizens were exempt from flogging. Indeed they were exempt from all degrading forms of punishment.

Paul was already weak from the beating he had received from the Jews. (Acts 21:32). Scourging would almost certainly have killed him. But his thought was not for himself but for the proclamation of the gospel. He had the protection of his status as a Roman citizen to fall back on and in this instance was compelled to use it, and to remind the centurion that he was uncondemned and had the privilege of a fair trial as a Roman citizen.

The centurion immediately stopped the soldiers from administering the torture and went to his superior officer. He said to the tribune, 'What are you about to do? For this man is a Roman citizen'. (Acts 22:26). It would of course have been wise to ascertain Paul's status before tying him up for scourging. The tribune's traction was immediate, for torturing a Roman citizen could have serious consequences if it were reported higher up the chain of command. His first question to Paul was a necessarily judicious one. 'Tell me, he said, "are you a Roman citizen?' And Paul said 'Yes'. The centurion replied, 'It cost me a lot of money to obtain my citizenship'. Paul said, 'But I was born a citizen'. (Acts 22:28).

Claudius Lysias had ample grounds for scepticism. At first, he had thought that Paul was an Egyptian terrorist commander, a rebel seeking to wrest Roman authority from Palestine. Then he was given to understand that Paul was a Jew as he listened to Paul's defence of himself; a member of that nation despised by the Romans on many grounds but chiefly on their insistence of there being only One God, in total contradistinction from the Roman pantheon of gods.

Now Paul was telling him that he was a Roman citizen.

It was possible to bribe one's way into citizenship, or the sale of citizenship, at great cost, as the tribune confessed to having done. It was a feature of life under the contemporary emperor Claudius. But Paul had no need to bribe anyone to acquire his citizenship. It was his birthright. How Paul's father before him had become a Roman citizen before him we are not told, either in Acts or in any of Paul's letters. It was enough for the tribune to back away from the punishment intended for Paul.

Those who were 'about to examine him' withdrew from him instantly, and the tribune was also afraid for he accepted that Paul was a Roman citizen and that he had bound him, (Acts 22:29) imposing on him the disgrace of being in public bonds, *in publica vincula,* (Barrett p 1050). Nevertheless in spite of his fear, he kept Paul in prison until the next day, for he was still desiring to know the real reason why the Jews accused him (Acts 22:30). He released him from his bonds but he did not allow him to go, and commanded the chief priests and all the council of the Jews, the Sanhedrin, to meet. And he brought Paul down and set him before them. (Acts 22:30).

Both Bruce and Barrett explain that if he had satisfied the Sanhedrin, Paul would have been set free. (Bruce p408; Barrett p 1051).

Acts Chapter 23

Acts 23:1-10. Paul before the Sanhedrin

And Paul, looking intently at the council said, 'Brethren, I have lived before God in all good conscience up to this day'. And the high priest Ananias commanded those who stood by him to strike him on the mouth. Then Paul said to him, 'God shall strike you, you whitewashed wall. Are you sitting to judge me according to the law and yet contrary to the law order me to be struck?' (Acts 23:1-3).

Paul had now moved, or had been moved from the fortress of Antonia to the temple. A cohort of Roman soldiers was regularly stationed in the barracks of Fort Antonia, situated to the north of the temple and communicating with it by a flight of stairs. These stairs led to the outer court of the temple, enabling the court to be under constant military surveillance. (Acts 21:31. Bruce p 396).

It was a simple matter for Claudius, together with Paul, to descend the steps into the temple and there to meet with the Sanhedrin, although as the tribune was not a Jew, it needed to be an informal setting for the trial. The presence of a non-Jew would cause defilement of the temple.

Claudius Lysias took no part in the discussion which followed but kept a low profile, only wanting to understand the reason for such animosity against Paul. His questioning of the crowd had produced no discernible reason why they would want to kill Paul. (Acts 21:33,34). He could not use torture because Paul was a Roman citizen. Perhaps allowing Paul to have some sort of informal trial before the Sanhedrin, the highest ruling body of the Jewish nation, who, if anyone, should know if the accusations brought against Paul were valid, was the only course open to him if he wanted to know the truth about Paul.

The informality of the occasion is underlined by the fact that Paul was the first one to speak. It would be inappropriate in a court of law for the defendant to be the first one to speak. But if Paul had broken the Jewish law in a way which disturbed the Roman peace, the *Pax Romana,* then the Roman governor had the authority to invoke a capital sentence. This is why it was necessary for the tribune to remain in the court both for Paul's sake and for the sake of the Sanhedrin, for they desperately wanted Paul's death but could only achieve this objective under the authority of the Roman tribune.

Claudius Lysias remained, if only incognito, to hear what defence Paul was going to make to the highest Jewish court in Jerusalem, the chief priests and the council. (Acts 22:30).

Paul's opening words were unusual. He did not say, 'I am innocent of the charges brought against me', but 'Brethren', for he regarded the Sanhedrin not as superiors or judges but as equals, as if to suggest that they were in this together. 'Brethren', he said, 'I have lived before God in all good conscience up to this day'. (Acts 23:1)

Conscience thought Claudius. What does Paul mean by conscience? For the concept of an inner consciousness of what was right and what was wrong in personal behaviour was not to be found in classical Greek philosophy.

Paul speaks of the conscience as being an independent personal witness to one's behaviour, and thus he could maintain that in an ethical sense, in spite of his persecution of believers, he had lived in all good conscience to this day in the sight of God, believing himself to have been doing the will of God. (Acts 26:9; Philippians 3:6).

He does not claim that the conscience is infallible. In Romans 2:15 he intimates that sometimes the conscience would produce conflicting thoughts, accusing or excusing the person who is seeking to obey the law. But in Acts 24:16, he claims that he has taken pains always to have a clear conscience, both towards God and towards men.

It was significant that his conscience had to be clear in the sight of God, for what he is saying is that God's righteousness is the standard; the standard set by the integrity of God. That was what he lived by.

This is not a new philosophy engineered by Paul. Peter also speaks of having a clear conscience. To the believers in 1 Peter 3:16 he writes, 'keep your conscience clear'. Paul, writing to Timothy who at that time was engaged with the church at Ephesus, urged him to charge them to love one another from a pure heart and a good conscience and sincere faith. (1 Timothy 1:5).

It would seem, as Paul discusses in Romans 9:1, that for the Chistian, the conscience is a means of determining the witness of the Holy Spirit, of examining one's own conscience and at this time, in Paul's case, his attitude towards his fellow Jews. The conscience was not just an indeterminate expression in a person's constituent being, but for the Spirit filled believer, a precious gift, bearing witness to the believer's spirit. It is as if all have a conscience, but when the Holy Spirit comes upon a person their conscience is transformed into a living witness. Again Paul writes in Romans, 'when we cry, "Abba, Father", it is the Spirit Himself who is witnessing with our spirit that we are children of God'. (Romans 8:10).

How absolutely necessary then for Paul to declare to the Sanhedrin that his conscience was clear in the sight of God. Given time, he might have gone on to explain more fully what exactly he meant by that, but he was interrupted by a blow on his mouth at the command of the high priest.

Paul had begun by trying to remind these Jews that there was a dimension to their thinking which was not appreciated by the Greek philosophers. This was not to suggest a universal immorality among either Greeks or Romans. There was kindness and love and loyalty within families, between friends and colleagues, but no authorized recognition of the hidden arbitration of behaviour. (Bruce p 409).

But Ananias, the high priest, is enraged by Paul's claim to have lived in all good conscience to this day. He recognizes that what Paul is saying is: You have accused me, Paul. I am accused, of rebellion against the faith of my fathers, of speaking against the law which God gave through Moses for the benefit and well being of His people, of defiling the temple and therefore denying God's gracious presence among His people, but I can genuinely say, before God, that my conscience is clear. I have acted before Him conscientiously in obedience to what I perceived to be God's will at the time of acting. My conscience is clear.

We are surprised at the reaction of violence exhibited by Ananias. As high priest, we would have expected a more measured, moderate approach to the situation imposed on him by the Roman tribune and not a violent response to Paul's opening statement.

Did he suspect that Paul's conscientiousness would ultimately destroy the kind of Judaism of which he was the highest representative? That theologically, the walls of Jerusalem were already tumbling down as they would do, not a few years hence in 70 A.D, when an effective revolt against Jewish subjugation by the Romans brought about the destruction of the temple in Jerusalem by Titus? For this was the year 60 A.D.

Ananias commanded those who stood by Paul to strike him in the mouth. (Acts 23:2), a wholly irrational thing to do, a reaction against what Paul had hardly begun to say, but probably confirming his fear that what what Paul was about to say was true.

Paul's reaction was also unexpected. Paul said to Ananias, 'God shall strike you, you whitewashed wall. Are you sitting to judge me according to the law and yet contrary to the law order me to be struck? (Acts 23:3).

Ananias was a thoroughly unpleasant character, a notoriously unscrupulous and rapacious politician and like most of the high priests before him, a Sadducee. He had been high priest since 47 A.D, and because of his pro-Roman policy was able to exert great authority. But for this policy he was assassinated in 66 A.D. In time, Paul's prediction was fulfilled. (Bruce p 409).

Paul did not know that he was the high priest, so why was Ananias so enraged? Perhaps because he could not claim as Paul had done that his conscience was clear. In fact it was far from clear and as he heard Paul speak, he regarded Paul's speech as an accusation against his own behaviour. Most people in positions of power expect to be recognized. He could not believe that Paul was speaking of his own way of living before God and that his speech was not an accusation, because he was not aware of Ananias' reputation.

But Paul, still not realizing that the order to strike him had been given by the man who was the high priest, turned to him and said 'God shall strike you, you whitewashed wall Are you sitting to judge me according to the law, and yet contrary to the law order me to be struck?'

Jesus had noticed on one occasion in Jerusalem that some graves or sepulchres of important people had been whitewashed or plastered over with a white plaster. This could be a sign of respect or reverence for the person who had died, a postmortem verdict that they had been especially devout or spiritually influential, when sometimes, perhaps often, this had not been the case and in fact was hypocrisy.

Jesus had said, 'Woe to you, scribes and Pharisees, hypocrites, for you are like whitewashed tombs, which outwardly appear beautiful, but within they are full of dead men's bones and all uncleanness. So you outwardly appear righteous to men, but within, you are full of hypocrisy and iniquity. (Matthew 23:28). Paul's words are reminiscent of those of Jesus, for Paul goes on to say in effect, you believe one thing and do another. You too are hypocritical. We are here together in this place for you to judge according to the law and yet you are breaking that very law by striking me. (Acts 23:3; Leviticus 19:15).

Paul was not retaliating in anger, but in measured logical response to what was going on, pointing out that someone guilty of hypocrisy was likely to have an uncomfortable end, for God would judge them. Though some scholars have considered that Paul was uttering a curse on Ananias, (Bruce p 409; Marshall p 365; and the discussion in Barrett pp 1059,1061), it is more likely that Paul was simply stating a fact, that hypocrisy *is* followed by the judgement of a just God. it was a reproof rather than a curse and a statement of the inevitable outcome if such behaviour continued.

Paul had not yet been formally accused of a crime, but only a vague reference to breaking or annulling the law of Moses. He had not been found guilty, although it appears that in such a court of law, however informal, the usual modus operandi was to assume the accused guilty until proven innocent.

Paul's comment however was immediately taken up by those who stood by. 'Would you revile God's high priest?' they said. (Acts 23:4). Leaving aside the question as to whether Ananias had truly been appointed by God to serve as high priest, a man as unlike Aaron as it was possible to be, it is of interest to gauge their reaction to Paul's words. Perhaps they regarded it as a curse, but in any case to imply that the high priest was a hypocrite could not be regarded with much favour, and this implication they had understood.

Paul withdrew his remarks. He said 'I did not know, brethren, that he was high priest, for it is written, "you shall not speak evil of a ruler of your people".' (Acts 23:5; Exodus 22:28).

Paul is making two points here. First, Ananias was unknown to him, and this was quite possible since Ananias had spent some time in Rome, having been deposed as high priest for a time because of an uprising in Judea, a province for which he had some responsibility. And secondly, that as high priest he should have known the law and not allowed Paul to be struck. If this was a court of law, however informal, it had to abide by the rules governing such an institution.

It is apparent that Paul did not know that Ananias was a Saducee, but because of his former life as a practising Pharisee, Paul could perceive that the Sanhedrin was divided, 'one part were Sadducees and the other Pharisees', (Acts 23:6). But his statement that he was a Pharisee was not to cause dissension among them. The dissension was already there. But to introduce the topic of resurrection, a topic of the utmost and ultimate importance to Paul especially because of the resurrection of Jesus Christ from the dead as evidence that He was truly the Son of God and the one for whom they had been waiting, the one of whom their scriptures spoke.

So first he established his own credentials. He cried out in the council, 'Brethren, I am a Pharisee, a son of a Pharisee', following this up with the statement, *'with respect to the hope and resurrection of the dead I am on trial'. (Acts 23:6).*

This was the spark which lit the fire. Resurrection from the dead was a firmly held belief of the Pharisees against the equally grimly held belief of the Sadducees that resurrection from the dead was nonsense, as were angels and spirits. 'For the Sadducees say that there is no resurrection, nor angels nor spirits, but the Pharisees acknowledge them all' (Acts 23:8). To believe in the resurrection from the dead, and angels and spirits as the Pharisees did, was to believe in an alternative world to this one.

There is a tradition that the Sadducee party grew out of a movement founded by the priest Zadok, commanded by Ezekiel at the time of the Babylonian exile while he was away with the exiles by the river Chebar. (Ezekiel 1:1; 44:15,31; 48:11). Ezekiel regarded the sons of Zadok as the spiritual heirs of the Levitical priesthood (Exodus 28:40; 32:26), decimated by the exile. They kept the charge of the sanctuary when the people of Israel went astray. 593-567 B.C. (Ezekiel 44:15).

The priestly family of Zadok represented purity of worship from those ancient times. In Paul's day they tried to cooperate as far as possible with the Roman authorities, since by doing so they were more likely to enjoy peace to practise their religion.

This policy however led them to have strong antipathy and objection to any nationalistic or rebellious aspirations among the people, which might encourage reprisals from the occupying power. Paul's teaching therefore they regarded as potentially politically dangerous. In addition, they repudiated any notion of immortality or resurrection to life after death or an alternative world of spirit beings, whether angels or demons. This new movement of which Paul appeared to be a leader believed firmly in the resurrection of a man named Jesus. It was necessary that both the movement and its leadership be eliminated.

It was obvious that Christianity would find itself in opposition to the Sadducees.

Paul proclaims himself to be a Pharisee, and the son of a Pharisee. In so doing he repudiates the theological position of the Sadducees and aligns himself with the Pharisees, a distinctly opposite theological standpoint. In standing on trial before a council of men of both persuasions what could he do but declare his own doctrinal position? He was legitimately stating his own view, that resurrection was at the heart of this new Christian faith, even if it led him on to a collision course with the Roman authorities.

Like so many before him, some of whose experiences are recounted by Luke, Christians *must* hold fast to this fundamental truth of the resurrection, whatever the consequences. It is absolutely foundational that though Jesus died a cruel death on the cross, God raised Him from the dead and He is now seated at His Father's right hand in heaven.

While the Pharisees, (a term derived from the Aramaic for 'separate'), were also pious, they derived their piety from strict study of the law and its application to their own way of life, and in so doing were guilty of opposing the popular Hellenizing tendencies of the period. The tradition regarding their origins lies in the Maccabean period, when Antiochus Epiphanes IV, 175-163 B.C. had desecrated the temple, offering up a pig upon the altar, 'the abomination of desolation' of Daniel 11:31, forbidding the worship of God because Antiochus wanted all his conquered people to worship in the same way, on the basis of having a unified empire over which he could rule.

The brave opposition of the Maccabees to this rejection of all that they stood for was supported by a courageous group of pious members of the community coming alongside their leaders. This primitive group was later to become the Pharisees (Bruce p 145). In New Testament times under Herod 37-4 B.C, their power increased, although they were a minority in the Sanhedrin. They were popular inasmuch as their opponents could not ignore them, united as they were to the scribes, those who had the understanding of the law, and were believed to be the spiritual leaders of the nation of Israel.

Though the Pharisees' concept of resurrection did not entirely fit with Paul's, Paul was consistent in his claim that it was in hope of the resurrection from the dead that he was called into question. He states unequivocally in 1 Corinthians 15:16, 17 'if the dead are not raised, neither has Christ risen, and if Christ be not risen you are yet in your sins'. He was not intending to cause disruption at this trial but setting out what he perceived to be its parameters, and what he believed to be the absolute focus and centre of his teaching, both among the Gentiles and the Jews. The hope of the resurrection from the dead was the hope of all Israel and in Paul's teaching, it was the gift to all, both Jews and Gentiles, for if Christ had not died and risen from the dead, there would be no redemption, no salvation.

As he said that he was on trial for the hope of the resurrection from the dead, there occurred a great uproar, and some of the scribes of the Pharisaic party stood up and began to argue heatedly, saying 'we find nothing wrong with this man. Suppose a spirit or an angel has spoken to him?'. And a great dissension was developing (Acts 23:6,9). In denying resurrection, the Sadducees were denying a doctrine which since post exilic times had been regarded throughout Judaism as genuine. These beliefs the Sadducees rejected as not being part of the Jewish faith, nor original to it. No wonder that at Paul's words, a great clamour arose and some of the scribes and Pharisees stood up and contended 'we find nothing wrong with this man'.

Was this intended as an insult to the Sadducees, or was it merely a statement of their own determination to support at all costs those whose views coincided with their own? Or at least those whom they imagined to have the same convictions that they had?

The clamour is growing insistent in its intensity. For the third time, Claudius had only one option, to remove Paul from the court, afraid that Paul would be torn into pieces by them (Acts 23:10). He commanded the soldiers to go down and take him by force from among them and bring him into the barracks, no doubt disappointed that once again, his desire to hear exactly why Paul was such a thorn in the side of the Jews was frustrated.

Acts 23:11. The Lord appears to Paul by night

The following night, the Lord stood by Paul and said,' Take courage, for as you have testified about Me at Jerusalem, so you must bear witness at Rome.

After all his ill treatment and abuse, Paul was very weary. He was still in prison and this was probably the safest place for him, for the Jews had by no means given up on their intention of killing him. But who would not prefer to be free than in prison, whatever danger lay outside the prison walls.

But Paul was not concerned so much for his own safety as for what he had perceived to be the next part of his ministry. He had been convinced that it had been in the will of the Lord for him that he should first visit Jerusalem, and from Jerusalem go on to Rome. (Acts 19:21). He had spoken to the Ephesian elders of his great desire to be at Jerusalem at Pentecost, the birthday of the church, but when he had reached Caesarea, the prophet Agabus had warned him in a prophecy not to go to Jerusalem. This did not deter Paul. He emphatically declared his conviction that it was the Lord's will that he should go to Jerusalem (Acts 21:9-15).

But here he was in Jerusalem, in prison, with no opportunity to preach the gospel which was so important to him, of having no real sense of having been able to preach the gospel in Jerusalem at this point and no prospect of being able to go on to Rome from a Jerusalem prison.

What Paul needed was affirmation that he was still in the will of the Lord, the only place he wanted to be. We do not know if he was alone in his prison cell. A dangerous prisoner would normally be chained to two soldiers, but perhaps Claudius Lysias had realised that Paul was chiefly dangerous to Judaism and not to his authority as tribune, and had given him the privilege of a cell to himself.

It was night time. There was no light anywhere. Paul was probably resting on the bench supplied for sleeping when he became aware of a presence in his cell, perhaps accompanied by a sensation of light. He was neither afraid nor surprised at the presence. He knew that it was the Lord who stood by him as He had on other occasions, some recorded for us by Luke. (Acts 9:5; 18:9; 22:17 27:23). And he lived his life in such close proximity with his Lord that to know that the Lord was with him and was standing by him was almost just an intensification of the way he normally lived. Bruised and bleeding he may well have been after his recent treatment at the hands of the Jews but his physical well being had become insignificant in the greater need he had for reassurance, for a word from his Lord. The Lord did not disappoint him. He never does. He said to Paul, 'Take courage Paul. As you have testified to Me in Jerusalem, so you must bear witness at Rome'.

What encouragement that must have been for Paul, for he had not been allowed to say all that he wanted to say, both to the tribune and to the Jews, and yet the Lord was telling him that he had testified to Him in Jerusalem. And the Lord had given him a promise, that as he had testified to Him in Jerusalem, so he would have an opportunity of testifying to Him in Rome.

Paul is being assured by the Lord that what he had been allowed to say had been adequate, that through it all he has been protected and that the Lord has commissioned him to testify to Him in Rome.

God has a plan for him. It will not be easy or comfortable. It will involve two trials, two years imprisonment and a difficult sea voyage including a shipwreck before he reaches Rome. But he is not told of the experiences which await him, nor of the outcome of that last trial and the sentence of death which will be passed on him. But what he is assured of is that God has initiated a plan for His servant and He will see it through. God will be in control of the course of events. God will guide what happens and what is equally important to Paul, He will always be there to give Paul courage as he testifies to Him in all the places He has chosen, and ultimately in Rome itself.

Paul had been aware of God's purpose for him to visit Rome as far back as when he had been in Corinth. Proposing to leave Corinth for Macedonia and Achaia, he had said, 'And then, after

I have been to Jerusalem I must also see Rome'. (Acts 19:21). Rome had been a burden laid on his heart for a long time and now that which had seemed impossible was coming to fruition. Now the Lord was confirming to him that he would not only 'see' Rome but witness to Him there.

But the Lord did not come to him first with a challenge, or an instruction, but with a promise of comfort and encouragement and strengthening for the task ahead. It was not going to be an easy experience. It would involve hardship, shipwreck, imprisonment; but Paul had the word of the Lord to him, and that was enough. On that word, he could go.

Acts 23:12-15. The plot against Paul

When it was day, the Jews made a plot and bound themselves by an oath neither to eat or drink till they had killed Paul. There were more than forty who made this conspiracy. And they went to the chief priests and elders and said, 'We have strictly bound ourselves by an oath to taste no food till we have killed Paul. You therefore, along with the council, give notice now to the tribune to bring him down to you as though you were going to determine his case more exactly. And we are ready to kill him before he comes near'.

The burden had been laid on Paul's heart, the burden of his destiny and of Rome's hearing and acceptance of the gospel, receiving the good news of Jesus. Now God was going to implement it. Paul could rest in the promise of God that as he had borne witness to him at Jerusalem, so he would also do at Rome.

The night time experience had come to an end. It was now day. (Acts 23:12). The Jews had not given up on their attempt to kill Paul. Their determination was if anything stronger than ever. They made a plot to kill Paul, and bound themselves by an oath neither to eat or drink till they had killed Paul, thus demonstrating their commitment to his death. There were more than forty who conspired together, and their oath makes it quite clear how serious they were.

But how were they to accomplish their objective? They had no legal right to do so. Their complaint before the tribunal had been ineffectual. It seemed that the only way they could get to Paul was through devising an ambush, when he was released from the prison environs. While he was in prison, he was safely in the custody of the tribune. If they could persuade Claudius Lysias that Paul needed to be examined more closely, and to be brought down from Antonia to another meeting of the Sanhedrin then they could ambush Paul on the way and kill him.

With this plan in view, they approached the chief priests and elders, perhaps that section of the Sanhedrin who were hostile to Paul. They told them everything, how 'they had bound themselves by an oath to taste no food until they had killed Paul' (Acts 23:14). And to ask the chief priests and elders along with the council 'to give notice to the tribune to bring him down to you as though you were going to determine his case more exactly. And we are ready to kill him before he comes near'. (Acts 23: 14,15).

There were several things wrong with this plan. It did not need forty men but only one with a sharp dagger to stab Paul and kill him. Forty men surrounding Paul would only get in the way of each other, though it may be that they thought all should all stab him so that no single one of them could take the blame; or indeed the congratulations of all.

Another factor which they had not considered was that it was not improbable that Claudius Lysias would provide a bodyguard for Paul, as he had good reason to do. Even forty men were unlikely to get the better of trained Roman soldiers, armed and ready to defend Paul. It was also unlikely that Claudius would respond quite so meekly and readily to a demand from more of these quarrelsome Jews (Acts 23:10), whom Claudius already knew to have designs on Paul's life. And who did they think they were, expecting a Roman tribune to be at their beck and call, when he had other ideas as to the best way to deal with Paul?

But this projected plan of the Jews had no further opportunity of being fulfilled anyway. Their plan for the tribune to allow the Jews to make further inquiry into Paul's case had been overheard before the Jews could even speak to the chief priests and elders. The Jews had not been careful enough to discuss their plans privately and securely and a young man had overheard their deliberations. He was Paul's nephew, the son of Paul's sister. (Acts 23:16). It appears that Paul was allowed to have visitors, and the young man did the only thing he could think of. He went and entered the barracks and told Paul of the plot.

Though a prisoner, it seems that Paul still had an aura of authority. He called one of the centurions and said to him, 'Take this young man to the tribune for he has something to tell him' (Acts 23:17). So the centurion took him and brought him to the tribune and said, 'Paul the prisoner called me and asked me to bring the young man to you as he has something to say to you'.

This marks a turning point in the narrative. From now on, Paul is removed from any jurisdiction the Jews may have thought to hold over him and to come under that of the Romans, as becomes clear when he comes before Feix the governor in chapter 24.

Now however, Claudius Lysias has to act, and to act quickly and decisively. He took Paul's nephew by the hand to give him confidence, for he was young and unsure of himself in the presence of this important person. 'The tribune took him by the hand and going aside, asked him privately "what is it you have to tell me?" (Acts 23:19) And he gave the whole story. 'The Jews have agreed to ask you to bring Paul down to the council tomorrow as though they were going to inquire somewhat more closely about him. But do not yield to them for more than forty of their men lie in ambush for him, having bound themselves neither to eat or drink till they have killed him. And now they are ready, waiting for the promise from you'. (Acts 23:20,21).

Obviously, the conspiracy had evolved into precipitate action. Convinced that Claudius would have no option but to comply with their request, according to the young man's statement, the forty Jewish men were already waiting, intensely aware that the tribune would shortly give the answer for Paul to be brought down to the Sanhedrin, for they believed it was the inevitable way for Claudius to act.

Claudius was not surprised at what the young man was telling him. By this time, he had come to realize that these would-be Jewish assassins were capable of any action, however foolish and impracticable. He had no suspicion of the account given him by Paul's nephew, for it tallied exactly with what he would have expected of the Jews. He took seriously what the young man had said and as he dismissed him, made him promise to tell no-one of the information passed on to him. (Acts 23:22).

An equally fierce determination came over the tribune, not only to protect Paul, but to show the Jews that he was protecting him by recruiting all the power and panoply available to an occupying power. He had had enough of these Jews. They were a nuisance and their small, mean plots were an irritation to him and wholly contemptible.

He did two things. First he organized a cavalcade of two hundred soldiers, with seventy horsemen and two hundred spearmen to take Paul mounted to Caesarea at the third hour of the night, bringing Paul to the governor Felix. He hoped that the cavalcade would also impress Felix. Secondly, he arranged for a letter to be taken to Felix, a report of the incident, detailing what had happened to Paul; and at the same time, exculpating himself from all responsibility.

Acts 23:25-30. The letter

And he wrote a letter to this effect. Claudius Lysias to his excellency the governor Felix, greeting.

This man was seized by the Jews and was about to be killed by them when I came upon them with the soldiers and rescued him, having learned that he was a Roman citizen; and desiring to know the charge of which they accused him, I brought him down to their council. I found that he was accused about questions of their law but charged with nothing worthy of death or imprisonment. And when it was disclosed to me that there would be a plot against the man, I sent him to you at once ordering his accusers also to state before you what they have against him.

The tribune wrote a letter 'to this effect'. (Acts 23:25). This may mean that though Luke may not have had access to the actual contents of the letter, this would clearly have been a summary of what the position had become regarding Paul, the prisoner whom he was sending to Felix the procurator.

It was necessarily an abbreviated account of all that had happened, but importantly included the fact that Paul was a Roman citizen, which may well have carried some weight with Felix. (Acts 23:27). It also included the major fact that Paul was not accused of any heinous crimes but that his attempted murder by the Jews was the outcome of a disagreement about their law. (Acts 23:29). In such a letter, Claudius Lysias would be keen to show the procurator that he had at all times acted wisely and precipitously, in bringing Paul down to the council of the Jews, (Acts 23:28) so that the case could be determined legally and without bloodshed.

The present letter was being written because it had 'been disclosed' to Claudius Lysias that there was a plot against Paul and he was therefore sending Paul to Felix 'at once', immediately, (Acts23:30). So that he could be the judge of that of which Paul had been accused by the Jews and that he was also ordering Paul's accusers to state before Felix what they had against him. (Acts 23:30).

Acts 23:31-35. Paul is taken to Caesarea

So the soldiers, according to their instructions, took Paul and brought him by night to Antipatris. And on the morrow they returned to the barracks, leaving the horsemen to go on with him.

When they came to Caesarea, and delivered the letter to the governor, they presented Paul also before him. On reading the letter, Felix asked to what province he belonged. When he learned that he was from Cilicia he said, 'I will hear you when your accusers arrive'. And he commanded him to be guarded in Herod's praetorium.

Having written this letter, commending it to the centurion in charge of the operation, Claudius sent off a detachment of soldiers, horsemen and spearmen to Caesarea, a journey of about forty miles.

Paul had been to Caesarea on other occasions, the last time when he was on the way to Jerusalem with contributions from the churches of Macedonia and Achaia for the believers in Jerusalem. He had begun the journey in Corinth (Acts 20:3), and on coming to Caesarea had stayed in the home of Philip who had four daughters who prophesied. (Acts 21:8). What a happy few days that had been! Now he was surrounded by half the Jerusalem garrison as he travelled to Caesarea via Antipatris as a prisoner of the Romans.

Caesarea was the capital city of the province of Judea under Roman jurisdiction, although it might have been expected that that honour should have gone to Jerusalem. Felix, the Roman governor of the province had his residence in Caesarea. He had been procurator since 52 A.D, and according to Stott p 355 was utterly ruthless in quelling any uprisings of the Jews.

F.F. Bruce, Stott and Marshall all quote the epigram about him by Tacitus. 'He exercised the power of a king with the mind of a slave'. (Bruce p 417; Stott p 335; Marshall p 370), suggesting that although he was a freedman, he had never grown out of a slave, servile mentality.

The letter to the governor had been a formal one. For the first time we learn that the name of the tribune was Claudius Lysias as he begins his letter in the accepted style of legal documents:

Claudius Lysias

To His excellency Governor Felix

Greeting.

This was the letter carried by the soldiers as they set out for Caesarea on the orders of the tribune. They had begun their preparations for the journey at the third hour of the night, (Acts 23:23), between nine and ten in the evening so that they could travel under cover of darkness. They travelled just over half of the way, arriving at Antipatris, (Acts 23:31), a city that had been founded by Herod the Great in honour of his father Antipater. It was a Hellenistic town on the Roman road and as such would have had little interest in Jewish wrangling over their law.

Reaching Antipatris, the large escort was no longer necessary. The soldiers were dismissed to return to their barracks at Jerusalem leaving the horsemen to go on with Paul to Caesarea. It was a long journey to complete on horseback in one night and a relief to the cavalry when they could hand over the letter to the governor, together with their prisoner. The dangers inherent and ever present on the Palestinian roads had been safely circumvented or overcome.

Barrett suggests that a large force was necessary to accompany Paul to Caesarea, for if he had been killed, Claudius could have been accused of accepting a bribe to allow this to happen. (Barrett, p 1079). Paul was a Roman citizen and entitled to a trial. Claudius Lysias was under an obligation to ensure that Paul was safe so that he, as yet uncondemned, could be given his day in court., and in all probability, be pronounced innocent.

In Roman terms, Paul was being well treated by the Roman authorities. He is being safely delivered to Felix. As an insignificant Jew, he would not have had that protection, for why would the Romans have taken steps to prevent even one such person from being killed by his compatriots? But God is using even the fact of Paul's Roman citizenship to bring him to that purpose which He had designed for him.

This factor of Paul's Roman citizenship was the focus of the letter of Claudius to Felix. The disagreement with the Jews is of course the springboard, causing Paul's case to be tried yet again, but this time by a Roman procurator and not as a trial concerning

Paul's alignment with this new religion called Christianity, a troublesome and probably heretical sect of Judaism.

Did Claudius ever learn the truth about the gospel, the truth which Paul had so longed to tell him about the Lord Jesus? But the Lord had spoken to Paul assuring him that he had testified to Him in Jerusalem, a testimony that Claudius had heard and perhaps responded to.

Felix received the letter prompted by the information passed on to Claudius by Paul's nephew, and also received Paul whom they presented before him. (Acts 23:33). Weary and travel-stained Paul did not look like a candidate for Felix's attention, but Felix could not ignore either the letter of the person of Paul.

However, he thought he had a solution to this particular problem. 'Where does he come from?' he asked. And learning that he came from the province of Cilicia, he discovered that he could at least postpone having to deal with him. There had been a custom for accused people to be referred back to their place of origin, and Paul of course was from Tarsus in Cilicia. But to have sent him back there would have been expensive, and also at that time, Cilicia was without an imperial legate. Perhaps in asking his question Felix had hoped that Paul could be shipped off somewhere else for his trial. As it was, Felix had no choice but to conduct the trial himself. Nevertheless he did have the option of waiting for Paul's accusers to arrive from Jerusalem. This took several days, and meanwhile, Paul was guarded in Herod;s praetorium.

Felix had said to Paul, 'I will hear you when your accusers arrive', and he kept his promise, after telling the guards to take Paul away to the praetorium within the palace built by Herod the Great. The palace had been taken over by the Roman administration. It was also the procurator's official residence.

Paul is a prisoner of Rome, totally vulnerable, but knowing that the Jews had nothing of which they could accuse him, and above all, believing, as God had promised, that he would be given an opportunity to witness to the Lord Jesus. Not only in Caesarea but in Rome.

Bruce enters a precious aside here. He says the praetorium in Phippians 1:13 is the proconsular headquarters at Ephesus, the prison from which Paul is writing to the Philippian believers. Paul writes, 'My imprisonment has become known to all the praetorian guards. What has happened to me has really served to advance the gospel'.

There was also the praetorium where Jesus was taken and where he was mocked by the soldiers before carrying His cross to the place of execution. (Mark 15:16).

And Paul also writes of 'they who are of Caesar's household' in Ephesus among whom were the 'saints', believers in the Lord, but also, significantly, members of the imperial civil service who were mostly freedmen. (Philippians 4:22; Bruce p 361). How amazing it would be if Paul had found some of those saints in the praetorium in Caesarea! For by this time, the church had become active in many places and had affected so many lives. There were believers everywhere! (Bruce p 361).

We do not know and must be careful not to speculate, but we do know that Paul had planned to visit Rome because he believed it to be God's will for him and though this may not have been quite the way he expected it to be, he knew that God's purpose would be achieved. He believed that this was another step along the way, forGod had spoken to him and he believed God's word. Even being in a Roman praetorium was part of God's plan for him.

Acts Chapter 24

Acts 24:1-9. Paul before Felix

And after five days, the high priest Ananias came down with some elders and a spokesman, one Tertullus. They laid before the governor their case against Paul and when he was called, Tertullus began to accuse him.

It had taken the Jews five days to accomplish what Paul and his Roman escort had achieved overnight, but perhaps they had spent some time in trying to find a suitable advocate for their theology as against Paul's. By this time they had discovered that Paul was a persuasive debater, needing no advocate of his own. He attributed any ability he had to the work of the Holy Spirit, who was the One taking the words spoken by him deep into the hearts of those who needed to come to Jesus.

It is unlikely that the whole Sanhedrin elected to go down to Caesarea, even with the tempting prospect of hearing Paul condemned to death. But Ananias came down with some elders and the spokesman, Tertullus. They hoped that their own inadequacy in finding the right arguments with which to accuse Paul would be more than compensated for by engaging Tertullus as their spokesman.

True to his word, Felix convened a court hearing and Paul was summoned. Tertullus did not immediately begin his accusation against Paul. First there appeared to be a short consultation between the Jews and the governor, as they discussed the case which they wanted to bring against Paul. Having done this, Tertullus was given permission to speak.

He began his speech with a fulsome exordium to Felix, which was the customary way of introducing a trial. He says, 'Since by you we enjoy much peace, and since by your provision, most excellent Felix, reforms are introduced on behalf of our nation, in every way and everywhere, we accept this with all gratitude'. (Acts 24:2,3).

Where Tertullus obtained this information is highly contestable. First he mentions 'the great peace enjoyed under Felix' proconsulship, which was far from the truth, and also the reforms which Felix had made 'for which the whole nation of Israel in every way and everywhere' accepted with all gratitude. (Acts 24:3). In fact Roman administration under Felix had been characterised by Jewish unrest and uprisings which Felix had put down with great brutality. (Stott p 360) But Tertullus was seeking to ingratiate himself with the governor and in this way achieve the verdict against Paul which the Jews had hired him to obtain.

Tertullus also promised to be brief. (Acts 24:4). This promise at least may have been gratefully received by Felix for he found all this wrangling of the Jews over their supposed differences regarding their law as wearying indeed.

Tertullus was not an eye witness of the events which had prompted both the actions of the Jews and the present trial. Nevertheless, he made three charges against Paul. First he made the accusation that Paul was a pestilent fellow. 'We have found' he says 'that he is a pestilent fellow, an agitator among all the Jews throughout the world'. He does not say who the 'we' are who have found Paul to be so, but this a serious accusation. It was political, not theological and it was seditious which in a Roman court would be taken very seriously and could not be ignored.

It was also marginally true. The Jewish nation had been dispersed to such an extent that it had become a universal presence throughout the empire, and a universal problem. Any disturbance which threatened the delicate relations between Jews and Romans was seditious, and on this basis, if this allegation had any substance, Felix had to take note of it. It was true that wherever Paul went throughout the known world, that the first place he sought out in which to preach the gospel was the local synagogue.

But Felix could see through their ploy to proceed against Paul as a trouble maker. Tertullus was seeking to persuade Felix that he was on the side of the Romans in this, that he and the procurator were working together to prevent such disturbance. But there was absolutely no chance of Jews and Romans ever working together in any kind of harmony. The whole history of the Roman occupation of Palestinewould obviate that conclusion.

The second accusation against Paul alleged that Paul was a 'ringleader of the sect of the Nazarenes'. (Acts 24:5), that is, the head of an illegal Jewish sect, and therefore dangerous. Tertullus uses the term 'sect of the Nazarenes' to describe the Christian movement, to imply, not simply that Jesus was from Nazareth, but that pejoratively, the term had come to consolidate the notion that these people who followed the teaching of Jesus were a group of rather backward people who reverenced Nazareth as the place from which Jesus had originated and whose main preoccupation was the re-interpretation of the Torah, the law of Moses in such a way as to nullify it and make it redundant.

Roman officialdom was always suspicious of anything associated with a Messianic movement. Bruce comments, they could not distinguish the religious from the political variety, (Bruce p 422), and indeed in most Messianic movements, such as that led by the Egyptian in Acts 21:38, and referred to by Claudius the tribune, there was little difference between the religious and the political.

The teaching of Jesus may well have been subversive, even revolutionary as those who loved the Lord sought to follow Him and to obey the twin commandments to love the Lord their God with all their hearts and their neighbour as themselves. (Matthew 22:37). But this was only a reinforcement of what the Jews already had, for it was in their own precious scriptures. By using the term, 'sect of the Nazarenes', Tertullus was trying to impress upon Felix that Paul was the ringleader of something not only alien to the Jews but also a potential threat to the established authority of Rome.

The third accusation was that Paul had profaned the temple. This may have seemed less important to a Roman procurator, but no doubt insisted on by the Jews who were employing Tertullus. But this could be an important charge, for that the charge could be brought at all was due to the provision made by the Romans to protect the sanctity of the temple. (Barrett p 1099). Tetullus claimed that Paul had 'even tried to profane the temple, but we seized him' (Acts 24:6), and arrested him.

This was not quite true either, for it was Claudius who had arrested Paul for his own safety. It was an extraordinary way to conduct a trial, for it made Tertullus a false witness. Paul was not arrested by the Jews as Tertullus claimed but lynched. Tertullus gave no credence to the fact that Claudius had saved Paul from sudden death by the Jews. Paul had not profaned the temple by taking Trophimus the Ephesian, a Gentile, into the temple. (Acts 21:29). Paul and Trophimus had simply been seen in Jerusalem together. Paul had not desecrated or defiled the holy place.

In spite of Trtullus' distortion of what little evidence there was, what he said did not fully satisfy the Jews. They were not completely happy with his performance. Tertullus' last plea had been to the governor, to examine Paul himself and 'to learn from him everything of which we accuse him'. (Acts 24:8). But at this point, not leaving it to Tertullus to make the case, not fully trusting that he *had* made the case against Paul, the Jews also 'joined inn the charge', quite literally joined in the attack on Paul', affirming that this was so'. (Acts 24:9).

Acts 24:10-21. Paul's defence before Felix

And when the governor had motioned to him to speak, Paul replied: 'Realising that for many years you have been judge over this nation, I cheerfully make my defence. As you may ascertain it is not more than twelve days since I went up to worship at Jerusalem and they did not find me disputing with anyone or stirring up a crowd either in the temple or in the synagogues or in the city. Neither can they prove to you what they now bring against me'.

Now it was Paul's turn to speak. He began with a brief complimentary exordium to Felix as custom demanded, but shorter than that of Tertullus. He reminded Felix that he had been governor over the province for many, in fact, five years. (Bruce p 423), and that he was cheerfully making his defence before a man of experience in these matters.

Paul then went on to outline the facts of the case from his own perspective, in a far more rational way than had Tertullus. He began by explaining that 'it is not more than twelve days since I went up to Jerusalem to worship'. (Acts 21:15; 24:11). He was on a pilgrimage to Jerusalem as were so many Jews. Paul never denied his Jewish heritage. He had neither the means nor the desire to stir up the crowds to revolt or insurrection against the Romans as Tertullus had suggested and in any case, twelve days, five or which had been spent in custody would not have given him the necessary time either.

There was no evidence that he had been disputing with any one, or stirring up a crowd 'either in the temple or in the synagogues or in the city'. (Acts 24:12). The Jews could not provide proof 'of what they now bring up against me'. (Acts 24:13). Disputing with someone was the first step in creating a disturbance. They could not find one person with whom Paul had had a dispute and the crowd which 'ran together against him' (Acts 21:30) was instigated by the Asian Jews, not by Paul. (Acts 21:27).

Paul is refuting the two accusations against him in Acts 24:5,6, but not the accusation of promoting world wide crimes of disturbance indicated by Tertullus, because Felix would have jurisdiction only within his own authority. Again, Tertullus is making a rather bad effort of being an advocate on behalf of the Jews.

Having dismissed fairly briefly the charges made against him as having no substantiation in fact, Paul then went on to confess or admit at greater length what his true position was. He says, 'I admit to you, Felix, that according to the Way which they call a sect, I worship the God of our fathers, believing everything laid down by the law or written in the prophets, having a hope which these themselves accept, that there will be a resurrection of both the just and the unjust. So I always take pains to have a clear conscience toward God and man'. (Acts 24:14-16)

Paul is making the point that it is to Felix that he is making this confession, for he is too well aware that the prejudice against him by the Jews would never allow them to to accept what he had to say. But here he was before a man who needed reality in his life. His wife Drusilla was a Jewess (Acts 24:24), and he had some knowledge of the Way, the term by which the Christian movement was referred to by Christians themselves. (Acts 16:17; 18:25; 19:9,23; 24: 14,22). But Felix had never committed himself to seeking out and following Jesus. Paul had before him, not an important Roman official but a man in need of forgiveness, a man who needed to come to Christ.

So he began by speaking to Felix of his own experience. Yes, he said, it was true that 'according to the Way which the Jews call a sect, I worship the God of our fathers'. He does not deny that he is a Jew, but that the God whom he worships *is* God, the same God who is the God of all their scriptures *and* the God who has done a new thing in the incarnation of His Son, Jesus. He is the God and Father of Jesus, who is the *Lord Jesus Christ*.

Paul believes that everything written in the law and prophets speaks of Jesus. The scriptures also provide a hope in God, which those Jews who agree with the Pharisees also believe, that there will be a resurrection from the dead at the end of time for all, both the just, those who have been made righteous, and the unjust, the unrighteous. (Acts 24:15). There were many Jews who anticipated a future time of judgement, prophesied in their scriptures.

Though many of the Jews accepted the idea of resurrection in theory, they could not accept that Jesus rose from the dead, preempting the final resurrection from the dead. But in Paul's reasoning, this is to obscure the facts. If God can raise the dead at the last, at the end of time, what is to prevent Him from raising Jesus from the dead ahead of time, seeing that He is the Son of God? And especially seeing that He was righteous as no one else had ever been and therefore the only One worthy to be the Judge before whom all must stand on the day of resurrection, as Paul explains in his letter to the Romans (Romans 14:9-12).

For this reason says Paul, I always take pains to have a clear conscience toward God and man, for judgment is coming. (Acts 24:16). Paul's conscience is clear; he would not obfuscate the issue raised by his trial by refusing to accept the truth of what had happened to Jesus, for His very resurrection proved His deity.

Paul goes on to explain the reason for his visit to Jerusalem. He says 'after some years I came to bring to my nation alms and offerings'. (Acts 24:17). It *was* some years. Paul had made a brief visit to Jerusalem, recorded by Luke in Acts 18:22, before going through the regions of Galatia and Phrygia. This was where communities of believers had been established, and Paul went through these regions, strengthening them in the faith.

Or Paul may have been remembering a visit he made to Jerusalem with Barnabas at the time of he Apostolic Council, when the important issue of whether believers needed to follow the Jewish practice of circumcision on becoming a Christian had been discussed and the apostolic decree formulated. (Acts 15:1,6,28).

Paul may also have remembered going to Jerusalem three years after his experience on the road to Damascus to visit Peter, with whom he stayed for fifteen days, (Galatians 1:18). And then fourteen years later when he went up to Jerusalem with Barnabas (Galatians 2:1).

But these opportunities of fellowship with the elders in Jerusalem were not so that he could align himself with them on any theological basis, but only on the basis of revelation. Paul writes in Galatians that it was because God had revealed to him that this was what He wanted him to do, and speak, that he went up to Jerusalem (Galatians 2:2). It was on the same basis that Paul had so recently been in Jerusalem. God had revealed to him that this was His purpose for him. (Acts 19:21). He came to Jeusalem 'to bring to my nation alms and offerings'. (Acts 24:17).

These were the offerings made by the Gentile churches for the poor believers in Jerusalem, who though they had become

Christians, were still of Paul's 'nation', the Jews. (Bruce p425). Paul had no ulterior motive in coming to Jerusalem and promoting any kind of insurrection. He was only fulfilling a promise made to the Gentile churches to deliver the money which they had collected out of love for their brothers and sisters in Jerusalem. It was an interesting and sincere attempt to unite the churches together rather than for each one to act and believe independently. The collection for the saints in Jerusalem was a demonstration of the truth that they were all one in Christ Jesus.

This may however have been construed by the Jews as an attempt to unite the churches together in such a way as to become a threat to the established Jewish synagogues which were often the centres of their community, meeting together to listen to and study the Torah, and to support each other in a world governed by those indifferent to, or antagonistic to, their faith.

Even a gift of love from a more prosperous section of the church to their less prosperous brethren could be seen as a threat by the more extremist Judaistic synagogues, and may have been a subsidiary reason for the treatment of Paul by the Asian Jews, (Acts 21:27), for the four men whom Paul had taken to the temple were Jews but also Christian believers, as James made clear. (Acts 21:23).

This visit which Paul was making to Jerusalem was innocent of any subterfuge, but his motivation was still suspect. The Jews had 'found him purified in the temple'. (Acts 24:18). Paul makes no mention of the four men who were with him, for if their identity were revealed, and they were discovered, that would put them in danger. But the Jews had found him in the temple 'without any crowd or tumult'. (Acts 24:18). Paul continues, these Jews who had found him in the temple were Jewish eyewitnesses who were no longer to be found either. If they had wanted to bring an accusation against him, they should be here, in court; or they should have been willing to to accuse him when he stood before the council (Acts 22:30) to describe what wrongdoing he had done. (Acts 24:20).

Paul insists that his defence before the council, the Sanhedrin, (Acts 23:1), was the same defence which he now used. In spite of all that these people had with which to accuse him in causing a revolt or profaning the temple, he perceived that the only charge against him, then as now, was a theological one and one which any of the Jews who had a Pharisaic background would adhere to, namely, that it was 'in respect of the resurrection of the dead I am on trial before you, Felix, this day'. (Acts 24:21).

Acts 24:22,23. Felix adjourns the trial

But Felix, having a rather accurate knowledge of the Way, put them off, saying, 'When Lysias the tribune comes down, I will decide your case'. Then he gave orders to the centurion that he should be kept in custody but should have some liberty and that none of his friends should be prevented from attending to his needs. (Acts 24:22, 23).

Why did Felix, having a rather more accurate knowledge of the Way, put them off saying, 'When Lysias comes down I will decide your case?' Why did Felix adjourn the proceedings so abruptly? So precipitately?

Felix was married to Drusilla, a Jewess. (Acts 24:24). It was probably through her that Felix had some knowledge of the Way. She was the younger daughter of Herod Agrippa 1; 11 B.C-44 A.D. Herod was an Idumean, not a Jew, but he cultivated good relations with the Jews. He was the Herod of Acts 12:1, who ordered the death of James the apostle because he thought it would please the Jews. (Acts 12:3). He himself died, smitten of God because he would not give God the glory and he was 'eaten of worms and died', (Acts 12:23) after having received the acclamation from the crowd, 'The voice of a god and not of a man!'

Drusilla herself had previously been married to Azizus, king of Emesa, but Felix persuaded her to leave her husband and become his wife, his third wife. (54 A.D). They had a son, also Agrippa, who died when Vesuvius erupted in 79 A.D. (Bruce p 427).

Had Felix adjourned the court because something of which Paul was speaking had affected him in some way? Acts 24:22 claims that he already had some knowledge of the Way, possibly from Drusilla, and of its cardinal principle that Jesus was the Son of God and had been raised by God from the dead. These Christians worshipped a God who had been dead and was now alive, and always present with them! Perhaps Felix was afraid that Paul's reasoning might take him to where he did not want to go, where he felt himself unable, or unwilling to go.

Drusilla was regarded as a Jewess, but was actually Idumean as was her father. Idumea was the area south of the Dead Sea which had later spread westwards. It had formerly been known as Edom and the Edomites as a people utterly opposed to the Israelites and to Israel's God. (The Book of Obadiah). So Idumeans were despised by the Jews. Felix may have had In addition a concern for his own religious position, as being married to an Idumean, and also he naturally wanted to retain a comfortable relationship with his wife. Felix used the absence of Lysias at the trial as an excuse for putting it off, saying to Paul, 'When Lysias the tribune comes down, I will examine your case'. (Acts 24:22).

Paul was not to be allowed to leave the praetorium. He was to be kept in custody, but allowed some liberty; and his friends, such as Philip the evangelist and his daughters, and others from the church in Caesarea should not be prevented from attending to his needs. (Acts 24:23).

Was Paul content with this verdict, still to be deprived of liberty although a less rigorous imprisonment than he had endured before? Yes, we may believe that he was. He wrote to the believers in Philippi that he had learned in whatever state he was, therewith to be content. (Philippians 4:11). He had heard, received and claimed the promise made to him by the Lord. Though he had no knowledge of how he was going to be able to go to Rome, he believed that this was in the will of the Lord for him, and this was a strong conviction What God had said,

He was able also to perform. (Romans 4:21). He always does what He says He will do. It is perfectly safe to trust the Lord.

Paul was in prison for *two years!*. Could not the Lord have intervened, hastened it so that Paul could testify at Rome as He had promised? No, for Paul's immediate concern was for Felix and Drusilla. His continued imprisonment of course provided Paul with protective custody. He will not be allowed to fall into the hands of the Jews but will still have friends who will provide him with food, comfort, encouragement.

At the same time, he was available for trial or punishment and had such a possibility continually hanging over him. We have no record that Claudius Lysias ever came down to Caesarea for a further trial of Paul, to provide that extra dimension that Felix would require of evidence in order to release Paul. In addition, perhaps because of the sum of money which Paul had been carrying to the church in Jerusalem for the relief of the poverty of some of its members, though now presumably distributed, Felix may have thought that Paul was a wealthy man, or had access to wealth. 'He hoped that money would be given to him by Paul', (Acts 24:26), an illegal but common form of bribery.

It was 'after some days' that Felix came with his wife Drusilla to see Paul. (Acts 24:24). This was to be Paul's ministry for the next period of his life, sharing the gospel with Felix and presumably, sometimes with Drusilla. There may also have been guards present on these occasions, listening to Paul as he preached the gospel, and of course Paul also had the joy and privilege of encouraging those faithful friends who came to encourage him, and to bring him gifts of food and other necessities.

After Paul had been in prison for some days, Felix sent for Paul and heard him speak about faith in Christ. (Acts 24:24). Felix had been described earlier as having some knowledge of the Way. Paul was able to expand on that knowledge, not as something reasoned about and accepted cerebrally, but taken deep into one's whole being, spiritual transformation of a high order, because faith in Jesus Christ has transforming power.

Paul spoke to Felix of righteousness, self control and the coming judgement. (Acts 24:25). These were deep, deep, considerations. What little knowledge we possess of the lifestyle of Felix and Drusilla might cause a belief that these subjects were ones pertinent to them. But we know our own hearts. We know that we need to learn about the righteousness of the God before whom we stand and our own unrighteousness before a holy God. We also need to learn more about the Holy Spirit's control, guiding our own self control, and the future judgement when we shall all stand before the judgement seat of Christ. (Romans 14:10).

Paul may have had private interviews with Felix as well as those including Drusilla, and there may have been others, servants and soldiers waiting on the procurator and also listening to Paul. But Felix became alarmed by what Paul was saying, and he said to Paul, 'go away for the present; when I have an opportunity I will summon you'. Felix was not like Gallio who cared for none of these things. (Acts 18:17). He truly wanted to know, and sent for Paul often in the beginning and conversed with him, (Acts 24:26) but as far as we know, never came to a place of commitment.

Acts Chapter 25

Acts 24:27-Acts 25:5. Felix is succeeded by Festus. Paul is left in custody

> But when two years had elapsed, Felix was succeeded by Porcius Festus; and desiring to do the Jews a favour, Felix left Paul in prison. (Acts 24:27). Now when Festus had come into his province, after three days he went up to Jerusalem from Caesarea. And the chief priests and the principal men of the Jews informed him against Paul; and they urged him, asking as a favour to have the men sent to Jerusalem, planning an ambush to kill him on the way. Festus replied that Paul was being kept in Caesarea and that he himself intended to go there shortly. 'So', said he,' let the men of authority among you go down with me and if there is anything wrong about the man, let them accuse him'. (Acts 25:1-5).

After two years, there inevitably came a change of governors. Felix was succeeded by Porcius Festus, and desiring to do the Jews a favour Paul was left in prison. Felix's decision to try to understand Paul's teaching had not, as far as we know, led him into a commitment to the Lord Jesus. For him and possibly for Drusilla too, the opportunity had gone by.

Festus inherited a troublesome situation. Felix had desperately wanted to do something about the continued opposition of the Jews against Paul, (Acts 25:2), but in the end, nothing had been resolved. Felix had vacillated between keeping Paul in protective custody, away from those Jews whose only ambition was to get rid of Paul, and his wish to ingratiate himself with these same Jews. Unable to come to a decision at Paul's trial when the opposing faction against Paul had failed to persuade him that Paul was guilty of the charges brought against him, he still failed ultimately, for Paul according to Roman law should have been released. Felix was about to leave Caesarea, and perhaps the problem could be solved by his successor. Desiring to do the Jews a favour, Felix left Paul in prison. (Acts 25:1-5).

Acts 25:1-5. Festus visits Jerusalem

The province is now to be governed by Festus, and when he had come into his new province, he needed to exert his authority, so after three days he went up to Jerusalem. Festus is now in charge, but the chief priests and the principal men of the Jews, the Sanhedrin, were there already with their complaint that justice still needed to be done in the case of Paul, even though Festus had been only three days in office.

Festus was acute enough to recognise that had it really been the open and shut case which they were attempting to describe to him, they were possibly not too familiar with Roman law, and certainly that their idea of justice differed from that which it was his responsibility to maintain as the governor.

He may not have known that the Jews had not abandoned their plan of ambushing Paul and killing him. (Acts 25:3), but he was generous enough to give them an audience, and to agree to their suggestion that Paul should have a retrial in Jerusalem, thus giving them the opportunity to ambush him and kill him on the way. However, he stipulated that the retrial should be in Caesarea rather than Jerusalem. Though this interfered with the ambush plan, he was meeting them halfway, and so they agreed.

These Jews may have been the ones who had bound themselves by an oath neither to eat or drink till they had killed Paul. (Acts 23:12). Given the time which had elapsed, they had either broken their oath or modified it in some way. But they were urgent in their request to Festus.

However, Festus had determined on this alternative site for a retrial. He informed them of his decision to keep Paul in Caesarea and that he himself would shortly be returning to Caesarea, inviting 'men of authority among you' to go down to

Caesarea with him so that 'if there is anything wrong with the man, let them accuse him'. (Acts 25:5).

Acts 25:6-12. Paul appeals to Caesar

When he had stayed among them not more than eight or ten days, Festus went down to Caesarea. And the next day he took his seat on the tribunal, and ordered Paul to be brought. And when he had come, the Jews who had gone down from Jerusalem stood about him, bringing against him many charges which they could not prove. (Acts 25:6,7).

Festus did not hurry to go down to Caesarea. He was not about to do the Jew's bidding lightly. He remained in Jerusalem 'not more than eight or ten days', and then went down to Caesarea.

The next day, he took his seat on the tribunal, the judgement seat, erected by Herod's palace, indicating that this was indeed a legal trial, and that his decision, whatever it was, had legal effectiveness.

He ordered Paul to be brought from the prison, expecting that the indictment against Paul may have been expanded, or changed in some way from the previous trial, since Paul had already been through a similar trial under Felix. Felix had not found Paul guilty, but it appeared that all the Jews could do was to repeat emphatically all the previous charges against him, 'bringing against him all the charges which they could not prove'. Tetullus appeared not to be with them on this occasion, perhaps because he had proved to be a weak reed for the Jews to lean on.

Without evidence or eyewitnesses how could the Jews expect Festus to take them seriously? Especially those charges which related to sedition in the empire, insurrection against the Roman authorities. Paul was then allowed to give his defence as he had at his trial under Felix. He began with a brief summary of what had been said before, and that neither against the law of the Jews, nor against the temple, nor against Caesar, had he offended at all. (Acts 25:8).

But again we find the Roman official seeking to ingratiate himself with the Jews, just as Felix had done. Festus, wishing to do the Jews a favour, said to Paul, 'Do you wish to go up to Jerusalem and be tried there on these charges before me?' (Acts 25:9).

This seemed plausible enough. After all, the alleged incident took place in Jerusalem and Festus was not entirely abdicating the responsibility of conducting the trial, stating that the trial would be before him. But there was the danger that having already tried to curry favour with the Jews, he would go further and find Paul guilty. Indeed, this may have been what the Jews were really after. Festus, deciding that this was only a matter of the interpretation of their law, would go to the extreme length of handing Paul over to their jurisdiction.

But the Jews had overreached themselves. They had accused Paul of treason and treason against the emperor, and Paul in his defence had stated that he had not offended against Caesar at all. (Acts 25:8). The Jews had raised the stakes, putting the whole affair on a completely different level, a level which Festus was bound to take seriously.

Paul, aware of the alternatives of being handed over to Jewish adjudication, or of being judged as a Roman citizen was quite sure which he preferred. Besides, was he not already standing before cCaesar's tribunal, for Festus was Caesar's representative and was seated on the tribunal as judge?

Paul said 'I am standing before Caesar's tribunal where I ought to be tried. To the Jews I have done no wrong as you know very well. If then I am a wrongdoer, and have committed anything for which I deserve to die, I do not seek to escape death, but if there is anything in their charges against me, no one can give me up to them. I appeal to Caesar.' (Acts 25:10.11).

The right to appeal to the emperor was one of the most ancient rights of the Roman citizen. The emperor had the power to veto and this power was invested in his representative, in this case, Festus. Paul had been quite willing to submit his case to Festus, for his previous experience with Roman officials had been favourable. Festus however needed to confer with his council about this new development. He was unwilling to take full responsibility for the decision he must now make, but eventually, 'after he had conferred with the council' and they had come to the conclusion that as Paul was a Roman citizen, he did have the right to appeal to Caesar, Festus gave his judgement. 'You have appealed to Caesar and to Caesar you shall go'. (Acts 25:12).

For Festus, this was an extremely difficult situation and he believed that he had found a way out of it. Instead of being tried before Caesar's representative, why should not Paul be tried before Caesar himself? He decided to take Paul's statement at face value; as a desire to have his case tried at Rome under the personal supervision of the emperor.

Paul was never concerned for his own safety, but he was concerned that the believers throughout the empire, the church, the *ecclesiae*, the gathered out ones, should be recognized, not as a sect of Judaism but as a movement, an actual phenomenon in its own right; a movement with the purpose of going into all the world and preaching the gospel to every creature, as their Lord had commissioned them. (Mark 16:15).

It was a movement completely distinct from Judaism. Perhaps Caesar himself would give them this recognition. Whether this meant an early death or a visit to Rome did not mean much to Paul, if only men and women could turn to Christ in penitence and faith and find new life in Him.

For Paul himself, he only wanted the will of God to govern his life, and though he had no knowledge of how God could bring this about, he believed that this was all part of God's purpose for him. Festus said to him, 'You have appealed to Caesar and to Caesar you must go'.

The emperor at that time was Nero, who succeeded his father Claudius in 54 A.D and ruled until 68 A.D. (Bruce p 432). Seneca, the philosopher, was a good influence on Nero during the first few years of his reign, but this is now 60 A.D. This was not going to be a good time for Paul going forward, viewed in purely earthly terms, but he was content.

Acts 25:13-22. Agrippa and Bernice visit Festus

Now when some days had passed, Agrippa the king and Bernice arrived at Caesarea to welcome Festus. And as they stayed there many days, Festus laid Paul's case before the king, saying 'There is a man left prisoner by Felix, and when I was at Jerusalem, the chief priests and the elders of the Jews brought charges against him, asking for a sentence of condemnation against him'. (Acts 25:13)

On the whole, Festus was a conciliatory and moderate procurator, and we have the statement in Acts 25:9 that he wished to do the Jews a favour by asking Paul if he would prefer to be tried in Jerusalem on the charges brought against him by the Jews. But this was an unsatisfactory alternative for Paul who had appealed to Caesar, and Festus, who had heard his defence, appeared determined to allow Paul to have the justice he deserved as a Roman citizen. On the other hand, so much of what the Jews had charged against Paul, and so much of Paul's defence, focussing as it did on the resurrection of Jesus, was outside the range of Festus' understanding. He called it 'theJewish superstition'. (Acts 25:19).

Roman law followed three stages. First, charges were brought by the prosecution. Then there would be a formal act of accusation. Thirdly, the case would be heard by 'the holder of the imperium', that is, the representative of the emperor, bringing the accused and the accuser together face to face. (Stott p 365).

This was what had happened. The charges against Paul by the Jewish leaders were: his offending against Jewish law and the temple. These were religious. But more importantly in the understanding of Festus was the political charge that Paul had offended against the emperor. (Acts 25:8).

Paul had denied that he had offended against Caesar but nevertheless, this charge had altered the course of events, for Paul had only one option open to him, to appeal to Caesar for a fair trial. Whether he was found guilty by Festus or handed over to the Jews for punishment, it was likely that the outcome would be the same; the death penalty.

So Paul had appealed to Caesar, the highest court in the empire, but symbolized by Caesar's representative here in Caesarea. What could Festus do? He was quite at a loss to know what to do. If he did not convict Paul, he was going against all that the Roman law and his own position as procurator stood for. Paul had said 'I appeal to Caesar' and Festus had complied to the extent of keeping Paul safely in prison, though knowing that he had to send Paul to Rome eventually, which was Paul's right as a Roman citizen.

Festus was full of perplexity.

Paul was full of hope that he would yet see Rome and witness in Rome to the saving power of his Lord.

Some days had passed when a state visit was announced. Herod Agrippa, the son of Herod Agrippa I of Acts 12, and his sister Berenice, were arriving at Caesarea to welcome Festus into his new role, and to pay their respects. This king was known as King Agrippa. On the death of his uncle, in 44 A.D. some years earlier while Agrippa was seventeen and being educated in Rome, Agrippa had been given his uncle's territory by Claudius in north east Palestine; but it was ruled by a Roman procurator until 50 A.D. Together with the kingdom of Chalcis, Claudius also gave Agrippa the right to appoint the Jewish high priest, and charge of the temple in Jerusalem. He died childless in about 100 A.D. (Josephus 'Antiquities XX, 9,4, 7. Bruce p 394).

Bernice, (latinized as Veronica), was the younger sister of Agrippa and of course, Herod of Chalcis had been her uncle too, the brother of her father Herod Agrppa I. Her father had given her in marriage to her uncle Herod of Chalcis, Herod's brother, and by him she had two sons.

After his death, she lived with her brother, Herod Agrippa II.

Though Agrippa was in effect, a puppet king, deriving what authority he had from Rome, he was still someone to be respected, and his visit to Festus was an honour. Agrippa and Bernice had been with Festus some days and Festus had attempted to entertain them. Perhaps there had been chariot racing or Greek plays in the basilica and certainly feasting. Perhaps Festus was running out of ideas when he had the inspiration of presenting Paul's case before the king. (Acts 25:14). This king, after all, with all his duties in Jerusalem, especially those of the temple and the high priest, might be able to help him write his report.

Festus said to the king,' There is a man left prisoner by Felix', and then went on to describe or relate to Arippa what he had done. He explains that shortly after he came to Caesarea, he had decided to go to Jerusalem, the second largest of his cities. While he was there, a deputation of the Jews came to him. Some of their chief priests and elders wanted to give information against Paul, asking for sentence against him. This of course he could not do. It was against Roman law and all legal procedure. If they wanted to accuse the prisoner, it had to be face to face. (Acts 25:16). Festus had invited the Jews to come to Caesarea so that Paul could meet his accusers face to face and make his defence.

The Jews had accepted his invitation to come to Caesarea. Festus immediately convened a court 'making no delay but on the next day taking his seat on the tribunal'. (Acts 25:17), only to discover that Paul was not being charged with crimes against the state 'but with certain disputes about their own superstition, and about one Jesus who was dead but whom Paul asserted to be alive'. (Acts 25:19).

Festus confessed himself to be at a loss to investigate these questions and explained to Agrippa that on the basis of *religious* dispute, he asked Paul whether he wished to go to Jerusalem to be tried there. But Paul had instead appealed to Festus 'to be kept in custody for the decision of the emperor' and so Festus had commanded him to be held 'until he could send him to Caesar'. (Acts 25:20,21). Festus had granted his appeal, remanding him to a higher court.

Agrippa listened carefully to all that Festus had told him. It intrigued him. He said, 'I should like to hear this man myself'. And Festus told him, 'Tomorrow you shall hear him'.

Acts 25:23-27. Paul brought before Agrippa

So, on the morrow, Agrippa and Bernice came with great pomp, and they entered the audience chamber with the military tribunes and the prominent men of the city. Then by command of Festus, Paul was brought in.

Agrippa and Bernice sat side by side as they did later when trying to avert the Jewish war and preserve peace (Josephus. *The Jewish War*). They had processed into the audience chamber or auditorium, used for conducting trials, into the privileged place reserved for them, with great pomp and ceremony. (Acts 25:23).

There were five cohorts of soldiers at Caesarea, each one of which would be commanded by a military tribune. These tribunes and the prominent men of the city would consist mainly of Gentiles, and would be there as a display of military and civil strength. (Bruce p 437). It was clear that Festus was enthusiastic about making this an occasion to be remembered, for it was important to him as a Roman official to maintain good relations with even minor royalty.

Stott gives a possible description of the scene. He suggests that Agrippa and Bernice would be wearing their purple robes of royalty and a gold circlet of a crown on their brows. Festus, to do honour to the occasion would be wearing the scarlet robe which a Roman governor would wear on state occasions. And following them would be all the pageantry of high ranking officers and leading men of the city. And then, when all these important people had taken their seats Paul was brought in by command of the governor.

From 'The Acts of Paul and Thecla', a pseudepigraphic writing of the post apostolic period, we have a description of Paul. He was short and slight. He was balding, with beetle brows, hooked nose and bandy legs. But he was 'full of grace'. (Stott p 369). Stott comments, wearing neither crown nor gown, but the tunic given to prisoners, and with his hands in chains, (Acts 26:29), Paul nevertheless dominated the court with his quiet, calm, Christian confidence and dignity. He was representing *his* king.

And Festus said, 'King Agrippa, and all who are present with us, you see this man about whom the whole Jewish people petitioned me, both at Jerusalem and here, shouting that he ought not to live any longer. But I found that had done nothing deserving of death and as he himself appealed to the emperor, I decided to send him'. (Acts 25:24,25). This was true in some measure. Certain Jews had petitioned Festus that he should hand over Paul for punishment, without allowing him any defence, for they considered that he had not so much committed a crime as indulged in heresy, basing his teaching on one called Jesus of Nazareth whom Paul claimed had been resurrected from the dead.

But it had not been the whole of the Jewish people who petitioned Festus for Paul's death, but members of the Sanhedrin, the chief priests and elders of the Jews, (Acts 25:2), and Festus had not found Paul guilty of any capital offence. In fact, neither had Felix, though Festus did not mention his predecessor.

The Jews had clamoured for, shouted for, Paul's death both in Jerusalem and here in Caesarea, Festus continued, but I examined him myself, listening to both sides of the argument, and when I found that he had done nothing worthy of death, I asked him if he would be willing to be judged before the Jews in Jerusalem, for that was where the original incident took place. But when I asked him, he said, 'I appeal to Caesar'. So Festus concluded, I decided to send him to Rome'. (Acts 25:25).

Though Festus is apparently seeking the more knowledgeable view of Agrippa in this case, it is obvious that he has already made up his mind what to do about Paul, seeking only Agrippa's confirmation and agreement that he has made the right decision. His problem is the report which he would need to send with the prisoner; what information about the prisoner would it contain. There is no evidence, no eye witnesses prepared to come forward. Sending a report which held no legitimate charges against the prisoner would be seen as seriously incompetent and at the very least, damaging to Festus' reputation as an efficient procurator.

Festus really did have a situation requiring great finesse. Since he had found Paul innocent, a man who had done nothing worthy of death, he could have released him. (Acts 25:25). But to release him into the community would almost certainly have brought about his death from the Jews, probably through lynching.

He had imagined that giving Paul the option of being tried in Jerusalem would give him some protection, but Paul had appealed to Caesar and there was no alternative but to comply with Paul's appeal, as a Roman citizen. But how ro convey all this in a report to the emperor, whom he calls 'my lord'? (Acts 25:26). This was an ascription common at the time of Nero, paying homage to Nero as his master and even his god, as emperors were reputed to be.

His report needed to be concise, couched in legal terminology and to have included all the charges against Paul. (Acts 25:27). So Festus looks to Agrippa for help in producing a document which will absolve him from any dereliction of duty, and perhaps also be an example of Roman justice. Festus says 'I have brought Paul before you, KIng Agrippa, that after we have examined him, I will have something to write. For it seems unreasonable in sending a prisoner, not to indicate the charges against him'. (Acts 25:27)

Sending Paul to Rome would have the effect of at once protecting him from the Jews and at the same time give the impression of Festus' determination to uphold Roman law. Festus was using the occasion of the visit to Caesarea of Agrippa and Berenice to present Paul to the king, and with Agrippa's knowledge of Judaism to help him in the writing of the report. This Agrippa seemed more than willing to do.

Acts Chapter 26

Acts 26:1-32. Paul's defence before Agrippa

Agrippa said to Paul,'You have permission to speak for yourself'. Then Paul stretched out his hand and made his defence. I think myself fortunate that it is before you, King Agrippa, I am to make my defence today against all the accusations of the Jews, because you are especially familiar with all customs and controversies of the Jews. Therefore I beg you to listen to me patiently.

Agrippa had said to Festus that he would like to hear the man himself, (Acts 25:22), probably both to help Festus and also to demonstrate how expert he was with Jewish beliefs.

Bruce describes Paul's defence as Paul's *Apologia pro vita sua,* a defence of his life experience leading him to an encounter with the Lord Jesus Christ, and cogent reasons for his way of life since, as a messenger of His gospel of reconciliation between God and man.

This title of a work by John Henry Newman had been the result of a controversy which Newman had had with Charles Kingsley, whose view was 'that Newman did not consider that truth was a necessity'. Bruce considered that this what Paul was seeking to establish through his defence, that *truth is a necessity,* absolute truth, the truth of who Christ is and the claim He has on men and women to listen to the truth and respond to it. Bruce considered this title to be relevant to Paul's situation as an apologetic, as a defence of what God had been doing in and through his life. (Bruce p 438) This is a helpful analogy. Paul does indeed speak truth to power in this, his last recorded summary of his own life and the truth which became his reason for living, the truth of who Jesus is and what he accomplishes in the lives of men and women. Paul is speaking truth to power in a way inimical to all that has gone before in the lives of those seated before him.

Bearing Professor Bruce's suggestion in mind, gives us a clue to what Paul is saying. What better way to provide a defence than to speak of his own life, his life in relation to his faith, and how his life has been transformed from a strict observation of all that the Jews maintained was the only way of righteousness to the utter transformation and revelation which Paul had received; the only way of approaching a Holy God.

This had begun for him on the road to Damascus, completely overturning all his preconceived ideas about holiness and access to the God of his salvation. God had prepared the way. He now knew that God had Himself provided access to Himself through Christ and his response of faith, and trust in His finished work on the cross.

It is possible even for a Christian to attribute a change in lifestyle and to ways of thinking, to circumstances, or to the influence of certain other people, who appear to live close to their Lord, and it is true that these may have tremendous repercussions on their lives. But Paul attributes everything to God. The Psalmist says, 'It is God who girds me with strength and makes my way perfect'. (Psalm 18:32), and this is Paul's testimony too. Paul would say, 'It is God and only God who has undertaken to be with me and to keep me in His will. It is Jesus, only Jesus who has provided the means whereby I may come to Him. It is the Holy Spirit who energises the life of Jesus within me. And so, all the honour and glory goes to Him. This was Paul's defence, his *apologia*. Agrippa said to Paul,' You have permission to speak for yourself'. Then Paul stretched out his hand and made his defence, (Acts 26:1).

Paul stretched out his hand to Agrippa, perhaps as a mark of respect, or as an appeal to him as one Jew to another, who understood the problems the Jewish nation was facing and who had an understanding of their inability to fit in with Roman concepts of justice, legality or virtue. In spite of everything Paul had suffered at the hands of the Jews, Paul never ceased to love them. He confessed to having great sorrow and unceasing anguish in his heart for them, his brethren, his kinsmen by race. (Romans 9:2). But knowing that what he was going to say was the gospel, perhaps Paul stretched out his hand in a gesture of beseeching, pleading with Agrippa to listen carefully and respond to the gospel, the good news of salvation.

Paul's exordium, the customary way of beginning or introducing his speech, was designed not just to tell Agrippa what he wanted to hear, that he was an expert in Jewish affairs. Paul really meant what he said. He knew his defence would take some time. His stretched out hand was also a plea for Agrippa to be prepared to listen carefully to what he had to say.

Acts 26:4-8. Paul's Pharisaic position

Paul said, I think myself fortunate that it is before you, King Agrippa, I am to make my defence today against all the accusations of the Jews, because you are especially familiar with all the customs and controversies of the Jews. Therefore, I beg you to listen to me patiently.

My manner of life from my youth, spent from the beginning among my own nation and at Jerusalem Is known by all the Jews. They have known for a long time if they are willing to testify that according to the strictest party of our religion, I have lived as a Pharisee. And now I stand here on trial for hope in the promise made by God to our fathers, to which our twelve tribes hope to attain as they earnestly worship night and day. And for this hope I am accused, O King! Why is it thought incredible by any of you that God raises the dead?

Paul first sets out his position as Pharisee. Beginning with his experience as a young man 'in his own nation', of Cilicia, (Acts 26:4), he then recounts his further education in Jerusalem. We know from the second account of his conversion, (Acts 22:3) that this was at the feet of Gamaliel, a highly respected teacher of the law and a member of the Sanhedrin. (Acts 5:33). Under Gamaliel's teaching, Paul lived according to the 'strictest (superlative) party of our religion', as a Pharisee. And this is well known of all the Jews. (Acts 26:4).

Paul claims that it is a Pharisee that he stands here on trial, 'for hope in the promise made by God to our fathers, to which our twelve tribes hope to attain, as they earnestly worship night and day. And for this hope I am accused by the Jews'. Surely Agrippa would be sympathetic to such a claim, for indeed the promise had been made to all the patriarchs, Abraham, Isaac and Jacob. Mary had spoken of it to Elisabeth in Luke 1:55, declaring that 'God spoke to our fathers, to Abraham and his descendants for ever'. Zechariah, the father of John the Baptist had also prophesied that God had raised up a horn of salvation for His people, to perform the mercy promised to our fathers and to remember His holy covenant, the oath which he sware to our forefather Abraham. (Luke 1:72). Paul later writes of what belongs to the Israelites, the covenant made through Abraham, Moses and David, the giving of the law, and the promises, all that God had promised. (Romans 9:4).

But now salvation has come through Jesus, who was so called because He would save His people from their sins. (Matthew 1:21) The promise made to the fathers has now been fulfilled in Him, the hope of Israel, to which Jews now had access, even the Twelve tribes of Israel. And for which they had been praying night and day.

It was for this hope 'the hope of in the promise of God made to our fathers' (Acts 26:6), that Paul claims that he is now being accused (Acts 26:8). The Jews had been worshipping God, praying to Him night and day for the hope, the promise of God to be realised. And when it happens, they find it incredible, unbelievable, impossible to believe that the hope of Israel, has come, has lived and died a terrible death but had been raised from the dead.

In Paul's thinking, the close connection between the hope of Israel, the promised Messiah to come and the resurrection, is indisputable. Paul continues, Why is it thought incredible by any of you that God raises the dead? And goes on to describe how he met with the resurrected Christ.

Acts 26:9-11. Paul's persecuting zeal

I myself was convinced that I ought to do many things in opposing the Name of Jesus of Nazareth. And I dId so in Jerusalem; I not only shut up many of the saints in prison, by authority from the chief priests, but when they were put to death, I cast my vote against them. And I punished them often in all the synagogues and tried to make them blaspheme; and in raging fury against them, I persecuted them even unto foreign cities. Thus I journeyed to Damascus.

Paul continues, that though he was a Pharisee, and as a Pharisee had a strong belief in the resurrection of men and women in general, he had not been satisfied about the resurrection of Jesus. He had heard rumours about Jesus of Nazareth, about His life of teaching and healing and that he had risen from the dead (Acts 26:9). But in Paul's view, Jesus must be seen as an imposter, and as a strict Pharisee, Paul ought to oppose such heresy. It was his duty to stamp out a movement which led people astray.

Armed with such evidence as he could muster, from people who had come to believe in, and follow Jesus, he had gone to the chief priests for documents of authority which they had been more than willing to give him, authorizing him to seek out such people. (Acts 26:10) Paul tells Agrippa that he not only shut up many of the saints in prison, but when they were put to death, he cast his vote against them.

This later Paul, speaking before Agrippa, older in experience and wisdom, now calls those whom he had imprisoned and killed, 'saints', meaning holy ones, separated to God for a life lived wholly for Him whether long or short. Paul had not considered them as such while he was persecuting them, punishing them often in all the synagogues and trying to make them blaspheme, and in raging fury against them, persecuting them even to foreign cities. (Acts 26:11). As Damascus was in Syria, this was the foreign city to which Paul referred.

But though in later life Paul was still contrite over the way he had persecuted Christians, saying that he was not worthy to be called an apostle because he persecuted the church of God, (1 Corinthians 15:9), yet God was able to use even the martyrdom of His saints for the blessing of many. The terrible experiences of those saints, as Paul describes them, caused to bring into being a man of God, an apostle to both Jews and Gentiles, a man who was prepared to suffer the loss of all things, to go through innumerable beatings, imprisonments, stonings, danger from many sources, if it only meant that he could be found in Christ; to have the surpassing knowledge of Jesus as Lord 'for whom I have suffered the loss of all things and do but count them as refuse that I might gain Christ'. (Philippians 3:8).

It was Paul's 'raging fury' against the saints that drove him to Damascus and into the transforming meeting with Jesus. (Acts 26:11).

Acts 26:12-18. The heavenly vision

Thus I journeyed to Damascus with the authority and commission of the chief priests. At midday, O King, I saw on the way a light from heaven, brighter than the sun, shining around me, and those who journeyed with me. And when we had all fallen to the ground I heard a voice saying to me in the Hebrew language, 'Saul, Saul, why do you persecute Me? It is hard for you to kick against the goads'. And I said, 'Who are you Lord'? And the Lord said, 'I am Jesus whom you are persecuting'.

Though Festus and Bernice were still in the audience hall with him, Paul appeared to address himself predominantly to Agrippa. Perhaps he sensed in Agrippa, whether or not he was aware of Agrippa's background, a real desire to know more of what Paul had to tell him of his conversion experience; how Jesus had come to him; how he had responded.

Paul, secure and confident in the Holy Spirit, had held out his hand to Agrippa. He had confessed that he had done many things contrary to the Name of Jesus of Nazareth which he also did in Jerusalem, (Acts 26:9) the place where he had received his religious education and where he had been well known by the Jews. They had known him personally and could testify to his absolute devotion 'to the strictest party of our sect'. (Acts 26:5).

It was this devotion, intensified by what he regarded as a putative movement damaging the purity of Judaism, which caused him to take the long journey to Damascus with the authority and commission of the chief priests. Paul says that at some point along the way, he and his companions were suddenly arrested by a light from heaven. Though it was the middle of the day, when the noonday sun was at its brightest, this was a light of such intensity that it could only have come from heaven. Whether voluntarily or involuntarily, the whole company fell to the ground. And Paul continues. 'When we had all fallen to the ground, I heard a voice speaking to me in the Hebrew language saying, 'Saul, Saul, why do you persecute Me? It hurts you to kick against the goads'.

And I said, 'Who are You Lord?' And He said, 'I am Jesus whom you are persecuting'. (Acts 26:14,15).

The bright light came from heaven. The voice came from heaven. This was not the normal or natural order of things that belong to the earth and sky. They were not superterrestrial but supramundane, not of this world but *out of this world*, the dwelling place of God, His abode; the place of His glory. That was why the light was so much brighter than the noonday sun.

Yet when Jesus spoke, He spoke in Aramaic, the common language of the Jews, and used Paul's Semitic name, perhaps childhood name, 'Saul'. For this brief moment the earth and the other world of heaven had come together, for God had a purpose in view and he was prepared to use even a man as full of prejudice as Paul/Saul to bring it together.

And yet Jesus was speaking to Paul in terms of endearment. Saul, SAUL, he was saying. Saul was used to speaking in Aramaic. Jesus could have spoken to him in classical Hebrew or Greek and he would have understood, but He chose to speak to him in the language of his childhood, of his growing up years, in the comforting tones of familiarity. Jesus did not speak in condemnation of all that Paul had done and was doing. He asked a simple question, 'Why do you persecute Me? It is hard for you to kick against the goads'.

Paul would have understood the reference, though it may be obscure to us. In order to encourage oxen to move more quickly and in a straight line when ploughing, they were pricked with goads, usually a sharp pointed stick.

Jesus was suggesting to Paul that he had been for too long obsessed with his religious studies, (as Paul had already intimated to Agrippa), because he so longed to be righteous before God. Philippians 3:6 confirms this. But persecuting the church and therefore Jesus Himself was not the way; he was only hurting himself. Like an ox, he was going in the wrong direction.

He had obsessively been going in one direction and finding it hard, because there were pricks which were causing him to think in another direction. He had been there at the death of Srephen. He had heard what Stephen had preached before he was stoned to death. He had held Stephen's garments while they threw the stones. He had seen how the church had grown after the death of Stephen, how it had scattered in so many different directions. All these had been 'pricks of the goads' to warn him that there was so much more to this new movement than he had supposed. Why had he not properly investigated the death and resurrection of Jesus? Why had he been so uneasy in his mind about the persecution of Christians even though he imagined it to be the righteous path to follow? Why had he not listened more carefully to Stephen's defence before he was stoned to death?

These were the goads which Jesus had allowed into Paul's life. Why was he still fighting against them?

Paul asked the question 'who are You, Lord'? But he already knew the answer. He had begun to realise that the Lord is Jesus, and it is only incidentally that he is resisting the goads. What he has really been resisting is Jesus. He recognizes that this is the Jesus who was crucified and rose from the dead. That He is the

Lord. And that further, when He says 'I am Jesus whom you are persecuting', He is identifying Himself with all those whom Paul had persecuted, these people who were and are extremely important to Him. They are His own special people. Paul will come to call them 'saints'.

The voice from heaven authenticated the position of authority which God had given to Jesus. And it is from that position of authority that Jesus has something further to say to Paul.' Saul', He says, 'Rise and stand upon your feet, for I have something of great importance to say to you. I have appeared to you for this purpose, to appoint you to serve and bear witness to the things in which you have seen and to those in which I will appear to you, delivering you from the people and from the Gentiles to whom I send you; to open their eyes that they may turn from darkness to light and from the power of Satan to God, that they may receive forgiveness of sins and a place among those who are sanctified by faith in Me'. (Acts 26:16-18).

In speaking to Festus, Agrippa and Bernice, Paul was not laying stress on his conversion, although the revelation of who Jesus is was seriously instrumental in what followed; but for Agrippa's sake, Paul was stressing the importance of the commission which he had received from the Lord Jesus who had appeared to him.

In this account of his conversion, Paul does not mention Ananias though Ananias was very dear to Paul, 'a devout man according to the law, well spoken of by all the Jews who lived there in Damascus (Acts 22:12) What Agrippa needed to hear was an abbreviated account of how Paul became a Christian and why he believed as he did, and not the part played by Ananias in his commissioning.

This was a serious commissioning. Jesus was sending Paul on a mission. He had appeared to Paul for a purpose. Paul was to be His servant, a minister of His. He had to bear witness to what he had seen now and when other experiences were given to him in the future, when Jesus would appear to him. Jesus assured him that He would deliver him from both the Jews and the Gentiles, 'to whom I send you'. (Acts 26:17). Both Jews and

Gentiles would have their eyes opened. They would turn from darkness to light, from the power of Satan to God, and receive forgiveness of sin and a place among those who are sanctified, made righteous by faith in Jesus (Acts 26:18).

Jesus says to Paul, 'I am sending you'. His is an apostolic commission.

One of the qualifications for being an apostle, a sent one, had been that he had personally accompanied the other disciples 'all the time that the Lord Jesus went in and out among us', (Acts 1:21) 'beginning with the baptism of John, until the day when He was taken up from us'. They were witnesses to Him, (Acts 1:8), they had seen the risen Lord, (1 Corinthians 15:8), who had said to them, 'as the Father has sent Me, so send I you' (John 20:21).

Paul had not had the privilege of being one of those disciples, those 'sent out' ones, apostles. But God was expanding the concept of apostleship. Paul was glad to be able to say, 'I am the least of all the apostles, born out of due time, yet He appeared to be also, though I was not fit to be an apostle because I persecuted the church of God. But by the grace of God I am what I am'. (1 Corinthians 15:8-10).

Paul redefines an apostle, not as one who had accompanied Jesus during his earthly life, for this precious experience had been given to few. But though he regarded himself as nothing, (2 Corinthians 12, 11,12), and not fit to be called to be an apostle, the signs of an apostle had been performed among the Corinthian believers in all patience, with signs and wonders and mighty works, And he says, the Corinthian church is the seal of his apostleship in the Lord. (1 Corinthians 9:2).

The point he is making to Agrippa is that his apostolic authority or any authority at all, comes from God. Jesus had appointed him to be His servant and His witness.

Though Paul is correct in saying exactly what Jesus had said to him, including his commissioning to the Gentiles as well as to the Jews, a comment which had occasioned much opposition from the Jews in Acts 22:21, neither Agrippa nor Festus appear to have taken exception to it. Perhaps Agrippa did not rate his

Jewish connection all that highly after all, and perhaps Festus feared no danger from an itinerant preacher, even one who was convinced of his status before God, but who was given to having visions and hearing voices from heaven.

But Paul's remembrance of the words of Jesus to him, that both Jews and Gentiles would turn from darkness to light and from Satan to God, had behind them enormous truths affecting the eternal destiny of so many, many people. It had a personal dimension for him too, for that was what Jesus was doing for him, forgiving his sins, giving him a place among those who were made righteous through faith in Jesus, liberating him from the power of Satan and bringing him into life giving relationship with God, something for which he had been striving and had striven in vain until his encounter with Jesus on the road to Damascus.

In the terminology which Paul reports Jesus as using here, this is conversion, turning from darkness to light, turning to God from the power of Satan. This is the gospel, received and understood and proceeding to sanctification, and all by faith in Jesus.

Acts 26:19,20. Paul's obedience to the heavenly vision

Wherefore, O King Agippa, I was not disobedient to the heavenly vision, but declared first to those in Damascus, then at Jerusalem, and throughout all the country of Judea and also to the Gentiles, that they should repent and turn to God and perform deeds worthy of repentance. (Acts 26:19).

Continuing to focus on Agrippa, Paul emphasises that the vision given to him was a heavenly one, originating from the Lord Jesus in heaven, and thus accounting for the glory that was revealed. Paul could of course have ignored it or repudiated it. Jesus always gives people the choice. When He says 'Follow Me', He never uses coercion or threats. He has given them free will and they are at perfect liberty to reject Him; to say 'No' to Him.

But Paul was not disobedient to the heavenly vision. He uses a figure of speech, *litotes*, which employs the negative to express the positive. He was *not disobedient*. Paul could only be obedient to something which was so obviously from heaven, from the place where God dwelt. It had so obviously appealed to all his faculties of reasoning, all his dissatisfaction with the life he now lived. When he saw the light; heard the voice, everything within him wanted to respond. Others had seen Jesus in the flesh, walked with Him, talked with Him. This was the only glimpse of Jesus which Paul had so far had, But it was enough. His heart was overcome with the wonder of it all, to know that Jesus cared for him so much that He had chosen Paul to be a witness to Him.

He could hardly wait to share the good news with others, the good news of the gospel. As he had now reached Damascus, what better place to start? Then returning to Jerusalem, possibly to give back to the chief priests the documentation he had been given, he took the good news with him, but did not stay in Jerusalem but travelled throughout Judea, taking the gospel not only to Jews but to Gentiles too, as Jesus had commanded him to do; the precious gospel of repentance towards God and faith towards the risen and ascended Lord Jesus Christ.

Acts 26:21. Paul's arrest and present circumstances

For this reason, the Jews seized me in the temple and tried to kill me. To this day, I have the help that comes from God and so I stand here testifying to small and great saying nothing but what the prophets and Moses said would come to pass, that the Christ must suffer and that by being the first to rise from the dead, He would proclaim light both to the people and to the Gentiles.

Paul says that for this reason, the preaching of the gospel and the truth of the resurrection, the Jews had seized him and tried to kill him. So he now brings his testimony to a conclusion.

This had been their intention that he should be arrested, which he now was, and even better from their point of view, that he should be killed either by them or judicially. This was now his fifth trial, although strictly speaking the present one was not a legal trial but an informal hearing. Paul's first trial had been before Felix. (Acts 22:3-21). His second had been before the Jewish council (Acts 23:1-8). The third had been insisted upon by Ananias the high priest with Felix In attendance (Acts 24:1-22), and then had been the first one before Festus. (Acts 25:21). And now this hearing before Agrippa and Berenice.

On each occasion, Paul had sought to defend himself on the grounds that the central theme of his message was the resurrection from the dead. Since men do not usually rise from the dead and eat and drink with their friends before being taken up in a cloud to heaven, the resurrection of Jesus logically gave rise to the assumption that He was divine, that He was indeed the Son of God. And Paul was speaking imperatively to Agrippa. This was the risen Jesus whom I encountered on the Damascus road.

It was this assertion that Jesus had already risen from the dead which clashed with the beliefs of the Pharisaic Jews concerning resurrection; the issue of time. These Jews had developed a belief over some years, especially since returning from exile in Babylon, that the whole person, body and soul would rise again from the dead *at some time in the future* expressed most clearly in Daniel 12:2 where it says, 'Many of those who sleep in the dust shall wake, some to everlasting life and some to shame and everlasting contempt'.

But Jesus had not been bound by some future date. He was alive. He had been resurrected from the dead and forty days later had ascended to heaven, there to share in the glory of God. This Man Jesus was simultaneously man and God, come to earth to live among human beings. This resurrected Jesus was the one who had appeared to Paul on the Damascus road.

It was the proclamation of the risen Christ and their need of repentance and of turning to God which had so infuriated the Jews that they wanted to kill him. But Jesus had fulfilled

His promise to Paul, delivering him from the people and from the Gentiles. (Acts 26:17).

But, Paul declares, why should this be a problem for the Jews? Why should they find it difficult to grasp? Paul is standing in the audience hall, 'testifying to both small and great', (Acts 16 22) for he realises that though he has been called by Festus to defend himself before Agrippa, there are many others present who are also listening to what he is saying. But Paul is saying nothing but what Moses and the prophets had said would come to pass, that the coming Christ must suffer and that by being the first to rise from the dead, He would proclaim light both to the people and to the Gentiles (Acts 26:23).

In speaking to Festus, Agrippa and Berenice, Paul knows that without the help of God he would not be here (Acts 26:22). For God had rescued him so many times when he had been in danger. It was through God's help that he had been enabled to proclaim the gospel message, and this was what he was now doing.

His was not a new message because it went back through all the Hebrew scriptures. And yet it was a new one, for all that Moses and the prophets had spoken of was now fulfilled in Jesus. He was the one who should come, the Messiah, the Christ, the Anointed of God, promised through the prophets.

This is an extraordinary claim to make, even to a believing Jew well versed in scripture. This is what Paul is testifying to, Jesus as the fulfilment of all scripture and scriptural revelation, as will be clear from his letters to the Romans and the Corinthians. (Romans 1:2; 16:26; 1 Corinthians 15:3).

Paul was convinced that the death of Jesus was not a last minute, eleventh hour decision by the Father, a sudden resolution that this could be the means of bringing many sons and daughters to glory, making the pioneer of their salvation perfect through suffering, (Hebrews 2:10); but that God had foretold by all the prophets that it was necessary that the Christ should suffer, (Acts 3:18), and to rise from the dead and that 'this Jesus, whio I proclaim to you is the Christ'. (Acts 17:3). And that He should be the *first* to rise from the dead, emphasizing not only the *particular* rising from the dead of Jesus, but the *general* resurrection leading to judgement.

Paul is insisting that this is not a proclamation of darkness, of confusion, of misunderstanding, but a proclamation of light. (Acts 26:23). The light had come into the world, and men loved darkness rather than light, (John 1:10), the light of the glorious knowledge of truth in the face of Jesus Christ, (2 Corinthians 4:6), a light to lighten, not only the Gentiles but also the glory of His people Israel. (Luke 2:32).

Jesus is proclaiming that light to Paul on the Damascus road, the light of His resurrection. This Is the hope of the resurrection, that because Jesus is risen from the dead, and seated at God's right hand, men and women can come to God. We have an advocate with the Father, Jesus Christ the righteous, and He is the expiation for our sins, and not for ours only, but for the sins of the whole world. (1 John 2:1).

Acts 26:24-29. Festus and Agrippa respond to Paul's defence

> As he thus made his defence, Festus said with a loud voice, 'Paul, you must be mad; your great learning is making you mad'. But Paul said, 'I am not mad, most noble Festus, but am speaking the sober truth. For the king knows about these things and to him I speak freely; for I am persuaded that none of these things has escaped his notice, for this was not done in a corner. King Agrippa, Do you believe the prophets? I know that you believe'. And Agrippa said to Paul, 'in a short time you think to make me a Christian'. And Paul said, Whether short or long, I would to God that not only you but all those who hear me this day might become as I am, except for these chains'. (Acts 26:24-29).

Paul's defence is concluded. It appears that Festus may have interrupted him, but Paul had said everything necessary. Festus was the first to react to what Paul had said. With a loud voice he said, 'Paul you are mad, much learning has made you mad'; possibly referring to Paul's knowledge of the scriptures.

Festus' remark was not intended to be offensive or pejorative. It was considered to be a prerequisite of poets and seers that they should be inspired with a kind of mania. (Bruce p 448). But Paul does not claim to have any special gift of inspired articulation but is speaking the sober truth; truth which is the direct antithesis of mania; solemn and sober truth, for eternal destinies are here at stake.

Paul says, 'I am not mad, most noble Festus, but am speaking the sober truth. For the king knows about these things and to him I speak freely. For these things were not done in a corner'. (Acts 26:26).

'None of these things was done in a corner' is another example of litotes, and makes it quite clear to Festus that this gospel activity, which not only Paul but so many others pursued openly, made no attempt at being esoteric or an exclusive arcane cult. The gospel was for all. It eliminated all distinctions of race or creed, or status in society, or gender. It was for all men and women everywhere for all time. Even if Festus had not himself investigated this amazing phenomenon, Paul was sure that Agrippa had.

Paul turned to Agrippa to corroborate this fact. Agrippa could testify that Paul was not mad and that Paul's statement concerning the prophets of the Hebrew scriptures was true; that nothing had happened except what the prophets had prophesied would happen had taken place, and this was indeed the sober truth.

Paul issued a direct challenge to Agrippa. 'King Agrippa, do you believe the prophets? I know that you believe'. (Acts 26:27). If Agrippa agreed with the prophets then he also must agree with what Paul said about the prophecies. The prophecies about the suffering and death and resurrection of Christ was indeed the sober truth.

If Agrippa does not agree with Paul's argument, his reputation as a Jewish sympathiser has gone forever. But if he agrees with Paul then he must of necessity accept that this man Jesus, this itinerant preacher from the despised backwater of Galilee, is also the resurrected Son of God.

Agrippa can see where this discussion is going. He said to Paul, 'In a short while you think to make me a Christian', or in another translation, 'Almost you persuade me to be a Christian'. (Acts 26:28). And Paul, with a heartfelt sigh, replies to Agrippa, Whether short or long, with few words or many, with ease or difficulty I would to God, I pray to God that not only you but also all who hear my words this day might become as I am' (Acts 26:29).

And as an afterthought he adds, 'except for these chains', indicating the chains upon his hands with a sweeping gesture, not to ignore them but to regard them as no obstruction to the gospel.

Acts 26:30-32. Festus and Agrippa agree that Paul is innocent

Then the king rose and the governor and Bernice and those who were sitting with them; and when they had withdrawn, they said to one another, 'This man is doing nothing worthy of death or imprisonment. And Agrippa said to Festus, 'This man could have been set at liberty if he had not appealed to Caesar'.

What could Festus, Agrippa and Bernice do? They had been challenged but they had had to come to a decision. They decide to withdraw in order to contemplate the next step. Together with those sitting in the judgement hall with them (Acts 26:30), they left the hall, not quite the same people who left as those who had entered, for they had much to think about, and contemplate, of the truth of what they had heard.

How long they discussed the situation is not known, but Festus, Agrippa and Bernice arrived at the same conclusion, that Paul was completely innocent of the charges brought against him. The next conclusion was a little more difficult. 'This man has done nothing worthy of imprisonment or death', they said.

'Is it possible to release him? (Acts 26:31). And Agrippa said to Festus, our hands are tied. We are bound by Roman law to send him to Caesar, for he has appealed to Caesar and to Caesar he must go. We can do nothing to save him. If he had not appealed to Caesar he could have been set free. (Acts 26:32). Paul's appeal has placed him squarely within the orbit of Roman law.

Acts Chapter 27

Acts 27:1-2. The voyage to Myra

And when it was decided that we should sail for Italy, they delivered Paul and some of the other prisoners to a centurion of the Augustan cohort, named Julius. And embarking on a ship of Adramyttium which was about to sail to the ports along the coast of Asia, we put out to sea, accompanied by Aristarchus, a Macedonian from Thessalonica.

This was Paul's first ship on the journey to Rome. Festus had decided to send him to Caesar. The emperor at that time was Nero. (54-68 A.D).

Paul may have continued for some time in prison, until a good strong sea going vessel became available, able to withstand what could be difficult sailing conditions. Now a suitable ship had arrived in Caesarea, and the journey to Rome could begin.

Festus had a trusty centurion called Julius. To him he delivered Paul, along with other prisoners, (Acts27:1). These other prisoners may have been in manacles to prevent them from committing suicide by jumping overboard and thus escaping whatever horrible death may have awaited them in Rome. Paul was regarded differently. He was a Roman citizen who had appealed to Caesar and was possibly free from restraints such as manacles.

The Augustan cohort of which Julius was a centurion was a popular name for a corps of officers who were also couriers, conveying messages between the emperor and his armies; an important communication service. They may also have had supervision of the 'corn ships', conveying supplies of wheat from the provinces, especially Egypt, to Rome, to feed its large population.

This ship had originated from Adramyttium, well up on the west coast of the province of Asia, and not far from Troas. It had probably sailed to Egypt and was now returning home, calling at ports along the way, and in this way had arrived at Caesarea. Marshall p404, suggests that Julius hoped that at one of these ports, he would be able to transfer to a ship bound for Italy with his prisoners.

These verses mark the resumption of the pronoun 'we'. It is now obviously Luke himself as an eye witness of the sea voyage to whom we owe the details of the narrative.

Paul is accompanied by Luke and also Aristarchus, both of whom probably travel as private citizens but with the aim of caring for Paul whose health may well have been affected as a result not only of the suffering he had endured, but also his long imprisonment. Luke may have remained in Palestine during this difficult period for Paul, to be near him and to help him whenever it was possible to do so.

Aristarchus is described by Paul in Philemon 24 and Colossians 4:10 as his companion and fellow worker. Since both these letters were written from Rome, it is possible that Aristarchus accompanied Paul right up to the prison in Rome. Paul writes to the Colossian believers that Aristarchus and another fellow prisoner called Justus are the only men of the circumcision, that is, of Jewish birth, 'among my fellow workers for the kingdom of God, and they have been a comfort to me'. (Colossians 4:10). What a privilege to be a comfort to Paul! As they sailed along the coast of Asia, these three men would have much to talk about, and perhaps to pray about.

About sixty nine nautical miles accomplished this first part of the journey, which brought them to Sidon, and which took a day. (Acts 27:3). At many of these ports, opportunities were taken to load and unload cargo, and because of the inevitable delay, 'Julius treated Paul kindly and gave him leave to go to his friends and be cared for', (Acts 27:3). 'Friends' was another name by which Christians recognized one another. It is possible that Luke, the doctor, had seen in Paul some medical condition for which he needed some 'care' which had not been available on board ship.

It was of course Julius' responsibility to deliver Paul to the custodial authorities who would then submit him for trial. This relaxation of the conditions on the part of Julius under which a prisoner, though an innocent man, was sailing under his authority, took some courage on the part of Julius, and also some certainty that Paul could be trusted not to escape but would return to the ship when she re-embarked.

Putting to sea again meant leaving the protection of the Phoenician coast and venturing out into the Great (Mediterranean) Sea. The ship, as a sailing ship, was reliant on the prevailing winds, so to minimize the effect of the west and north winds which were against them they sailed under the lee of the island of Cyprus. (Acts 27:4)

This gave them some protection, but to get to Myra, they had to leave the coast of Cyprus and sail across the open sea to the Lysian coast of Asia Minor. (Bruce p 443). Bruce estimates that this voyage would have taken nine days.

Acts 27:6-8. From Myra they sail to Crete

And when we had sailed across the sea which is off Cilicia and Pampmpylia, we came to Myra in Lycia. There the centurion found a ship of Alexandria sailing for Italy and put us on board. We sailed slowly for a number of days and arrived with difficulty off Cnidus and as the wind did not allow us to go on, we sailed under the lee of Crete off Salmone. Coasting along it with difficulty, we came to a place called Fair Havens, near which was the city of Lasea.

Paul had visited Myra before, on his way to Jerusalem (Acts 21:1), according to some ancient manuscripts. Myra was one of the chief ports for the Egyptian courier service, but there was no time on this occasion for Paul and his companions to leave the ship to spend time with friends, for a new ship was quickly found; a ship from Alexandria which was sailing for Italy. (Acts 27:6).

This ship appears to have been a cornship, (Acts 27:38), and therefore a more robust and larger ship, capable of carrying two hundred and seventy six people. (Acts 27:37). Luke describes it as a ship of Alexandria (Acts 27:6), sailing between Rome and Egypt with supplies of wheat, and of the greatest significance, since being commissioned to the corn fleet meant that it was a department of the state, organized on almost military lines. Provided that the west wind remained steady, the best route from Alexandria to Rome for such a ship would take them past Myra, and followed by a northern wind would take them to Sicily. From there a westerly wind would bring them to Ostia or Puteoli on the west coast of Italy. (Bruce p 454).

Though this was the normal expectation of the voyage, and evidently the aim of the ship's captain, the ship had been able to make headway only with difficulty. It took a number of days to reach Cnidus, a promontory on the south west extremity of Asia Minor. (Acts 27:7). Though Cnidus had two harbours, and was safe enough for the time being, the ship had to continue the journey before winter set in when sailing would be nearly impossible. The usual route would have taken them north of the island of Crete, but because of the northeast wind they sailed south and east of Crete taking shelter from the north west wind. (Acts 27:7). So they sailed under the lee of Crete, protected from the wind, coasting along the coast of Crete off Salmone (Acts 27:7) on the west side of the island until they reached a small bay called Fair Havens. (Acts 27:8).

This was now a dangerous time for sailing. The voyage had already taken longer than was usual, and 'the fast had already gone by'. (Acts 27:9). Luke is using the Jewish calendar, the Fast being the Jewish Day of Atonement, *Yom Kippur*, the tenth day of the month Tishri. (Marshall p 406). Marshal is informative on these dates, explaining that the Jewish calendar was based on the moon and could vary from year to year. But generally speaking, the dangerous season for navigation lasted from September 14th to November 11th. After November, navigation on the open sea ceased for the remainder of the winter. (Bruce p455).

Acts 27:9-12. Paul's advice neglected

As much time had been lost and the voyage was already dangerous because the fast had already gone by, Paul advised them saying, 'Sirs, I perceive that the voyage will be with injury and much loss, not only of the cargo and the ship, but also of our lives'. But the centurion paid more attention to the captain and to the owner of the ship, than to what Paul said.

Though Paul was neither a sailor nor a part of the group of three which decided the course of the ship, the owner, the captain and the centurion, he felt that he needed to make some intervention. Paul was a prisoner but a prisoner with access to the centurion and therefore, by extension, to the owner of the ship and the ship's captain. But his remarks were substantially prudent advice. Paul advised them saying 'Sirs, I perceive that the voyage will be with injury and much loss, not only of the cargo and the ship, but also of our lives'. (Acts 27:10).

This was a ship which was commissioned by the state, and the owner, was a contractor for the state transport of corn, who employed the captain to take the cargo safely to Rome. But the centurion was the higher official on board, the commanding officer, and though impressed by Paul's acute summary of the situation chose to ignore what he had to say. 'The centurion paid more attention to the captain and to the owner of the ship than to what Paul said'. (Acts 27:11). He may have said, 'Look at this harbour of Fair Havens, how small it is, and how large this ship. It would be inconvenient to spend the winter here. We can at least attempt to reach Phoenix, a harbour of Crete where there will be more amenities and where the climatic conditions would be more favourable, 'looking noth east and south east, and winter there'. (Acts 27:12).

This apparently pleased all the ship's company. 'The majority advised to put to sea from there', (Acts 27:12), looking forward to the prospect of spending the winter at Phoenix in Crete. At first, all seemed well. A south wind had sprung up and 'blew gently' (Acts 27:13) which would favour their journey westwards.

Weighing anchor, they sailed close to the shore of Crete, keeping into the land.

Acts 27:13-20. They are caught in the wind Euraquilo

But soon, a tempestuous northeastern wind called Euraquilo struck down from the land; and when the ship was caught and could not face the wind we gave way to it and were driven. And running under the lee of a small island called Cauda we managed with difficulty to secure the boat. After hoisting it up, they took measures to undergird the ship, then, fearing that they should run on the Syrtis, they lowered the gear and so were driven.

This state of affairs was not to last however. The wind changed. A tempestuous wind rushed down from Crete striking down from the land. (Acts 27:14). It was a northeaster, known as Euraquilo, (R.S.V) or Euroclydon (K.J.V). The term tempest indicates a wind of hurricane force, a typhoon, the whirling motion of the clouds and the sea caused by the meeting together of opposing currents of air as the wind blew down from the mountains to the north east of of Crete, stirring up the waves enough to catch the ship, to hold it so that the sailors 'gave way to it and were driven'. (Acts 27:16).

Responding to the danger they were in, the sailors had to do three things. First they hauled on board the small boat which was normally towed behind the ship, not kept on deck. 'We managed with difficulty to secure the boat', writes Luke with feeling. With all hands on deck, he may well have been one of those hauling on the ropes. (Acts 27:16). This was to prevent the boat from colliding with the ship in the gale, with damage either to the ship, or boat, or both. Then, after hoisting up the boat they took steps to 'undergird' the ship. There is some doubt as to what 'undergird' might mean but the most plausible explanation would seem to be ropes tied round the ship im order to hold the wooden planks more firmly together and prevent the ship from breaking up in the violence of the waves.

This may well have taken all the daylight hours.

The next day, fearing that they might be cast upon the Syrtis, a sheet of water off the coast of Libya which was dangerous because it was shallow and unpredictably liable to shiting sandbanks by the tide, the sailors 'lowered the gear and so were driven'. (Acts 27:17). Again, the meaning of the term 'gear' is uncertain. Marshall has two suggestions. Gear could mean either the mainsail, to 'lower it or set it'. Or to lower the gear could mean to drop some kind of sea anchor, to enable the ship to slow down, causing it to go towards the north and avoid the dangerous Syrtis area.

Bruce, p460; Stott p387 and Barrett p1197 also regard the dropping of the anchor as a possibility, although Barrett also considers the alternative of reefing the ship's sails with the view of sailing as close to the wind as they could. However, the original text remains obscure.

On the following day, the storm continued. The storm-tossed crew had to make another decision. They must jettison the cargo. (Acts 27:18).' They began to throw the cargo overboard', descriptive of how desperate they had become, for by losing the cargo, the owner would also lose the money which would have been paid to him on the delivery of the wheat, part of which would have been for the wages of the crew.

But worse was to come. The third day 'they cast out with their own hands the tackle of the ship'. (Acts 27:19). Marshall p 409 and Bruce p 460 both assume that this was to cast the spare gear overboard, perhaps the heavy mainsail and yard, with the object of lightening the ship. Luke comments that it was by their own hands they did it. Could this mean that they at least had concurred with Paul's assessment of their situation, 'that the voyage could end with 'loss, not only of the cargo and the ship, but also of our lives'. (Acts 27:10), and that they had taken upon themselves to cast the tackle into the sea without being ordered to do so by the captain?

By this time, no-one had any idea where they were. They could normally reckon their position by the sun and the stars, for this was before the advent of compasses and sextants. But 'for many a day neither sun nor stars appeared. They knew there was absolutely no chance of survival, no hope of being saved. Luke writes again in his signature fashion, using litotes, 'no small tempest lay on us and all hope of our being saved was at last abandoned'. (Acts 27:20).

To give up all hope is the last stage of despair. But there was one man who was not despairing. Though the situation was desperate and was daily growing more so, Paul had a message of encouragement which he wanted to bring to everyone on board.

Acts 27:21-26. Paul's encouragement

As they had been for a long time without food, Paul then came forward among them and said,' Men, you should have listened to me and should not have sailed from Crete and thus incurred this injury and loss'. (Acts 27:21).

Paul is addressing 'men'. Does this include the owner, the captain and the centurion? Does it indicate that the sailors, and the soldiers guarding the prisoners and the prisoners themselves had also heard what Paul had said on a previous occasion? And did Paul's intervention give them a reason for listening to Paul more closely now, for he had so obviously been right in his earlier assessment of their situation. Space is limited on board ship. It is quite possible that anything said could be heard by any number of others.

These men had long been without food. (Acts 27:21). This may have been due to sea sickness among the crew because of the tempest, or the loss of cooking facilities, or of the spoiling of the food in the storm. But Paul says, 'I bid you take heart! For there will be no loss of life among you but only of the ship'. (Acts 27:22)

How could Paul say that? What authority did he have to predict the future, to know what was going to happen?They were glad of course of his encouraging words, but somewhat sceptical too. So Paul proceeds to explain. He said, 'this very night there stood by me an angel of the God to whom I belong, and whom I worship'. Well yes, Paul, they might have said, we have heard that you are somewhat given to having visions. What is it this time and will it get us out of our present predicament?

But Paul went on, 'the angel said, do not be afraid Paul. You must stand before Caesar; and lo, God has granted you all those who sail with you'. (Acts 27:25).

Paul is declaring publicly, proclaiming that in spite of every appearance to the contrary, he has faith. He believes that God will do all that He has said He will do. But then he says, 'But we shall have to run on some island'. (Acts 27:26). They will be cast ashore but Paul will no doubt be praying for his fellow travellers and they will be saved.

Acts 27:27-29. They approach the island of Malta

When the fourteenth night had come, as we were drifting across the sea of Adria, about midnight the sailors suspected that they were nearing land. (Acts 27:27)

Luke was keeping an accurate log. With no daylight or starlight, (Acts 27:20), with having taken no food (Acts 27:21), the sailors had given up counting the days, but fourteen days was exactly the time needed to reach Malta from Cauda, under these terrible climatic conditions.

The Adriatic sea across which they were drifting was considered in those days to extend from the Ionian Sea, south of Italy, westwards to Gibraltar and between Italy and the Balkan peninsula to the east, including in ancient times the area of the sea between Crete and Sicily. (Marshall p411). Bruce simplifies it by describing it as the sea between Italy, Malta, Crete and Greece, (Bruce p462). Drifting across this sea in the dark, not altogether trusting Paul's vision that there would be no loss of life, was a frightening experience.

But when the fourteenth day had come, 'as we were drifting across the sea of Adria, about midnight the sailors suspected that they were nearing land'. They may have heard the sound of breakers on the sea shore. Although it was midnight, they may have seen, even if obscurely, some light on the island. This was hopeful, but it could be dangerous if they were drifting on to rocks. They decided to take a sounding.

The first sounding revealed a depth of twenty fathoms. A little farther on, they sounded again and found fifteen fathoms (Acts 27:28). This was a little too near the land for safety, especially in the dark. They let out four anchors from the stern to prevent the ship from drifting further 'and prayed for the day to come'. (Acts 27:29). The anchors would act as a brake until they could see what further action to take, and they chose to anchor the ship by the stern so that it could swing round from the wind but keep the bow of the ship facing the shore ready for landing. (Bruce p 463). For this same reason, Bruce rather enigmatically adds, Nelson anchored by the stern in the Battle of the Nile.

Acts 27:30-32. The sailors attempt to escape

And as the sailors were seeking to escape from the ship, and had lowered the boat into the sea under pretence of laying out anchors from the bow, Paul said to the centurion and the soldiers 'Unless these men stay in the ship you cannot be saved'. Then the soldiers cut away the ropes of the boat and let it go.

This was land, and although the sailors did not know what exactly the land was, any kind of land would be more acceptable than remaining on a storm tossed ship. They had an impulsive desire to escape.

A sort of plan emerged. They would pretend to be laying out anchors from the bow of the ship while actually lowering the boat into the sea, and by this means escape to the land. They had already lowered the boat when Paul again intervened. He said to the centurion and the soldiers, 'Unless these stay in the ship, you cannot be saved'. The sailors were obviously crucial to the manning of the ship and without them there would not be sufficient men to handle the ship. But Paul also, no doubt, had in mind what the angel of God had said to him. There was no need for the sailors to take such a drastic step, for God had promised that there would be no loss of life among them but only the loss of the ship. The sailors had only to wait for the wind to die down; for the storm to abate; for the daylight to come.

The soldiers were impulsive too. They could have hauled the boat back on deck, but instead they 'cut away the ropes of the boat and let it go'. (Acts 27:32). This act did indeed prevent the sailors from escaping, but it also made getting ashore more difficult for everyone.

Acts 27:33-38. Again, Paul encourages everyone

As day was about to dawn, Paul urged them to take some food saying 'Today is the fourteenth day that you have continued in suspense and without food, having taken nothing. Therefore I urge you to take some food; it will give you strength since not a hair of your head is to perish from the head of any of you'.

And when he had said this, he took bread and giving thanks to God in the presence of all, he broke it and began to eat. Then they were all encouraged, and ate some food themselves. We were in all two hundred and seventy six persons in the ship. And when they had eaten enough, they lightened the ship, throwing out the wheat into the sea.

There was apparently no lack of food on board. It was not lack, but abstinence that concerned Paul, for though the cargo of grain had been cast overboard, there was other food in the galley. (Acts 27:18).

Why had they abstained from food? Did they believe that their gods, to whom they prayed, (Acts 27:29) would look favourably on them if they fasted? Was it some kind of inadvertent suicide because they were convinced that they were going to die anyway? Or was it simply that the unusual turbulence of the ship during the storm had made eating impossible? They had lost some physical strength without food, and Paul was concerned for them, perhaps prompted by Luke the physician. He knew that suspense, anxiety, fear, had played some part in their abstaining from food. (Acts 27:33). The sailors had prayed. Now Paul took some bread and giving thanks to God in the presence of all, he broke it and began to eat.

This normal Jewish practice of thanking God before eating had become part of Christian practice too. But it goes beyond mere practice. Paul is witnessing to the presence of God in his life, of his dependence on Him. That in spite of all evidence to the contrary, God is in control and will fulfil His word to His servant by ensuring that he arrives in Rome. He is also witnessing to these men on board that he believes that there will be no loss of life among them for so his God has promised.

Some expositors have found sacramental significance in Paul's action, that he was sharing the Lord's supper, presumably with Luke and Aristarchus. He may well have done so on other occasions but this occasion was sacramental only in the sense that Paul was witnessing to his faith in God and in the Lord Jesus Christ.

Nevertheless, when the people in the ship saw Paul begin to eat, 'they were all encouraged and began to eat some food themselves'. (Acts 27:36). Luke, faithful, meticulous Luke, says, 'We were in all two hundred and seventy six persons in the ship'. (Acts 27:37). And because it was important that the ship should be as light as possible if there was any chance of her being able to come ashore safely, 'they lightened the ship, throwing out the wheat into the sea', bringing the ship ashore with as little load as possible.

Acts 27:39-41. The shipwreck

Now when it was day, they did not recognize the land, but they noticed a bay with a beach on which they planned if possible to bring the ship ashore. So they cast off the anchors and left them in the sea at the same time loosening the ropes that tied the rudders; then, hoisting the foresail to the wind, they made for the beach.

Daylight had come, and with it the possibility of being able to get safely to land. From the deck of the ship, they could see land but did not recognize it as Malta, only learning that later. (Acts 28:1). But they could see a bay with a beach. (Acts 27:39). They could now visualize how they might get the ship to shore.

The recent soundings had given them a depth of water of fifteen fathoms. (A fathom is about six feet, the combined length of the outstretched arms. Barrett p203). They needed to be very careful how they approached the island, for these two soundings had indicated that the entrance to the bay could well be a shifting sea bed. They had reduced speed by casting out four anchors from the stern. (Acts 27:29). Now they cast off the anchors and left them in the sea. (Acts 27:40), for that procedure had prevented the ship from taking on the heavy seas broadside, and they could now look for a suitable place in which to beach the ship. (Acts 27:39).

They also loosened the ropes which held the rudders. These were the steering paddles, fastened by ropes to a yoke or crossbar, and loosening the ropes meant that the ship could no longer be steered and that they were reliant on on the wind to drive them to the beach. This was the case; hoisting the foresail, relying on the wind, they made for the beach as the wind filled the sail. (Acts 27:40). Though a small sail, attached to the foremast, it achieved its purpose, and the ship made for the beach.

But striking a shoal, 'a place between two seas', (R.S.V. margin), they ran the vessel aground. (Acts 27:41). Bruce explains that a ship driven by a gale would inevitably expose a bow to being 'stuck and immovable' (Acts 27:41), while the stern would be exposed to the full force of the waves and be broken up by the surf. (Acts 27:41).

Acts 27:42-44. They all get safely to land

The soldiers plan was to kill the prisoners lest any should swim away and escape, but the centurion, wishing to save Paul, kept them from carrying out their purpose. He ordered those who could swim to throw themselves overboard first and make for the land and the rest on planks or on pieces of the ship. And so it was that all escaped to land.

Little by little, the stern of the ship was breaking up and now the soldiers had a problem. What to do with the prisoners? According to Roman law, if a prisoner escaped, then the soldier on guard would be held responsible and would incur the punishment which would have been awarded to the prisoner. In some cases, this would be the death penalty.

The soldier's plan was to kill all the prisoners lest any should swim away and escape. (Acts 27:42). Once they had managed to swim ashore they could easily be lost in the countryside and might never be recaptured. From the prisoner's point of view, even if they did not reach land but died in the attempt, this might be a less painful death than that which awaited them at Rome.

But the soldiers had reckoned without their commanding officer. This may have been Julius who had shown Paul unusual consideration before, or another centurion. 'But the centurion, wishing to save Paul, kept them from carrying out their purpose' (Acts 27:43), for of course, Paul, as a prisoner would have been part of the extermination of the prisoner contingent.

The centurion however could not make too much of his intention to save Paul, and so he ordered that those prisoners who could swim should throw themselves overboard first and make for land, and those who could not swim should acquire a piece of timber, or a plank, a piece of wreckage which could float, and by this means reach the shore.

In spite of this hit and miss procedure, 'All escaped to land', (Acts 27:44), prisoners, soldiers, sailors, officers; some who could not swim being helped by those who could. What had been told Paul by the angel, the mouthpiece of God, had come to pass. It came to pass that all escaped safely to land. Paul refers to his many experiences of sea voyages which ended in disaster. He says in 2 Corinthians 11:25, 'Three times I have been shipwrecked. A night and a day I have been adrift at sea'. But whether or not he could swim, he does not tell us.

Acts Chapter 28

Acts 28:1-6. Paul and the viper

After we had escaped, we then learned that the island was called Malta. And the natives showed us no little kindness for they kindled a fire and welcomed us all, because it had begun to rain and was cold. Paul had gathered a bundle of sticks and put them on the fire, when a viper came out because of the heat and fastened on his hand.

And so it was that all escaped to land. Bruce comments that the island's Phoenician name, Melita, means refuge, escape, and that the island deserved its name. (Bruce p470). The inhabitants of the island are called 'natives' in R.S.V. and barbarians in K.J.V. This does not mean that they were uncivilized but of Phoenician extraction and spoke a Phoenician dialect. This was why to the Greeks they were barbarians. Perhaps Paul, though a well travelled and well educated man, had at last come across a people with whom he could not easily communicate; but God provided him with a way.

Luke, who of course was also there, was greatly impressed by these barbarians or natives. Using the litotes figure of speech once again, he says that 'the barbarians showed us no little kindness'. (Acts 28:2). Seeing that the refugees from the shipwreck were wet and cold from being in the water they lit a fire and 'welcomed us all'. In addition to being wet from the sea, it now began to rain.

A bonfire was soon alight around which they sat, their clothes steaming in the heat, their hands outstretched to the blaze.

Paul had gathered a bunch of sticks and put them on the fire when a viper came out of the fire because of the heat and fastened on his hand. (Acts 28:3). Vipers do not coil, they fasten on their prey, and the viper fastened on Paul. The inhabitants watched in wonder, expecting that the poisonous venom from the snake would cause Paul to swell up and die. (Acts 28:6).

But they drew a different conclusion when they saw the creature hanging from his hand. They said to one another, 'No doubt this man is a murderer. Though he has escaped from the sea, justice has not allowed him to live'. (Acts 28:4). Paul however shook off the creature into the fire and suffered no harm. They waited, expecting him to swell up or suddenly fall down dead, but when they had waited a long time, and saw no misfortune come to him, they changed their minds and said that he was a god.

How easily we jump to conclusions and judge others. For a long time, the inhabitants waited, staring at Paul. Paul had shaken off the viper into the fire and so far had suffered no harm. But when they had waited a long time, and saw no misfortune come to him they changed their minds and said that he was a god.

In Acts 14:11, the crowd at Lystra, speaking in Lycaonian, had the same reversal of opinion, first acclaiming Paul and Barnabas as the Greek gods Zeus and Hermes, or Jupiter and Mercury in the Roman pantheon, and afterwards attempting to stone them to death.

Paul's experience may also be reflected in the final contested chapter of Mark's gospel, where it is claimed that believers may pick up serpents, and if they drink any deadly thing, it will not hurt them. They will lay hands on the sick and they will recover. (Mark 16:18).

This latter gift of healing had been given to Paul at Lystra when a lame man, crippled from birth had been healed, (Acts 14:9), and in Ephesus, when God did extraordinary things by the hand of Paul, so that handkerchiefs, napkins and aprons were carried away from his body to the sick, and diseases left them and evil spirits came out of them. (Acts 19:11). The most extreme healing came to Eutychus, who fell asleep and fell from the window while Paul was preaching. But Paul bent over him, embracing him and restoring him to life. Paul was neither a

murderer or a god, but a man who lived by faith in the One
True God.

Acts 28:7-10. Healings in Malta

*Now in the neighbourhood of that place were lands belonging
to the chief man of the island, named Publius, whio received us
and entertained us hospitably for three days. It happened that
the father of Publius lay sick with a fever and dysentery; and
Paul visited him and prayed and, putting his hands on him,
healed him.*

The ship's crew and all who were on board had come to this
hospitable island and as Paul had promised on the authority he
had had from God, there was no loss of life, in spite of all they
had been through the tempest.

It appeared that the wreck of the ship had happened in that
part of the island where there was an estate belonging to the
chief man of the island named Publius. This man received
them hospitably and entertained them for three days. Did this
hospitality extend to all the ship's company? This would seem to
be unlikely. Perhaps Luke is only referring to Paul, his friends,
and those men in authority. Or had Publius heard about the
snake episode and wanted to see Paul for himself?

It happened, it came to pass, that the father of Publius lay
sick with a fever and dysentery; and Paul visited him and prayed,
and putting his hands on him, healed him. (Acts 28:8). As in
Mark 16:18, it seems that healing was often accompanied by the
laying on of hands, making it clear to any observer that it is
through the Holy Spirit, and through Him alone, that the healing
has taken place, and that the healer, in this case Paul, is merely
the vehicle. And so the glory goes to Him. By laying hands on
him Paul is saying in effect, there is nothing special about me.
Look to Jesus for He is the one who heals.

Bruce notes p472, that as early as in the writing of
Hippocrates, (The Hippocratic oath), dysentery is associated
with pyrexia, that is, a high temperature.

As had been so often the case when Jesus healed people, when one person had been healed, others hoped that healing could be for them too; and when the healing of Publius' father had taken place, the rest of the people on the island who had diseases also came and were cured (Acts 28:9).

What a time of rejoicing ensued! With our relatively easy access to advanced medical treatment, it is difficult to imagine the enduring pain of a disease or complaint without the most basic of painkillers, suffering which could endure for a lifetime. No one who needed medical help on that island needed it any longer. The power of the Lord was present to heal. (Luke 5:17).

How grateful they were is indicated by the many gifts presented to Paul and his companions. (Acts 28:10). The R.S.V margin reads, 'they were honoured with many honours'. They were honoured guests on the island for three months and when it was time for Paul and the others to leave, 'they put on board whatever we needed'. (Acts 28:10), making sure that the travellers were well supplied for the journey.

Paul, a prisoner on his way to Rome for a trial on a capital charge was being accorded the best that the island could provide. It was not only the people who were honouring Paul. God Himself was honouring His servant.

Acts 28:11-15. And so we came to Rome

After three months we set sail in a ship which had wintered in the island, a ship of Alexandria with the Twin Brothers, (Castor and Pollux), as figurehead. Putting in at Syracuse we stayed there for three days and from there we made a circuit and arrived at Rhegium. And after one day a south wind sprang up, and on the second day we came to Puteoli. There we found brethren and were invited to stay with them for seven days. And so we came to Rome. (Acts 28:11-15).

The ship of Alexandria was in all probability another grain ship on iots way to Rome. Paul's voyage on the ship which was shipwrecked began after the Fast, the Day of Atonement (Acts 27:9), and it is reasonable to assume that they reached Malta by the end of October or possibly by the beginning of November.

This would indicate the start of this final voyage to be about the end of January or beginning of February, which could still be subject to adverse weather conditions. It was an early date to be attempting a sea voyage to Rome. It was important however that a grain ship should reach its destination as soon as possible with its precious cargo for the people of Rome.

The ship was known by the figurehead on the prow as 'the Twin Brothers', the heavenly twins, twin gods, Castor and Pollux, sons of Zeus. These gods were commonly worshipped by sailors and called upon in time of need as their patron gods. Ships like inns, took their names from their figureheads. Their constellation was Gemini. This was a sign from the Zodiac arrangement of the universe that they were being looked after by their gods, especially in rough weather.

The ship set out for Syracuse on the east coast of Sicily, but on reaching Syracuse there was some delay, perhaps a change in wind direction or even a calm, so 'putting in at Syracuse they stayed there for three days' (Acts 28:12), is the commentary from the faithful Luke with his meticulous detail.

Luke goes on to say that from there they made a circuit and arrived at Rhegium. (Acts 28:13). The phrase 'made a circuit' is probably a nautical term whose meaning has become obscure. In any case, it is clear that the ship was progressing northwards and came to Rhegium. After one day in Rhegium, a south wind arose and they crossed to Puteoli.

Puteoli was a principal port in southern Italy and one of the chief ports for the corn ships from Alexandria. Travellers to Rome would also have disembarked at Puteoli and from there made their way overland to Rome, a distance of one hundred and thirty miles. It is not surprising that in such a cosmopolitan port there should be Christian believers. There, Paul and his companions found 'brethren', and were invited to stay for seven days. And so we came to Rome.

They still had some little way to go to the heart of the city, but they were on their way, being welcomed by the brethren who had come to meet them. (Acts 28:15). Just as if Paul was a dignitary on some important visit to the city, a deputation had come out of the city to greet him and escort him there. But this deputation was not from the important people of the city, but from the Roman Christians.

This was not a church which had been founded by Paul, but he immediately recognized them as 'brothers'. (Acts 28:15). How amazing that in these comparatively few years since Pentecost, Christianity had become an empire wide phenomenon. Perhaps some of these believers had been in Jerusalem when the Holy Spirit came, and the church had been born, and had taken the gospel back to Rome with them.

These beloved brethren had travelled down the Appian Way to meet Paul at the Appian Forum about forty three miles from Rome and the same or another group were at the Three Taverns or Tres Tabernae, about thirty three miles from Rome.

With every mile, Paul is becoming nearer to what he knows is his immediate destiny, further imprisonment. At this stage he does not know what we know from post canonical writings that he is to be martyred. The thought of imprisonment is enough for the moment. But here there are believers with him, who are with him spiritually, ideologically and physically as he enters Rome. When Paul saw them, Paul thanked God and took courage. (Acts 28:15). He had longed for this, believing it to be the Father's will for him, His loving purpose for His servant. (Acts 19:21). God had fulfilled His promise to him and whatever followed, Paul knew that he could trust his God.

Now the soldiers appointed to guard him took over, but Paul knew that ultimately he was in God's hands.

Acts 28:16. Paul is handed over to be kept under guard

And when we came into Rome, Paul was allowed to stay by himself, with the soldier that guarded him.

With this sentence, the third 'we' section of Acts comes to an end. Luke undoubtedly stayed as close as possible to Paul's dwelling, Luke the beloved physician, as Paul calls him. (Colossians 4:14). Luke alone is with me, says Paul when writing to Timothy (2 Timothy 4:11). Luke, his fellow worker, Paul describes him in Philemon 24. What a lot we would have missed without the Acts of the Apostles. Its narrative throws light on Paul's letters to the churches, and gives us an understanding of the background to them. We owe a debt of gratitude to Luke.

Paul was still of course a Roman prisoner, but he was permitted to stay on his own rather than in a public prison. But though he was living in his own hired dwelling, (Acts 28:30), in private accommodation, he was compelled to remain with soldiers who were taking shifts in guarding him. He may even have been chained by the wrists to them. (Acts 28:20). This was on the orders of the Praetorian prefect, the prefect of the Praetorian guard to whom provincial prisoners were committed. (Barrett, p1233; Bruce p476).

Acts 28:17-22. Paul's first interview with the Jews of Rome

After three days, Paul called together the local leaders of the Jews; and when they had gathered he said to them, 'Brethren, though I had done nothing against the people or the customs of our fathers, yet I was delivered prisoner from Jerusalem into the hands of the Romans. (Acts 28:17).

Paul had settled quickly into his temporary home. He had allowed himself three days to recover from the unusually problematic journey from Caesarea. Now he was again a prisoner, but a prisoner with a certain amount of liberty, and the first thing he did was to suggest a meeting with the Jewish leaders in Rome.

We might have expected that Paul's first thought would be for the Christians in Rome, but throughout Acts, we have seen that Paul followed the principle of 'to the Jew first and also to the

Greeks'. (Romans 1:16). The Jews were God's own people. He had chosen them for Himself, 'Israel for His own possession', (Psalm 135:4).

Paul wants to explain to the Jews that the scripture on which their lives were based foretold time and again the coming of the Messiah, God's anointed One, and that the Messiah was Jesus. They knew that this was so, that God was going to send His anointed One. Paul wanted them to know that Jesus had been identified as the Messiah by the resurrection from the dead. This is the gospel. This was the Christian message.

Paul's earlier custom was to go to a synagogue whenever he reached a different city. This of course was now not possible. But he is able to invite the Jewish leaders into his dwelling and this is his first intention. He welcomes them by addressing them as 'Brethren'. He never denied his Jewish heritage, his Jewish upbringing, his Jewish education, but always regarded himself as a Jew.

Paul wants them to know that he had done nothing against the people or customs of 'our fathers', yet he had been delivered prisoner from Jerusalem into the hands of the Romans. (Acts 28:17). He did not give them details about his attempted assassination by the Jews of Jerusalem, or their hounding of him to the Roman authorities. Whatever had happened to him, he believed that he was always in the hands of his God, who had rescued him from many dangers. God had said to him, 'My grace is sufficient for you, for My power is made perfect in weakness. I am content with.... persecutions and calamities, for when I am weak then am I strong'. (2 Corinthians 12:9,10).

But he wanted them to know that the reason for his presence in Rome was so that he could be examined in Rome as he had been in Caesarea and Jerusalem, and then set at liberty. (Acts 28:18). These experiences had been painful because the charges against him had been brought by the Jews. The Roman authorities, Felix, Festus, Agrippa and Bernice had found in him nothing worthy of the death penalty, but to avoid that penalty being executed by the Jews, Paul had appealed to Caesar. (Acts 28:19).

This was Paul's situation, and the reason for his being in Rome, as he explained to them. But Paul wanted them to know too that behind all the outward circumstance of his presence there, was his desire to share with them 'the hope of Israel', (Acts 28:20), the identification of their coming Messiah with Jesus, and it was for the proclamation of this hope that he was bound 'with this chain'.

Paul was hoping that the Jews in Rome might have had some communication with the Jews in Judea about him, but neither by letter nor by Jews returning to Rome from Judea had they heard any evil about him. (Acts 28:21). But they desired to hear from Paul what his views were, for 'with regard to this sect, we know that it is everywhere spoken against'. (Acts 28: 22).

Acts 28:23-29. Paul's second interview with the Jews of Rome

When they had appointed a day for him, they came to him at his lodging in great numbers. And he expounded the matter to them from morning till evening, testifying to the kingdom of God and trying to convince them about Jesus both from the law of Moses and from the prophets. And some were convinced by what he said while others disbelieved. (Acts 28:23,24).

The Jewish leaders desired to hear from Paul what his views were. This was not just a polite request. The Jewish leaders really wanted to know. They appointed a day for him, and when the day came, 'they came to him at his lodging in great numbers'.

It was a long day. Paul expounded the matter to them from morning till evening, 'testifying to the kingdom of God and trying to convince them about Jesus both from the law of Moses and the prophets'. (Acts 28:23).

God had promised that Paul would be witness to the truth, that he would testify to Jesus and the resurrection, that he would be a chosen instrument of God's, to carry His Name before the Gentiles and kings and sons of Israel, and that he would suffer for that Name. (Acts 9:15,16). And that he would be a witness for

Jesus to all men (Acts 22:15), sending him to the Gentiles to open their eyes that they might turn from darkness to light and from the power of Satan to God, that they might receive forgiveness of sins and a place among all who are sanctified by faith in Jesus. (Acts 26:12,18).

There was no half hearted response from Paul's hearers, The group was completely divided. Some were convinced by what Paul said, while others disbelieved; and as evening drew on, they departed, arguing among themselves.

But Paul had one last thing to say to them before they left. He said, 'The Holy Spirit was right in saying to your fathers through Isaiah the prophet, 'Go to this people and say,"You shall indeed hear, but not understand, and you shall see but never perceive. For this people's heart has grown dull, and their ears are heavy of hearing and their eyes they have closed, lest they should perceive with their eyes, and hear with their ears, and understand with their hearts, and turn to Me to heal them". (Acts 28:24-27; Isaiah 6:9,10).

How true was this vital prophecy from Isaiah. Paul as a Jew had been deaf and blind to all that the Holy Spirit had done through the earthly ministry, the life and death and resurrection of Jesus. But by God's grace, his eyes had been opened, his ears unstopped and understanding given to his heart, so that he had turned to the Lord for healing. Many Jews had turned to the Lord. Paul longed that all these Roman Jews would also turn to Him, but he had ended with a warning that God had not finished with men and women. He had given His word, the scriptures, to the Jews and if they rejected it, if they refused to believe that Jesus was the promised and anointed Son of God, He would offer salvation to the Gentiles. *They* would listen. Acts 28:29).

Acts 28:30,31. The gospel continues unhindered in Rome

And Paul lived there two whole years at his own expense, in his own hired dwelling, and welcomed all who came to him,

preaching the kingdom of God and teaching about the Lord
Jesus Christ quite openly and unhindered. (Acts 28:30,31)

The story of Paul as told by Luke is coming to an end. For two further years, Paul lived in his own hired dwelling, at his own expense. Bruce p 480 and Stott p 400, both suggest that Paul may have used his tent making skills to provide him with a source of income, but using his hands while chained would have been difficult. In spite of the relative liberty he enjoyed, he was still a prisoner of the state. It is surely more plausible to suggest that the believers in Rome would have been glad to supply Paul with whatever he needed.

This was now 62 A.D, and Luke's whole volume of the acts of the apostles and the acts of the Holy Spirit draws to its close. The Neronian persecution began in 64 A.D; the Jewish war was between 66 and 70 A.D., and the Fall of Jerusalem in 70 A.D. There are various possibilities as to what happened to Paul after two years. He may have been released without any charge because his accusers did not appear to testify against him. He may have been tried and acquitted. He may have been tried and executed. He may have been tried, acquitted, released and then re-arrested during Nero's pogrom. He may have been martyred.

We do know that during those two years, Paul wrote some of the sublimest theology ever to be penned, the three prison letters to the Ephesians, Philippians and Colossians, and the pastoral letters to Philemon, Timothy and Titus. And the letters were authenticated by his sufferings. He writes to the Philippians 'I want you to understand, brethren, that the things which happened to me have fallen out to the furtherance of the gospel. It has served to advance the gospel so that it has become known throughout the whole praetorian guard and to all the rest that my imprisonment is for Christ'. (Philippians 1:12).

Paul was prepared to die for the sake of the gospel. He was a prisoner on account of the gospel and for it he was ready to die, but for the gospel he encouraged believers to live, to bring the gospel to the uttermost parts of the earth so that men and women might be saved. (Psalm 2:8; I Thessalonians 2:16; Acts 1:8).

For two whole years, Paul welcomed all who came to him, preaching the kingdom of God and teaching about the Lord Jesus Christ quite openly and unhindered.

Paul was bound, but the word of God was not bound. (2 Timothy 2:9).

Select Bibliography

Barrett, C.K., *The Acts of the Apostles Volume 1,* (Edinburgh: T and T Clark, 1994)

Barrett, C.K., *The Acts of the Apostles Volume 2,* (Edinburgh: T and T Clark, 1998)

Bruce, F.F., *The Acts of the Apostles* (London: The Tyndale Press, 1965)

Jervell, Jacob, *The Theology of the Acts of the Apostles* (Cambridge: Cambridge University Press, 1996)

Marshall I.H., *The Acts of the Apostles* (Sheffield: Sheffield Academic Press, 1992)

Marshall, I.H., *Acts* (London: Inter- Varsity Press, 1980)

Sanders, E.P., *Paul and Palestinian Judaism* (London: SCM Press, 1989)

Sanders, E.P., *Paul* (Oxford: Oxford University Press, 1991)

Stott, John R.W., *The Message of Acts* (London: Inter-Varsity Press 1990)

www.ingramcontent.com/pod-product-compliance
Lightning Source LLC
Chambersburg PA
CBHW021132090426
42740CB00008B/749